WITHDRAWN BY THE
UNIVERSITY OF MICHIGAN

*Athenian Prostitution*

# ATHENIAN PROSTITUTION

*The Business of Sex*

EDWARD E. COHEN

OXFORD
UNIVERSITY PRESS

# OXFORD
UNIVERSITY PRESS

Oxford University Press is a department of the University of
Oxford. It furthers the University's objective of excellence in research,
scholarship, and education by publishing worldwide.

Oxford  New York
Auckland  Cape Town  Dar es Salaam  Hong Kong  Karachi
Kuala Lumpur  Madrid  Melbourne  Mexico City  Nairobi
New Delhi  Shanghai  Taipei  Toronto

With offices in
Argentina  Austria  Brazil  Chile  Czech Republic  France  Greece
Guatemala  Hungary  Italy  Japan  Poland  Portugal  Singapore
South Korea  Switzerland  Thailand  Turkey  Ukraine  Vietnam

Oxford is a registered trademark of Oxford University Press
in the UK and certain other countries.

Published in the United States of America by
Oxford University Press
198 Madison Avenue, New York, NY 10016

© Oxford University Press 2015

All rights reserved. No part of this publication may be reproduced, stored in
a retrieval system, or transmitted, in any form or by any means, without the prior
permission in writing of Oxford University Press, or as expressly permitted by law,
by license, or under terms agreed with the appropriate reproduction rights organization.
Inquiries concerning reproduction outside the scope of the above should be sent to the
Rights Department, Oxford University Press, at the address above.

You must not circulate this work in any other form
and you must impose this same condition on any acquirer.

Cataloging-in-Publication data is on file at the Library of Congress
ISBN 978-0-19-027592-1

Printed in the United States of America
on acid-free paper

*To The Memory of*
*Abigail Rebecca Cohen*
*(1973–2000)*

*Contents*

| | |
|---|---|
| *Conventions* | ix |
| *Acknowledgments* | xiii |
| *Abbreviations* | xv |
| Introduction | 1 |
|     Lack of Statistics and Archival Material   12 | |
|     Forensic, Comic, and Other Literary Sources   14 | |
|     Material Remains   20 | |
| 1. Aphroditê's Workers in Democratic Athens | 25 |
| 2. Prostitution as a Liberal Profession | 39 |
|     Athenian Work Ethics   40 | |
|     Weaving a Web of Dependence   44 | |
|     Selling "Free" Love   59 | |
| 3. (Commercial) Sex and the City: Restrictions on Prostitutes as Political Leaders | 69 |
|     "Improper Behavior that People Actually Do Engage In"   70 | |
|     In Conflict: Purchased Sex and Elite Homoerotic Culture   81 | |
|     Protecting the City against Erotic Greed   88 | |
| 4. "Prostitution pursuant to Contract" | 97 |
|     Consensual Agreements at Athens   103 | |
|     Contractual Capacity of Women and Slaves   106 | |
|     Private Contracts and Public Interests   112 | |
| 5. Beyond Legalization: Laws Affecting Prostitutes | 115 |

Prohibition of Pimping (Proagôgeia)  118
Protecting Slaves from "Outrageous" Victimization (*Hybris*)  124

6. Mothers and Daughters in a Family Business  131

Women as Merchants of Sex  138
Mothers and Daughters  145

7. The Costs, and Rewards, of Sexual Services  155

The Pricing Process at Athens  157
The Price of Sex  162
The Rewards of Sexual Services  171

*Works Cited*  181

*General Index*  223

*Index of Passages Cited*  227

# Conventions

## Terminology

The conundrum: Although the institutions and terminologies describing and underlying the sale of sex in ancient Greece and in modern societies differ considerably, comprehensibility mandates that authors writing in English employ terms cognizable to their readers. Our "escorts," "companions," "hookers," "whores," and "mistresses" are not equipollent with the *pornoi,-ai, hetairai,-oi, pallakai, gynaikes,* and *kitharistrides* of ancient Athens. All of these terms, embedded in cultural contexts, carry their own individualized (often highly variable) denotations and connotations. Accordingly, I eschew the absolute retention of original Greek terms and instead adopt a hybrid practice: where feasible, I use Hellenic vocabulary; where appropriate, I explain Greek terms; where necessary, I have tried to use the English word closest in meaning and suggestion to describe a Greek practice or practitioner. But readers should always remember that in reality the Athenians had no "courtesans" or "prostitutes" or "sex workers"—and that the choice of terminology in English is at best a rough approximation to the Hellenic original.[1] Similarly, modern terms such as "heterosexuality," "homosexuality," and "bisexuality" (and many others) are inherently problematic when applied anachronistically to Athenian phenomena.[2] The transposition of ancient usage into modern vocabulary (or of modern coinages into Athenian life) can optimally convey no more than the "imitated" pronunciation offered by phrase books to travelers in foreign lands attempting to communicate in the local language.

---

1. Other solutions are possible, but no more satisfactory. Thus Glazebrook (2006b: 135) "avoid(s) using 'courtesan'" for *hetaira* (because of its "inappropriate connotations"), preferring "sexual companion" (which generates its own transcultural difficulties).

2. The use of modern terminology is merely "a convenient shorthand" for ancient practices not "covering the same semantic range as the modern concept" (Hubbard 2003: 1).

## The "Fourth Century B.C.E."

I have sought to derive themes and conclusions solely from Athenian evidence that happens to fall largely within the modern denotation of "fourth century B.C.E." (albeit expansively construed, as explained in the "introduction, 'Later Literature,' pp. 18–20"). Yet phenomena attributed to the "fourth century" often originated a few years before the chronological start of the "fourth century," or otherwise do not exactly correspond to this modern numerology. (Unless otherwise indicated or clear from the context, all chronological references in this volume are to be understood as "B.C.E.") References to other periods and places are intended essentially for clarification or for their perceived intrinsic interest, sometimes as confirmation of conclusions drawn from Athenian material, but never as independent proof by analogy concerning Athenian practices otherwise unknown.

## Money

Most monetary values in this book are expressed as ancient Athenian *drachmas*.[3] We should not, however, attempt to relate the value of this Athenian silver coinage to the unstable modern values of equivalent physical amounts of precious metals.[4] In my opinion, the best (although not entirely satisfactory) choice is to understand the *drachma* in the context of its purchasing power at Athens (approximately a day's labor by a not unskilled individual; see E. Cohen 1992: 22, n.92)—although even this conversion must be adjusted for variations in labor costs and purchasing power in individual modern countries.[5]

---

3. The Athenian *drachma* was divided into six *obols*. One hundred *drachmas* equaled a *mna*; 6,000 *drachmas* equaled a *talent*.

4. A talent of silver, equivalent to 6,000 *drachmas*, weighed approximately 688 ounces (about 26 kilograms or slightly more than 57 pounds). Between 1970 and 1990, the market value of silver ranged from about $2 per ounce to a momentary high (in 1980) of $48.70 per ounce (*New York Times*, Jan. 6, 1991, 3.11). On April 25, 2011, the spot market price of silver reached a record $49.82 (INO.com [FOREX: Metals]). Even at prices approaching $50 per ounce, however, the composition of a single drachma would represent a metallic value of only about $5.50.

5. Economists acknowledge the difficulty of establishing meaningful exchange equivalencies for freely traded modern monies. In theory, "absolute purchasing power parity" should prevail where exchange ratios are being set by market forces. (The formulaic expression is $P/P^* = E$, where E represents the exchange rate (domestic currency units per foreign unit), P the domestic price index, and $P^*$ the foreign price index. In actual practice, wide

## *Textual Matters*

Unless otherwise indicated, all translations and paraphrases of ancient sources are my own. Greek authors who are edited in Oxford Classical Text editions are generally quoted from that series; for other Greek authors, the text usually is that of the Budé edition. Unless the distinction is relevant to my discussion, I do not differentiate between speeches or other works properly bearing the name of an ancient author, and those of doubtful attribution.[6]

My manuscript was delivered to Oxford University Press in late 2014, and it has accordingly been impossible to consider systematically secondary literature that has appeared thereafter.

---

and fluctuating variations predominate, for reasons much disputed. See Bain and Howells 2003: 289–94; Walsh 2003: 269–321; Handa 2000: 518–19, 557–61.

6. Thus, I generally cite as "Demosthenes" those speeches traditionally included in the Demosthenic corpus, as "Aristotle" those works similarly included in the Aristotelian corpus, and as "Loukianos" the *Erôtes* so attributed traditionally.

# Acknowledgments

I AM THANKFUL to all those who have aided me in the preparation and production of this volume.

I early received much stimulation from the challenging questions and insightful comments of students participating in my Penn seminars devoted to aspects of Power, Money and Sex at Athens. I also benefited greatly from the reactions of academic audiences worldwide who attended my lectures covering, in incipient form, a good portion of the material presented here—in the United States, at Princeton, Harvard and Columbia Universities; at Colby and Dartmouth Colleges; at the Massachusetts Institute of Technology; at the Universities of Texas at Austin, Colorado at Boulder, and Wisconsin at Madison; and at a meeting of the Society for Classical Studies in New Orleans. I also am appreciative of audiences in Spain at the University of La Coruña; in Portugal, at the University of Coimbra; in the Netherlands, at the University of Leiden; in Italy, at "La Sapienza" (the University of Rome), the University of Cassino, and at Salerno (Symposion di Diritto Greco ed Ellenistico XV); in France, at the Sorbonne (Université de Paris 1), the Université François Rabelais de Tours, and the Galerie Colbert in Paris (XVIII$^e$ Congrès de droit grec et hellénistique); and in Greece at the Universities of Athens and Komotini, and at a conference organized by the Institute for Philosophical Research, Patras.

I am grateful for valuable input from Profs. Adele Scafuro (Brown), Adriaan Lanni (Harvard), Thomas Hubbard (Texas), Paul Cartledge (Cambridge), Robert Wallace (Northwestern), Joseph McGinn (Vanderbilt), Athina Dimopoulou-Piliouni (Athens), Allison Glazebrook (Brock), and Gerhard Thür (Vienna). None of these scholars necessarily endorses any of my views (and at least one has dissented most helpfully).

At Oxford University Press, Stefan Vranka has provided encouragement and good judgment, for which I am most grateful. Oxford's anonymous readers have offered a number of valuable suggestions. Meenakshi Venkat has excelled at copyediting. Joe Sheppard (presently of Columbia University) has skillfully prepared the List of Abbreviations, the General Index, and the Index of Passages Cited. In Philadelphia, Sue Taylor has, as always, been enormously helpful. Above all, my deepest and ever- continuing appreciation is to my wife, Betsy.

This book is dedicated to the memory of our daughter, Abigail Rebecca Cohen, whose early death from congenital heart disease is belied by her iconic photographs (many included in her acclaimed collection, "One Cycle of My Journey"), by the continuing importance of the arts foundation that has succeeded to the Internet site for artists co-founded by Abby, and by her living presence through her ubiquitous kind deeds that have survived her.

"For the good and talented have the whole earth for their tomb—a memorial preserved through the heart."

# *Abbreviations*

| | |
|---|---|
| Aiskhin. | Aiskhinês |
| Alkiphr. | Alkiphrôn |
| Andok. | Andokidês |
| *Anth. Pal.* | *Anthologia Palatina* |
| Antiph. | Antiphôn |
| ARV² | J.D. Beazley, *Attic Red-Figure Vase-Painters*, 2nd ed. (1963) |
| Aristoph. | Aristophanês |
|   Akh. | *Akharneis* |
|   Batr. | *Batrakhoi* |
|   Eir. | *Eirênê* |
|   Ekklês. | *Ekklêsiazousai* |
|   Hipp. | *Hippeis* |
|   Lys. | *Lysistrata* |
|   Neph. | *Nephelai* |
|   Orn. | *Ornithes* |
|   Plout. | *Ploutos* |
|   Sphêk. | *Sphêkes* |
|   Thes. | *Thesmophoriazousai* |
| Ar. Byz. | Aristophanês of Byzantion |
| Aristot. | Aristotle |
|   Ath. Pol. | *Athênaiôn Politeia* |
|   Metaph. | *Metaphysics* |
|   N.E. | *Nicomachean Ethics* |
|   Oik. | *Oikonomika* |
|   Poet. | *Poetics* |
|   Pol. | *Politics* |
|   Rhet. | *Rhetoric* |
| Asc. | Asconius |
|   Verr. | *Commentary on Cicero* In Verrem |

| | |
|---|---|
| Athên. | Athênaios |
| BGU | *Berliner Griechische Urkunden* (Ägyptische Urkunden aus den Kgl. Museen zu Berlin) |
| Dein. | Deinarkhos |
| Dem. | Demosthenes |
|   Ep. | *Epistulae* |
|   Or. | *Orationes* |
| Dêmêtr. | Dêmêtrios of Phalêron |
| Diod. Sik. | Diodôros of Sicily |
| Diog. Laert. | Diogenês Laertios |
| Dion. Hal. | Dionysios of Halikarnassos |
|   Ant. | *Antiquitates Romanae* |
| Donat. | Donatus |
| Eup. | Eupolis |
| Eur. | Euripides |
|   Hipp. | *Hippolytos* |
|   Hiket. | *Hiketidês* |
|   Mel. Des. | *Melanippê Desmôtês* |
|   Or. | *Orestês* |
| FGrH | F. Jacoby, *Fragmente der griechischen Historiker* (1923– ) |
| Gai. | Gaius |
|   Inst. | *Institutiones* |
| Harp. | Harpokratiôn |
| Hdt. | Herodotus |
| Hêrôd. | Hêrôdas |
| Hyper. | Hyperidês |
|   *Ath.* | *Against Athênogenês* |
| IG | *Inscriptiones Graecae* (1873–) |
| Isai. | Isaios |
| Isok. | Isokratês |
| KA | R. Kassel and C. Austin, *Poetae Comici Graeci* (1983–1991) |
| Kallim. | Kallimakhos |
| Lib. | Libanios |
| Louk. | Loukianos |
|   Apol. | *Apologia* |
|   Erôt. | *Erôtes* |
|   Herm. | *Hermotimos* |
|   Hetair. Dial. | *Hetairikoi Dialogoi* |
|   Symp. | *Symposion* |

| | |
|---|---|
| Lyk. | Lykourgos |
|   Leôk. | *Kata Leôkratous* |
| Lys. | Lysias |
| Makh. | Makhôn |
| Men. | Menander |
|   Dys. | *Dyskolos* |
|   Epitrep. | *Epitrepontes* |
|   Perik. | *Perikeiromenê* |
|   Sam. | *Samia* |
| Mon. Anc. | *Monumentum Ancyranum* |
| Naev. | Naevius |
|   fr. com. | *Fragmenta Comoediarum* |
| OGI | *Orientis Graeci Inscriptiones Selectae* |
| P Berol. | *Berlin Papyri* |
| PG | Migne, *Patrologia Graeca* |
| P Hamb. | *Papyri Hamburgenses* |
| P Mag. | *Papyri Graecae Magicae* |
| P Oxy. | *Oxyrhynchus Papyri* (1898–) |
| PRev. Laws | B. Grenfell, *Revenue Laws of Ptolemy Philadelphus* (1896) |
| P Teb. | *Tebtunis Papyri* (1902–76) |
| Paus. | Pausanias |
| Petron. | Petronius |
|   Sat. | *Satyricôn* |
| Phôt. | Phôtios |
| Pind. | Pindaros |
|   Ol. | *Olympian Odes* |
| Pl. | Plato |
|   Alk. | *Alkibiadês* |
|   Gorg. | *Gorgias* |
|   Khrm. | *Kharmidês* |
|   Krit. | *Kritôn* |
|   Lys. | *Lysis* |
|   Men. | *Menexenos* |
|   Nom. | *Nomoi* |
|   Plt. | *Politikos* |
|   Prôtag. | *Prôtagoras* |
|   Rep. | *Republic* |
|   Symp. | *Symposion* |
|   Tht. | *Theaitêtos* |

| | |
|---|---|
| Plaut. | *Plautus* |
|   Asin. | *Asinaria* |
|   Bacch. | *Bacchides* |
|   Cist. | *Cistellaria* |
|   Curc. | *Curculio* |
|   Epid. | *Epidicus* |
|   Men. | *Menaechmi* |
|   Merc. | *Mercator* |
|   Mil. | *Miles Gloriosus* |
|   Mostell. | *Mostellaria* |
|   Pers. | *Persa* |
|   Pseud. | *Pseudolus* |
|   Trin. | *Trinummus* |
|   Truc. | *Truculentus* |
| Plin. | Pliny the Elder |
|   N.H. | *Naturalis historia* |
| Plut. | Plutarch |
|   Erôt. | *Erôtikos* |
|   Mor. | *Moralia* |
|   Symp. Prob. | *Symposiakôn Problêmatôn* |
|   Camill. | *Camillus* |
|   Per. | *Periklês* |
|   Phôk. | *Phôkiôn* |
|   Sol. | *Solôn* |
| Poll. | Pollux |
| Polyain. | Polyainos |
| Polyb. | Polybius |
| Quint. | Quintilian |
|   Inst. Or. | *Institutio Oratoria* |
| schol. | *scholia* or scholiast |
| SEG | *Supplementum epigraphicum Graecum* (1923–) |
| Sêmon. | Sêmonidês |
| Sen. | Seneca the Younger |
|   De ben. | *De beneficiis* |
| S.I.G. | *Sylloge Inscriptionum Graecarum* (1915–24) |
| Ter. | Terence |
|   An. | *Andria* |
|   Eun. | *Eunuchus* |

| | |
|---|---|
| Heaut. | *Heauton Timoroumenos* |
| Hek. | *Hekyra* |
| Theophr. | Theophrastos |
| Khar. | *Kharaktêres* |
| Thouk. | Thucydides |
| UPZ | U. Wilcken, *Urkunden der Ptolemäerzeit* 1 (1922–27), 2 (1957) |
| Xen. | Xenophôn |
| Anab. | *Anabasis* |
| Apom. | *Apomnêmoneumatôn* |
| Ath. Pol. | *Athênaiôn Politeia* |
| Hell. | *Hellênika* |
| Kyn. | *Kynêgetikos* |
| Lak. Pol. | *Lakedaimoniôn Politeia* |
| Oik. | *Oikonomikos* |
| Por. | *Poroi* |
| Symp. | *Symposion* |

# *Introduction*

> PROSTITUTION COMPRISES (A) A SET OF DESIRES, BELIEFS, AND PRACTICES THAT, UNDER PATRIARCHY, HAVE BEEN GENDER-BIASED, EXTREMELY DISCRIMINATORY TO AND OF WOMEN, *AND*
> (B) AN EXCHANGE RELATIONSHIP IN WHICH SEX IS OFFERED FOR SALE—PROSTITUTION'S SEX-ECONOMIC DIMENSION. THESE TWO DIMENSIONS CAN BE DISENTANGLED...
> —LYNN CHANCER, *Toward a Sociological Feminist Theory of Prostitutes and Prostitution* (1998)

> IN OTHER *POLEIS* SEXUAL CONVENTIONS ARE EASY TO UNDERSTAND AND WELL-DEFINED, BUT AT ATHENS THEY ARE *POIKILOS* (COMPLEX, INTRICATE, MANY-HUED).
> —PLATO *SYMPOSIUM* 182A7–9[1]

GREEK HISTORY HAS long eschewed the mundane details of Athenian commerce and labor: "So long as classics is dominated by the concerns of liberal humanism, economic questions will be marginal" (Morris 2001: 14).[2] The standard volume on many aspects of Athenian business endeavors (Boeckh's *Die Staatshaushaltung der Athener*) was written in 1817.[3] Not

---

1. ὁ περὶ τὸν ἔρωτα νόμος ἐν μὲν ταῖς ἄλλαις πόλεσι νοῆσαι ῥᾴδιος, ἁπλῶς γὰρ ὥρισται· ὁ δ'ἐνθάδε καὶ ἐν Λακεδαίμονι ποικίλος.

2. Similarly Cartledge 2002: 12: classicists have persisted in "an avoidance of pure (or mere) economic history." Cf. Will 1954; Stroud 1998: 27–28; Morris and Manning 2005: 26–27.

3. When its forthcoming English translation is issued, Bresson 2007/2008 (French) is likely, finally, to supersede Boeckh 1817 as an introductory handbook.

surprisingly, then, business factors have been virtually ignored in the cascade of valuable recent studies directed to cultural, anthropological, sexual, or gender aspects of the purchase of Athenian sex.[4] My focus is different. I discuss the Athenian sex worker[5] in the context of the economic structure of fourth-century Athens[6] and examine the societal and professional values ("business ethics") influencing this métier. And because Athenian prostitution was a trade functioning within a "slave society" of towering cultural accomplishment, I pay attention both to the element of compulsion immanent in an economy dependent on unfree labor[7] and to Athenian prostitution's social contours and implications, its place in the Athenian *imaginaire*.[8]

---

4. Important insights, emanating from a variety of useful methodologies and approaches, are contained in a plenitude of recent work on Greek prostitution: see, for example, McGinn 2014; Kennedy 2014: 68–96; Glazebrook and Henry, eds. 2011; Lanni 2010; Faraone and McClure, eds. 2006; Davidson 2007 (Chapter 16) and 1997; McClure 2003b; Kurke 1999b. This sudden "flurry" of work on prostitution (Golden 2003: 5, n. 12) contrasts with the twentieth century's "general neglect of this area of ancient studies" (Davidson 1997: xviii). Modern studies have seen a similar explosion of interest in prostitution: Chancer 1998: 183; Chapkis 1997.

5. In the modern world, "'sex work' and 'sex worker' have become the accepted value-free terms for [prostitution]," but some ancient historians purposely "avoid the terms because they ... imply that prostitution is just a job and the prostitute free to choose his or her profession" (Glazebrook and Henry 2011: 13, n. 1). See also McGinn 2014: 85.

6. This attention to structure and performance, and to Athenian economic, legal, and social "institutions," is consistent with the transformative New Institutional Economics, which emphasizes institutions in the sense of "background constraints" or "rules of the games" (Frier and Kehoe 2007: 113–14) and suggests that "the task of economic history [is] to explain the structure and performance of economies through time" (North 1981: 3). See Morris, Saller, and Scheidel 2007.

7. Despite the ubiquitous presence of unfree individuals in virtually all human communities prior to the nineteenth century (Klees 1998: 1–18), Attika constitutes one of the world's few attested true "slave economies"—those in which the contribution of a huge number of unfree persons to the totality of wealth production is so substantial that a society's overall production, distribution, and consumption is highly dependent on slave labor. On the significance of unfree labor at Athens, see Nafissi 2004: 395–99; E. Cohen 2000: 130–31; Fisher 1993b: 3; Garlan 1988: 201–203; Marx 1970–72: III.332, 384–85, 594–95 (cf. Mazza 1978).

8. Now an important focus for much historical writing, the French *l'imaginaire* (originally popularized by Sartre and Lacan) originated in French psychoanalysis (where it has functioned as a flexible rendering of Freud's "fantasy"). Transposed into social theory as the equivalent of "social imaginary," it has come to mean, when applied to Athenian history, "the city's 'self-image,' how it sees itself in fantasy, with a large element of idealization and wish fulfillment" (Loraux [1984] 1993: 3 [Translator's Note]). See also Castoriadis 2002: 15–37; 1975. For recent studies focused on Athenian prostitution and Athenian self-image, see Glazebrook 2006b (ideology of womanhood) and Lape 2006 ("psychology of prostitution" and "democratic reproduction"). Cf. Lape 2004: 76–80; McClure 2003b: 3–9 (prostitute as "fetish" = "illusion").

Although modern scholars tend to treat male prostitution at Athens as a subfield of the study of male homosexuality[9] and to isolate Athenian female prostitution within the field of women's studies,[10] in this book I treat prostitution as a commercial function in which both men and women provided sex for compensation—and often under compulsion. Athenian pottery is replete with portrayals that have been identified as brothel scenes.[11] Men and women working in these bordellos are alike described as *kathêmenoi (-ai) epi tôn oikêmatôn*—"ensconced in a brothel," or (literally) "sitting in a cubicle."[12] This graphic description corresponds to the physical layout of Athenian houses of prostitution—which seem to have consisted either of a single large (and sometimes even labyrinthine) edifice containing a number of rooms (*oikêmata*) that could be entered from the interior of the building,[13] or of a line of small chambers (*oikêmata*), each accessible directly from the

---

9. Gay Studies has appropriated Athenian male prostitution as a significant element in "the erotics of male culture in ancient Greece" (Halperin 1995: 3), and has used those "erotics" as an important basis for "the social construction of homosexuality" (Mohr 1992: 222).

10. Thus Pomeroy's pioneering work on "Women in Classical Antiquity" is titled *Goddesses, Whores, Wives and Slaves* (1975) and a "Suggested Undergraduate Syllabus for 'Women in Classical Antiquity'" (Pomeroy 1984) features a unit on female prostitutes. A similar segregation prevails in studies of Roman prostitution. McGinn explicitly limits his extensive survey to "female prostitution" (1998: 3), and Stumpp 1998, although entitled "Prostitution in der römischen Antike," in fact deals almost entirely with female sexual commerce.

11. See, for example, Hydria, Leningrad Painter, Chicago 1911.456, $ARV^2$ 572.88; Bell-krater, Dinos Painter, London BM F65, $ARV^2$ 1154.35; Cup, Makrôn, Paris Louvre G 143, $ARV^2$ 469.148; Cup, Ambrosios Painter, Munich Private Collection (Immerwahr 1984: Pls. 2–3); Cup, Euaiôn Painter, Berlin Schloss Charlottenburg 31426, $ARV^2$ 795.100, Beazley Add. 142; Hydria, Harrow Painter, Maplewood, Noble Coll., $ARV^2$ 276.70. On the difficulty of interpreting visual portrayals on ceramic ware, see pp. 20–24.

12. τοὺς (τὰς) ἐπὶ τῶν οἰκημάτων (καθημένας). As a servile pursuit, "sitting in a brothel" was no less contemptible than working in a shoemaking operation or in a retail shop (Pl. *Khrm.* 163b5–8). (For Athenian deprecation of "employment," see chapter 2.) As a term for servile prostitution, "sitting in a brothel" was applied by the Greeks even to foreign—and fantastic—situations. Thus Herodotos describes episodes where Egyptian pharaohs (purportedly to catch a thief or to increase royal revenues) placed their own daughters in a brothel cubicle (*oikêma*) (see 2.121e2, 126).

13. Some brothels seem to have contained a sizeable entrance hall and even large interior courtyards (cf. Building "Z" in the Kerameikos, discussed in chapter 2, n. 98 and accompanying text). Comic fragments suggest that these open areas may have been used for the presentation of female prostitutes to potential customers (see Xenarkh. Fr. 4 [K-A]; Euboulos Frs. 67 and 82 [K-A]).

street.¹⁴ (The word *oikêma* [plural *oikêmata*] denoted both the "individual chamber" or "hut" where a prostitute "sat" and [by metonymy] the larger prostitutional complex with its individual quarters.¹⁵) Although both the unified and the linear establishments were familiarly known by many other names—*porneia, matryleia, khamaitypeia, ergastêria, synoikiai, dêmosiai oikiai, tegê, kinêtêria*, etc.—the term "sitting in an *oikêma*" is used consistently to describe the plight of both male and female workers relegated to the abject circumstance and slavish conditions of these brothels. Aiskhinês claims that there could be no doubt concerning the prostitutional calling of the men who "sat in the *oikêmata*," practicing "the trade" "under compulsion."¹⁶ Thus Phaidôn of Elis "was compelled" to work as a male prostitute in a brothel (*oikêma*) before his liberation by the Sokratic circle and his subsequent immersion "like a free man" (*eleutheriôs*) into philosophy.¹⁷ Arkhestratos, a male "domestic companion" (*symbiôtês*) of one of the sons of Periklês, is said to have labored under circumstances similar to those of "the women working in the brothels (*oikêmata*)."¹⁸ Isaios describes how one such woman, Alkê, "sat in an *oikêma* for years" (that is, was a brothel prostitute), before becoming the manager of a multi-unit house (*synoikia*) in the Kerameikos section of central Athens, and ultimately coming to live with Euktêmôn, a wealthy Athenian who owned a number of buildings in which women operated brothels.¹⁹ Conditions in these *oikêmata* were so abject that the

---

14. This openness explains why female prostitutes are attested as visible to potential customers passing by on the street and as able even to "snare" persons walking along the road. Cf. Fauth 1967: 359–60: " 'das Hinauslehnen aus dem Fenster' zu einer hetärenhaften Praxis erotischer Anlockung gehörte." For various testimonia, especially passages from Aristophanês (e.g., *Thes.* 797–99, *Ekklês.* 878–82) confirming this pattern, see Graham 1998a: 23–27.

15. The individual chambers and less grandiose houses were known as τὰ μικρὰ οἰκήματα (Athên. 220d). Representations of the interiors of brothels are frequently identified on Athenian pottery: see, for example, Meyer 1988; Pls. 2 and 3 of Immerwahr 1984.

16. ὁρᾶτε τουτουσὶ τοὺς ἐπὶ τῶν οἰκημάτων καθημένους τοὺς ὁμολογουμένως τὴν πρᾶξιν πράττοντας. . . . εἰ δή τις ὑμᾶς ἔροιτο τοὺς ὁδῷ πορευομένους τί νῦν οὗτος ὁ ἄνθρωπος πράττει, εὐθὺς ἂν εἴποιτε τοῦ ἔργου τοὔνομα (Aiskh. 1.74).

17. Φαίδων Ἠλεῖος . . . ἠναγκάσθη στῆναι ἐπ' οἰκήματος· ἀλλὰ τὸ θύριον προστιθεὶς μετεῖχε Σωκράτους, ἕως αὐτὸν λυτρώσασθαι τοὺς περὶ Ἀλκιβιάδην ἢ Κρίτωνα προὔτρεψε· καὶ τοὐντεῦθεν ἐλεθερίως ἐφιλοσόφει (Diog. Laert. 2.105).

18. Athên. 220d: τούτων γὰρ τὸν μὲν Ἀρχεστράτου φησὶν εἶναι συμβιωτὴν τοῦ παραπλήσια ταῖς ἐπὶ τῶν μικρῶν οἰκημάτων ἐργαζομένου.

19. Αὕτη δὲ ἡ Ἀλκὴ ὠνηθεῖσα πολλὰ μέν ἔτη καθῆστο ἐν οἰκήματι, ἤδη δὲ πρεσβυτέρα οὖσα ἀπὸ μὲν τοῦ οἰκήματος ἀνίσταται . . . ἐπιμελεῖσθαι τῆς ἐν Κεραμεικῷ συνοικίας (Isai. 6.19–20).

Athenians reportedly executed Euthymakhos for placing an Olynthian woman in an *oikêma*.²⁰ Antiphôn 1 deals with the fatal outcome of a woman's desperate efforts to avoid being forced into a brothel (*porneion*).²¹

At first glance, the relative abundance of surviving evidence for commercial sex at Athens suggests that an economic analysis of Athenian prostitution is highly feasible. Prostitution is the gravamen of a number of surviving court speeches (and fragments)—and is often alluded to in others—and is the occupation practiced by numerous characters in surviving comedies (and extracts therefrom). Venal sex is often encountered in many other genres of Greek literature, and purchased *eros* is tantalizingly present in material remains, including inscriptions, pottery, and architectural vestiges. These sources seem to provide, for an ancient subject, an unusually rich trove of "factual" material. Or do they?

For decades, scholars have differed concerning the evidentiary value of the multitudinous ancient material on Athenian prostitution and its practitioners—the apparently brutally exploited brothel slaves (*pornai*) and the seemingly exalted courtesans (*hetairai*, sing. *hetaira*). Some commentators have uncritically accepted, or reluctantly acquiesced in, the "plent(itude) of evidence for the *hetaira*'s political, historical, social, cultural and religious centrality" (Davidson 2004b: 173). But for other scholars, the *hetaira* is "a socially marginal figure" recreated as a cultural icon by the "representational modes and textual strategies" of male commentators in antiquity.²² In turn, some recent commentators have been decrying the "hyper-skepticism" of those who "at times" tend totally to disregard surviving testimonia (McGinn 2011: 266). Other scholars have suggested that "more work needs to be done not only on the cultural construction of the prostitute but also on the social and economic history of prostitution" (Glazebrook and Henry 2011: 3). This book is offered as such a contribution to social and economic history, intended to demonstrate that attention to economic factors and social context can often

---

φοιτῶν γὰρ ὁ Εὐκτήμων . . . καταλιπὼν καὶ τὴν γυναῖκα καὶ τοὺς παῖδας καὶ τὴν οἰκίαν ἦν ᾤκει. . . . διῃτᾶτο ἐκεῖ (Isai. 6. 21).

20. ὑμεῖς . . . ἀπεκτείνατε . . . Εὐθύμαχον δέ, διότι τὴν Ὀλυνθίαν παιδίσκην ἔστησεν ἐπ' οἰκήματος (Dein. 1.23). See Fisher 1995: 69–70; E. Cohen 2000: 163–64.

21. On the personal status of this "concubine," see Heitsch 1984: 22–23.

22. McClure 2003b: 2–3. McClure faults the naïveté of scholars like Havelock (1995: 42–49) and Dimakis (1988: 53: "Celles-ci (hetaïres) étaient presque les seules femmes libres disposant d'une culture plus étendue et capables de discuter sur des sujets de niveau supérieur").

illuminate—without extirpating—evidence that on its face may seem implausible or repugnant.

Two major evidentiary obstacles, however, do impede an economic analysis of commercial sex at Athens: (a) the lack of statistical and archival data and (b) the potential misdirection inherent in the two principal classes of surviving evidence—comedic material (which seeks laughs rather than the transmission of reliable information) and forensic testimonia (which seek persuasion rather than factual truth). The deficiencies of humor and rhetoric as source material are exacerbated by the complicated—and often conflicting—emotional reactions, in both the modern West and in ancient Athens, to money, sex, and their exchange, sometimes through coercion.[23] Although we may prefer "functionalist" doctrines that stress the "social solidarity," "structural equilibrium," or "cultural uniformity" of societies,[24] a striving for theoretical consistency too often, in my opinion, obliterates the discontinuities, contradictions, and unintegrated deviations inherent in complex and dynamic civilizations[25]—inconsistencies that will not be purposefully suppressed in this book. The Athenians were well aware of the complexities and irregularities of their civilization, especially as to erotic mores: "In other *poleis* sexual conventions are easy to understand and well-defined, but at Athens they are *poikilos*" (complex, intricate, many-hued).[26] Economically, Athens was a thriving entrepreneurial megalopolis—in fact, in the fourth century the dominant commercial center of the eastern Mediterranean[27]—but she nevertheless harbored a conservative tradition that objected to all profit-making

---

23. On the increasing attention to emotional factors in economic analysis, see Berezin 2005; Loewenstein 2000; Elster 1998. For the importance of affect in social scientific studies generally, see Turner 2000; Barbalet, ed., 2002.

24. See Leach's early criticism (1965: 7) of British anthropologists' adherence to functional ideology. Cf. Holmwood 2005: 103; D. Cohen 1995: 9–13.

25. For the social and economic dissonance to be expected in vital, multiplex societies, see Keiser 1986; Rueschemeyer 1984: 134; Bourdieu 1977: 98. Dougherty properly urges us "to read the multiplicity of narratives that represent Athenians as Athenians in such a way that we preserve their contradictions" (1996: 251). Similarly Fisher 2001: 34.

26. Pl. *Symp.* 182a7–9: ὁ περὶ τὸν ἔρωτα νόμος ἐν μὲν ταῖς ἄλλαις πόλεσι νοῆσαι ῥᾴδιος, ἁπλῶς γὰρ ὥρισται· ὁ δ'ἐνθάδε καὶ ἐν Λακεδαίμονι ποικίλος, below, pp. 11–12.

27. See Migeotte 2009: 132; Picard 2008b: 159. Cf. Oliver 2007: 15–41; Moreno 2007: 3–33, 323–34; Bissa 2009: 169–91.

endeavors,²⁸ including those relating to sex. Xenophôn, for example, finds the commercialization of *eros* no less disgusting than charging for education.²⁹ But Athens was not monolithic, and such views had to coexist with the reality of the "monetised and money-using economy of fourth-century Athens,"³⁰ of a "city (that) lived entirely by cash transactions" (Humphreys 1978: 148),³¹ producing a culture "fraught with ambivalence, ambiguity and conflict,"³² in which legislative disincentives to "citizen" prostitution paralleled the open and lawful purchase of sex from "citizen" prostitutes.³³ Athenian commercial life was rife with the "multiplicity of narratives" (Dougherty 1996: 251) that bring consistency to few institutions at Athens—or in the modern world.

In fact, the modern world still struggles to understand, even to define,³⁴ contemporary prostitution, and does so without reliable statistical or archival material, and with a plethora of contradictory emotionally charged orientations and conflicting agendas. Western antagonism to the sale of sex, long grounded in religious and moral beliefs, has been somewhat attenuated by the emergence of secular liberal societies but has been concomitantly intensified by feminist analyses and by the increasing (or at least increasingly more publicized) coercive aspects of commercial sex. Despite greater public awareness of the existence of male prostitutes (and of female customers for both female and male providers

---

28. "[T]he trade of Athens, its monetary commercialism, its naval policy, and its democratic tendencies ... were hated by the oligarchic parties of Athens" (Popper 1950: 173, with regard to the fifth century).

29. *Apom.* 1.6.13: παρ' ἡμῖν νομίζεται τὴν ὥραν καὶ τὴν σοφίαν ὁμοίως μὲν καλόν, ὁμοίως δὲ αἰσχρὸν διατίθεσθαι εἶναι. τήν τε γὰρ ὥραν ἐὰν μέν τις ἀργυρίου πωλῇ τῷ βουλομένῳ, πόρνον αὐτὸν ἀποκαλοῦσιν, ἐὰν δέ τις, ὃν ἂν γνῷ καλόν τε κἀγαθὸν ἐραστὴν ὄντα, τοῦτον φίλον ἑαυτῷ ποιῆται, σώφρονα νομίζομεν. καὶ τὴν σοφίαν ὡσαύτως. . . . For the equation of scholars and courtesans, see Athên. 567–573b. For the causes and some manifestations of aristocratic disdain for commerce, including prostitution, see pp. 25–27.

30. Shipton 2000: 14. See also Shipton 1997; Gofas 1994; Kanellopoulos 1987: 19–22; Theokharês 1983: 100–14.

31. On the increasing monetization of Athens during the classical period, especially in the fourth century, see Schaps 2004, 2008; Shipton 2000 (esp. 5–14), 2001; Davies 2001; Picard 2008b: 147–51.

32. D. Cohen 1991a: 21. Cf. Larmour et al. 1998: 27.

33. For the implications of legislation restricting the political activity of those citizens who were or had been male prostitutes, see chapter 3.

34. See pp. 82–83.

of sex),³⁵ prostitution in the modern world remains largely a phenomenon in which female prostitutes, working within male-dominated business structures, service male customers.³⁶ This configuration conforms to what is generally believed to have been "a persistent pattern through much of history" in which women have been the "providers of sexual labor" and men "the group deriving profits and power" (Kempadoo 1998: 5). Not surprisingly, then, many recent critiques of prostitution insist on the commodification of female sexuality as the cause of the persistence of prostitution: on this premise, the commercial exploitation of women's sexuality is a byproduct of the perpetuation of patriarchal regimes, and the persistence of prostitution is a symptom of severe social malaise.³⁷ Much feminist theorizing and feminist activity have accordingly been devoted to efforts to eradicate prostitution.³⁸ Concurrently, however, and in counterpoint, recent years have seen the growth of prostitutes' rights organizations,³⁹ originated by and composed almost entirely of women. This movement insists that the provision of sexual services should be free from governmental strictures and juridical harassment, and that the practitioners of a trade in which women traditionally have been able to earn exceptionally high income should enjoy

---

35. MacKinnon 2005: 437, n. 1; Zelizer 2005: 31–32; Pisano 2002: 114–28; Weitzer 2000a: 2; Whitaker 1999; Longo and Parker 1992; Pheterson 1996: 27; Chapkis 1997: 6–7; Pruit and Lafont 1995; Bishop and Robinson 1998: vii; von Zoticus 1997. According to one survey, almost 40 percent of single women tourists to certain locations in the Caribbean had engaged in sex with local men whom they had paid directly or indirectly (Davidson and Taylor 2004: 338). About 5 percent of foreign women visiting Kenya are said to be "sexual tourists" coming to purchase the sexual services of men (*New York Times*, February 14, 2002, p. A12).

36. See the various studies in Kempadoo and Doezema 1998, and in Delacoste and Alexander 1998. Cf. Edlund and Korn 2002: 184–87.

37. See, for example, McGinn 2004: 5 ("prostitution as a fundamental component of the enduring institution of patriarchy"); Bromberg 1998: 310–11; Chancer 1998: 181 ("numerous historical and anthropological accounts depict prostitution as originating coercively, in social groups already patriarchally organized"); Overall 1992 (prostitution "a manifestation of capitalistic patriarchy"). Similarly, see Bishop and Robinson 1998: 241; Weisberg 1996: 242; Hoigard and Finstad 1992; Harsin 1985; Rubin 1975.

38. See MacKinnon 2005: 1987; Bishop and Robinson 1998: 221 (prostitution "institutionalizes the alienated sexuality constructed by current economic and social forces"). Cf. Wynter 1998; Barry 1995, 1984; Russell 1993; Davis and Stasz 1990; Heyl 1979b.

39. See, for example, the websites of the Prostitutes' Education Network (www.bayswan.org/penet.htm) and of the Sex Workers Outreach Program (www.swop-usa.org). Cf. Askola 2007: 25–27; Bindman 1997; McClintock 1993; Jenness 1993. For organizations outside the United States, see Kempadoo and Doezema 1998: 167–225.

the same legal benefits and protections as those provided to other workers. These groups have been vocally resentful of what they see as condescendingly "maternalistic" and "colonialistic" attempts by economically secure feminists of Western European origin seeking to deprive "sex workers"[40]—overwhelmingly "sisters of color" and/or otherwise impoverished women[41]—of the legal rights, and social and economic benefits, available to those engaged in other (lawful) occupations.[42] Opposing the claim that prostitution is inherently harmful to its practitioners, who supposedly "suffer degradation by being treated as sexual commodities" (Shrage 1989: 347), these activists reject the attachment of moralistic cultural interpretations to commercial sexual acts.[43] Instead they insist that ' "sex work" actually falls within the category of "emotional labor"— vocations that include caring for the disabled and the handicapped, for the young and the aged, and occupations such as teaching, airline cabin service, psychotherapy, and even acting.[44] Overall, they argue, "emotional labor" seems not to be inherently harmful to its practitioners, who are generally able to separate their private emotions from their occupational duties and "summon and contain emotion within the commercial transaction" (Chapkis 1997: 76). Likewise, it is argued that persons engaged in sexual labor "are able to distinguish intimacy and love from the sexual act itself."[45] By the closing years of the twentieth century, such views had gained considerable acceptance among feminists and others, while the human rights group Amnesty International has recently characterized the sale of sex as a basic human right and has called for total

---

40. For the origins and growing prevalence of this term, see L. Bell, ed. 1987; McClintock 1993; S. Bell 1994; Leigh 1997; Montgomery 1998: 150, n. 4.

41. See Mohanty 1991: 56; Wijers 1998; Porter and Bonilla 2000. Cf. Mohanty 1997. The Collective in Defense of Prostitutes' Rights estimates that the majority of Spain's prostitutes are immigrants (*New York Times*: January 18, 2004). Only 20 percent of prostitutes in the United Kingdom are British (*The Economist*, September 4, 2004). For Holland and Germany, chapter 5, nn. 3 and 4.

42. See Carmen and Moody 1985; Collins 1990: 164; Shrage 1994: 142.

43. Cf. Reynolds 1986: 195–96: "Rehabilitating prostitutes is not a reasonable direction for public policy, since most prostitutes are willing and often eager participants."

44. See Pheterson 1989; Troung 1990; Highleyman 1997: 152; Chapkis 2000.

45. Kempadoo 1998: 5. Cf. Brewis and Linstead 2004; Montgomery 1998; Pheterson 1996; Overall 1992: 716, 718 (dissenting: "sex work differs in a crucial way from other forms of women's labor . . . (which) would still be socially necessary in a postcapitalist, postpatriarchal world").

decriminalization of prostitution.⁴⁶ (At the same time, many "academic feminists" continue to insist that commercial sex should not be legalized under any conditions and that prostitutional arrangements should not be recognized as legitimate contracts of employment.⁴⁷)

Finally, and yet more recently, intense worldwide antagonism to prostitution has been generated by globalization's fostering of cross-border trafficking in human beings, especially women and children, under brutally coercive conditions. An earlier "globalization"—the expansion of Hellenic civilization and trade into distant portions of the ancient world—likewise fostered mobility in commercial sex. Most scholars, in fact, see Athenian prostitution as "the special preserve of foreigners."⁴⁸ Retinues of prostitutes reportedly accompanied armies on their far-flung journeys through Hellas and neighboring lands;⁴⁹ officers often were accompanied by more than one *hetaira*.⁵⁰ Thus, Kharês, the Athenian general who spent much of his career outside Athens (largely in the northern Aegean), traveled about on campaigns with variegated groups of prostitutes, supposedly dedicating to erotic expenditures a portion of his military budget.⁵¹ Monuments to Pythionikê, a *hetaira* who among others serviced the Macedonian general Harpalos, reportedly stood in Athens—and hundreds of kilometers distant in Babylon!⁵² Stratôn, the king of Sidon, is said to have made use of courtesans from "the whole of Hellas," including Ionia and the

---

46. See *New York Times*, November 4, 2001, August 2, 2015; Griffin 2001; *San Francisco Bay Guardian*, January 18, 2004; Nussbaum 1998, 1999; Bell 1994; Sullivan 1994. Cf. Jeffreys 1997: 2: "In the last two decades the ideas of many feminists about prostitution have changed."

47. Pateman 2006, 1988; Carter and Giobbe 2006; Spector 2006: 422, n. 5.

48. Dover [1978] 1989: 34. The " 'untouchability" of those members of "the privileged citizen class" and their right to "throw their weight around to intimidate metics and slaves" supposedly precluded for *politai* the demeaning dependence inherent in functioning as prostitutes (Winkler 1990b: 49). Cf. chapter 3, n. 22.

49. See, for example, Xen. *Anab.* 4.3.19, 5.4.33. Alexis of Samos noted the women who accompanied Periklês (Athên. 572f): ἑταῖραι . . . αἱ συνακολουθήσασαι Περικλεῖ ὅτε ἐπολιόρκε τὴν Σάμον.

50. See Garlan 1975: 135; Cox 2003: 8.

51. FGrHist 115. F213 (Theopompos of Chios = Athên. 532c): Χάρητος . . . . ὅς γε περιήγετο στρατευόμενος αὐλητρίδας καὶ πεζὰς ἑταίρας, καὶ τῶν χρημάτων τῶν εἰσφερομένων εἰς τὸν πόλεμον τὰ μὲν εἰς ταύτην τὴν ὕβριν ἀνήλισκε. See Flower 1994: 126–28.

52. Poseidonios FGrH 87 F 14 (= Athên. 594e); Theopomp. FGrH 115 F 254 (= Athên. 595b-c). Cf. pp. 30–31.

Peloponnesos.[53] Commercial sex flourished at the recurring Hellenic festivals and games, at which crowds of visitors gathered for sport, enlightenment, pleasure, and tourism (Scanlon 2002: 226–27), and to which operators of sexual businesses (*pornoboskoi*) led "herds of women following the seasons and the festivals" (Davidson 1997: 92). Neaira, for example, resident in Attika for decades and long accepted as a citizen, had "worked the circuit of the entire (Hellenic) world," allegedly whoring "over all the Peloponnesos, in Thessaly and Magnesia, in Chios and through most of Ionia."[54] Sinôpê supposedly came from Thrace to work as a whore on Aigina, but ultimately "moved her practice of prostitution" to Athens.[55] Pythionikê is said to have worked as a *hetaira* in Korinth, and in Athens.[56]

But both for the modern world and for ancient Hellas, dependable statistical documentation of coerced sexual travel is nonexistent, and anecdotal information (often generated by partisan sources) is often unreliable.[57] Consider, for example, the disputed frequency of voluntary versus forced recruitment of aliens to present-day sexual service: opponents of prostitution insistently claim that coercion is rampant,[58] but proponents of the legitimization of "sex work" find trafficking generally to be merely "facilitated migration" of willing employees.[59] In the absence of numerical evidence, wild speculation abounds: between 2001 and 2005, for example, in a variety of communications, the US State Department reported the number of individuals trafficked to the United States annually "for sexual exploitation" to be as low as 14,500 and as high as 50,000 (Shafer 2006). But a senior State Department adviser on trafficking told the *New York*

---

53. FGrHist 115 F114 (Theopompos of Chios = Athên. 5531b): ὁ δὲ Στράτων . . . μετεπέμπετο πολλὰς δὲ μουσουργοὺς ἐξ Ἰωνίας, ἑτέρας δὲ παιδίσκας ἐξ ἁπάσης τῆς Ἑλλάδος.

54. Dem. 59.108: ἐν Πελοποννήσῳ μὲν πάσῃ, ἐν Θετταλίᾳ δὲ καὶ Μαγνησίᾳ μετὰ Σίμου τοῦ Λαρισαίου καὶ ἐν Ἰωνίᾳ τῇ πλείστῃ μετὰ Σωτάδου τοῦ Κρητὸς ἀκολουθοῦσα, μισθωθεῖσα. . . . γῆς περίοδον εἰργασμένην. Kapparis (1999: 400) finds this enumeration of work locations "perfectly credible" (but cf. Carey's skepticism [1992: 141]).

55. Athênaios 595a: Σινώπης τῆς Θρᾴττης τῆς ἐξ Αἰγίνης Ἀθήναζε μετενεγκαμένης τὴν πορνείαν.

56. Paus. 1.37.5: ἑταιροῦσαν δὲ ἔν τε Ἀθήναις καὶ ἐν Κορίνθῳ.

57. For the twenty-first century, Vermeulen 2010: 107–108; Stefanizzi 2010; Askola 2007: 1–3.

58. See Kara 2009: 4–37; Gerdes, ed. 2006: 107–09, 164–65, 175; MacKinnon 2005: 157–58; Leidholdt 2003: 175–80.

59. Doezma 2001; Network of Sexwork Projects 2002.

*Times* in 2004 that "we're not finding victims in the United States because we're not looking for them."⁶⁰ One expert estimates at 1.2 million the number of "young women and children who were deceived, abducted, seduced, or sold by families to be prostituted across the globe" (Kara 2009: 2); another commentator denies the accuracy of even far lower numbers, claiming that "most women volunteer for the trip westward because of the money they can make" and that "anti-trafficking activists use exaggerated sex slavery stories to get international media coverage of their cause" (McAleer 2006: 42).

The difficulty of ascertaining the "reality" of modern prostitution presages the greater difficulty of investigating commercial sex in an ancient society whose actual functioning we cannot adequately perceive, and whose social and economic institutions are only imperfectly known. For Athenian prostitution, statistics and archival material do not exist; literary testimonia and references are often, at best, uncontextualized, and sometimes even purposefully misleading; interpretation of relevant material remains, preserved in relative abundance, presents complex challenges.⁶¹ And yet, in contrast to other trades at Athens, for which information is often almost entirely absent,⁶² prostitution is relatively well-attested—in some regards (because commercial sex was lawful at Athens) better attested, *mirabile dictu*, than certain aspects of modern prostitution.

## *Lack of Statistics and Archival Material*

We know of no effort, in the whole of classical antiquity, to assemble, classify, and tabulate numerical data in a systematic fashion so as to present significant information about a specific ancient subject.⁶³ The "ignominious truth" is that "there are no ancient statistics."⁶⁴ Accordingly, we

---

60. *New York Times* Magazine, January 25, 2004.

61. See pp. 20–24.

62. Wrenhaven 2009: 368; Labarre 1998: 795.

63. On this absence of statistics in the ancient Mediterranean world, see Picard, 2008a: 27–30; Morris and Manning 2005: 133–34; Cohen 1992: 27.

64. Jones, Introduction to his inaugural lecture (1948). Cf. the similar observation by Momigliano in his own inaugural lecture (1952).

have no reliable information concerning even the number of Athenian citizens, or their quantity relative to that of slaves and free aliens (*metics*) resident at Athens.⁶⁵ And so, as with many aspects of modern prostitution (pp. 11–12), a statistical approach to Athenian prostitution is not possible. But an ancient investigator would have had access to material that the criminalization of modern commercial sex precludes. The Athenian state annually delivered precise data and detailed information on individual sex-workers to the private tax-collectors who actually extracted the tax imposed on prostitutes: according to Aiskhinês, there was no need to speculate (*eikazein*); the number and composition of Athenian sex-workers was known with precision (*akribôs*).⁶⁶ This information, however, has not survived. Although the Athenians did maintain an archive in the Mêtroön,⁶⁷ where such materials might have been kept,⁶⁸ its contents are not extant. Because of these losses, we cannot today determine, for example, the relative number of prostitutes of each sex, the frequency of purchased erotic encounters with male rather than female prostitutes, the relative ratios of free versus enslaved prostitutes, or the numbers of those working under compulsion.⁶⁹

---

65. For surveys of the widely divergent modern estimates of the number of adult male citizens at Athens during the fourth and fifth centuries, see Scheidel 1998: 197–98; Oliver 2007: 79–83. Cf. Gomme 1933: 26, 29; Ehrenberg 1969: 31; Ruschenbusch 1979: 146; 1981: 112; Hansen 1985b: 67–69; Oliver 1995: 9–38. Uncertainty concerning the composition of the population: Scheidel 2007: 45; Jones 2008: 34; Whitby 1998: 109–114.

66. καθ' ἕκαστον ἐνιαυτὸν ἡ βουλὴ πωλεῖ τὸ πορνικὸν τέλος· καὶ τοὺς πριαμένους τὸ τέλος οὐκ εἰκάζειν, ἀλλ' ἀκριβῶς εἰδέναι τοὺς ταύτῃ χρωμένους τῇ ἐργασίᾳ. (Aiskh. 1.119). See further, chapter 5, pp. 117–118ff. On the process of "tax farming" at Athens, see Athenian Grain-Tax Law (374/3)(esp.) 27–30 (Stroud 1998); Aristot. *Ath. Pol.* 47.2; Andok. 1.73, 133–36; Aristoph. *Sphêk.* 657–59. Cf. Faraguna 2010; Migeotte 2001.

67. Sickinger 1999: 93–195; Thomas 1989: 68–83.

68. Even in the fourth century, however, the items on deposit in the Athenian archive(s) (or elsewhere) were necessarily limited: there was no land register (Gabrielsen 1986: 113, n. 40; Christ 1990: 158), no list of *politai* (Davidson 1997: 215; Biscardi 1991: 140 and 1970), only rudimentary financial accounts (Finley 1982), although in the postclassical period, economic matters appear to have been more extensively and more sophisticatedly memorialized (Sickinger 1999: 69–70, 125–27).

69. This lacuna has not deterred scholars from speculation: "Male sex-workers were, I think, nowhere near as numerous as their female counterparts" (Davidson 1997: 77); "Female (prostitutes) greatly outnumbered males" (Skinner 2005: 98); "[the] majority of prostitutes in the ancient world" were working under compulsion (Glazebrook and Henry 2011: 13, n. 2).

## Forensic, Comic, and Other Literary Sources

The study of Athenian prostitution is greatly facilitated, however, by the abundance of relevant information that *is* preserved in literary sources, especially in the "situation comedies" of Menander and other comedic sources, and in the multitude of law-court presentations—long recognized as providing "the best image of contemporary society"[70]—that deal with or allude to aspects of meretricious arrangements (especially the speeches entitled Aiskhinês 1, Demosthenes 59, Lysias 3, and Lysias 4). In addition, material remains from Athens (ceramic representations, inscriptions preserved on stone, floor plans, and other architectural remnants) provide further potential insights. But again, the interpretation of this material presents substantial evidentiary challenges.

### Forensic Material

Although Athenian forensic speeches are rhetorical contrivances that virtually always present evidence tendentiously (and often dishonestly), the presuppositions underlying litigants' claims are generally reliable: since forensic presentations were made to panels composed of hundreds of jurors—with persuasion being the speaker's dominant motive[71]—the presence of a general phenomenon may be confirmed by a claim that presupposes such a phenomenon, even if we cannot establish (or strongly doubt) the truth of the speaker's specific factual assertion.[72] An assertion dependent on premises blatantly inconceivable would be inherently unpersuasive. When Simôn insists that he has entered into a formal commercial contract with Theodotos providing for the exchange of sex for money (Lysias 3.22), we may be unable to confirm the truth or falsity of Simôn's contention, but we *can* be sure that such arrangements were not implausible in

---

70. Garlan 1988: 16. Cf. Mossé [1962] 1979: 179–215.

71. Although some scholars view Athenian private litigation as largely "theatre" (Humphreys 2007) or as a venue for the venting of elite social animosities (D. Cohen 1995: 70, 82), with litigants sometimes seeking actually to lose their cases (E. Cohen [forthcoming (b)]; Todd 2011: 138, 1994: 131, n. 180), I view Athenian litigation as essentially the effort of real people to prevail in real conflicts by persuading a majority of jurors to vote in their favor (cf. Harris 2013: 12–13). In my opinion, therefore, the proffering of absurd or transparently untrue underlying factual assumptions would have been devastatingly negative to a proponent's case—and would likely be avoided in a forensic presentation.

72. Cf. E. Cohen 1990b: 178, 186–90; Millett 2000: 25–26, 1991: 2; Todd 1990.

fourth-century Athens. When Apollodôros claims that Nikaretê presented as her own offspring the child prostitutes whom she owned, because the "highest prices" might be obtained from customers desiring to have sex with young girls whom they believed to be the free offspring of the woman providing the children's services,[73] we may be unable to evaluate the true personal status of these prostitutes, or to confirm Nikaretê's actual business practices, but we can safely conclude that pricing of sexual services did in fact vary in accordance with a prostitute's perceived status and a customer's psychological predispositions. When a number of Athenian political leaders are accused, in a number of individual speeches, of having prostituted themselves in their youth, again we cannot determine the likely truth of any individual accusation or even exclude the possibility that all such surviving charges are false (or true). But we may reasonably infer that Athenian audiences would not categorically rule out such charges as inherently implausible (just as modern Western political audiences might not find inherently implausible the recurrent charges of sexual misconduct leveled against European and American political leaders).

## Comic Sources

In contrast to scholars' long acceptance of material from forensic speeches as valuable for an understanding of Attic society, comedy has only recently been gaining recognition as a useful source of information on the actualities of Athenian life. Although the fourth-century plays of Menander and his contemporaries constitute a genre centered (unlike earlier comic works[74]) on the private lives of individuals, nineteenth-century scholars made almost no historical use of this so-called New Comedy, whose value as source material they deprecated.[75] In part this disregard reflected the

---

73. Dem. 59.18–19: Ἑπτὰ γὰρ ταύτας παιδίσκας ἐκ μικρῶν παιδίων ἐκτήσατο Νικαρέτη ... προειποῦσα δ' αὐτὰς ὀνόματι θυγατέρας, ἵν' ὡς μεγίστους μισθοὺς πράττοιτο τοὺς βουλομένους πλησιάζειν αὐταῖς ὡς ἐλευθέραις οὔσαις. ...

74. Yet even fifth-century comedy—despite its frequent engagement with public policy and its indulgence in wild fantasy—can be fruitfully mined for factual information relating to social history (Buis 2014: 322): see MacDowell's discussions of allegations of politicians' foreign origin (1993: 359–71) and of charges of cowardice against public figures (1995: 24–26). In fact, "both domestic and political themes and subjects were already in the (comic) repertory when our attestation begins ca. 440" (Henderson 2014: 181).

75. See, for example, Mahaffy: "[W]hen we come to inquire from [Menander] and from the New Comedy what they have to tell us about their age, the outcome is miserably small. ... It

relative paucity of surviving material (which increased exponentially during the twentieth century as a result of fresh papyrological publications); in part it reflected the traditional academic fascination with Athens as a paragon of high culture (inhibiting interest in surviving literature that was perceived as low-brow popular pap[76]).

Through the twentieth century, however, the continuing discovery and elucidation of comic plays and fragments made scholars increasingly aware of the valuable information on contemporary life contained in this material. Concurrently, a shift in academic interests has generated renewed attention to the social dimensions—romantic attachments, class conflict, gender issues—that form the subject matter of Attic New Comedy. Despite the distortions inherent in the authors' pursuit of love and of laughs, the assumptions—of contexts and relationships—underlying fourth-century comedy provide insight concerning Athenian social practices. In particular, scholars have recurrently demonstrated how Menander's comedies (in which prostitutes often appear[77]) provide considerable information about Athenian life, offering even highly specific details about the laws of property and succession.[78] For example, the marriage alliances in the *Dyskolos*—although fashioned to meet the exigencies of humorous scheme and artifice—replicate contemporary marital and inheritance practices.[79] The structure (and even the amounts) of dowries in Menander's work are consistent with arrangements epigraphically and historically attested.[80]

---

is usual to lament the irreparable loss of the plays of Menander, but it may be doubted whether history would gain from a further knowledge of him" (1896: 125).

76. "Seductions and unwanted children, coincidences and recognitions of long-lost daughters, irate fathers and impertinent slaves ... New Comedy." Tarn [1927] 1952: 273.

77. No less than thirty-seven *hetairai* appear by name in comedies dated from 380 to 320 (Henderson 2014: 192). On Menander's treatment of such prostitutes, see Brown 1990: 254; Henry 1985.

78. See Buis 2014: 334–37; Cox 2002: 391; Hunter 1994: 85, 217, n. 26; Patterson 1998: 191–205.

79. See Zagagi 1995: 94–113. Some scholars have summarily rejected as mere "comedy" Menander's portrayal of marriage between members of relatively wealthy and relatively poor families (Rosivach 2001: 133). But Cox 2002 has demonstrated that epigraphic evidence supports the occurrence of marriages between men and women of sharply differing economic situations. Cf. Hoffmann 1986.

80. See Golden 1990: 174–76; Casson 1976: 53–59; Gomme and Sandbach 1973: 298. Finley earlier, and falsely, assumed the size of Menandrian dowries to be excessive ([1951] 1985: 266–67, n. 29).

Similarly the portrayal of the *hetaira* Khrysis in *Woman of Samos* reveals the extent to which free Athenian residents might preserve their independence even while providing for themselves through the provision of sex to others—and confirms further aspects of the business of prostitution known through more prosaic sources (see section "Selling 'Free' Love" in chapter 2). Although Menandrian plots may be unrepresentative of the actual daily lives of the overwhelming majority of the population of Attika (who presumably did not spend a considerable portion of their time at dinner parties celebrating the happy conclusion of social and familial strife), "what Menander offers us through his comic lens is an image of the life of the society as a whole and its central human relationships,"[81] an image that informs the pages of my book.

Despite the discovery of fresh papyrological texts of Athenian comic writing, much of Greek New Comedy is still known primarily from the work of the Latin comic authors Plautus and Terence (Nesselrath 2014: 672–73). Their *palliatae* ("plays in Greek garb") are adaptations from Hellenic originals, generally preserving the essence of the plots, contexts, characters, and institutions of the earlier Greek plays. Since female prostitutes and their customers, families, and associates are not infrequently at or near the epicenter of action and characterization,[82] and brothels are frequently featured on the stage (often in close proximity to aristocratic households),[83] these Roman *palliatae*, the only complete Latin comedies to have survived from antiquity, are invaluable sources for the study of Athenian prostitution. But as products and adaptations—not translations—of a distinct (and non-Hellenic) society, these works must be used with focused care: the separation of Greek and Roman elements has been a preoccupation of scholars active in this field and will affect my investigation, especially in chapters 6 and 7.[84]

Linguistic considerations, especially those inherent in the Latin language, present a further challenge. For example, the Roman term *meretrix*, a female provider of commercial sex, does not encompass (or convey) the nuanced characteristics of the Greek *pornê* and the Greek *hetaira*, female

---

81. Patterson 1998: 195. See also Zagagi 1995: 113.

82. See, for example, Plaut. *Cistellaria*; Ter. *Andria, Eunuchus, Heauton Timoroumenos*.

83. See, for example, Plautus's *Menaechmi, Mostellaria* and *Pseudolus*.

84. On the proper use of Roman comic material as evidence for Athenian legal and social practices see Scafuro 1997: 16–19; Paoli 1976: 76–77. See also McCarthy 2000: 5; Paoli 1951.

providers of commercial sex in a civilization and language inherently binomial (see chapter 1, pp. 31–38). Roman society offered no division of sexual workers comparable to that of Greek society, and no duality of nomenclature and structure. Yet in Latin "adaptations" of the prostitute-laden works of Greek New Comedy[85] the single word *meretrix* had to convey to Roman audiences the subtle and variant significations of the two Hellenic terms.[86]

Closely related to comedy is the mimiamb, a genre mixing iambic poetry (traditional verse of realistic passion) with the "mime" (bawdy popular entertainment in prose). In Mimes 1 and 2, recovered from the sands of Egypt and first published in 1891, Hêrôdas provides striking pictures of those in control of commercial sex—a procuress, a brothel-keeper—and the sexual workers whom they used and coveted. Here again—although the content is presumably fictitious—the context, allusions, background, and coloration necessarily reflect actual practices and institutions. Yet, like the Atticists of later antiquity, Hêrôdas is not writing exclusively of the first half of the third century and of the Hellenistic culture in which he lived. Instead, he recreates a world of Hellenic tradition manifested through stock characters—"sometimes female panderers or adulterers, sometimes a man arriving for drunken sexual revelry with his love."[87]

## "Later" Literature

Virtually all the forensic and comedic evidence discussed above dates from the fourth century B.C.E. (and the years immediately before and after the fourth century), and this book accordingly chronicles conditions prevailing during this classical period—and not necessarily at other times. Some fourth-century evidence, however, is preserved in the works of authors who lived long after the classical period of Athens—most significantly in the *Hetairikoi Dialogoi* ("Courtesans' Dialogues") of Loukianos, and in the *Deipnosophistai* ("Scholars at Dinner") of Athênaios, both of whom were

---

85. On the ubiquity of prostitutes as characters in fourth-century Comedy, see Henderson 2014: 186, 191–93; Lape 2004: 161, n. 72.

86. See Halporn 1993: 201–202. Despite the dominant ubiquity of *meretrix*, Latin offered, in fact, numerous nuanced terms for people who engaged in sex for compensation: Adams 1983 enumerates some fifty such Latin words. Cf. Foxhall 2013: 103; James 2006: 225–28; McClure 2006: 7–8.

87. ποτὲ μὲν γυναῖκας καὶ μοιχοὺς καὶ μαστροπούς, ποτὲ δὲ ἄνδρα μεθύοντα καὶ ἐπὶ κῶμον παραγινόμενον πρὸς τὴν ἐρωμένην (Athên. 621c5–7) (Translation: I. Cunningham, 1993: 204).

active roughly half a millennium after the fourth century, writing in Greek at the acme of the Roman Empire.[88] While Athênaios preserves the *ipsissima verba* of earlier authors, Loukianos consciously seeks to recreate, linguistically and historically, the world of classical Athens. His *Courtesans' Dialogues* "look back to fourth-century comedy" (Davidson 1997: 332), offering a setting "vaguely Hellenistic" (Jones 1986: 158). Working from classical sources now lost, Loukianos offers allusions, historical settings, values, and contexts that recreate, in shadow and mist, the world earlier adumbrated by Menander[89]—and he provides modern scholars with valuable material to test or expand the evidence of the fourth-century sources.[90] As with fourth-century comedy itself, we learn most from the framework of relationships and the social assumptions that underlie Loukianos's comic portrayals and amorous exaggerations.

A similar effort to recreate the fourth century, "borrowing from New Comedy and from the authors of the classical period,"[91] was undertaken by Alkiphrôn, an author of the second or third century C.E., whose writing provides striking parallels with the *Courtesans' Dialogues* of Loukianos. Alkiphrôn's *Courtesans' Letters* (*Epistolai Hetairikai*), fictitious correspondence largely attributed to famed prostitutes of classical Athens, offers details of amour and commerce in a cultivated style patterned after the classical Greek of centuries earlier.

Athênaios's work—consisting of literary excerpts and other citations inserted into the framework of a banquet attended by a large number of learned guests—preserves thousands of citations, especially from fourth-century Middle and Late Comedy, thus potentially providing our largest single repository of information about aspects of daily life in fourth-century Athens.[92] The guests at the banquet discourse learnedly on many subjects, but their tales of

---

88. Loukianos: fl. 160–80 C.E.: see Pellizer and Sirugo 1995: 37–41; Haley 2002: 289. Athênaios: fl. *c.* 200 C.E.: see Zecchini 1939.

89. In *the Courtesans' Dialogues*, "types and situations are plainly drawn, for the most part, from New Comedy" (Robinson 1979: 11), and its "world is essentially the same as that of New Comedy" (Rosivach 1998: 145). See Branham 1989: 128. For Loukianos's familiarity with, and frequent citation of, Menander, see Schmid 1959: 157–58; Jones 1986: 151. For his deep knowledge of classical literature, see Helm 1927: 1766; Householder 1941 (pace Anderson 1976 and 1978, whose "argumentation is thin" [Jones 1986: 150, n. 9]).

90. See generally Reardon 1971: esp. 179; Bompaire 1958, 1975; Delz 1950, 1960.

91. Benner and Fobes 1949: 5. See also Trapp 1996, s.v. Alciphron.

92. See Sidwell 2000: 137; McClure 2003a: 260–61.

famous courtesans (13.555 ff.), buttressed by a vast collection of quotations from Athenian literature, are a potentially invaluable exegesis of commercial sex in classical Athens. Athênaios, Alkiphrôn, Loukianos, and other later authors, however, present a fresh historiographical challenge: throughout this book I have therefore endeavored to note both possible conflicts between these sources and material directly preserved from the fourth century, to interpret these citations in context, and to record suggestions made by others concerning the unreliability of such later testimonia.[93]

A further challenge arises from the overrepresentation of "literary" material in the corpus of surviving evidence. Authors of imaginative works are by definition creators of fiction, not chroniclers of facts. A fortiori, a collection—like that of Athênaios—encompassing multiple citations from multiple authors is a compendium of fictitious inventiveness that must be read with attention to context. As contemporary critical theory teaches, uncontextualized interpretations may propagate superficiality and inaccuracy.[94] Yet—as with law court presentations, where the literal truth of a litigant's specific factual assertions generally are beyond our evaluation, but the speaker's presuppositions may provide sound evidence (see pp. 14–15)—the implicit assumptions and overt allusions of comedy and vignette frequently illuminate historical institutions and behavior. These assumptions and allusions often provide insight into actual practices—although the comic dimension and cultural context usually underlie, and often distort, even a seemingly straightforward surface.

## *Material Remains*

Material remains are an important—but difficult—source of information concerning Athenian prostitution. Archaeologists claim to have identified "red-light districts" in Athens, and have even unearthed ground plans of buildings believed to have been brothels, within which artifacts supposedly

---

93. For Athênaios, historiographical factors have been assayed with a thoroughness not yet attained for Alkiphrôn, Loukianos, and other later authors on whom I rely: see Chapters 5 through 17 of Braund and Wilkins, eds., 2000. Regarding the subjectivity often shown by modern historians in accepting or rejecting specific items of evidence relating to earlier periods but preserved in the writings of later antiquity, especially on legal questions, see D. Cohen 1990: esp. 293. Cf. Wolff 1975.

94. Cf. Glazebrook and Henry 2011: 6–7; McClure 2003b: 2; Dalby 1996: 176–77; Flower 1994: 7.

relating to prostitution have been found.⁹⁵ Many representations on ceramic material ("pottery") have been identified as meretricious scenes.⁹⁶ Evaluating such evidence, however, is methodologically challenging.⁹⁷ For instance, modern illustrations of prostitutes, selected from Attic vases, offer multitudinous portrayals of female sex workers, but supposedly none of males ⁹⁸—a manifestation, in my opinion, of a practice whereby "critics tend to assume that the women in sexually explicit heterosexual scenes are prostitutes," while explicit portrayals of male homosexual relations are termed "courtship scenes." ⁹⁹ Identification of Athenian locations for commercial sex is likewise subject to preconception: brothels seem to have occupied all or part of structures that might have served numerous other purposes when not used as bordellos (Aiskhinês 1.124); many prostitutes worked in individual chambers that seem often not to have been part of larger complexes devoted to commercial sex (see pp. 3–5).

In fact, much of Athenian visual iconography (the interpretation of ceramic representations on surviving Attic vases and fragments)—and accordingly much of the profuse information on prostitution believed to be offered by pottery—rests, to greater or lesser extent, on two now-contested bases: the assumption that because of the alleged seclusion at Athens of "respectable" women, females portrayed on ceramic material were unlikely to be free women, and certainly not the wives and daughters of Athenian citizens; and the assumption that ceramic representation depicts actual life in a manner directly cognizable by modern scholars. Because of the belief that respectable women were invisible, "the resulting descriptions of visual imagery suggest that any woman receiving a gift is a prostitute of some sort and not a potential or actual wife" (Rabinowitz 2011: 128). Yet the underlying concept of the invisibility of respectable women at Athens is itself questionable.¹⁰⁰ Moreover, although art historians and archaeologists

---

95. See Knigge 2005; Glazebook 2011: 39–46; see also chapter 2, p. 52.

96. Lear and Cantarella 2008: 137–38; Lewis 2002: 196; Ferrari 2002: 178, 300 (nn. 89, 90).

97. Consider the heated dispute regarding the woman on an alabastron (Ethn. Mus., Athens, 1239) that arguably depicts a youth leading a customer to a prostitute (Robert 1919: 125–29). On this controversy, see Schnapp 1986; Meyer 1988. Cf. Immerwahr 1984.

98. Rabinowitz 2002: 161, n. 101; Shapiro 1992

99. Rabinowitz 2002: 111; 154, n. 32. Cf. Lear and Cantarella 2008: 80; Rodenwalt 1932; Beasley 1947: 195–244. Keuls does identify a scene on a cup by Douris (ARV 437, 114: Metropolitan Museum of Art, N. Y., 52.11.4) as "men negotiating the price of sex with a boy."

100. See D. Cohen 1996; Sourvinou-Inwood 1995: 111–18; Reeder 1995: 22–23.

had long tended to see scenes adorning Attic vases as reflections of reality—illustrations of actual Athenian life—these pictures are now often construed as mere deco or, alternatively, as pictures of life suffused within the Athenian *imaginaire*, systems of signs and symbols requiring decoding—but on either interpretation not transparently direct illustrations of actual life.[101] Even extreme expounders of such interpretations concede, however, that ceramic portrayals may nonetheless reveal mundane reality—furniture, clothing, physical activity—whose banality may result in its going unrecorded in literary sources, despite its importance for the modern reconstruction of ancient life. In actual practice, however, scholars often use vase-paintings as at least a partial reflection of an underlying historical reality—albeit a reality somewhat obscured by iconographic alterations—an approach reflecting "a belief that visual media are, at least when representational, inherently more realistic than literary genres" (Lear and Cantarella 2008: 24). In this book, I follow a moderate position, emphasizing careful analysis of surviving images: "as tempting as it is to interpret scenes of women in a literal way, especially in the absence of other evidence, one must be cautious" (Bundrick 2008: 284).

Consider sex-workers' "social status." Visual iconography is often said to confirm the universally low juridical and civic status of prostitutes. Scholars accordingly have tended to attribute slave status to all persons identified as whores in scenes on Athenian pottery—and a fortiori to deny ceramic presence to courtesans of elegance and wealth. Female prostitutes of high status and accomplishment are never seen on pottery—either because they do not exist or because the so-called *megalomisthoi* ("high-earning" prostitutes) are increasingly denigrated by modern commentators as "nothing more than the product of (lustful) imaginings of older (male, heterosexual?) scholars" (Davidson 2005: 182). Yet the interpretative removal of free *hetairai* from ceramic scenes is almost always tautological—arising from a priori assumptions that a decent woman would not be appearing on ceramic representations and that a prostitute (merely because of his or her sexual function) must necessarily be a slave. In fact, "in most cases it is impossible to identify clear expressions of citizen, non-citizen or slave status, direct or symbolic" (Lewis 2002: 8), or even to distinguish *hetairai* from (other) free

---

101. See Lissarrague 1990: 1–12; Bérard et al. 1989; Schmitt, Pantel, and Thelamon 1983; Zinserling 1977.

women in erotic or commercial settings.[102] Broader studies (especially Peschel 1987) have shown the unreliability of the stereotypical modern bases—nudity, hairstyle, purses, garter amulets, the presence of inscribed names—for identifying Athenian prostitutes on ceramic work.[103] Literary evidence suggests that this absence of clear indications of status on pottery merely replicates the actual homogeneous appearance of the various residents of Attika, making it difficult to distinguish, by dress or by physical characteristic alone, free persons from slaves, citizens from aliens. Although some modern scholars have sought to find in sepulchral art and obtuse literary allusions markers of attire differentiating slaves from free persons,[104] the author of the satiric *Constitution of the Athenians* insists that at Athens no difference in dress or physical appearance distinguishes citizen, foreigner, or slave,[105] an egalitarianism confirmed—and decried—by Plato.[106] Court presentations routinely posit a similarity of appearance among local inhabitants. During a raid on a citizen's farm, for example, by persons seeking to enforce a judgment, the debtor's son was carried off: he was assumed to be a slave (Demosthenes 47.61). The maltreatment

---

102. Llewellyn-Jones 2003: 140, 151, n. 76; Miller 1997: 165 ff.; Bazant 1987: 37; Kilmer 1993. Yet some literary scholars, seeking to explain away a pictorial record in conflict with academic preconceptions, insist that the absence on pottery of clear differentiation between *hetaira* and citizen is itself a sophisticated subversion of the true, and blatant, distinctions found in real life (see Beard 1991).

103. Purses offer a good example. While Lewis questions the prevailing belief that the presence of a purse in male/female scenes is an indication of a prostitutional theme (2002: 194–99), Stewart finds the mere absence of a purse ipso facto sufficient reason to dismiss the possibility of prostitution (1997: 157). Cf. Ferrari 2002: 16; von Reden 1995: 206–209.

104. Dalby 2002 finds in literary materials a suggestion that courtesans wore more elaborate clothing (and of finer quality) than other female residents of Attika. But he concedes that in general "their dress was like that of other women" (2002: 119). Bäbler claims that "female slaves on grave-stelai are usually depicted wearing a characteristic long-sleeved dress or '*kandys*,' which seems to have been a kind of 'slave garment'" (2001, n. 5 and related text). Cf. Bäbler 1998: 20–32. But other specialists disagree: "slave figures dress in the same way as the (free) women with whom they appear" (Lewis 2002: 140). Rihll (2011: 50) finds slaves "generally indistinguishable" from citizens "in appearance and, apparently, in demeanour." Davies 1994 sees the iconography of grave stêlai as suggestive of the "solidarity" of women and their slaves.

105. Xen. *Ath. Pol.* 1.10: εἰ νόμος ἦν τόν δοῦλον ὑπό τοῦ ἐλευθέρου τύπτεσθαι. . . . πολλάκις ἂν οἰηθεὶς εἶναι τόν Ἀθηναῖον δοῦλον ἐπάταξεν ἄν· ἐσθῆτά τε γὰρ οὐδὲν βελτίων ὁ δῆμος αὐτόθι ἢ οἱ δοῦλοι καὶ οἱ μέτοικοι, καὶ τὰ εἴδη οὐδὲν βελτίους εἰσίν. Similarly: Sommerstein 2009: 136.

106. *Rep.* 563b: . . . οἱ ἐωνημένοι καὶ αἱ ἐωνημέναι μηδὲν ἧττον ἐλεύθεροι ὦσι τῶν πριαμένων. ἐν γυναιξὶ δὲ πρὸς ἄνδρας καὶ ἀνδράσι πρὸς γυναῖκας ὅση ἡ ἰσονομία καὶ ἐλευθερία γίγνεται . . .

of a free woman, described at Demosthenes 47.58–59, demonstrates the difficulty of differentiating female slaves from other women. We even hear of a young man who was sent into a neighbor's garden to pluck flowers in the hope that, mistaking the intruder for a slave, the neighbor might strike or bind him and thus become subject to damages for *hybris* (Demosthenes 53.16).

Visual iconography, however, does not always confirm literary reports or scholarly preconception. In some contexts, it may challenge written testimonia or may even suggest fruitful areas of exploration not obvious from other sources. In short, in my opinion, material remains do constitute valuable evidence for Athenian prostitution, but visual iconography and architectonic identification must always be employed only in the context of, and with the aid of, all other relevant material.

# I
## Aphroditê's Workers in Democratic Athens

AT ATHENS TRADITIONAL aristocratic ethics idealized leisurely dedication to cultural and social activities, condemned all commerce as inherently servile, and insisted that farming alone provided a proper economic arena for the "free man" (anêr eleutheros).[1] Xenophôn decried the presence in the Athenian Assembly of clothes-cleaners, leather-workers, construction workers, blacksmiths, traders, and men involved in retail activity.[2] For Plato, "market people" (agoraioi anthrôpoi) were "defective men" (phauloi) who pursued monetary profit because they were incapable of more acceptable cultural and political pursuits.[3] Aristotle and Xenophôn explicitly group the "commercial crowd" (agoraios okhlos) with slaves and servants.[4] Xenophôn decried the commercialization of sex.[5] Since Greeks tended to construe work not merely as an economic function but also as a mechanism of self-definition,[6] by aristocratic standards men involved in nonagrarian, so-called banausic callings—production or

---

1. Xen. Oik. 5.1; Eur. Or. 917–22, Hiket.; Pl. Nom. 889d; Men. Fr. 338 (Kôrte/Thierfelder 1953); Aristoph. Eir. passim, Akh. 32–36. See Hanson 1995: 214–19.

2. Τοὺς γναφέας αὐτῶν ἢ τοὺς σκυτέας ἢ τοὺς τέκτονας ἢ τοὺς χαλκέας ἢ τοὺς γεωργοὺς ἢ τοὺς ἐμπόρους ἢ τοὺς ἐν τῇ ἀγορᾷ μεταβαλλομένους . . . ἐκ γὰρ τούτων ἁπάντων ἡ ἐκκλησία συνίσταται (Apom. 3.7.6). Plato agrees: Ὁμοίως μὲν τέκτων, ὁμοίως δὲ χαλκεύς, σκυτοτόμος, ἔμπορος, ναύκληρος . . . (Prôtag. 319d). Cf. Humphreys 1978: 148.

3. Pl. Rep. 371c. Cf. Pl. Prôtag. 347c; Polit. 289e.

4. See Aristot. Pol. 1291b14–30, 1289b26–34; Xen. Hell. 6.2.23.

5. Apom. 1.6.13. See introduction, pp. 6–7 and n. 29.

6. See von Reden 1992; Loraux 1995: 44–58; Vernant 1971: 2.17. Cf. Schwimmer 1979.

trading of goods, labor for monetary compensation, even professional acting or musical performances—were unworthy of "citizenship,"[7] and many oligarchic states wisely and absolutely (according to Aristotle) prohibited citizens (*politai*) from engaging actively in business.[8] Even at Athens, the right of laboring men, even practitioners of a skilled trade, to be citizens and to participate actively in public affairs was justified primarily on the basis that engagement in such occupations was a matter not of choice but of economic necessity.[9] But, in Aristotle's opinion, political instability was an inherent result of the extension of political rights to persons engaged in trade and commerce: possessors of wealth would naturally object to sharing power with persons lacking assets sufficient to shield themselves from having to work for a living.[10] When antidemocratic forces briefly seized power at Athens in 413, their Constitution of the Five Thousand explicitly limited political participation to the 5,000 Athenians who were "best" in body and wealth.[11] By traditional standards, those engaged in trade and business would have been judged "worst" in body and wealth: aristocratic doctrine insisted that banausic activity deformed the body[12]; one should thus pity the impoverished person forced by financial necessity into such pursuits.[13] Aristotle's conclusion is explicit: "The best community will not make a working man a citizen."[14]

This pervasive aristocratic contempt for productive labor is frequently disturbing to modern observers who themselves are often

---

7. On the virulent opposition to *banausia*, see, e.g., Arist. *Pol.* 1337b18–22; 1258b25–27, 33–39; 1260a41–b2; 1277a32–b7; 1277b33–1278a13; 1341b8–18. Cf. Kamen 2013: 99; Welskopf 1980; Balot 2001: 22–43; Humphreys 1978, esp. 148–49.

8. Χρηματίζεσθαι. Cf. Ober 1991: 125.

9. Aiskhin. 1.27: ὁ νομοθέτης διαρρήδην ἀπέδειξεν οὓς χρὴ δημηγορεῖν καὶ οὓς οὐ δεῖ λέγειν ἐν τῷ δήμῳ. Καὶ οὐκ ἀπελαύνει ἀπὸ τοῦ βήματος, εἴ τις . . . τέχνην τινὰ ἐργάζεται ἐπικουρῶν τῇ ἀναγκαίᾳ τροφῇ . . . Cf. Thouk. 2.37, 40.

10. *Pol.* 1316b1–5: οἱ πολὺ ὑπερέχοντες ταῖς οὐσίαις οὐ δίκαιον οἴονται εἶναι ἴσον μετέχειν τῆς πόλεως τοὺς κεκτημένους μηθὲν τοῖς κεκτημένοις· ἐν πολλαῖς τε ὀλιγαρχίαις οὐκ ἔξεστι χρηματίζεσθαι, ἀλλὰ νόμοι εἰσὶν οἱ κωλύοντες.

11. Aristot. *Ath. Pol.* 29.5: τὴν δ' ἄλλην πολιτείαν ἐπιτρέψαι πᾶσαν Ἀθηναίων τοῖς δυνατωτάτοις καὶ τοῖς σώμασιν καὶ τοῖς χρήμασιν λῃτουργεῖν μὴ ἔλαττον ἢ πεντακισχιλίοις. . . . Thouk. 8.65.3: οὔτε μεθεκτέον τῶν πραγμάτων πλέοσιν ἢ πεντακισχιλίοις, καὶ τούτοις οἳ ἂν μάλιστα τοῖς τε χρήμασι καὶ τοῖς σώμασιν ὠφελεῖν οἷοί τε ὦσιν.

12. βαναυσόταται δ' ἐν αἷς τὰ σώματα λωβῶνται μάλιστα (Aristot. *Pol.* 1258b37).

13. Isai. 5.39; Dem. 57.45.

14. *Pol.* 1278a8: ἡ δὲ βελτίστη πόλις οὐ ποιήσει βάναυσον πολίτην.

highly admiring of the aesthetic accomplishments of Athenian ceramic workers and other artistic producers of what were for the Greeks often merely utilitarian products. Modern veneration of Athenian trades not surprisingly does not extend to prostitution, but for the Greeks the provision of sex for compensation was not differentiated structurally or linguistically from other métiers. Thus, brothels were *ergastêria* ("work-houses")[15]; prostitution was alluded to dispassionately as an *ergasia* ("business"),[16] sometimes even as a *tekhnê* (a profession requiring a high degree of skill).[17]

As a mercantile activity, however, prostitution was not untouched by Athenian antagonism toward commercial and manual pursuits, and numerous negative allusions toward prostitutes and prostitution are found in Greek sources—often implicitly, sometimes explicitly. However, a detailed study of the terminology of Greek prostitution finds that for prostitution "terms that imply moral shame are not widely attested before the second to third century CE" (Kapparis 2011: 228), a half-millennium and more after the classical period. Many other commercial activities did not fare as well: pursuits today not evoking negativity were often denigrated in classical Athens. Bankers were denounced as "most pestiferous."[18] Selling ribbons or serving as a wet-nurse evoked contempt[19]—as did auctioneering, cooking, inn-keeping, tax collecting, brothel-keeping, and gambling.[20] Employment as an actor evoked contempt similar to that engendered by operating a primary school.[21] Any form of hired daylabor, even agricultural work requiring personal effort, was seen by some

---

15. Although the Greeks had numerous other terms for prostitutional locations, *ergastêrion* is the earliest attested word for brothel (Kapparis 2011: 226) and seems to have been the official term: places of prostitution were so designated in legal texts and contexts (see, e.g., Dem. 59.67; Lys. 10.19; Plut. *Sol.* 23.1—cf. Johnstone 2002). Cf. Alkiphr. 3.27 and Fr. 4; Aiskhin. 1.124.

16. Venal sex as an *ergasia:* Hdt. 2.135; Dem. 18.129. For *ergasia* as the general term for a profit-making business, see E. Cohen 1992: 111, n. 1.

17. For prostitution as a *tekhnê*, see Dem. 59.18.

18. Τοὺς τραπεζίτας· ἔθνος τούτου γὰρ οὐδέν ἐστιν ἐξωλέστερον. (Antiphanês Fr. 157 [K-A]).

19. Dem. 57.29, 35.

20. Theophr. *Khar.* 6.2–10: ὁ δὲ ἀπονενοημένος . . . δεινὸς δὲ καὶ πανδοκεῦσαι καὶ πορνοβοσκῆσαι καὶ τελωνῆσαι . . . κηρύττειν, μαγειρεύειν, κυβεύειν.

21. See the ridicule heaped on Aiskhinês for his involvement in these activities: Dem. 19.70, 246, 249.

as offensively inappropriate for an Athenian woman.²² Some citizens so disdained Athenians working in retail trade that "sitting in a brothel was no more despicable to the elite than working in the agora" (Glazebrook 2011: 35)—a contempt so virulent that a law had been passed prohibiting insults targeting business activity in the market (*agora*) by male or female citizens.²³ Aristotle's contemporary, Hêrakleidês Pontikos, found the pursuit of leisure and pleasure and the avoidance of manual labor to be the essential separator of "free men" from slaves and persons of low birth.²⁴

But beyond attitudes toward work, prostitution as the "business of sex," melding money and eroticism, further evoked negativity from segments of Greek opinion uncomfortable with carnality *tout court*. Some of Plato's writings, vividly expressing antagonism toward all forms of physical eroticism,²⁵ are often cited as evidence of pervasive Athenian antagonism toward purchased sex: Krenkel, for example, in an encyclopedia article on prostitution in Greece and Rome, notes that "prostitution . . . according to Plato (*Laws* 841a–e) jeopardized familial ties, public health, morality and the birth of offspring required for maintaining the community."²⁶ Even courtesans at the apex of commercial sex are denigrated as "socially marginal" (McClure 2003b: 3). Male citizens who had taken money for sex were deprived of the opportunity to participate in certain political and civil activities (see chapter 3). For modern scholars, virtually without exception, Athenian prostitution is assumed or judged to have been the object of Athenian antagonism or contempt.²⁷

---

22. Dem. 57.45: πολλὰ δουλικὰ καὶ ταπεινὰ πράγματα τοὺς ἐλευθέρους ἡ πενία βιάζεται ποιεῖν . . . πολλαὶ καὶ τιτθαὶ καὶ ἔριθοι καὶ τρυγήτριαι γεγόνασιν. . . .

23. Dem. 57.30: τοὺς νόμους οἳ κελεύουσιν ἔνοχον εἶναι τῇ κακηγορίᾳ τὸν τὴν ἐργασίαν τὴν ἐν τῇ ἀγορᾷ ἢ τῶν πολιτῶν ἢ τῶν πολιτίδων ὀνειδίζοντά τινι. See Wallace 1994b: 116.

24. *Peri Hêdonês* (quoted in Athen. 512b4–6): ἐστὶ γὰρ τὸ μὲν ἥδεσθαι καὶ τὸ τρυφᾶν ἐλευθέρων . . . τὸ δὲ πονεῖν δούλων καὶ ταπεινῶν. See Wehrli 1969, fr. 55.

25. See Plato *Rep.* 458d–461b, *Nomoi* 840d–841e; Aristot. *Pol.* 1334b29–1335b37, 1335b38–1336a2.

26. 1988: 1293. Plato in *Laws* 841a–e actually censures every manifestation of nonmarital sex as damaging to public welfare. He does, however, posit "purchased" sex as the least harmful alternative to marriage, provided that it occurs clandestinely (ἢ τὸ μὲν τῶν ἀρρένων πάμπαν ἀφελοίμεθ' ἄν, τὸ δὲ γυναικῶν, εἴ τις συγγίγνοιτό τινι . . . ὠνηταῖς εἴτε ἄλλῳ ὁτῳοῦν τρόπῳ κτηταῖς, μὴ λανθάνων ἄνδρας τε καὶ γυναῖκας πάσας: 841d5–e2). See Morrow [1960] 1993: 441.

27. McGinn 2014: 84. See, for example, Wrenhaven 2009: 381–84; Glazebrook 2006b (courtesans "socially marginal"); Herter [1960] 2003: 108; Kapparis 1999: 5; Sissa 1999: 153; Rosivach 1998: 115, 139; Pierce 1997: 166; Davidson 1997: 89; Brock 1994: 338, 341; D. Cohen 1991a: 179; Henry 1986.

Yet ancient sources also adumbrate another view, in which work in general is admired (see chapter 2, pp. 41–42), and the sale of sex is presented alluringly. In fact, at Athens prostitution was lawful,[28] pervasive,[29] and, if practiced in compliance with Athenian work ethics, commensurable with other means of earning a living (see chapter 2, pp. 39–44). In a state that accorded legal recognition to "whatever arrangements a party has willingly agreed upon with another"—a state which never did restrict "victimless sexual conduct"[30]—written arrangements for the sale of sex were commonplace, and complex contracts for erotic services were so widespread that the phrase "whoring under contract" had become idiomatic in local discourse.[31] Trumpeted by comic poets as a democratic and ethically desirable alternative to other forms of nonmarital sex,[32] prostitution gained social legitimacy from its association with the goddess Aphroditê,[33] for whom prostitutes "clearly functioned as mediators, their sexual skills a sort of 'technology' that canalized her potent force" (Thornton 1997: 152). Aphroditê was even believed to aid courtesans in securing wealthy clients.[34]

---

28. See chapter 5, n. 1 and related text.

29. Xen. *Apom.* 2.2.4 (prostitutes available everywhere: τῶν γε ἀφροδισίων ἕνεκα . . . τούτου γε τῶν ἀπολυσόντων μεσταὶ μὲν αἱ ὁδοί, μεστὰ δὲ τὰ οἰκήματα). Cf. Theopompos of Chios (FGrH 115 F213 = Athên. 532c): ὁ δῆμος ὁ τῶν Ἀθηναίων . . . αὐτοὶ τοῦτον τὸν τρόπον ἔζων, ὥστε τοὺς μὲν νέους ἐν τοῖς αὐλητριδίοις καὶ παρὰ ταῖς ἑταίραις διατρίβειν. . . .

30. Wallace 1997: 151–52 and ff.; Lape 2006: 139–41. For occasional limitations on other personal freedoms, however, see Wallace 1993, 1994a, 1994b, and 1996 (cf. Rahe 1992: 196; Sissa 1999: 154–55).

31. The significance of these "consensual contracts" is the subject of chapter 4.

32. See Euboulos Frs. 67 and 82 (K-A); Philêmôn Fr. 3 (K-A).

33. "Hetairai in ancient Athens prayed and made offerings to their patron deity Aphroditê, just as wives and pregnant women worshipped Hera and Artemis respectively" (Neils 2000: 216). See Thornton 1997: 152. At Korinth, supplicants to Aphroditê actively sought prostitutes' help: Athên. 13.573c. On the perceived power of Aphroditê in human affairs ("les puissances de l'amour en Grèce antique"), see Calame 1996: 11–20.

34. Athên. 588c. Opinion is divided concerning the presence of "sacred prostitutes" at some of the goddess' cult sites. Budin 2008, 2006 denies that there is any credible classical evidence for the practice of temple prostitution. Cf. Budin 2003a: 148–53, 2004: 102–103; Pirenne-Delforge 1994: 112–13. *Contra:* Davidson 2004b: 172–73; Dillon 2002: 199–202; Glinster 2000: 27–31; Legras 1997: 250–58, who (at p. 250, n. 5) provides references to earlier literature. See Beard and Henderson 1997. Archaeologists have even identified possible sites for sacred prostitution in Greece (Merenda: Kakavoyianni and Dovinou 2003: 34–35; Piraeus: Steinhauer 2003: 42–43). For the "Hellenization" of Aphroditê and her loss or minimization of some of her Near Eastern characteristics, see Budin 2003b: 273–82.

Within Attika, the shrine of Aphroditê Pandêmos, near the Akropolis,[35] was said to have been built from the proceeds of one of Solôn's innovations, the state's purchase and employment of female slaves as prostitutes. Despite the doubtful historicity of this tale,[36] the laudatory connection of democracy's founder with the foundation of brothels does provide startling insight into a fourth-century Athens that treated prostitution as a "'democratic' reform" (Kurke 1999: 199), "as an intrinsic element of the democracy" (Halperin 1990: 100). And through its "tax on prostitution" (*pornikon telos*), Athens was an active accessory to the sexual labors of its residents.[37] Female prostitutes may even have been welcome at the Thesmophoria,[38] religious rites of high exclusivity,[39] and appear to have participated prominently in the sacred Adônia festival.[40] The city's goddess, Athêna, titular deity of crafts, listed prostitutes among her benefactors (Harris 1995: 144–49), and a monument honoring a famed courtesan

---

35. For the temple of Aphroditê Pandêmos (located immediately below that of Athêna Nikê at the Propylaia), see Paus. 1.22.3; Beschi 1967–68; for Aphroditê's temple on the Sacred Way, see Travlos 1937; I.G. II² 4570, 4574–85.

36. Athên. 13.569d-f = Philêmôn Fr. 3 (K-A), Nikandros of Kolophôn FGrH 271/2 F 9. Some scholars flatly dismiss the report as ahistorical (Rosivach 1995; Frost 2002; Henry 2000: 505–506); others accept it (Herter 1960 [1985]: 73 and Pellizer and Sirugo 1995: 9); most seem to find the connection plausible but unproven, sometimes suggesting that municipal brothels may have existed at a later time but might have been anachronistically attributed to Solôn (cf. Lape 2004: 77; Hartmann 2002: 248–49). Henry (2011: 31) insists that "we should not discount the possibility of a 'municipal brothel' in sixth-century Athens. . . . Solôn may well have provided female sex slaves for Athens' finest youth."

37. Pausanias 1.23.2. Andreadês ([1928] 1992: 358) terms Athens' fiscal involvement "scandalous" (σκανδαλώδη). See also Lentakis 1998: 130–54; Pirenne-Delfore 1994: 117. Athenian sources treat this involvement as unexceptional: see Aiskh. 1.119. On this prostitutional tax at Athens and elsewhere in Greece, see chapter 5, nn. 8 and 11.

38. Sakurai 2008: 42–43; Brumfield 1981: 84–88; Dahl 1976: 96. See Men. *Epitrep.* 749–50; Aristoph. *Thes.* 293–94; Louk. 80.2.1; Isai. 3.80.

39. Participation in these ceremonies (from which men were excluded) was based on household affiliation: Burkert 1985: 242 and nn. 7, 8 thereto. Some scholars (following Aristoph. *Thes.* 329–31: τελέως δ'ἐκκλησιάσαιμεν 'Αθηναίων εὐγενεῖς γυναῖκες) have concluded that participation was limited explicitly to *politides*: women "legitimately married to an Athenian citizen in full possession of his political rights" (Just 1989: 24). In accord: Detienne 1977: 78. Other scholars, following Isaios 6.49–50, see the festival as open to "women of the community" (Pomeroy 1975: 78; cf. Fantham et al. 1994: 87)—variant positions that are reconcilable if the terms *astai* and *politides* are distinguished: see E. Cohen 2000: Chapter 2.

40. Diphilos Fr. 42, 39 (K-A); 49 (K-A); Alkiphr. 4.14.8. For the important involvement of prostitutes in this festival, see Detienne 1977; Parker 1996: 194; Thornton 1997: 152. See also Winkler 1990: 198–200 and (for detailed consideration of the Adônia festival) Attalah 1966.

stood on the Athenian Akropolis next to a statue of Aphroditê.[41] On the Sacred Way from Eleusis to Athens, an enormous fourth-century dedication to the prostitute Pythionikê commanded for centuries the prestigious position where one could first glimpse the Parthenon and the Akropolis—an imposing memorial in a choice location on the most hallowed of Attic thoroughfares (a site and construction, as an ancient commentator observed, truly worthy of a Miltiadês, or a Periklês, or a Kimôn).[42] Throughout the city, sites for prostitution appear to have been subject to no locational bias: brothels "appear mixed in with other businesses and residential buildings" (Glazebrook 2011: 53).

This dichotomy in Athenian testimonia about commercial sex is consistent with the bifurcated view of prostitution embedded in the very language of ancient Athens, comprising two principal clusters of ancient Greek words relating to "prostitution,"[43] those cognate to *pernanai* ("sell") and those cognate to *hetairein* ("be a companion"), verbs that in turn yield the nouns *hetairos(-a)* and *pornos(ê)*, male and female "prostitutes." These two terms encompass what in modern Western societies is a single, albeit intractably undefinable, concept of "prostitution."[44] This Greek binomialism reflects the Hellenic tendency to understand and to organize phenomena not (as we do) through definitional focus on a specific subject in isolation, but through contrast, preferably through antithesis.[45] Where

---

41. Similarly at Sparta, the famous *hetaira* Kottina had dedicated a statue of herself that stood proximate to that of Athêna Khalkioikos (Athên. 574c–d). On monuments to prostitutes in Greek sanctuaries, see Keesling 2006.

42. Dikaiarkhos FGrH 2. 266 (= Athên. 594f–595a): ἀφικνούμενος κατὰ τὴν ἀπ' Ἐλευσῖνος τὴν ἱερὰν ὁδὸν καλουμένην ... καταστὰς οὗ ἂν φανῇ τὸ πρῶτον ὁ τῆς Ἀθηνᾶς ἀφορώμενος νεὼς καὶ τὸ πόλισμα, ὄψεται παρὰ τὴν ὁδὸν αὐτὴν ᾠκοδομημένον μνῆμα οἷον οὐχ ἕτερον οὐδὲ σύνεγγυς οὐδέν ἐστι τῷ μεγέθει. τοῦτο δὲ τὸ μὲν πρῶτον, ... ἢ Μιλτιάδου φήσειεν ἂν σαφῶς ἢ Περικλέους ἢ Κίμωνος. Poseidonios FGrH 87 F 14 (=Athên. 594e): Ἅρπαλος ... ἐρασθεὶς Πυθιονίκης πολλὰ εἰς αὐτὴν κατανάλωσεν ἑταίραν οὖσαν· καὶ ἀποθανούσῃ πολυτάλαντον μνημεῖον κατεσκεύασεν. Cf. Paus. 1.37.5: μνῆμα πάντων ὁπόσα Ἕλλησί ἐστιν ἀρχαῖα θέας μάλιστα ἄξιον.

43. But ancient Greek (even within its constricted surviving attestations) contained a vast multitude of words, at least 200, at different registers of usage, relating to venal sexual exchange. See Kapparis 2011.

44. For the etymology of *pernanai*, see Benveniste 1969: 1.133, 1973: 112; Chantraine [1968–70] 1999: 888 (πόρνη "franchement different [et plus péjorative] de ἑταίρα"). For *hetairein*, see Chantraine [1968–70] 1999: 380–81.

45. On this dualistic opposition so central to Hellenic culture that it has been said to have "dominated Greek thought" (Garner 1987: 76), see Lloyd [1966] 1987: 15–85; E. Cohen 1992: 46–52, 191–94.

modern Western thought generally posits a broad spectrum of possibilities and seeks to differentiate a multitude of slightly varying entities,[46] ancient Greek assumed not a medley of separate forms, but only a counterpoised opposition, complementary alternatives occupying in mutual tension the entire relevant cognitive universe. For modern thinkers, opposites are mutually exclusive; for the Greeks, antitheses were complementary (and thus tended to be inclusive). Greek commercial institutions accordingly tend to derive their meaning from their binomial interrelationships with their putative opposites.[47] Thus, interest (*tokos*, literally "yield") is either "maritime" (*nautikos*) or "landed" (*eggeios*): there is no alternative.[48] Where Anglo-American law sets "real property" and "personal property" at different points on a spectrum that allows for items sharing certain characteristics of both ("fixtures"), for the Greeks all property is either "visible" (*phanera ousia*) or "invisible" (*aphanês ousia*)[49]: even the differentiation between realty and personalty tends to be expressed through this antithesis.[50] And so it is not surprising that every manifestation of commercial sex tended to be encompassed within a binomial antithesis.

Modern scholars have generally recognized the fundamental importance of this dualism to an understanding of Greek prostitution, but—instead of seeking to identify the counterpoised opposition underlying this dichotomy—have tended to interpret these terms "as marking different degrees on a continuum" (Miner 2003: 21), ignoring the business context within which prostitution occurred and the cognitive processes of antithesis through which Athenians interpreted and described this (and every other) activity. To differentiate *hetaira* from *pornê*, discursive

---

46. For the modern tendency "to divide each difficulty into as many parts as necessary the better to solve it," extolled by Descartes, see Lévi-Strauss and Eribon 1991: 112.

47. Differing contexts yield differing antitheses. As Davidson notes, "The Greeks often talked about the world in binary terms as polarized extremes . . . (but) the terms of the opposition might change all the time. . . ." (1997: xxv).

48. By modern Western criteria, attributions to one or the other category frequently seem arbitrary. A loan secured by land may be characterized as a "maritime" loan because its traits as a whole seem to a speaker to fit the "maritime" grouping rather than the "landed" category. See E. Cohen 1990a; Lipsius [1909–15] 1966: 721; Harrison 1968–71, I.228, n. 3; Korver 1934: 125 ff.

49. Modern scholars have again been entirely unsuccessful in abstract efforts to find distinct qualities inherent in specific objects which would render them predictably either "invisible" or "visible." See Gabrielsen 1986: esp. 101, n. 7; Bongenaar 1933: 234–39; Koutorga 1859: 6–11, Schodorf 1905: 90 ff.; Weiss 1923: 173, 464, 491; Schuhl 1953.

50. Harp. s.v.: ἀφανὴς οὐσία καὶ φανερά; Lys. Fr. 79; Dem. 5.8.

analysis literally evokes a conceptual continuum "constituted along the axis of gift- vs. commodity-exchange, identified with the *hetaira* and the *pornê* respectively."[51] Conventional philologists have sought to separate the *hetairos (-a)* from the *pornos (-ê)*[52] by identifying, impressionistically, characteristics seemingly common to one term or the other. The result has been the joining, not the separation, of the two functions—literally the creation of a progression focused on "the overlap of their function (exchange of sex for something of value)."[53] Some scholars argue that "in general" promiscuity is the key to this continuum: a *pornos* is a man "who constantly sells his body to different men, whereas a *hetairos* has a more long-term relationship with one partner" (MacDowell 2000: 14); a *hetaira* engaged in relationships that were "not merely occasional."[54] For other commentators, "emotional attitude" supposedly identifies a *pornos (-ê)* as "a common prostitute" while a *hetairos (-a)* is "nearer to 'mistress' than to 'prostitute.'"[55] But for most analysts, not promiscuity or affection, but "status" has been the linking characteristic: social position is believed to differentiate the high-class *hêtairos (-a)* from the street or brothel *pornos (-ê)*—through gradations of status mediating the many variations in actual practice.[56]

---

51. Kurke 1999b: 179 (paraphrasing Davidson). Cf. Kurke 1997: 145; Davidson 1994: 141–42, 1997: 117–27; Reinsberg 1989: 80–86. Proponents of a cultural approach have constructed, even for the archaic period, elaborate, albeit varying, explanations for the origin and differentiation of the two terms. For example, Reinsberg (1989: 161) believes that *hetaira* as "courtesan" appeared in the early sixth century in response to the growth of maritime commerce, which provided surplus wealth to substantial numbers of itinerant traders, a view advanced earlier by Schneider (1913: col. 1332). But Kurke (1997:111) deems it "no accident that the category of the *hetaira* appears roughly contemporaneously with the adoption of coinage by the Greek cities." Cf., however, von Reden's important insistence (1997) that the *polis* developed only after coinage had already come into general usage in Greece.

52. The Greek terms for male prostitute—*pornos* (plural *pornoi*) and *hetairos* (plural *hetairoi*)—are paralleled by *pornê* (plural *pornai*) and *hetaira* (plural *hetairai*), Greek for female prostitutes. Menander puns on the similarity of name and task for both male and female prostitutes (*hetairoi* and *hetairai*): Men. *Parakatathêkê* (K.-A. 287 = Athên. 571e): πεποιήκατ' ἔργον οὐχ ἑταίρων γάρ . . . | μὰ Δι' ἀλλ' ἑταιρῶν · ταὐτὰ δ' ὄντα γράμματα | τὴν προσαγόρευσιν οὐ σφόδρ' εὔσημον ποιεῖ. (Μὰ . . . ἑταιρῶν added by Zedelius [following Casaubon]).

53. Miner 2003: 21. Cf. Calame 1989: 103–104; Gomme and Sandbach 1973: 30; Herter 1957: 1181–82.

54. Cantarella 1987: 50. Cf. Brown 1990: 263, n. 38; Dover 1984: 147.

55. Dover [1978] 1989: 20–21. Cf. Lentakis 1999: 162.

56. Cf. Hauschild 1933: 7–9; Herter 1957: 1154, 1181–82, and Herter 1960 [1985]: 83; Peschel 1987: 19–20; Harvey 1988: 249; Calame 1989: 103–104.

All these interpretations, however, flounder on a common difficulty: actual usage seems to demonstrate a conflation, rather than a distinction, in the employment of the terms. Comic writers fuse the two categories. Diphilos portrays a *hetaira* sumptuously celebrating the Adônia festival "with other *pornai*,"[57] thus explicitly describing a single woman in a single sentence as both *hetaira* and *pornê*. Anaxilas similarly describes the same women indiscriminately as both *hetairai* and *pornai*, while Aristophanês in the *Ploutos* interchanges *hetairai* and *pornoi*.[58] The philosopher Kynoulkos illustrates his allusion to the *hetairides* of Aspasia by quoting Aristophanês's reference to the *pornai* of Aspasia (Athênaios 569f–570a). Athenian legislation prohibiting male prostitutes' participation in political life treats the terms as a couplet, applying the law explicitly, but without differentiation, to both *pornoi* and *hetairoi*.[59] In court presentations, a single person is sometimes referred to indiscriminately in a single forensic speech by both words.[60] A good example of this interchangeability is the characterization of Neaira (and of her daughter Phanô) throughout Demosthenes 59 where Apollodôros oscillates "between treating Neaira as a classy and expensive *hetaira* and as a common prostitute."[61] In his speech against Timarkhos, Aiskhinês employs a similar fluidity of terminology: dealing with legislation precluding certain political activity by those who have acted as either *pornoi* or *hetairoi*, Aiskhinês acknowledges explicitly that Timarkhos could be characterized as either (§§50–51)—but expresses reluctance even to use the term *pornos*[62] and entirely refrains from designating Timarkhos as *hetairos*. In contrast, other speakers sometimes employ the word *hetaira* to encompass all aspects of female prostitution (from the most dependently

---

57. πολυτελῶς Ἀδώνια | ἄγους' ἑταίρα μεθ ἑτέρων πορνῶν· (Fr. 42 [K-A], lines 39–40).

58. Anax. Fr. 22 [K.-A.], lines 1, 22, 31 (*hetairai* at the beginning and end, but in the middle *pornai*). Aristoph. *Plout.* 149–55 describes Corinthian *hetairai* and *pornoi* as acting in exactly the same fashion (καὶ τάς γ' ἑταίρας φασὶ τὰς Κορινθίας ... καὶ τούς γε παῖδάς φασι ταὐτὸ τοῦτο δρᾶν ... τοὺς πόρνους).

59. ἢ πεπορνευμένος ἢ ἑταιρηκώς (Aiskhin. 1.29). Cf. Dem. 19.233.

60. See Dem. 48.53, 56; Aiskhin. 1 passim. Cf. Dem. 22.56.

61. Fisher 2001: 185. Similarly: Gilhuly 2009:44, 1999: 23; Carey 1992: 140–41; Kapparis 1999: 408–409. Miner argues that the seemingly "remarkable level of inconsistency" (Davidson 1997: 73) in prostitutional terminology here is actually "an integral part of (Apollodoros's) rhetorical strategy" (Miner 2003: 20).

62. See especially Aiskhin. 1.37–38, 40–41, 45, 51–52, 74–76.

debased to the most independently magnificent),⁶³ while the word *pornê* is occasionally used to describe a woman clearly in a long-term relationship.⁶⁴ Even advocates of a clear differentiation between *hetaira* and *pornê* concede that, in practice, "the distinction" between the two terms "is not always sharp" (MacDowell 2000: 14), "the boundaries between these roles" "not precise . . . not clearly defined" (Miner 2003: 20, 35). Dover, in his detailed study of "popular morality," concludes that for the Greeks, "submission in gratitude for gifts, services or help is not so different in kind from submission in return for an agreed fee" (Dover [1974] 1984: 152). For this reason, perhaps, the *hetaira* of discursive poetics is sometimes a chameleon: "The pressure and anxieties of the male participants occasionally refashion her as a *pornê*" (Kurke 1997: 145–46), and in certain contexts "*hetaira* and *pornê* (become) interchangeable terms."⁶⁵

This interchangeability in usage has caused some scholars to call for yet more research to resolve these contradictions.⁶⁶ Others have increasingly despaired of identifying meaningful distinctions between the two terms and have proclaimed the uselessness of impressionistic or semiotic searches for objectively distinguishing characteristics inherent in the specific terms.⁶⁷ Less equivocally, certain social historians (for whom *hetaira* and *pornê* are two words covering a single form of exploitation⁶⁸) eschew all

---

63. See, e.g., Dem. 59.122, where the term "encompasses all forms of prostitution . . . from expensive courtesans to common prostitutes established in brothels" (Kapparis 1999: 422–23).

64. See Lysias 4.19; Dem. 59.30.

65. 1997: 219, n. 110, speaking of their relation to "the sacralized public space identified with the Basilinna."

66. Miner, who has analyzed the use of these words only in Demosthenes 59, envisions a future research program focusing in detail on their employment in other orators, especially Aiskhinês (2003: 20, n. 3). A decade earlier, Brown was already lamenting the absence of a systematic exploration of prostitutional nomenclature (1990: 248).

67. Kapparis 2011: 223 ("despite a long debate the results remain inconclusive"); McClure 2003: 266 ("the word [*hetaira*] is used later, and interchangeably, with *porne*"). Cf. Kapparis 1999: 408; Davidson 1997: 74; Flemming 1999: 47 (regarding Greek-speaking areas of the Roman Empire).

68. For these observers, all women in Attika, other than "wives" or "potential wives," supposedly constitute a single group "open to free sexual exploitation" (Just 1989: 5, 141). Similarly: Brown 1990: 248–49; Keuls 1985: 153–54, 199–202; Henry 1992: 262, 2000: 504. Some savants, following Hesiod (*Works and Days* 373–75), even deem marriage the functional equivalent of prostitution, and therefore term the *hetaira* an "ersatzfrau" (Reinsberg 1989: 87), indistinguishable in her nullity from a wife. Davidson 1997: 125: "Hetaeras are closer to wives than (to) prostitutes." Cf. Davidson 1997: 132–33; Henry 1986: 147 (pace Ogden 1996: 102).

real distinction between the terms, as do some commentators of a symbolic orientation (for whom "imaginary history" is more real than "historical reality"[69]). Both of these schools summarily reject the abundant testimonia purporting to describe how glamorous and brilliant *hetairai*, wealthy and independent, occupied a prepossessing position in Athenian life, and (like Periklês's Aspasia) sometimes even made important contributions to Attic civilization and politics.[70] Read literally, such accounts present the *hetaira* "as the first 'liberated woman,' a desirable, refined companion" (McClure 2003b: 2), a sharp contrast to the slave *pornai* laboring in brothels (see the section "Weaving a Web of Dependence" in chapter 2). But for both the school of exploitation and that of symbolism, these passages are not to be read literally. For the former, the recurring allusions to sophisticated and successful *hetairai*, and the stories illustrating their wit and prosperity, are deleterious myth and false romanticization: the "refined hetaira" is "a fabrication of the male mind" (Keuls 1985: 199). For the latter, the *hetaira* is "a socially marginal figure" recreated as a cultural icon by the "representational modes and textual strategies" of male commentators in antiquity (McClure 2003b: 3). No consideration is given to recurrent forensic assertions that male *hetairoi* sometimes occupied positions of high state importance.[71] Evidence for highlypaid, socially significant *hetairai* is scorned as "superficial and uncontextualized reading . . . that cannot be taken as an accurate assessment of the lives of actual courtesans, nor even of the Greek literary tradition" (McClure 2003b: 2). The actual content of surviving manuscripts is considered mere "facticity" obscuring "the discursive structures of our texts" (Kurke 1999: 23). Thus, separated from her fictive cultural pretensions, her putative independence exposed as a mere false manifestation of the Athenian male *imaginaire*, her wealth a manifestation of her true poverty (see McGinn 2004: 52–53), the intellectually capable and highly paid *hetaira* emerges as indistinguishable from the contemptible *pornê*.

---

69. Kurke 1999: 23; 2002: 88.

70. See, for example, Pl. *Men.* 236b5; Xen. *Oik.* 3.14 ff.; Plut. *Per.* 24; Alkiphr. 4.19; Athên. Book 13. For further evidence and context, see the section "Selling 'Free' Love" in chapter 2; Davidson 2004; Pirenne-Delforge 1994: 283, n. 49; Brulé 2001: 230–31; Garrison 2000: 294: n. 28; Mossé 1983: 63–66; Dimakis 1988; Reinsberg 1993: 80–86; Helbig 1873: 195; Henry 1985 passim.

71. For the alleged political prominence of some male prostitutes, see chapter 3, pp. 70–72.

But an investigation of commercial factors—the conditions and values governing sexual labor—offers an alternative approach to understanding these two terms, one through which we need not conflate (at least in business contexts) the terms *hetairos,-a* and *pornos, -ê*. The Athenian work ethics discussed in chapter 2 confirm and explain, in an economic context, the theoretical antithesis distinguishing the terms *hetairos, -a* and *pornos, -ê*. Conforming to society's expectations of a free person, the *hetairos, -a* functioned independently, that is, not under the control of another person. A *pornos, -ê* labored under servile conditions. *Pornê* and its cognates therefore tended to be derogatory,[72] and *hetaira*, euphemistic[73]—an "urbane" distinction in usage explicitly attributed to the Athenians by later Greek commentators.[74] Accordingly, Antiphanês in *Hydria* denominates *hetaira* as a term inherently "fine" (*kalon*), although sometimes tarnished by the actual behavior of some of its practitioners.[75] Menander in the *Parakatathêkê* illustrates the euphemistic sense of *hetaira* by punning on the similarity in sound between the words for male and for female courtesans (which are identical in the genitive case [hetairôn] except for a difference in the syllable emphasized in the masculine and feminine forms).[76] Similarly Dionysios of Halikarnassos notes that the term *hetaira* had come to be applied euphemistically to those formerly referred to as "sex-workers" (*tais mistharnousais taphrodisia*).[77] But this euphemism carried economic significance. According to the speaker in Demosthenes 57, from servile (*doulika*) activity "many Athenian women (*astai*) rose from poverty to

---

72. "the more disgraceful and slanderous of the two terms" (Miner 2003: 20, n. 3).

73. See Pirenne-Delforge 1994: 283, n. 49 ("exalted" or "high-class" not an inappropriate characterization of *hetaira*); McClure 2003b: 13 ("the term [*hetaira*] by definition functions as a euphemism").

74. Plut. *Solôn* 15.2–3: Ἃ δ'οὖν οἱ νεώτεροι τοὺς Ἀθηναίους λέγουσι τὰς τῶν πραγμάτων δυσχερείας ὀνόμασι χρηστοῖς καὶ φιλανθρώποις ἐπικαλύπτοντας ἀστείως ὑποκορίζεσθαι, τὰς μὲν πόρνας ἑταίρας, τοὺς δὲ φόρους συντάξεις κ.τ.λ. καλοῦντας.

75. ὄντως ἑταίρας. Αἱ μὲν ἄλλαι τοὔνομα | βλάπτουσι τοῖς τρόποις γὰρ ὄντως ὂν καλόν. Fr. 210 (K-A). Cf. Brown 1990: 248.

76. Μένανδρος ἐν Παρακαταθήκῃ ἀπὸ τῶν ἑταιρῶν τοὺς ἑταίρους διαστέλλων φησι· πεποίηκατ' ἔργον οὐχ ἑταίρων γάρ, φίλαι, | μὰ Δι' ἀλλ' ἑταιρῶν· ταὐτὰ δ'ὄντα γράμματα | τὴν προσαγόρευσιν οὐ σφόδρ' εὔσχημον ποιεῖ.

77. Ant. 1.84.4: τὴν Λούπαν· ἔστι δὲ τοῦτο Ἑλληνικόν τε καὶ ἀρχαῖον ἐπὶ ταῖς μισθαρνούσαις τἀφροδίσια τιθέμενον, αἳ νῦν εὐπρεπεστέρᾳ κλήσει ἑταῖραι προσαγορεύονται.

riches" (Translation: Bers 2003).⁷⁸ Myrtilos characterizes "true companions" (*hetairôn*) as able to provide affection without taking inappropriate economic advantage.⁷⁹ Anaxilas similarly distinguishes *pornê* from *hetaira* precisely on monetary grounds: unlike the *pornê*, a *hetaira* is in a position to generate *kharis* by providing her services without charge (when she considers the situation appropriate).⁸⁰ *Kharis*, the undertaking and dispensing of reciprocal obligations and favors, is often seen to lie at the heart of free Athenian culture.⁸¹ In chapter 2, therefore, I consider in detail—from an economic perspective—how *hetairai* sought (and often were able), to conform to Athenian free work ethics, unlike *pornai*.

---

78. §45: πολλὰ δουλικὰ καὶ ταπεινὰ πράγματα τοὺς ἐλευθέρους ἡ πενία βιάζεται ποιεῖν. . . . ἀσταὶ γυναῖκες, πολλαὶ δ ἐκ πενήτων πλούσιαι νῦν.

79. Athên. 571c: περὶ τῶν ὄντως ἑταιρῶν τὸν λόγον πεποίημαι, τουτέστιν τῶν φιλίαν ἄδολον συντηρεῖν δυναμένων.

80. ἐὰν δέ τις μετρίως ἔχουσα χρημάτων | τοῖς δεομένοις τινῶν ὑπουργῇ πρὸς χάριν, | ἐκ τῆς ἑταιρίας ἑταίρα τοὔνομα, | προσηγορεύθη. Καὶ σὺ νῦν οὐχ ὡς λέγεις | πόρνης, ἑταίρας δ'εἰς ἔρωτα τυγχάνεις | ἐληλυθώς (*Neottis*: Fr. 21 [K-A]).

81. See the section "In Conflict: Purchased Sex and Elite Homoerotic Culture" in chapter 3.

## 2
# *Prostitution as a Liberal Profession*

AT ATHENS A working individual might seek recognition as a practitioner of a "liberal profession" (*eleutherios tekhnê*, "an occupation appropriate for a free person").[1] For the Athenians, the social acceptability and moral standing of human labor was largely determined by the conditions under which work was performed. Pursued in a context characteristic of servile endeavor, prostitution—like all forms of slave labor—was contemptible. Pursued under conditions appropriate to nonservile endeavor, prostitution—like all forms of free labor—was not violative of Athenian work ethics. Thus Plato finds retail selling, craftsmanship, and prostitution all reprehensible if performed under someone else's control, but honorable (*kalon*) when undertaken on one's own behalf.[2] Medicine was often practiced by slaves, but dung-collection was supervised by free persons functioning as state officials.[3] Athenian work ethics, in short, focused on the structure of vocational relationships, not on the typology or nature of the labor undertaken—although a strand of opinion considered

---

1. ἐλευθέριος (-α) τέχνη: Plu. *Mor.* 122D. (On the characteristics of *tekhnai* ["professions"], see E. Cohen 1992: 62–64.) Although the English use of "liberal" as "suitable for free persons" ("liberal profession," "liberal education") is derived from the Latin *liberalis*, the Athenians employed *eleutherios* (and its cognates) in the same sense. See, for example, Xen. *Apom.* 2.7.4 (ἐλευθερίως πεπαιδευμένους). Cf. Xen. *Apom.* 2.84; Pl. *Nomoi* 823e; Aristot. *Pol.* 1338a32. In contrast, "prostitution appropriate to slaves" was ἡ τῶν πορνῶν ἐργασία (Dem. 59.113).

2. οὐδενὶ ἂν ὄνειδος φάναι εἶναι σκυτοτομοῦντι ἢ ταριχοπωλοῦντι ἢ ἐπ᾽ οἰκήματος καθημένῳ ἀλλὰ ... καὶ ποίημα μὲν γίγνεσθαι ὄνειδος ἐνίοτε, ὅταν μὴ μετὰ τοῦ καλοῦ γίγνηται. ... φάναι δέ γε χρὴ καὶ οἰκεῖα μόνα τὰ τοιαῦτα ἡγεῖσθαι αὐτόν, τὰ δὲ βλαβερὰ πάντα ἀλλότρια· ... τὸν τὰ αὑτοῦ πράττοντα τοῦτον σώφρονα καλεῖν.(*Khrm.* 163b6–8, c1–8).

3. Dung-collectors: Aristot. *Ath.Pol.* 50.2 (ἀστυνόμοι δέκα· καὶ ὅπως τῶν κοπρολόγων μηδεὶς ἐντὸς ι σταδίων τοῦ τείχους καταβαλεῖ κόπρον ἐπιμελοῦνται). Doctors as slaves:see n. 77 and p. 49.

disreputable, ipso facto, all "banausic" and/or "parasitic" labor[4] (that is, virtually all undertakings other than agriculture, public service, cultural activities, and nonmercenary military duty: see chapter 1, pp. 1–4). "Sitting in a brothel was no more despicable to the elite than working in the agora" (Glazebrook 2011: 35). For the residents of Attika, however, the carnal aspect of prostitution presented issues beyond those of work ethics: facets of elite male social society would have been threatened by a male citizen's sexual submission in a commercial or quasi-commercial context; a female citizen's functioning as a prostitute complicated, at the least, the transmission of Athenian citizenship through the union of two citizens (see chapter 3, pp. 76–77, 83–88) In short, because of the erotic dimension inherent in the provision of sex, prostitution at Athens could never be merely a "job like any other" (Foxhall 2013: 101). Its position in the Athenian economy and in Athenian society must be analyzed and understood not anachronistically, but in the context of Athenian values and of the Athenian economy.

## Athenian Work Ethics

For free Athenians, a pervasive moral tenet was "the obligation to maintain an independence of occupation . . and at all costs to avoid seeming to work in a 'slavish' way for another."[5] In Aristotle's words, "The nature of the free man prevents his living under the control of another"[6]— "living for another" is inherently "slavish" (*doulikon*).[7] Plato praises the man working for himself and censures as inherently immoral "doing the tasks of others."[8] Isokratês equates hired employment (*thêteia*)

---

4. A calling might be perceived as inherently servile. In Xenophôn's *Symposion* (3.10, 4.56), for example, *mastropeia* ("the trade of procurer": Loeb translation) as portrayed is termed "dishonorable" (ἀδόξῳ οὔσῃ τέχνῃ). *Mastropeia*, however, tended to be synonymous with or confused with *proagôgeia*, which was actually unlawful in certain contexts: see chapter 5, pp. 118–23.

5. Fisher 1998a: 70. Similarly: Cartledge 1993: 148–49; Fisher 1993.

6. Aristot. *Rhet.* 1367a33: ἐλευθέρου γὰρ τὸ μὴ πρὸς ἄλλον ζῆν. Jameson 1997: 100 notes free persons' "reluctance to admit to the need of working for someone else." Cf. Humphreys [1983] 1993:10; Finley 1981: 122.

7. n. E. 1124b26–1125a1: ἀναγκαῖον . . . πρὸς ἄλλον μὴ δύνασθαι ζῆν ἀλλ' ἢ φίλον· δουλικὸν γάρ. Cf. *Metaph.* 982b25–26: ἄνθρωπος, φαμέν, ἐλεύθερος ὁ αὑτοῦ ἕνεκα καὶ μὴ ἄλλου ὤν.

8. *Khrm.* 163c3–8: τὰ γὰρ καλῶς τε καὶ ὠφελίμως ποιούμενα ἔργα ἐκάλει, . . . φάναι δέ γε χρῆ καὶ οἰκεῖα μόνα τὰ τοιαῦτα ἡγεῖσθαι αὐτόν, τὰ δὲ βλαβερὰ πάντα ἀλλότρια· . . . τὸν τὰ αὑτοῦ πράττοντα τούτων σώφρονα καλεῖν.

with slavery.⁹ Isaios laments the free men, and Demosthenes the free women, compelled by a "lack of necessities" to labor for pay: free people "should be pitied" if economic necessity forces them into "slavish" (*doulika*) employment.¹⁰ Pollux, paraphrasing fourth-century sources, characterizes as servile a free person who works for wages.¹¹ In fact, receipt of a salary (*misthophoria*) was the hallmark of a slave. When the Athenian state required coin-testers and mint-workers for continuing service, legislation explicitly provided for the payment of *misthophoriai* to the skilled public slaves (*dêmosioi*) who provided these services on a regular basis (and for their punishment in the event of absenteeism).¹² Even lucrative managerial positions were disdained by free persons: most supervisors accordingly were slaves,¹³ even on large estates where high compensation had to be offered to motivate unfree but highly skilled individuals.¹⁴ Thus, in Xenophon's *Memorabilia* (§2.8), Sôkratês proposes permanent employment as an estate supervisor to Euthêros, an impoverished free man. Such stewards, Sôkratês notes, were well compensated (§6) for even routine services (§3). But Euthêros curtly rejects the suggestion: managing an employer's property was only appropriate for a slave (§4).

In a society permeated by the demeaning use of nonfree labor,¹⁵ antagonism to work under a master should not be confused with antipathy to

---

9. 14.48: τίνα γὰρ ἡμᾶς οἴεσθε γνώμην ἔχειν ὁρῶντας... πολλοὺς μὲν μικρῶν ἕνεκα συμβολαίων δουλεύοντας, ἄλλους δ' ἐπὶ θητείαν ἰόντας; Cf. Aristot. *Rhet.* 1367a30–32: ἐλευθέρου γὰρ σημεῖον· οὐδὲν ποιεῖν ἔργον θητικόν.

10. Isaios 5.39: δι' ἔνδειαν τῶν ἐπιτηδείων. Dem. 57.45: πολλὰ δουλικὰ καὶ ταπεινὰ πράγματα τοὺς ἐλευθέρους ἡ πενία βιάζεται ποιεῖν, ἐφ' 'οἷς ἐλεοῖντ'' ἄν... πολλαὶ καὶ τιτθαὶ καὶ ἔριθοι καὶ τρυγήτριαι γεγόνασιν ὑπὸ τῶν τῆς πόλεως κατ' ἐκείνους τοὺς χρόνους συμφορῶν ἀσταὶ γυναῖκες. On *misthôtoi*, see Martini 1997: 49.

11. 3.82: πελάται δὲ καὶ θῆτες ἐλευθέρων ἐστὶν ὀνόματα διὰ πενίαν ἐπ' ἀργυρίῳ δουλευόντων. Similarly: Aristot. *Ath. Pol.* 2.2, *Pol.* 1337b20–21 (ὁ δὲ αὐτὸ τοῦτο πράττων δι' ἄλλους πολλάκις θητικὸν καὶ δουλικὸν δόξειεν ἂν πράττειν), 1341b10–15. Some of this feeling carried over into the Roman period. See Chrysippus (ap. Sen., *De ben.* 3.22.1 = Stoicorum Veterum Fragmenta 3, fr. 351): servus est perpetuus mercennarius.

12. S.E.G. 26.72, lines 49–55. See Figueira 1998: 536–47; Alessandri 1984; Stumpf 1986. Cf. I.G. II² 1492.137; I.G. II² 1388.61–62.

13. As employees, unfree labor fell into two categories: "management slaves" (*epitropoi*) and workers (*ergatai*): δούλων δὲ εἴδη δύο, ἐπίτροπος καὶ ἐργάτης. *Oik.* 1344a26–27. (attributed to Aristotle).

14. See Xen. *Oik.* 12.3; 1.16–17.

15. For Attika as a "slave economy," see introduction, p. 2, n. 7.

labor itself.[16] Even Plato (who condemned all commerce as inherently servile) approvingly quotes Hêsiod's judgment that work itself "is no disgrace."[17] In the Funeral Oration, often cited as a quintessential statement of Athenian values,[18] Periklês insists that "we place the real disgrace of poverty not in owning to the fact but in declining the struggle against it," as a result of which "our ordinary citizens (are) occupied with the pursuits of industry" (Crawley translation).[19] Athenian law—like that of certain modern Communist nations before 1990—even seems to have forbidden "idleness" (*argia*), which Demosthenes contrasts with "working" (*ergazesthai*).[20] A law attributed to Solôn required a male parent to teach his son a trade (*tekhnê*): otherwise the offspring need not support his father in old age.[21] In fact, numerous Athenians are known to have been self-employed in a great variety of activities. Many followed entrepreneurial pursuits,[22] and many others pursued numerous specialized callings, including prostitution.[23] In about half of all *politai* (perhaps 10,000 citizens) pursued nonagricultural work in hundreds of individual *métiers*.[24]

---

16. For the distinction, and an analysis of its historical basis, see Wood 1988: 126–45, esp. 139. Some Athenians, however, did tend to view work as essentially the obligation of unfree persons: see chapter 1, pp. 27–28 and n. 24; Vernant 1983a.

17. *Khrm.* 163b4–5: ἔμαθον γὰρ παρ᾽ Ἡσιόδου, ὃς ἔφη ἔργον δ᾽ οὐδὲν εἶναι ὄνειδος. Plato valorized agricultural pursuits: see *Nomoi* 889d, *Rep.* 371c, *Prôtag.* 347c, *Polit.* 289e.

18. "Perhaps the strongest statement ever made" of Athenian principles (Popper 1950: 182); "the privileged locust of democratic theory" (Loraux [1981] 1986: 173); "the most instructive" presentation (Jones [1957] 1978: 42). See also Hussey 1985: 123–25; 11; Flashar 1969.

19. Thouk. 2.40.1–2: καὶ τὸ πένεσθαι οὐχ ὁμολογεῖν τινὶ αἰσχρόν, ἀλλὰ μὴ διαφεύγειν ἔργῳ αἴσχιον . . . . ἔνι τε τοῖς αὐτοῖς οἰκείων ἅμα καὶ πολιτικῶν ἐπιμέλεια, καὶ ἑτέροις πρὸς ἔργα τετραμμένοις. On textual issues raised by the phrase ἑτέροις πρὸς ἔργα τετραμμένοις, see Gomme 1956: II.121; on possible interpretations of Thouk. 40.1–2, see Rusten 1985.

20. Dem. 57.32: ἔστι καὶ ἕτερος περὶ τῆς ἀργίας νόμος, ᾧ αὐτὸς ἔνοχος ὢν ἡμᾶς τοὺς ἐργαζομένους διαβάλλεις. Cf. Lysias Fr. 11 (Gernet—Bizos) Gernet 1926: 240 proffers "absence de travail" as the meaning of *argia*. Although the detailed provisions of this statute are unknown, Harrison 1968, 1971: I.80 conjectures that "its main *raison d'être* was protection of the rights of the family," presumably against dissipation of the estate through "idleness."

21. Plut. *Sol.* 22.1: νόμον ἔγραψεν, υἱῷ τρέφειν πατέρα μὴ διδαξάμενον τέχνην ἐπάναγκες μὴ εἶναι. Cf. Pl. *Krit.* 50d.

22. See Thompson 1983; Garnsey, ed., 1980. For the significance of such activities in the ancient world: Goody 1986: 177–84; Silver 1995: 53–79.

23. Cf. Schaps 2004: 150–59. For the male and female "citizens" alleged to have been prostitutes, see chapter 3, pp. 70–74.

24. Harris 2002: 70; 2006: 145 ("the number of people working in nonagricultural occupations was so large that it was probably more than half of the population of Attica"). For the variety of female occupations at Athens, see Foxhall 2013: 100.

Confounding modern expectations, the same labor functions might be performed indiscriminately by slave workers or by free "foreign residents" (*metics*) or by "citizens" (*politai*).[25] (In fact, the shoes for the public slaves working at Eleusis were made by a cobbler who was a *politês*![26]) In the Athenian navy, *politai*, metics, and slaves served as crew members without differentiation of status or work assignment: a master and his slave even appear often to have been rowers on the same trireme.[27] Free and unfree women are attested as retail workers in markets,[28] while free women worked alongside domestic slaves at many tasks.[29] Yet the willingness of Athenian "citizens" to do the same work as foreigners or slaves was accompanied by a scrupulous effort to avoid even the appearance of being "employed" at a job. Service outside the Athenian household by free persons was usually for a single specific task or for a limited period of time and seldom exclusive to a single employer: we typically encounter Athenian businessmen working on their own for a variety of customers, or agents undertaking a limited task for an individual client.[30] Even slaves attempted to avoid the appearance of "slavish employment": the Athenian institution of "servants living independently" (*douloi khôris oikountes*) permitted unfree persons to conduct their own businesses, establish their own households, and sometimes even to own their own slaves[31]—with little

---

25. R. Osborne 1995: 30; Hopper 1979: 140; Finley 1981: 99; Ehrenberg 1962: 162, 183, 185; Loomis 1998: 236–39. This concurrence is especially well-attested in the construction trades: Randall 1953; Burford 1972; E. Cohen 2000: 134–35, 187.

26. I. G. II² 1672.190. Cf. I. G. II² 1672.70–71.

27. See I. G. I³ 1032 and Thouk. 7.13.2, which together confirm that "slaves regularly formed a substantial proportion of the rowers on Athenian triremes, and their masters included fellow oarsmen" (Graham 1998: 110). See Graham 1992; Welwei 1974; Burke 1992: 218 (discussion of Isokratês 8.48).

28. The *phialai exeleutherikai* inscriptions (n. 100) record the manumission of formerly enslaved female retailworkers (Wrenhaven 2009: 381). For free women working in public markets, see Dem. 57 and 59 and chapter 6, p. 136.

29. See, for example, Iskhomakhos's spouse at Xen. *Oik*. 7.6. The wife's role, however, was often essentially managerial: see E. Cohen 2000: 37–38.

30. Note the maritime entrepreneur who introduces a client to the bank of Hêrakleidês in Dem. 33.7; Agyrrhios who serves Pasiôn as a representative in litigational matters (Isok. 17.31–32; cf. Stroud 1998: 22, Strauss 1987: 142); Arkhestratos who provided the bond for Pasiôn (Isok. 17.43); Stephanos's relationship with the banker Aristolokhos at Dem. 45.64.

31. See I.G. II² 1570. 78–79, with regard to [. . .]leidês (whose name has been incompletely preserved); Athên. 595a, for prostitutes owned by other prostitutes, themselves enslaved (Πυθιονίκη . . . ἢ Βακχίδος μὲν ἦν δούλη τῆς αὐλητρίδος, ἐκείνη δὲ Σινώπης τῆς Θράττης τῆς

contact, and most importantly, virtually without supervision from their owners.[32] The presence, or absence, of supervision and control was thus a critical, perhaps the central, factor in Athenian evaluation of work situations. Sexual labor was no exception.

## Weaving a Web of Dependence

Athenian aversion to the dependence inherent in salaried employment meant that providing sex in brothels was appropriate only for slaves. In fact, numerous opportunities for self-employment of free persons in craft or trade,[33] and the wide availability of remuneration for public pursuits,[34] left only slaves (and family members) as potential employees for the many Athenian businesses (workshops, stores, brothels, banks, and numerous other *ergasiai*[35]) that needed the labor of individuals over a continuing period of time.[36] "Nowhere in the sources do we hear of private establishments employing a staff of hired workers as their normal operation" (Finley 1981: 262–63, n. 6). Athenians assumed, correctly, that persons performing repetitive functions in a commercial context—whether bank functionaries[37]

---

ἐξ Αἰγίνης μετενεγκαμένης τὴν πορνείαν· ὥστε γίνεσθαι μὴ μόνον τρίδουλον . . .). (McClure dismisses this report "since slaves could not own property" [2003: 75]). For the mechanisms by which slaves could effectively acquire ("own") assets, see E. Cohen 2000: 145–54; Hervagault and Mactoux 1974; Perotti 1974. For the banking *oikoi* of slaves and former slaves, see E. Cohen 1992: Chapter 4. Ownership of slaves by persons themselves enslaved is not unique to Athens: under Roman practice, for example, slaves routinely owned other slaves—sometimes in large numbers (Watson 1987: 95).

32. See chapter 7, pp. 172–75.

33. See p. 42.

34. The Athenian state offered paid service in the armed forces, and compensation for frequent jury duty and assembly meetings; for "incapacitated" *politai* of limited means, there were outright public grants (Aristot. *Ath. Pol.* 49.4). Cf. Lysias 24, in which an Athenian unable to work easily at his own business but too poor to buy a slave doesn't even consider the possibility of hiring a free man to work for him: instead he seeks public assistance (§6).

35. Ἐργασία ("operation") is literally the income resulting from business endeavors, for example, the earnings of a slave (Hyper. *Ath.* 22: ἐὰν ἐργασίαν εὕρῃ ὁ οἰκέτης) or even "money-making" itself (Aristot. *E.N.* 1160a16: πρὸς ἐργασίαν χρημάτων). But by extension the Athenians came to use it to describe businesses as varied as banking (Dem. 36.6, 11, 13, 29) and prostitution (Hdt. 2.135; Dem. 18.129).

36. For the complex commercialization of the overall fourth-century Athenian economy, see pp. 86, nn. 90–92, and p. 155, n. 1; for the systemization of manufacturing, see Acton 2014: 248–88.

37. Bank workers were assumed to be enslaved: see, for example, Dem. 49.51 (τίς ὁ παραλαβὼν τῶν οἰκετῶν τῶν ἡμετέρων;).

or sexual workers—were likely to be slaves.[38] At Kolonôs Agoraios, the site of Athens' incipient version of a labor market,[39] *douloi* constituted virtually all of those standing for hire.[40]

Most slaves, however, worked "at home," that is, within the household (*oikos*), with which virtually all persons at Athens, both free and unfree, were affiliated.[41] The members of a particular *oikos* formed, in Aristotle's words, a "natural association for everyday purposes."[42] Slaves are explicitly included by Aristotle as members of the *oikos*, along with husband, wife, and children.[43] As an entity encompassing the physical attributes of a residence, the complement of members now (and/or in some cases previously) living in that residence, and the assets and business activities relating to those members,[44] the *oikos* was the physical location of virtually

---

38. A few free persons—motivated by abject circumstance or financial incentives—might occasionally have accepted paid employment (see n. 10 and accompanying text).

39. Marx believed that the formation of a labor market necessarily meant the introduction of "wage slavery," a precursor to classical capitalism (1970–72: I.170; cf. Lane 1991: 310–11). But this proposition is not confirmed by the continued dominance of the Athenian economy by household-based businesses primarily utilizing household members.

40. Pherekratês Fr. 142 (K-A). See Fuks 1951: 171–73; Garlan 1980: 8–9; Schaps 2004: 153–55. Cf. Hemelrijk [1925] 1979: 140; Biscardi 1989. The prime ancient Greek term for "slave" was *doulos* (masc. plur. *douloi*, fem. sing. *doulê*, fem. plur. *doulai*). For the complex terminology of slavery, and the wide variety of terms in use in classical Greece, see Zelnick-Abramovitz 2005: 27–39.

41. Aristot. *Pol.* 1253b6–7: πρῶτα δὲ καὶ ἐλάχιστα μέρη οἰκίας δεσπότης καὶ δοῦλος, καὶ πόσις καὶ ἄλοχος, καὶ πατὴρ καὶ τέκνα. See *Pol.* 1253b4–7: οἰκία δὲ τέλειος ἐκ δούλων καὶ ἐλευθέρων. In a ceremony analogous to that which greeted the entry of a bride, a newly purchased slave was welcomed into the *oikos* with an outpouring of figs, dates, and other delicacies intended to portend a "sweet and pleasant" future. See Lex. Seguer. (Bekker) 269.9. Cf. Aristoph. *Plout.* 768 and schol.; Dem. 45.74; Pollux 3.77; Harpokratiôn and Suidas, s.v.καταχύσματα. (Acceptance of slaves as inferior members of a family has been characteristic of many societies [see for example, precolonial slavery in West Africa: Miers and Kopytoff 1977: 11]).

42. *Pol.* 1252b12–14: ἡ μὲν οὖν εἰς πᾶσαν ἡμέραν συνεστηκυῖα κοινωνία κατὰ φύσιν οἶκός ἐστιν. See 1253b4: οἰκία δὲ τέλειος ἐκ δούλων καὶ ἐλευθέρων.

43. *Pol.* 1253b4–7. In fact, the slave, as a member of the *oikos*, was frequently referred to as an *oiketês*. Inclusion of unfree persons as members of the master's family is not an exceptional phenomenon in ancient societies: see Schumacher 2001: Chapter 3.

44. Although "the different senses of the word" can be studied separately (as MacDowell [1989] does)—and in context a particular aspect may be emphasized (as with the physical premises in Antiph. 2d.8)—the unique signification of the term lies in its denotation of an *entity*. For each of the separate notations of physical place, the human beings associated with that place and assets of value belonging to those persons, Greek offers a plenitude of alternative terms, most particularly *oikia* for the physical house, *klêros* for the assets, and *agkhisteia* for a circle of related persons.

all retail establishments, workshops, and craft and trade activities.[45] Even the permanent physical premises of an Athenian bank (*trapeza*) were usually coextensive with the personal residence of the *trapeza*'s proprietor.[46] As a result, at Athens, "'firm' and private household" were, in Moses Finley's words, "one and the same,"[47] and so, for those slaves working in brothels, their *oikos* was likely to be both their place of work and their residence.[48] Aiskhinês actually describes a single house that was used in turn as a business place and home by a doctor, smith, fuller, carpenter, and as a brothel.[49]

Substantial ancient evidence shows that "the prostitution of slaves was paradigmatically based in brothels" (*porneia*)[50] and that *pornai*—in contrast to the predominantly free *hetairai* chronicled in the literary tradition[51]—were predominantly slaves (*doulai*). Aiskhinês makes explicit the contrast between free *hetairoi* and slave *pornoi* when he urges Timarkhos, charged with prostitution, to respond to the accusations not as a *pornos*, but as a free man.[52] Aristophanês, in the *Ekklêsiazousai*, explicitly contrasts the chorus of free citizen-women to the *pornai* who are slaves (*doulai*), and comically proposes to have the free women hereafter service free men, relegating the *pornai doulai* to sleeping with unfree males.[53] Demosthenes warns that if Athenian juries do not uphold laws relating to citizenship, the work of *pornai* will fall to the daughters of "citizens," but that *hetairai* will be indistinguishable from (other) free

---

45. See Dem. 47.56; Men. *Sam.* 234–36; Pollux 1.80. See also Nevett 1999: 66–67, 88; Jameson 2002: 168–69; E. Cohen 2000: 42–43.

46. See Dem. 49.22, 52.8, 52.14.

47. [1953] 1981: 69. Cf. Plácido 1997. Identity of firm and household appears to have been widespread in antiquity: for the ancient Near East, see Silver 1995: 50–54; for Rome, Kirschenbaum 1987: 122–23.

48. Kapparis 1999: 228 ("prostitutes working in brothels lived on the premises"). Cf. Bettalli 1985; Jameson 1990: 185; Pesando 1987: 47–55.

49. 1.124. Cf. Hêrôdas 2.36 (Cunningham 1971: 88).

50. Flemming 1999: 43. Cf. Davidson 1997: 90–99; Kapparis 1999: 228–29.

51. See pp. 59 ff.

52. ἃ δὲ πείθει σε Δημοσθένης λέγειν, οὐκ ἀνδρός ἐστιν ἐλευθέρου, ἀλλὰ πόρνου περὶ τῶν τόπων διαφερομένου (1.123).

53. *Ekklês.* 717–24: (Πρ.) ἔπειτα τὰς πόρνας καταπαῦσαι βούλομαι | ἁπαξαπάσας. Βλ. ἵνα τί; Πρ. δῆλον τουτογί· | ἵνα τῶν νέων ἔχωσιν αὗται τὰς ἀκμάς. | καὶ τάς γε δούλας οὐχὶ δεῖ κοσμουμένας | τὴν τῶν ἐλευθέρων ὑφαρπάζειν Κύπριν, | ἀλλὰ παρὰ τοῖς δούλοισι κοιμᾶσθαι μόνον κ.τ.λ.

women.⁵⁴ Menander sets the *pornê* in direct antithesis to a free woman. The abject slave whore of *Epitrepontes*, working for a *pornoboskos* who has hired her out for 12 *drachmas*, is a *pornê*.⁵⁵ In the *Woman from Samos*, the confident sex-mate of the wealthy Dêmeas is a free *hetaira*.⁵⁶ For Menander there is a natural conflict between the free woman and the slave *pornê*: the slave is more manipulative and in her knavery knows no shame.⁵⁷ Herôdas likewise assumes that *pornai* are slaves: to protect his *pornai*, Battaros invokes a law dealing with *doulai*.⁵⁸ In fact, the words *pornê* and *doulê* occur together so commonly that a study by the Italian scholar Citti has concluded that mention of the term *pornê* in ancient Greek necessarily evokes the mental image of a *doulê*: the two words form "*una coppia nominale*," "a verbal coupling."⁵⁹ Thus the defendant in Lysias 4, seeking to have a woman give evidence under torture, refers to her not merely as a "slave"⁶⁰ but as a "slave *pornê*" (in Greek *doulê pornê*).⁶¹ In fact, her characterization as a "*doulê*" is based only on the defendant's

---

54. Dem. 59.113: . . . προπηλακισθέντος δὲ τοῦ νόμου . . . ἡ μὲν τῶν πορνῶν ἐργασία ἥξει εἰς τὰς τῶν πολιτῶν θυγατέρας . . . τὸ δὲ τῶν ἐλευθέρων γυναικῶν ἀξίωμα εἰς τὰς ἑταίρας, ἂν ἄδειαν λάβωσι τοῦ ἐξεῖναι αὐταῖς παιδοποιεῖσθαι ὡς ἂν βούλωνται καὶ τελετῶν καὶ ἱερῶν καὶ τιμῶν μετέχειν τῶν ἐν τῇ πόλει. Cf. Gilhuly 2009: 1, 56.

55. Cf. lines 136–37 (πορνοβοσκῷ δώδεκα τῆς ἡμέρας δραχμὰς δίδωσι); 430–31 (ἐᾶτέ μ', ἱκετεύω σε, καὶ μή μοι κακὰ παρέχετ'); 646 (παιδάριον ἐκ πόρνης).

56. Cf. lines 30–31 (Σαμίας ἑταίρας εἰς ἐ<πι>θυμίαν τινὰ | ἐλθεῖν ἐκεῖνον); 748–49 (Σὺ δ' ἐπ' ἐλευθέραν γυναῖκα λαμβάνεις βακτίσην καὶ διώκεις). On Khrysis's self-assured decision making, see, for example, lines 137–45.

57. *Epitrep.* Fr. 7: χαλεπόν, Παμφίλη, |ἐλευθέραι γυναικὶ πρὸς πόρνην μάχη· | πλείονα κακουργεῖ, πλείον' οἶδ', αἰσχύνεται | οὐδέν, κολακεύει μᾶλλον.

58. Mime 2: 30, 36–37, 46–48: ἐγὼ δ|ὲ πό[ρ]νας ἐκ Τύρου . . . οὐδὲ τῶν πορνέων βίηι λαβὼν οἴχωκεν· . . . ἐπὴν δ' ἐλεύθερός τις αἰκίσηι δούλην . . . τῆς δίκης τὸ τίμημα διπλοῦν τελείτω.

59. 1997: 92. Citti sees the two terms as virtually synonymous: "Uno dei due termini comportasse l'altro" (1997: 95). See Marzi 1979: 29.

60. Only unfree persons were putatively subject to examination under torture in private disputes. But—despite much surviving rhetorical posturing—no slave is known to have actually given testimony under torture in private disputes. Todd 1990: 33–34 summarizes: "On forty-two occasions in the orators we find the challenge, either 'torture my slaves for evidence' or 'let me torture yours.' Forty times this challenge was flatly rejected; twice (Isoc. 17.15–16, Dem. 37.42) it was accepted but not carried through." See Kamen 2013: 13–14. Various explanations have been proffered for this phenomenon: see Thür 1977; Gagarin 1996, 2001; Mirhady 1996, 2000; Allen 2000: 365–66, n. 14.

61. Lys. 4.19: ἀγανακτῶ δ', ὦ βουλή, εἰ διὰ πόρνην καὶ δούλην ἄνθρωπον περὶ τῶν μεγίστων εἰς κίνδυνον καθέστηκα.

characterization of her as a *pornê*: the plaintiff insists that she is free,[62] and no evidence (other than her characterization as a *doulê*) suggests that she is enslaved. Theopompos, the fourth-century historian, emphasizes the linkage between the two terms in describing a certain Pythionikê, a slave who had belonged to three separate owners, and was therefore "thrice a *doulê* and thrice a *pornê*" (*tri-doulon kai tri-pornon*).[63] A scholiast explains a passage in Demosthenes by offering the example of "*douloi* and sons of *pornai*."[64] Libanios, in a rhetorical critique, brands Aiskhinês as an individual born of a father who was a *doulos* and a mother who was a *pornê*.[65] And, as one might expect, the fullest examples of this verbal combination are to be found in patristic works.[66]

Within their brothels, Athenian prostitutes—like other slaves—would have received instruction in the provision of sexual services. Athenian society functioned through an enormous network of hundreds of distinct occupations, most unrelated to agriculture.[67] To maintain this diverse specialization, in the many fields requiring knowledge and skill (*tekhnai*)[68]— handicraft, catering, and medicine, for example—*douloi* and *doulai* normally received substantial training,[69] vocational education that free persons often lacked.[70] Slaves working in *trapezai* were taught the intricacies

---

62. §12: φησὶν αὐτὴν ἐλευθέραν εἶναι. §14: αὐτὴν ἐλευθέραν ἐσκήπτετο εἶναι.

63. μὴ μόνον τρίδουλον, ἀλλὰ καὶ τρίπορνον αὐτήν (Athên. 595a = FGrHist 115 F 253).

64. Εἴα ἂν ἐκεῖνα λέγων, ἅπερ ἀπαιτῶν τὰς εἰσφορὰς ὁ Ἀνδροτίων ἐλοιδορεῖτο, δούλους καλῶν καὶ ἐκ πορνῶν. Y L (Dilts 1986: 274, Scholion 69).

65. Libanios 8.301–302 (Foerster): θαυμαστὸν οὐδὲν εἰ γεγονὼς ἐκ δούλου πατρὸς καὶ τούτου πονηροῦ καὶ πόρνης μητρὸς κ. τ. λ.

66. John Chrysostom, *In Joannem* PG 59.165.23; *De Mansuetudine* PG 63.554.12.

67. For a survey of "the extensive horizontal specialization in the Athenian economy" and the resultant profusion of discrete labor functions, see Harris 2002.

68. Xen. *Oik.* 1.1: ἆρα γε ἡ οἰκονομία ἐπιστήμης τινὸς ὄνομά ἐστιν, ὥσπερ ἡ ἰατρικὴ καὶ ἡ χαλκευτικὴ καὶ ἡ τεκτονική; Ἡ καὶ ὥσπερ τούτων τῶν τεχνῶν κ. τ. λ. Cf. Pollux 4.7, 22. On prostitution as a *tekhnê*, see Dem. 59.18.

69. Xen. *Oik.* 7.41, 12.4; Aristot. *Oik.* 1344a27–29 and passim. Training of artisans and caterers: see, for example, Dem. 45.71 (τοῦτον εἰ συνέβη μάγειρον ἢ τινος ἄλλης τέχνης δημιουργὸν πρίασθαι, τὴν τοῦ δεσπότου τέχνην ἂν μαθὼν κ. τ. λ.). Medicine: Klees 1998: 96–100; Sigerist 1970: 74.

70. Contrasts the vocationally useless "liberal education" of free persons with slaves' training in *tekhnai* (crafts or trades requiring knowledge and skill: Xen. *Oik.* 1.1; Pollux 4.7.22): his female relatives lack the knowledge and skills of slaves (ὁ μὲν γὰρ τεχνίτας τρέφει, ἐγὼ δ'ἐλευθερίως πεπαιδευμένους: *Apom.* 2.7.4).

of finance and accounting.⁷¹ Operators of meretricious businesses (*mastropoi*) were expected to teach their sex-workers skills that would generate substantial monies,⁷² and in fact slaves working as prostitutes are known to have received specialized training, sometimes starting in childhood,⁷³ including lessons in dance.⁷⁴ Yet even the best educated and most highly skilled *douloi* often performed multiple tasks. Slaves who were skilled frequently combined the provision of entertainment with the practice of prostitution.⁷⁵ Domestic servants often worked at both household tasks and commercial pursuits.⁷⁶ Thus slaves working as doctors or as doctors' assistants are known to have devoted part of their time to household duties.⁷⁷ (Aiskhinês, charging Timarkhos with betraying his free status by acting in a slavish fashion, specifically accuses him of combining work as a prostitute with a purported pursuit of training in medicine.⁷⁸)

This pattern of multiple tasking provides the context for a division of labor in which some female slaves worked as both prostitutes and wool-workers.⁷⁹ Brothel prostitution and wool-working, even at supervisory

---

71. Dem. 45.72 (with regard to the great *trapezitês* Phormiôn, who entered banking as a slave): ἐπειδὴ δ'ὁ πατὴρ ὁ ἡμέτερος τραπεζίτης ὢν ἐκτήσατ' αὐτὸν καὶ γράμματ' ἐπαίδευσεν καὶ τὴν τέχνην ἐδίδαξεν.... The *douloi* Xenôn, Euphrôn, Euphraios, and Kallistratos—while still enslaved—as principals operated the largest bank in Athens, that of Pasiôn (see chapter 7, p. 173).

72. Xen. *Symp.* 4.59–60: ὁ ἀγαθὸς μαστροπὸς τὰ συμφέροντα εἰς τὸ ἀρέσκειν διδάσκοι ἄν... εἴ τις τοιούτους δύναιτο ἐξεργάζεσθαι ὧν προστατοίη, δικαίως ἂν μέγα φρονοίη ἐπὶ τῇ τέχνῃ καὶ δικαίως ἂν πολὺν μισθὸν λαμβάνοι.

73. See, for example, Dem. 59.18: Νικαρέτη ... δεινὴ δὲ καὶ δυναμένη φύσιν μικρῶν παιδίων συνιδεῖν εὐπρεπῆ, καὶ ταῦτα ἐπισταμένη θρέψαι καὶ παιδεῦσαι ἐμπείρως, τέχνην ταύτην κατεσκευασμένη. Kapparis comments: "She knew how to educate them to become commercially successful courtesans" (1999: 207). See Alkiphrôn 4 passim; Louk. *Hetair. Dialek.* 4.3, 10.4. Cf. Vanoyeke 1990: 33–35.

74. Instruction in dance is a frequent motif on Attic pottery, often interpreted as an integral aspect of the training of young prostitutes. See Delavaud-Roux 1993: 131–32. Cf. Aristoph. *Thes.* 1177–98.

75. See chapter 7, pp. 163–164.

76. Garlan 1988: 62: "Domestic slaves devoted part of their time" to the production of goods: "slaves were, in most cases, simply general 'dogsbodies.'" Cf. Jameson 2002: 168–70.

77. Garlan 1988: 68. Cf. Kudlien 1968; Joly 1969.

78. Aiskhin. 1.40: ἐκάθητο ἐν Πειραιεῖ ἐπὶ τοῦ Εὐθυδίκου ἰατρείου, προφάσει μὲν τῆς τέχνης μαθητής, τῇ δ'ἀληθείᾳ πωλεῖν αὐτὸν προῃρημένος....

79. In the modern world, prostitution is often a part-time pursuit: "In few cases are women and men engaged full-time ... sex work is commonly just one of the multiple activities

levels, were major Athenian industries in which women's roles were dominant. Female *pornai*, believed to be far more numerous than male *pornoi*,[80] typically worked as prostitutes under a senior woman who "knew how to run her business ... and how to keep the women under strict control."[81] Similarly wool-working—"the characteristic area of feminine expertise normally cited by ancient authors"[82]—was entirely dependent on female labor.[83] Although many free women were skilled in this craft, and often supervised or even worked along with their slaves,[84] the actual production and servicing of textiles were almost entirely the work of unfree women.[85] Aristotle, in defending slavery as natural and necessary, focuses on this *tekhnê* and its slave workers: so long as shuttles could not spin by themselves, owners would have need for slaves.[86] Even under the sting of unwonted poverty, the Athenian Aristarkhos only reluctantly put his free female dependents to work producing wool, and even then he himself

---

employed for generating income" (Kempadoo 1998: 3–4). Prostitutes often work additionally in retail trade, office occupations, domestic service, and in street activities such as shoe-shining. Cf. Azize et al. 1996; Senior 1992; Kane 1993; Bolles 1992.

80. Davidson 1997: 77. But for the impossibility of determining actual ratios of male and female sex workers at Athens, see introduction, pp. 12–13.

81. Kapparis 1999: 207. Cf. Carey 1992: 94. For female *mastropoi*, see chapter 6, pp. 140–42.

82. Brock 1994; 338. Cf. Wrenhaven 2009: 371: "(W)eaving was the primary task of women in ancient Greece." See Pl. *Alk.* 126e, *Lysis* 208d–e, *Nomoi* 805e–806a; Xen. *Apom.* 3.9.11, *Lak. Pol.* 1.3.

83. "Una delle attività di competenza esclusiva delle donne" (Faraguna 1999a: 70). Cf. Lewis 2002: 62–65. Market trade seems to have been centered in the ἱματιόπωλις ἀγορά (Pollux 7.78): see Wycherley 1957: 200, no. 663 and 187–88, no. 614. Clothing for slaves seems to have been an important retail product: Bettalli 1982: 264, 271–72.

84. Aristoph. *Batr.* 1349–51, *Lys.* 519–20, 536–37, 728–30, *Neph.* 53–55; Pl. *Rep.* 455c; Xen. *Oik.* 7.6, 21, 36; Plut. *Mor.* 830c (citing Kratês the Cynic). Cf. the older woman looking on while two younger women fold finished cloth (stamnos attributed to the Copenhagen painter) and the weighing of wool by two women under the supervision of their seated mistress (black-figure lekythos by the Amasis painter): Lewis 2002: 62–63.

85. *Dyeing*: Eup. Fr. 434 (K-A), Aristoph. *Ekkl.* 215; *Weaving*: SEG 18.36 B2; *Linen-working*: Aiskhin. 1.97, Alexis Fr. 36 (K-A); *Sewing*: I.G. II² 1556.28, Antiphanês *Akestria* Fr. 21–24, Jordan 1985: n. 72. *Wool-working*: Scenes on Attic vases: Webster 1972: Chapters 16 and 17. The best treatment of "l'importanza della mandopera servile nella manifattura tessile" is Faraguna 1999a: 72–79. Cf. Jameson 1977/78: 134, n. 63; Tod 1950: 10–11.

86. εἰ γὰρ ἠδύνατο ἕκαστον τῶν ὀργάνων κελευσθὲν ἢ προαισθανόμενον ἀποτελεῖν τὸ αὑτοῦ ἔργον ... οὕτως αἱ κερκίδες ἐκέρκιζον αὐταί ... οὐδὲν ἂν ἔδει ... οὔτε τοῖς δεσπόταις δούλων (*Pol.* 1253b33–1254a1).

refused personally to be involved in the labor.[87] With good reason: because wool-working was identified as a strictly female activity, a man so engaged was ipso facto marked as effeminate.[88]

Reflecting such factors as slaves' personal characteristics, owners' economic situation, and numerous other elements of chance and opportunity, the actual work assignments of unfree persons would have varied greatly. Many *pornai* would likely have had no involvement in textile work, and many wool workers, no involvement in commercial sex[89]—but substantial evidence suggests that numerous female slaves functioned both as wool workers and as brothel prostitutes.[90] This combination of tasks was in fact consonant with the traditional Athenian association of wool-working and feminine sexuality: "the connection between a girl's attaining sexual maturity (and) acquiring the prerequisite skill in wool-working" (Sebesta 2002: 126) was exemplified by the important Athenian rite of the *arrhêphoroi*, for example, in which selected young girls nearing puberty were secluded on the Akropolis, taught the wool-working skills needed to weave the elaborate *peplos* presented each year to Athena, and then sent on a journey to a temple of Aphroditê carrying baskets of sexual significance—biscuits shaped like phalluses and snakes![91] In turn, Athêna (as goddess of female crafts) joined Aphroditê in receiving the real-life offerings of Athenian prostitutes[92]—and was portrayed in literature as the recipient of dedications by wool-workers who were also working or hoped to work as prostitutes. Attic pottery arguably reinforced the linkage between wool-working and sexual commerce through its frequent presentations of Aphroditê's gestures of spinning and of her elaborate headdress and embroidered bust ornament (Fischer 2013).

---

87. Xen. *Apom.* 2.7.12: Αἰτιῶνται αὐτὸν μόνον τῶν ἐν τῇ οἰκίᾳ ἀργὸν ἐσθίειν.

88. Cf. Midas (Athên. 516b), Sardanapalos (Diod. Sik. 2.23), Kallôn (Diod. Sik. 32.11). Robert identifies as a slave the male figure interacting with women engaged in textile work depicted on an epinetron from Attika (Athens, Ethn. Mus. 2179; Robert 1892: Pl. 13, contrary to Sutton 1981: 224–25). Acton points out, however, the existence of specialist male tailors and "celebrated male weavers" (2014: 154–55).

89. Sutton 2004: 335: "Not all spinning women on vases are prostitutes."

90. Rodenwaldt 1932; Keuls 1983; Neils 2000; Acton 2014: 157–58. Davidson summarizes: "A large group of women . . . were forced (or chose)" to work at both pursuits (1997: 89).

91. Aristoph. *Lys.* 641–47, Harp. s.v.ἀρρηφορεῖν, Suda s.v.ἀρρηφορία, *Etym. Magn.* 149.14–23. Cf. Reeder 1995: 248–49; Loraux [1984] 1993: 164, n. 74; Calame 1977: 1: 68 and 238–39.

92. Parthenon dedications to Athêna from *hetairai*: Harris 1995: 244–49. Aphroditê as patron goddess of prostitutes, chapter 1, pp. 29–31.

Surviving Athenian vases offer a number of scenes linking female erotic and textile labor, including depictions of young men bringing gifts or money-bags to women working with wool[93] and scenes of women with names appropriate to prostitutes (Aphrodisia and Obolê) putting aside their wool while male customers approach or wait.[94] A water-jar depicts a naked woman spinning wool before a clothed seated woman, "clearly the madam who forces her *pornai* to work during the off hours."[95] Strikingly, a number of ceramic vessels portray woven work baskets "of the type often depicted in wool-working scenes" hanging on brothel walls, again "strongly suggest(ing)" the connection between wool-working and commercial sex.[96] So pervasive is the fusion on Greek vases of wool-work and monetary eroticism that for many art historians, "spinning and textile activity have become synonymous with prostitution."[97] And beyond ceramic representation, material culture provides the evidence of more than one hundred loom-weights found (along with hundreds of drinking vessels) in virtually every room in the classical levels of a labyrinthine building that has been identified as a *porneion*[98]—physical evidence of "courtesans who attended both to the loom and to the guests" (Knigge [1988] 1991: 93).

---

93. See, for example, ARV² 101.3 (Robert 1919: 125–29); ARV² 557.123; ARV² 795.100; Antikensammlung, Staatliche Museen zu Berlin, F 2254; Heidelberg 64/5 (kalpis by the Nausikaa Painter). Cf. ARV² 276.70 (discussed in Meyer 1988). Other examples: von Reden 1995: 206–209. Ferrari (2002: 14–16) argues that the pouches depicted in a number of these scenes did not contain coins but knucklebones, a strange suggestion since "knucklebones are associated with children, not grown women" (Wrenhaven 2009: 372). Cf. introduction, p. 23, n. 103, and related text.

94. Munich, Zanker: Münzen und Medaillen AG, *Auktion* 51 (Basel 1975), discussed at Williams 1983: 96–97. Cf. ARV² 189.72.1632; ARV² 275.50. For an overview of erotically charged representations of women engaged in spinning and related duties, see Sutton 2004: 333–37; Reinsberg 1989: 122–25. Lewis surveys Athenian ceramic treatment of wool-work (2002: 62–65).

95. Neils 2000: 209. Cf. Sebesta 2002: 125–26; Wrenhaven 2009: 374 (fig. 1). The vase is in Copenhagen (Nat. Mus. 153= ARV² 1131, 161 and Williams 1983: 96, fig. 7.4). Cf. ARV² 795.10294–7.

96. Wrenhaven 2009: 375. See, for example, London, British Museum E71; Basel, Antikenmuseum Basel und Sammlung Ludwig Ka415; New Haven, Yale University Art Gallery 1913.163; Florence, Museo Archeologico 3921. Cf. Gilhuly 2009: 161.

97. Ferrari 2002: 13. The relationship between wool-working and prostitution was first emphasized in Rodenwaldt 1932. More recent affirmations include Wrenhaven 2009: 371–78; Reeder 1995: 181–87, nos. 36–38; Meyer 1988; Sutton 1992: 19–20. Ferrari is skeptical (2002: 13–14), as is Bundrick (2008: 296).

98. So-called Building Z located by the city wall at the Sacred Gate, in an area long identified as one of the red-light districts of ancient Athens. Among the remains was an

This involvement of individual women in both erotic and wool-working commerce explains a series of dedications that have baffled scholars. The *phialai exeleutherikai* tablets—our prime source of information on the manumission of Athenian slaves—document the freeing (in the 320's) of approximately 375 slaves,[99] each of whom offers a 100 *drachma* silver bowl (*phialê*) after his or her acquittal in formalistic, that is, fictitious actions (*dikai apostasiou*) brought by ex-owners.[100] In these inscriptions, occupations are recorded for 52 of 86 ex-slaves who are probably or certainly female, but for only 62 of 110 probable or certain males.[101] For scholars accustomed to thinking of Athenian women, and especially slave women, as hapless objects of male domination locked away in the interior of society, consigned to ignorance and reserved for exploitation,[102]

---

amulet depicting Aphroditê Ourania riding a goat across the night sky. For the site, structure, excavation, and contents of this building, see Knigge 2005; Lentakis 1998: 64–65; Lind 1988; Glazebrook 2012: 46.

99. These documents have been published in I.G. II² (1553–78) and republished (in part) by Lewis in 1959 and 1968 (to incorporate additional finds from the Athenian Agora excavations) and by Meyer 2010: 81–146. See also Agora I 4665 (= Walbank 1996: 452–53). Kränzlein 1975 surveys scholarly work on these texts; for early treatments of the original nineteenth-century fragments, see Calderini [1908] 1965: 424–34.

100. On the *dikê apostasiou*, see Dem. 35.47–49, Aristot. *Ath. Pol.* 58.3. Harp., s.v. ἀποστασίου. Cf. Klees 1998: 348–54; Todd 1993: 190–92; Gernet [1950] 1955: 168–72; Calderini [1908] 1965: 330–35. Zelnick-Abramovitz (2005: 274–92) suggests that these actions were not "fictitious," and that the *phialai exeleutherikai* "record the verdicts of genuine trials" (2005: 285), but that only the acquittals, leading to full manumission, have been preserved, giving rise to the dedications recorded in I.G. II² 1553–78 (2005: 289–90). See also Papazarkadas 2012; Zelnick-Abramovitz 2013: 71–107. Meyer offers an "unconvincing" (Vlassopoulos 2011), "contrived" (Sickinger 2013: 206) suggestion that the *phialai exeleutherikai* do not relate to freedmen, but to metics.

101. I follow calculations made by Todd, who produced, as he notes, "deliberately conservative figures" (1997: 121). For example, he disregards twelve *talasiourgoi* as being of "uncertain sex," even though five of the twelve have names that are typically feminine, and wool-working seems to have been an overwhelmingly female pursuit (see above). As apparent confirmation of the undercounting by Todd of female *talasiourgoi*, there is not a single *talasiourgos* among the 110 slaves who (by Todd's reckoning) are "probably" or "certainly" male (1997: 121–22). Of the total of 375, Todd found 179 to be of "uncertain sex" (meaning that without regard to other possible indicia of sex, their names were not followed by the formulaic language οἰκῶν [male]/οἰκοῦσα [female] or ἀποφυγών [male]/ ἀποφυγοῦσα [female]). (Many of these omissions, however, reflect the fragmentary nature of the surviving inscribed materials.)

102. Ancient literature in general stereotypically attributes to women and slaves similar negative attributes (see Murnaghan and Joshel 1998: 3–5; Just 1985). Aristotle, for example, treated women and slaves together: the woman's inferiority possibly was to be contrasted with the slave's utter worthlessness (Poet. 1454a21–2: καίτοι γε ἴσως τούτων τὸ μὲν χεῖρον, τὸ δὲ ὅλως φαῦλόν ἐστιν. For the impact of slavery on Greek women, see Dubois 2003: 131–52. For the prevailing scholarly view of male citizen dominance, see, for example, Cartledge 1993: 4.

this information—showing manumitted slave women as more likely than slave men to have had an occupation—is "most surprising" and "too straightforward an inference" (Todd 1997: 122). As a result, scholars have resorted to a "corrective approach" in an effort to make the ancient evidence conform to modern expectation.[103] Todd dismisses the testimony of the *phialai exeleutherikai* as an "illusion" (1997: 122). Rosivach (1989), noting that a majority (twenty-nine) of the fifty-two working women are designated as *talasiourgoi* ("wool-workers"), finds a simple solution: the standard Liddell-Scott Greek/English Lexicon must be corrected. He insists that the word *"talasiourgos"* here does not mean "wool-worker" as the Lexicon (1996 Supplement) claims:[104] with a "diagnostic reading," *"talasiourgos"* actually means "housewife."[105] So "corrected," the inscriptions would report just the opposite of the actual unrevised texts: relatively few Athenian freedwomen would have had occupations. With this alteration, however, the inscriptions would now present what even Todd sees as "a curious omission from the texts"—the absence of "female household slaves" (Todd 1997: 23).

But scholars need not manufacture such a "curious omission" through "corrective" revision of the actual texts. In my opinion, the "plain meaning" of the inscriptions—interpreted in the context of the linkage between prostitution and wool-working—makes good sense without "corrective" interpretation.

Scholars have long conjectured that slaves obtaining manumission at Athens were likely to be disproportionately those who had special access

---

103. In French terms, "documentation 'surdéterminée'" requires "une lecture 'symptomale'" (Garlan 1982: 31). "Diagnostic reading," a popular tool of francophone methodology, is defended as merely an appropriate response to the inevitable subjectivity of those espousing objective pretensions: "Very few of the apparently purely scholarly debates on [Greek slavery] avoid, in one way or another, consciously or unconsciously, adopting a particular ideological perspective" (Garlan 1988: 23). For decades, scholars dismissed the evidence that Building Z (n. 98) was a brothel, and denied that the sale of sex had some coherent relationship to the many scenes on vases showing young men bringing gifts or money-bags to women working with wool (see Davidson 1997: 85–90).

104. Even Rosivach (1989: 365) concedes that the word in all other ancient citations means "wool-worker." *Talasiourgia* ("wool-working") sometimes refers only to the process of spinning wool into thread, but often encompasses the entire process, including weaving. See Blümner 1912: 104; Tod 1901–02: 204, n. 8.

105. Although Rosivach sometimes substitutes "home-maker" for "housewife," he generally uses "wife" in its literal sense, even trying to identify de facto husbands. But this interpretation is impossible: on Lewis's "Great Inscription," two *talasiourgoi* are grouped with a single man (Side B, Col. I, lines 253–66).

to a free person's support or possessed skills that produced relatively high compensation.¹⁰⁶ Olympiôdoros, for example, who never married, spent a large part of his assets—far too much, in the opinion of his relatives—in paying for the manumission of a prostitute (who thereafter supposedly strode about arrogantly, bedecked with gold jewelry, wearing fine clothes and accompanied by a retinue of attendants).¹⁰⁷ The wealthy Apollodôros, although married, is said to have funded the manumission of one female prostitute, and to have provided for the marriage of another courtesan.¹⁰⁸ Misgolas, an esteemed Athenian active in Athenian cult life and known to be "marvelously" committed to purchasing the sexual services of musical performers, provided (with his brother) for the manumission of two slaves.¹⁰⁹ In Lysias 4, two men shared the cost of buying freedom for a slave woman whose sexual services they had previously been purchasing.¹¹⁰ For their part, skilled slaves were often able to retain a portion (termed *apophora*) of the income they produced¹¹¹—thus providing funds for the purchase of freedom or, at the least, offering a source of repayment of monies advanced by others.¹¹² But enslaved wool-workers would have had virtually

---

106. See Zelnick-Abramovitz 2005: 153–83, 216–22; Kruger 2001: 153; Faraguna 1999a: 72; Blavatskaja 1972: 73–74 (who infers the superior capacity of prostitutes to obtain manumission). For Leôgoras's lavish expenditures on the *hetaira* Myrrina, see a recently published graffito from Athens confirming an allusion in Eupolis 50 (44) (K-A): Sourlas 2014: 248–50.

107. γυναῖκα μὲν ἀστὴν . . . . οὐδεπώποτε ἔγημεν . . . ἑταίραν δὲ λυσάμενος ἔνδον ἔχει . . . τὴν μὲν τούτου ἑταίραν περαιτέρω τοῦ καλῶς ἔχοντος καὶ χρυσία πολλὰ ἔχουσαν καὶ ἱμάτια καλά, καὶ ἐξόδους λαμπρὰς ἐξιοῦσαν καὶ ὑβρίζουσαν ἐκ τῶν ἡμετέρων . . . .(Dem. 48.53, 55). See chapter 7, p. 178.

108. Καὶ τὴν μὲν λέλυσαι, τὴν δ'ἐκδέδωκας ἑταίραν, καὶ ταῦτα γυναῖκ' ἔχων ποιεῖς (Dem. 36.45). On Apollodôros as examplar "of a wealthy and privileged young citizen," cf. Trevett 1992: 167–70.

109. Sexual involvement with musicians: Aiskhinês 1.41 (see chapter 1, n. 85 and accompanying text). Manumission of slaves: I.G. II² 1554 (=S.E.G. 18.36: 335, 339). Misgolas's involvement in cult of Artemis: I.G. II² 2825: 2. Reputation at Athens: ἀνὴρ τὰ ἄλλα καλὸς κἀγαθός (Aiskhin. 1.41).

110. This is the contention of the speaker's opponent: φησὶν αὐτὴν ἐλευθέραν εἶναι . . . αὕτη δὲ ὑπῆρχε κοινή, ὁμοίως ἀμφοτέρων ἀργύριον κατατεθηκότων . . . . διὰ πόρνην καὶ δούλην ἄνθρωπον (§§ 12, 16, 19). For exegesis of this elliptically preserved case, see Cox 1998: 188–89.

111. See chapter 7, pp. 172–74.

112. See Faraguna 1999a: 72, Finley [1951] 1985: 104–105. Lenders (operating as groups of *eranistai*) appear with frequency on the *phialai exeleutherikai* inscriptions. See I.G. II² 1553.7–10, 20–23; 1556 B27–29; 1557 B105–107; 1558 A37–43; 1559 A II 26–31; 1566 A27–29; 1568 B18–23; 1569 A III 18–21; 1570.24–26, 57–62, 82–84; 1571.8–13; and 1572.8–11; Lewis 1959: Face A, lines 141–42 and 566–67, Face B, lines 2 and 153; Lewis 1968: 368, line 8. The silver bowls

no opportunity to earn or accumulate personal funds, or to gain access to possible benefactors: they generally toiled in anonymity at repetitive chores in a supervised process requiring the joint labor of a number of workers,[113] often producing goods intended not for the market (and the generation of cash) but for the *oikos* itself.[114] Loukianos contrasts the meager wages of wool-work with the anticipated prosperity of prostitution;[115] elegiac literature records the plaintive complaints of women relegated to the famished poverty of wool-work.[116] Prostitutes by contrast earned "good money" (Lewis 2002: 99), not less than one-half *drachma* per act, and possibly much more (Loomis 1998: 185).[117] Through *apophora*, slave prostitutes, especially those in high demand, were sometimes able to share—by agreement with their master—in a portion of these payments. Surviving material even explains in detail how Neaira, a slave prostitute, allegedly bought her freedom through a combination of her own earnings and assistance from several of her "lovers," who had developed an emotional relationship with her.[118] This contrast between the impoverished wool-worker and the potentially high-earning prostitute (and the linkage between the two pursuits) are confirmed by a number of Hellenistic epigrams that describe dedications to Athêna or to Aphroditê offered by women aspiring to abandon the impoverishment of wool-working in order to devote

---

themselves are generally believed to have been paid for by the freed persons. This again would have required considerable funds. (We have no reliable information on prices paid to owners at Athens in connection with manumissions.)

113. See Xen. *Oik.* 2.7; Timoklês Fr. 33 (K-A: comm.), Συνέριθοι: συνέριθοι Ἀττικοί, συνυφαίνουσαι Ἕλληνες.

114. Rosivach 1989: 366–67. But there were some workers of high skill producing specialized product for sale in the market, such as the craftswoman expert in lace making described at Aiskhin. 1.97 (ἀμόργινα ἐπισταμένην ἐργάζεσθαι καὶ εἰς τὴν ἀγορὰν ἐκφερούσαν). An otherwise ordinary female slave skilled at wool-working might be worth twice the price of an untrained *doulê* (Xen. *Oik.* 7.41). For wool-working directed toward cash sales outside the *oikos*, see Kennedy 2014: 130–33; Labarre 1998; Kosmopoulou 2001: 301.

115. 80.6.: νῦν μὲν ὑφαίνουσα, νῦν δὲ κρόκην κατάγουσα ἢ στήμονα κλώθουσα ἐποριζόμην τὰ σιτία μόλις· . . . τὴν ἐλπίδα περιμένουσα.

116. See *Anth. Pal.* 6.285 (κακῶν λιμηρὰ γυναικῶν ἔργα); 6.283 (μίσθια νῦν σπαθίοις πενιχροῖς πηνίσματα κρούει); 6.48 (λιμηρῆς ἄρμενον ἐργασίης); 6.284 (εὔκλωστον δὲ γυναικῶν νῆμα καὶ ἠλακάτην ἀργὸς ἔχοι τάλαρος).

117. On the range of fees for sex, and their superiority to other compensation at Athens, see chapter 7, pp. 164–71.

118. See Dem. 59.29–32 (and the discussion in Kapparis 1999: 227–35).

themselves entirely to sexual commerce.[119] In a clever ditty by Nikarkhos, a woman has placed on a raging fire spindles and other equipment connected with Athêna. For this woman, wool-working is an impoverished ("famished") occupation appropriate only for "base females" (*kakôn gynaikôn*).[120] In contrast, prostitution offers a "pleasured life" (*terpnon bioton*) of festivals, revelry, and music in which Aphroditê, freeing her from wool-working, and "sharing in the (new) labor," will be her 10 percent partner.[121] In another epigram, a woman named Bittô dedicates to Athêna the textile apparatus of the work she hates, "the tools of impoverished enterprise": emulating Paris, she's casting her vote for Aphroditê's labor instead (*Anth. Pal.* 6.48). Yet another woman—whose sexual labors have reaped finery through lucrative assignations—would choose now entirely to abandon wool-working (*Anth. Pal.* 6.284), an option not available to the subject of a further epigram, an aging female who in contrast has had to abandon lucrative prostitution and is now left only with the impoverished yields of wool-working (*Anth. Pal.* 6.283). Following the opposite trajectory, Chrysis in Terence's *Andria* (adapted from Menander's *Andria* and *Perinthia*) moved into prostitution at Athens after previous impoverished and difficult labor as a wool-worker.[122]

The unexpurgated texts of the *phialai exeleutherikai*—showing that "women seem just as likely to have jobs as do men" (Todd 1997: 122)—thus make good sense: slaves working in wool can be properly described as *talasiourgoi* ("wool-workers"). They need not be denominated by modern scholars as "housewives." Earnings from prostitution—and useful relationships developed from this métier—would have provided a financial and personal mechanism for obtaining freedom,[123] and slaves who commanded earnings from prostitution would likely have figured prominently

---

119. For a survey of these poems and similar material, see Davidson 1997: 87–88.

120. *Anth. Pal.* 6.285: κακῶν λιμηρὰ γυναικῶν ἔργα (5–6).

121. Ibid., lines 7–10. For the mechanisms through which slaves might share their revenues (or profits) with their owners, and otherwise maintain an independent existence, see E. Cohen 1998: 114–23.

122. Primo haec pudice vitam parce ac duriter | agebat, lana ac tela victum quaeritans; | sed postquam amans accessit pretium pollicens | unus et item alter, ita ut ingeniumst omnium | hominum ab labore proclive ad lubidinem, | accepit condicionem, de(h)inc quaestum occipit (lines 74–79).

123. See, for example, the purchase of freedom, through her earnings and her relationships, by Neaira, an alleged slave prostitute: chapter 7, pp. 172–74.

among those gaining manumission. Not surprisingly, therefore, some of the freed slaves carry names that are typical Athenian designations for sex-workers—Glykera ("Sweetie") and Malthakê ("Softie"). Others—like the musicians (a flute-girl, a harpist) who "entertained" at male social functions—are recorded under callings that are known frequently to have been coupled with the provision of sexual services.[124] But, most explicitly, the *phialai exeleutherikai* inscriptions record a relatively large number of freed persons (both male and female) who are denominated "*pais*" (or "*paidion*," diminutive of *pais*). (Of the 185 persons for whom occupations are recorded, 16 are so denominated, of whom 3 are definitely female, 2 certainly male, and the others of uncertain sex.) This term—although often carrying the meaning of "servant" or "child"—frequently refers to persons engaging in sexual activity at the behest of an importuning male who offers something of value.[125] Appearing in a formulaic list of occupations, "prostitute" (as Todd notes [1997: 123]) is an appropriate possible translation.[126] In contrast, neither *pornai (-oi)* or *hetairai (-oi)* would be suitable designations for these newly liberated persons: *pornê (-os)*—as we have seen (pp. 46–48)—was a virtual synonym for "slave," an incongruous appellation for a dedication attesting to free status and perhaps a term of opprobrium to be avoided.[127] *Hetaira*—as we shall see (in the next section)—was a term scrupulously trumpeted as the calling of a free person, an honorific perhaps overly ostentatious for a formerly enslaved worker. Of course, many females are recorded in these inscriptions as *talasiourgoi*. Were they women whose identity was primarily as wool-workers but whose freedom was owed to the wages of sex, or were they persons now retired from compensated sexual activity? Or were some of these *talasiourgoi* part of the small minority of highly skilled (and possibly highly compensated)

---

124. These musicians "might also be called on to provide sexual entertainment" (Rhodes 1981: 574). See this chapter, p. 49; chapter 7, pp. 163–64.

125. According to Dover, in (homo)sexual relationships, "... the passive partner is called 'pais,' ('boy'), a word also used for 'child,' 'girl,' 'son,' 'daughter,' and 'slave'" (1978 [1989]: 16). "Pais" frequently appears on vases as a denomination for attractive young men or women. For male and female *paides* identified as objects of sexual desire, see Pl. *Nomoi* 836a7 (ἐρώτων παίδων τε ἀρρένων καὶ θηλειῶν).

126. Cf. I.G. IX (1) 1² 102: manumission of a *paidarion* which Blavatskaja (1972: 73–74) groups with a number of other Aitolian inscriptions that he believes to involve manumission of prostitutes.

127. Wrenhaven 2009: 382: "The fact that prostitution was a legal trade and was widely practiced in ancient Greece need not imply that it bore no social stigma."

specialist producers of exquisite textile products crafted to meet market demand?¹²⁸ Or because of the dominant importance of "wool-work" as a female pursuit, could "wool-work" generically denote "female labor?"¹²⁹ We will never know. The extraordinarily elliptical language of the inscriptions, the highly fragmentary state in which they have survived, and our ignorance of their social and legal contexts leave us unable to determine even whether the choice of occupation attributed to each worker was made by the newly freed persons, by their former owners, by some *polis* official—or perhaps even by the stone cutter(s).¹³⁰ Yet these lists of *paides* and *talasiourgoi* and other freed persons, evidence for a process of manumission otherwise unknown, do offer a context for the situations portrayed in epigrammatic literature. They help explain a paradox otherwise inexplicable, a mystery raised by the anonymous poet of the Palatine Anthology and, I think, answered by our discussion—of how Philainion, the woolworker, made herself a gray coat sleeping in the embrace of Agamêdês.¹³¹

## *Selling "Free" Love*

Free Athenian purveyors of *erôs*—prominent or even dominant among the courtesans of Athens¹³²—sought to avoid all indications of dependence, and to manifest their autonomy. (In this, they would have been joined by those nonbrothel prostitutes who, although juridically unfree, aspired, and were able, to conform to the prevalent Athenian work values guiding free labor.) Accordingly, our sources provide vivid portrayals of meretricious arrangements that complied with the vocational ethics of free Athenians: the ability to select one's clients and to establish the parameters of service (the antithesis of compulsory sexual submission to any would-be purchaser); control over one's physical and familial surroundings, including the ownership of

---

128. See n. 114.

129. As Lewis 2002: 62 suggests. On epitaphs, "wool-work" appears generically to encompass a broad category of female activity (see Stears 2001).

130. "The truth of the matter is that our evidence is inadequate." Lewis 1959: 238.

131. *Anth. Pal.* 6.284: λάθρη κοιμηθεῖσα Φιλαίνιον εἰς Ἀγαμήδους | κόλπους τὴν φαιὴν εἰργάσατο χλανίδα.

132. "Unter der Gruppe der renommierten Hetären, die als Spitzenverdienerinnen galten (*megalomisthoi*) (Athênaios 570b; 558a–e), waren Sklavinnen kaum anzutreffen" (Klees 1998: 147, n. 16). Cf. Lentakis 1999: 146, 165.

valuable personal property[133] and the capacity to host one's own *symposia* ("dinner-parties")[134] (the antithesis of servile confinement in a brothel and relegation exclusively to other people's entertainment); the provision of reciprocated largess to one's lovers; the appearance of leisurely dedication to cultural and social activities;[135] the pursuit of work not only as an economic necessity but also as a mechanism of self-definition;[136] the independent negotiation of business arrangements reflecting the reciprocal (and not dependent) nature of a commercial sexual relationship (the antithesis of agreements providing for the commodity-use of an enslaved prostitute offered no formal voice in the arrangements to which [s]he was subject).[137]

The occupational situation and behavior of a prostitute endeavoring to comply with Athenian work ethics are displayed compellingly in Xenophôn's description of Sôkratês's meeting with the *hetaira* Theodotê ("a woman of the sort who sleeps with men who are persuasive"—emphasizing her freedom of selection—and whose livelihood comes from the benefactions of men who have become "friends"—an elevation of her relationships from master/servant or customer/commodity into the independence inherent in personalized reciprocity[138]). Sôkratês is awed by the domestic world she controls:[139] Theodotê lives in extravagant

---

133. Courtesans' luxurious possessions are frequently mentioned in Athenian literature. See, for example, Loukianos 80.4.1 (θοἰμάτια γὰρ καὶ τὰ χρυσία ταῦτα προείμην ἡδέως). Cf. the sumptious lifestyles and impressive property attributed to Khrysis in Menander's *Samia* and to Theodotê in Xenophôn's Memoirs of Sôkratês, discussed below, this chapter, pp. 60–62, 63–64. On women's rights of "ownership" at Athens, see Foxhall 1989; Sealey 1990: 45–49. Cf. Aristot. *Rhet.* 1361a.

134. See Gnathaina's famous *Nomos Sussitikos*, dining rules for her clients and associates: chapter 6, n. 105 and related text ). Cf. Makhôn 11.252, 258, 262–84 (Gow); Kallimakhos Fr. 433 (Pfeiffer).

135. For the Athenian elite idealization of such pursuits, see Fisher 1998b: 84–86; Stocks 1936; de Ste. Croix 1981: 114–117.

136. See n. 149 in this chapter and accompanying text.

137. "Contracts" negotiated by prostitutes (or their mothers) are discussed in detail in chapter 4. Lysias 4 offers a good example of an (alleged) sexual contract for the use of a slave (§1: ἀρνεῖσθαι τὰ περὶ τῆς ἀνθρώπου, μὴ κοινῇ ἡμᾶς χρῆσθαι συγχωρῆσαι). Cf. Dem. 59.71 (agreement between Stephanos and Epainetos for use of Phanô).

138. *Apom.* 3.11: §1: Γυναικὸς ... καλῆς ... καὶ οἵας συνεῖναι τῷ πείθοντι .... §4: Πόθεν οὖν, ἔφη, τὰ ἐπιτήδεια ἔχεις; Ἐάν τις, ἔφη, φίλος μοι γενόμενος εὖ ποιεῖν ἐθέλῃ, οὗτός μοι βίος ἐστί. On the importance attached by Athenians to egalitarian reciprocity, especially in the provision of personal services, see chapter 3, pp. 85–87.

139. Athenian courtesans are frequently presented as enormously wealthy: see chapter 7, pp. 175–79.

surroundings in a home furnished sumptuously in every way; she dresses and adorns herself luxuriously, and is accompanied by a retinue of finely outfitted and attractive "maid servants." Her mother is present, likewise wearing noticeably fine jewelry and clothing.[140] Exploring the sources of her prosperity, Sôkratês's queries ("do you own land? rental property? craftsmen?"[141]) assume that she herself might be a citizen (*politis*) whose possessions include real-estate and slaves. When Theodotê shows total indifference to Sôkratês's efforts to help her increase her income from her "friends" through systematic pursuit of "fine and wealthy" benefactors (§9), they each are conforming to third-party expectations. Xenophôn, seeking to refute the charge that Sôkratês was a deleterious "destroyer" of the young,[142] offers in these *Memoirs* examples of how the sage was in fact a practical dispenser of sound ideas,[143] including business advice (such as the suggestions that brought prosperity to Aristarkhos and his female relatives in the wool business (see pp. 50–51). Theodotê, in her turn, is careful to manifest the values of "free" Athenian labor. She herself has no desire or capacity to implement Sôkratês's schemes to maximize profit,[144] but she is willing to let *him* work for *her*.[145] She spends her time posing for artists, leaving potential customers waiting.[146] Whatever the reality of her situation[147]—and here Xenophôn, as so often, presents a portrait

---

140. ὁ Σωκράτης ὁρῶν αὐτήν τε πολυτελῶς κεκοσμημένην καὶ μητέρα παροῦσαν αὐτῇ ἐν ἐσθῆτί τε καὶ θεραπείᾳ οὐ τῇ τυχούσῃ, καὶ θεραπαίνας πολλὰς καὶ εὐειδεῖς καὶ οὐδὲ ταύτας ἠμελημένως ἐχούσας, καὶ τοῖς ἄλλοις τὴν οἰκίαν ἀφθόνως κατεσκευασμένην . . . . νὴ τὴν Ἥραν, ἔφη, ὦ Θεοδότη, καλόν γε τὸ κτῆμα . . . . (§§4, 5).

141. ἔστι σοι ἀγρός; . . . Ἀλλ' ἄρα οἰκία προσόδους ἔχουσα; . . . Ἀλλὰ μὴ χειροτέχναι τινές; (§4).

142. Cf. 1.1.1 (πολλάκις ἐθαύμασα τίσι ποτὲ λόγοις Ἀθηναίους ἔπεισαν οἱ γραψάμενοι Σωκράτην ὡς . . . ἀδικεῖ δὲ καὶ τοὺς νέους διαφθείρων) and 2.7.1 (καὶ μὴν τὰς ἀπορίας γε τῶν φίλων τὰς μὲν δι' ἄγνοιαν ἐπειρᾶτο γνώμῃ ἀκεῖσθαι, τὰς δὲ δι' ἔνδειαν διδάσκων κατὰ δύναμιν ἀλλήλοις ἐπαρκεῖν).

143. Sôkratês explains how she might acquire clients and maximize their contributions to her (§9: ὅπως ἐμβάλῃ αὐτοὺς εἰς τὰ σὰ δίκτυα . . . §12: οὕτω γὰρ ἂν μάλιστα φίλοι γίγνοιντο καὶ πλεῖστον χρόνον φιλοῖεν καὶ μέγιστα εὐεργετοῖεν; §14: τηνικαῦτα γὰρ πολὺ διαφέρει τὰ αὐτὰ δῶρα ἢ πρὶν ἐπιθυμῆσαι διδόναι).

144. §10: Μὰ τὸν Δί', ἐγὼ τούτων οὐδὲν μηχανῶμαι.

145. §15: Τί οὖν οὐ σύ μοι, ὦ Σώκρατες, ἐγένου συνθηρατὴς τῶν φίλων;

146. §2: οὕτω μὲν δὴ πορευθέντες πρὸς τὴν Θεοδότην καὶ καταλαβόντες ζωγράφῳ τινὶ παρεστηκυῖαν ἐθεάσαντο. Παυσαμένου δὲ τοῦ ζωγράφου . . .; § 3: ἡμεῖς δὲ ἤδη τε ὧν ἐθεασάμεθα ἐπιθυμοῦμεν ἅψασθαι καὶ ἄπιμεν ὑποκνιζόμενοι καὶ ἀπελθόντες ποθήσομεν.

147. Cartledge 2001: 159–60 offers an economic, Goldhill 1998 a cultural, interpretation of this vignette.

of shimmering but unconfirmable verisimilitude, highly seasoned with Sokratean irony—Theodotê, providing services in a manner and context appropriate to a free person, is the reification of the Athenian *imaginaire*:[148] she works for her living but is convinced that she does so to her own benefit and that of her "friends." By Modern Western Standards, she is at best a pretentious prostitute or madam earning a fine living from a dubious occupation, but in Athenian context she is pursuing an erotic métier in a fashion appropriate to a free woman. For Athenians such independence was, morally, far more commendable than the slavish conditions of brothel labor.

Because of the Athenians' tendency to idealize labor not as a form of production but as "cultural self-definition,"[149] the interconnection of work with intellectual and artistic pursuits offered further indicia of compliance with Athenian ethics. Not surprisingly, then, the lives of leading *hetairai* were often intertwined, frequently in a mutually supportive fashion, with those of great artists and men of affairs.[150] Consider Periklês and Aspasia. A *hetaira* of legendary charm and beauty, a renowned literary stylist who (according to Suda) taught rhetoric,[151] a businesswoman of considerable wealth,[152] Aspasia reportedly worked closely with Periklês on matters of public policy—an activity for which she was lampooned by Athens' comic dramatists.[153] Plato claims that she was even a principal author of Perikles's famed "Funeral Address."[154] Phrynê, another woman

---

148. See introduction, n. 8.

149. On the linkage at Athens of labor and "kulturellen Selbstdefinition," see von Reden 1992; Loraux 1995: 44–58; Vernant 1989; Schwimmer 1979.

150. For the recent tendency to dismiss the evidence for sophisticated and successful *hetairai* as mere myth and false romanticization, see introduction, p. 5.

151. For the verses in dactylic hexameter extant under her own name (τοῖς φερομένοις ὡς αὐτῆς ἔπεσιν), see Athên. 219c–d.

152. See chapter 6, p. 139.

153. On Aspasia, see esp. Plut. *Perikl.* 24.2–10. The ancient literary sources for her persona and accomplishments are set forth in Judeich 1896. For modern treatments, see Kennedy 2014: 68–96; Henry 1995; Stadter 1989: 233–42; Dover 1988: Chapter 13. Kennedy believes that Aspasia may have been a *hetaira*, but argues reasonably that in English, "girlfriend" or "companion" may be more appropriate denominations than "prostitute" or "whore" (2014: 85–87): see my discussion of nomenclature in Conventions, p. ix. Henry characterizes Aspasia as a "concubine" (*pallakê*) (1995: 15).

154. Men. 236b5: συνετίθει τὸν ἐπιτάφιον λόγον ὃν Περικλῆς εἶπεν. In the *Menexenos*, a teasing Sôkratês even proffers the alleged text of a Funeral Oration composed by Aspasia (236b7–c1).

of renowned wealth,[155] was the sexual companion of men such as the prominent Athenian statesman Hypereidês and the preeminent sculptor Praxitelês. She famously was the subject of Apellês's *Aphroditê Rising from the Sea* and of Praxitelês's *Knidian Aphroditê*.[156] Praxitelês's depiction of Phrynê in gold (or gilt) stood in a prominent position at Delphi between royal depictions of King Philip II of Macedon and Arkhidamos III, the famed Spartan king.[157] But less exalted portrayals in pottery of sometimes nameless courtesans confirm the egalitarian posture and presence of Athenian *hetairai*. In ceramic renderings of symposia, *hetairai* are garbed like male participants: men and women catch their long hair in a filet; both brandish garlands around their heads; both drape their clothing around their torsos in such a way as to display their naked chests or busts. "To all intents and purposes, *hetairai* and symposiasts look like equal partners" (Llewellyn-Jones 2003: 143). And even on the street, *hetairai* are portrayed in ceramic-ware as dressed modestly, sometimes even veiled—in sharp contrast to the portrayal, in literary sources, of street-walkers as provokingly dressed (or half-undressed) (Dalby 2002).

Athenian literature also portrays *hetairai* living in a lover's home as self-assertive, confident, and prosperous. Thus the free *hetaira* Khrysis in Menander's *Woman from Samos* is depicted as sumptuously garbed,[158] with personal servant(s) (line 373), and other personal possessions (line 381). She is so confident of her situation—correctly, as the play's dénouement demonstrates—that she is willing to offend her lover Dêmeas by pretending to have given birth to a child, seemingly by another man, and then to have kept the child without Dêmeas's consent—a manifestation of the considerable power that she yields within the household.[159] Now upset

---

155. Athên. 567e, 591d (ἐπλούτει δὲ σφόδρα ἡ Φρύνη). See Timoklês, *Neaira* Fr. 25 (K-A). Cf. Amphis, *Kouris* Fr. 23 (K-A).

156. On Phrynê, see Athên. 590d–592f; Plut. *Mor.* 849e; Alkiphr. 4.5.2. Cf. Eur. *Hipp.* 522; Pliny, *N. H.* 35.10.6. For modern reconstructions of her life, see Raubitschek 1941; Cooper 1995.

157. Athên. 590b–c; Plut. *Mor.* 400f–401b, 753f. Gold: Plut. *Mor.* 401a. Gilded: Paus. 9.27. On this statue, see Keesling 2002: 66–71; Jacquemin 1999: 166–67 and 238; Arafat 2000: 196–97.

158. A late mosaic from the so-called "House of Menander" at Mytilênê on Lesbos depicts Khrysis richly adorned in a multi-colored tunic and gown. See Charitonidis et al. 1970: 38–41 and color plate 4; Webster 1995: I.93 (XZ 31) and II.469 (6DM 2.2); Berczelly 1988.

159. Lines 80 ff.: (MO) Ὁ πατὴρ χαλεπανεῖ <σοι>. (XP) πεπαύσεται πάλιν | ἐρᾷ γάρ ... | ... τοῦτο δ' εἰς διαλλαγὰς | ἄγει τάχιστα καὶ τὸν ὀργιλώτατον. | ... ἔγωγε πάντ' ἂν ὑπομεῖναι δοκῶ ....

with her, Dêmeas threatens to deprive her of his financial support. Then, he claims, she will experience the life of an ordinary *hetaira*: working in town, attending parties, having to accept mere 10 *drachma* fees (perhaps US$500–$1,000 calculated on purchasing power equivalence).[160] Not so bad by modern Western standards, or even by Athenian. Dêmeas, however, adds a foreboding warning, devastating to a free Athenian (albeit a threat that for us reflects an ordinary, unremarkable aspect of earning a living): Khrysis would have to follow directions. "If she didn't do as instructed happily and quickly, she'd die of starvation."[161] But not to worry. It's only comedy—not real life—and the play has a happy, and (by Athenian standards) true-to-life ending: Khrysis remains Dêmeas's *hetaira*—presumably now more independent than ever before.[162]

In real life, wealthy patrons were expected to provide gifts of expensive jewelry, clothing, and servants to Greek *hetairai*.[163] In addition to costly presents, however, the fourth-century Athenian *hetaira* Neaira, as sketched in Demosthenes 59,[164] expects from her lover Phryniôn not only assistance in obtaining her freedom, but also love, obedience to her desires, and respect for her *persona*. When Phryniôn instead treats her with *hybris*, she leaves him—taking her valuable personal possessions (and whatever else Phryniôn had in his house) and her two personal servants.[165] She later agrees to live with Stephanos only after he appeals to her grandiose expectations, agrees to protect her,

---

160. Lines 390, 392–94: ἐν τῇ πόλει | . . . αἱ κατά σε, Χρυσί, πραττόμεναι δραχμὰς δέκα | μόνας ἕτεραι τρέχουσιν ἐπὶ τὰ δεῖπνα καὶ | πίνουσ' ἄκρατον . . . On "purchasing power parity," see Conventions, p. x.

161. Lines 394–95 ff: ἀποθάνωσιν, ἢ | πεινῶσιν, ἂν μὴ τοῦθ' ἑτοίμως καὶ ταχὺ πολῶσιν.

162. Because Khrysis remains a courtesan, modern scholars tend to be unhappy with the play's ending: see Jacques 1989: xli–xliii.

163. See, for example, Dem. 48.55; Louk. 80.5.4, 80.6.2; Alkiphr. 4.17.5. Cf. Piccirili 1978: 320–24. For *hetairai* as symbols of luxury, see McClure 2003b: 68 and 212, n. 23.

164. Here again, the actual truth of Apollodôros's claims cannot today be refuted or confirmed—Neaira may well have not been a *hetaira* at all—but the presuppositions underlying his claims offer insight into popular perceptions of the potential values and experiences of actual *hetairai*.

165. Dem. 59.32–35: προσθεὶς τὸ ἐπίλοιπον αὐτός, κατατίθησιν αὐτῆς τὰς εἴκοσι μνᾶς τῷ Εὐκράτει καὶ τῷ Τιμανορίδᾳ ἐπ' ἐλευθερίᾳ . . . ἐπειδὴ τοίνυν ἀσελγῶς προὐπηλακίζετο ὑπὸ τοῦ Φρυνίωνος καὶ οὐχ ὡς ᾤετο ἠγαπᾶτο, οὐδ' ὑπηρέτει αὐτῇ ἃ ἐβούλετο, συσκευασαμένη αὐτοῦ τὰ ἐκ τῆς οἰκίας καὶ ὅσα ἦν αὐτῇ ὑπ' ἐκείνου περὶ τὸ σῶμα κατεσκευασμένα ἱμάτια καὶ χρυσία, καὶ θεραπαίνας δύο . . . ἀποδιδράσκει. Cf. §37: διηγησαμένη πάντα τὰ πεπραγμένα καὶ τὴν ὕβριν τοῦ Φρυνίωνος.

promises to marry her, and commits to treating her children as his own.¹⁶⁶

Athênaios preserves a multitude of tales attesting to the proud independence—sometimes deprecated as *hybris*—of Athenian *hetairai*. In fact, the much-coveted Laïs, defying popular expectations of courtesans' arrogant treatment of clients, gained notoriety for treating lovers without disdain, reportedly showing similar respect to both rich and poor customers.¹⁶⁷ Her charges, however, were almost perversely willful: the wealthy philosopher Aristippos supposedly incurred huge expense; the impecunious Cynic, Diogenês, supposedly enjoyed her services without charge.¹⁶⁸ Similarly, Gnathainion, granddaughter of the famous whore Gnathaina, refused to engage in "equestrian" sex with her lover Andronikos despite repeated requests, but supposedly indulged a handsome coppersmith from whom she had initially not wanted any compensation.¹⁶⁹ In her servanted, well-provisioned home, Herôdas's Mêtrikhê receives Gyllis, a procuress (*mastropos*). Mêtrikhê provides the hospitality of finely measured gourmet wine, but rejects categorically Gyllis's proposal of a new lover whose wealth would be bestowed on Mêtrikhê in amount beyond expectation.¹⁷⁰ Gyllis stresses the reciprocity of the proposed relationship: Mêtrikhê will obtain sexual pleasure as well as monetary compensation. But the courtesan chooses to remain faithful to Mandris "at whom no one laughs" (lines 76–77).

Similar indicia of independence are found frequently in the *Courtesans' Dialogues* (*Hetairikoi Dialogoi*) of Loukianos.¹⁷¹ These *hetairai* retain for

---

166. Dem. 59.38: ἐπάρας δὲ αὐτὴν οὗτος τῷ λόγῳ καὶ φυσήσας, ὡς κλαύσοιτο ὁ Φρυνίων εἰ ἅψοιτο αὐτῆς, αὐτὸς δὲ γυναῖκα αὐτὴν ἕξων, τούς τε παῖδας τοὺς ὄντας αὐτῇ τότε εἰσάξων εἰς τοὺς φράτερας ὡς αὑτοῦ ὄντας καὶ πολίτας ποιήσων, ἀδικήσει δὲ οὐδεὶς ἀνθρώπων, ἀφικνεῖται αὐτὴν ἔχων δεῦρο . . .

167. Athên. 588e4–6: ἡ Λαῒς . . . πολὺν ἐραστῶν ἔσχηκεν ὅμιλον, οὐ διακρίνουσα πλούσιον ἢ πένητα οὐδ' ὑβριστικῶς αὐτοῖς χρωμένη.

168. Athên. 588e8–10: Ἀρίστιππος δὲ κατ' ἔτος δύο μῆνας συνδιημέρευεν αὐτῇ . . . καὶ ὀνειδιζόμενος ὑπὸ Ἰκέτου ὅτι "σὺ μὲν αὐτῇ τοσοῦτον ἀργύριον δίδως, ἡ δὲ προῖκα Διογένει τῷ κυνὶ συγκυλιέται" . . . .

169. Athên. 581c2–e6: ἐν ταῖς Ἀθήναις χαλκοτύπος σφόδρ' εὐφυής . . . οὐχ ὑπομένουσαν τὴν Γναθαίνιον λαβεῖν μίσθωμα . . . κατεσχόλαζε τῆς Γναθαινίου λέγων, ἑτέρῳ τρόπῳ μὲν συγγεγενῆσθαι μηδενί ἑξῆς καθιππάσθαι δ'ὑπ' αὐτῆς πεντάκις. Μετὰ ταῦτ' ἀκούσας Ἀνδρόνικος τὸ γεγονὸς . . . ὀργιζόμενος πικρῶς τε λοιδορούμενος . . . ταῦτ' ἔλεγε τῇ Γναθαινίῳ, αὐτὸν μὲν ἀξιοῦντα μὴ τετευχέναι τούτου παρ'αὐτῆς μηδέποτε τοῦ σχήματος.

170. Mime 1 ("amount beyond expectation": καί σοι δοθήσεταί τι μέζον ἢ δοκεῖς, lines 64–65).

171. For the methodological considerations affecting my use of material from Loukianos, see introduction, pp. 18–19.

themselves the option of accepting, or rejecting, individual customers, and they exercise control (sometimes ostentatiously) over their professional and personal surroundings. Often disdaining narrow considerations of economic gain (*kerdos*), on occasion they instead valorize humanistic concerns. In practice, their own access to valuable compensation is sometimes offset by excessively generous largess to their lovers. Within (because of?) this congeries of values, Athenian *hetairai* assert the freedom to suffer the jealousies,[172] plot the vengeances,[173] and experience the triumphs and denigrations of erotic affection and sexual passion.[174]

To these courtesans (as portrayed fictionally by Loukianos) the proffer of monetary incentives is often unpersuasive if acceptance is conditioned on acquiescence in male affronts to their *persona*: the element of self-definition central to the Hellenic conceptualization of free labor tends to preclude sacrifice of personal image through nonreciprocal cash transactions. Thus Philinna—despite her financial dependence on Diphilos—refuses to let fear of poverty compel her to sleep with him after he violates their understanding regarding mutual sexual exclusivity,[175] reducing Diphilos to tears of mortification, and leading her mother to remind her of the proverb "Don't kill the golden goose!"[176] Tryphaina insists that she would not have accepted an assignation had she known that its overarching purpose was to make another woman jealous.[177] Hymnis, espousing Athenian concepts of humanism,[178] objects to the soldier Leontikhos's

---

172. See 80.1.1: τὸ πρᾶγμα οὐ μετρίως μου ἥψατο . . . εἰωθὸς γίγνεσθαι ὑφ' ἡμῶν τῶν ἑταιρῶν. Prostitutes' jealousy (ζηλοτυπία) is also an animating theme of Satires 2, 11, and 14. For men, jealousy was seen as a fundamental element of purchased *eros*: was a lover not painfully possessive really a lover? (Ὅστις μήτε ζηλοτυπεῖ μήτε ὀργίζεται . . . ἔτι ἐραστής ἐκεῖνός ἐστιν; 80.8.1).

173. See, in particular, 80.4, devoted to the pursuit of magical potions with which to take vengeance on a rival prostitute who has purloined a customer/lover. Cf. Faraone 1999: 9 and passim; Herzig 1940: 12–19; Kofler 1949: 86–98.

174. In 80.11, for example, Tryphaina, although well-paid (§1: πέντε δραχμὰς τὸ μίσθωμα) is affronted by her client Kharmidês's yearning for Philêmation (§3).

175. See 80.3.3 (mother's admonition): πτωχαί ἐσμεν,οὐδὲ μέμνησαι ὅσα παρ'αὐτοῦ ἐλάβοιμεν ἢ οἷον δὴ τὸν πέρυσι χειμῶνα διηγάγομεν ἄν, εἰ μὴ τοῦτον ἡμῖν ἡ Ἀφροδίτη ἔπεμψε . . .— (Philinna's reply): ἀνέχωμαι διὰ τοῦτο [τὸ μίσθωμα] ὑβριζομένη ὑπ'αὐτοῦ;

176. 80.3.3: ὅρα μὴ κατὰ τὴν παροιμίαν ἀπορρήξωμεν πάνυ τείνουσαι τὸ καλῴδιον. Literally: "Stretching the string, let's not break it!" Diphilos's tears: Ἀλλ'οὐδὲ τῆς νυκτός, οἶμαι, συνεκάθευδες, καταλιποῦσα δὲ δακρύοντα (80.3.1).

177. 80.11.3: οὐκ ἂν ἧκον, εἴ μοι προεῖπέ τις ὡς ἐπὶ τούτοις παραλαμβανοίμην, λυπῆσαι ἄλλην.

178. Athenian concepts of *philanthrôpia* ("kindliness," "benevolence") encompassed concern for vulnerable or helpless persons: see Fisher 1995.

boasting of his mutilation of the vanquished: a bloody butcher will not share her bed even at double the usual rate.[179] Rejecting lucrative relationships with wealthy would-be clients, Mousarion insists on giving gifts to her lover (who is unable, or unwilling, to pay her anything).[180]

Yet narrow, and sound, commercial calculations did govern the actions of some of Loukianos's *hetairai*. Pannykhis, for example, is determined to accommodate a former lover newly returned with wealth from war booty—but also seek to retain her present patron who has already paid much but has promised much more.[181] When Kharmidês is unable readily to pay Philêmation's suggested fee, she "shuts him out" and receives Moskhiôn in his place.[182] Although customers generally seem to have accepted the *hetaira*'s right to bestow services as she wished,[183] a few clients did respond with indignation or even with violence, sometimes to their own grave harm. Krokalê, for example, refused even to see Deinomakhos after his failure to pay her the daunting sum of two talents, the suggested cost of an exclusive relationship.[184] Deinomakhos in anger then breaks down Krokalê's outer door, and proceeds through her house to inflict life-threatening injuries on the wealthy farmer Gorgos, a new client, with whom she had been drinking and dancing. The happy ending (from a prostitutional rights' perspective): Krokalê escapes unharmed to

---

179. 80.13.4: ΥΜΝΙΣ· Ἄπαγε, ὦ Λεόντιχε, μιαρὰ ταῦτα καὶ φοβερὰ περὶ σαυτοῦ διηγῇ, καὶ οὐκ ἄν ἔτι σε οὐδὲ προσβλέψειέ τις οὕτω χαίροντα τῷ λύθρῳ, οὐχ ὅπως συμπίοι ἢ συγκοιμηθείη. Ἐγὼ γοῦν ἄπειμι. ΛΕΟΝΤΙΧΟΣ· διπλάσιον ἀπόλαβε τὸ μίσθωμα. ΥΜΝΙΣ· οὐκ ἂν ὑπομείναιμι ἀνδροφόνῳ συγκαθεύδειν.

180. 80.7.1–3: τοῦ νεανίσκου ... ὃς ὀβολὸν οὐδέποτέ σοι δέδωκεν, οὐκ ἐσθῆτα, οὐχ ὑποδήματα, οὐ μύρον .... τὸν δακτύλιον δέδωκας ... καὶ πάλιν τὰ δύο περιδέραια ... ὀθόνας γὰρ καὶ χιτωνίσκους τί ἂν λέγοιμι; .... ὁ Ἀχαρνεὺς ἧκε δύο μνᾶς κομίζων ... σὺ δὲ ἐκεῖνον μὲν ἀπεσκοράκισας, καθεύδεις δὲ μετὰ τοῦ Ἀδώνιδος Χαιρέου. ... Τί καὶ Ἀντιφῶντα μνᾶν ὑπισχούμενον οὐδὲ τοῦτον ἐδέξω;

181. 80.9.3: οὔτε γὰρ τοῦτον ἀποπέμψαι καλὸν τάλαντον ἔναγχος δεδωκότα καὶ τὰ ἄλλα ἔμπορον ὄντα καὶ πολλὰ ὑπισχνούμενον, οὔτε Πολέμωνα τοιοῦτον ἐπανήκοντα χρήσιμον μὴ παραδέχεσθαι·

182. 80.11.3: ἐπειδὴ χιλίας αἰτούσῃ οὐκ εἶχον διδόναι ῥᾳδίως ... Μοσχίωνα ἐσδεξαμένη ἀπέκλεισέ με.

183. See, for example, Louk. 80.9.5 (Ἐλευθέρα ἐστι καὶ ἀκολουθήσει, ἢν ἐθέλῃ) 80.14.1 (ἐγὼ καὶ πρὸ τῶν θυρῶν ἕστηκα δακρύων). In contrast, the public slave Pittalakos refused to accept Timarkhos's decision to end his relationship with the slave and instead to provide services to the wealthy Treasurer of the Athenian fleet, Hêgêsandros. For Pittalakos's harassment of courtesan and client, their abusive response, and Pittalakos's ultimate resort to the Athenian courts, see Aiskhin. 1: 54–64.

184. Loukianos 80.15.2: ἡ Κροκάλη δύο τάλαντα αἰτήσασα, εἰ βούλεται μόνος ἔχειν αὐτήν, ἐπεὶ μὴ ἐδίδου ὁ Δεινόμαχος, ἐκεῖνον ἀπέκλεισεν ...

a neighbor's home, but Deinomakhos winds up dealing with a posse of citizens seeking his arrest.[185] (While Krokalê's experience is presumably fictitious, the assault on Gorgos resembles the real-life experience of the male prostitute Theodotos, who likewise escaped harm when Simôn, a dismissed would-be lover whom he had come to dislike,[186] attacked Theodotos and his new patron [Lysias 3.6, 12]). In this case, however, Theodotos, pursuant to a formal contractual commitment of sex for money, had actually received 300 *drachmas* from Simôn, but preferred the foreign travel and other enticements offered by Simôn's wealthy rival.[187])

---

185. 80.15.2: τὸν Γόργον δὲ Οἰνοέα τινὰ γεωρὸν εὔπορον . . . προσιεμένη ἔπινε μετ' αὐτοῦ . . . ἡ αὔλειος ἡράσσετο, καὶ μετὰ μικρὸν . . . ἀνετέτραπτο πάντα καὶ ὁ Γόργος ἐπαίετο . . . ἡ Κροκάλη ἔφθη ὑπεκφυγοῦσα παρὰ τὴν γείτονα . . . ἀπέρχεται δὲ καὶ ὁ γεωργὸς ὀψόμενός τινας φίλους τῶν ἀστικῶν, οἳ παραδώσουσι τοῖς πρυτανεῦσι τὸν Μεγαρέα.

186. Τούτῳ μὲν οὐδὲ διελέγετο, ἀλλ' ἐμίσει πάντων ἀνθρώπων μάλιστα (Lys. 3.31).

187. See chapter 4, n. 1 and accompanying text.

## 3

## (Commercial) Sex and the City

RESTRICTIONS ON PROSTITUTES
AS POLITICAL LEADERS

LAWS HAVE BEEN ENACTED ABOUT OFFENSES THAT ARE SIGNIFICANT, BUT CONTINUING TO OCCUR, I BELIEVE, IN ATHENS. FOR OUR PREDECESSORS MADE LAWS TO DEAL WITH IMPROPER BEHAVIOR THAT PEOPLE ACTUALLY DO ENGAGE IN.—Aiskhinês 1.13 (with regard to Athenian citizen involvement in prostitution)[1]

TWO BELIEFS HAVE long dominated academic discussion of the involvement of Athenian citizens in prostitution—that (1) the provision of sex for compensation was a function relegated almost exclusively to foreigners and slaves[2] and (2) Athenian legislation proscribing male prostitutes' right to participate in certain political activities confirmed Athenian disparagement of "prostitution as an unsavory occupation," a seemingly unique denigration since "we do not find such restrictions for practitioners of other trades" (Wrenhaven 2009: 382). This chapter seeks to show that in fact, contrary to the first assumption, Athenian citizens were far from invisible in meretricious activity, and that the limitation on male prostitutes' political rights constitutes only a portion of Athenians' complex, and sometimes contradictory, reactions to commercial sex (as has already been adumbrated in chapters 1 and 2).

---

1. Νομοθετεῖ (sc. ὁ νομοθέτης) περὶ ἀδικημάτων μεγάλων μέν, γιγνομένων δ'οἶμαι ἐν τῇ πόλει· ἐκ γὰρ τοῦ πράττεσθαί τιν' ὧν οὐ προσῆκεν, ἐκ τούτου τοὺς νόμους ἔθενθ' οἱ παλαιοί.

2. See, for example, Dover [1978] 1989: 34; Kennedy 2014: 2 ("metic women have been almost exclusively discussed as sexual labor"), 124.

## *"Improper Behavior that People Actually Do Engage In"*

Despite traditional concepts of manliness (*andreia*) that deemed agricultural pursuits the only economic activity appropriate for male citizens,[3] many male inhabitants of Attika practiced trades and crafts entirely unrelated to farming, including prostitution.[4] Surviving ceramic representations illustrate the chasm between aristocratic Athenian nostalgia for a world based exclusively on husbandry and the actuality of a society dependent on a specialized division of labor to produce the assets needed to import food and to pay for a multitude of services. On pottery Athenians are almost never presented as engaged in farming; business activity, however, including prostitution, is frequently portrayed on surviving pots and fragments (Lewis 2002: 8). Literary sources provide context and specificity. Although Athenian prostitution is often seen as "the special preserve of foreigners,"[5] citizens functioning as courtesans are the focus of the only surviving materials dealing in detail with male prostitution (Aiskhinês 1 and Lysias 3),[6] and citizens, male and female (*politai, politides*), are explicitly characterized as prostitutes in many other contexts. For example, a prominent member of the Council (*Boulê*) under the rule of the Thirty, Epikharês, is charged by Andokidês with having been a promiscuously inexpensive male whore, compliantly and shamefully "taking small sums from any one inclined."[7] Aiskhinês claims that "one of the citizens" prominently involved in public affairs made idiomatic the phrase "whoring under contract" by working as a male prostitute under written covenants deposited with a third party.[8] Scholars since antiquity have suggested that

---

3. For the impact of masculine conventions on economic activity, see chapter 6, pp. 131–35.

4. On the diversity and specialization of labor functions, see chapter 2, p. 42.

5. See introduction, pp. 10–11.

6. For a detailed discussion of these two cases, see E. Cohen 2000: 167–77.

7. σὺ .. ὅς ἑνὶ μὲν οὐχ ἡταίρησας (καλῶς γὰρ ἄν σοι εἶχε), πραττόμενος δ' οὐ πολὺ ἀργύριον τὸν βουλόμενον ἀνθρώπων, ὡς οὗτοι ἴσασιν, ἐπὶ τοῖς αἰσχίστοις ἔργοις ἔζης (Andok. 1.100). There is no reason to identify this Epikharês with his even more important homonym, who was one of the Ten, successors to the Thirty.

8. πόθεν οὖν ἴσχυκε καὶ σύνηθες γεγένηται λέγειν, ὡς κατὰ γραμματεῖον ἤδη τινὲς ἡταίρησαν, ἐρῶ. ἀνὴρ εἷς τῶν πολιτῶν ... λέγεται κατὰ συνθήκας ἡταιρηκέναι τὰς παρ' Ἀντικλεῖ κειμένας· οὐκ ὢν <δ'> ἰδιώτης, ἀλλὰ πρὸς τὰ κοινὰ προσιὼν καὶ λοιδορίαις περιπίπτων, εἰς συνήθειαν ἐποίησε τοῦ λόγου τούτου τὴν πόλιν καταστῆναι, καὶ διὰ τοῦτο ἐρωτῶσί τινες, εἰ κατὰ γραμματεῖον

this anonymous citizen-prostitute was the political leader Androtiôn,[9] who in an unrelated action is explicitly characterized as a prostitute by Diodôros.[10] Aiskhinês also identifies the influential political leader Hêgêsandros as a "whore" (*pornos*) and as Laodamas's paid "woman."[11] In turn, Demosthenes makes allegations of prostitution against Aiskhinês's brother Aphobêtos and his brother-in-law Nikias.[12] In Lysias 3, Theodotos is the citizen-prostitute balancing lucrative compensation from two citizen-patrons.[13] In Demosthenes 22, the parents of two *politai* are alleged to have been prostitutes:[14] since the children were Athenian citizens, the two prostitutes were necessarily holders of Athenian citizenship (*politeia*) under the Periklean law that restricted *politeia* to the offspring of two citizen parents.[15] In a letter attributed to Aiskhinês, prostitution is attributed to the mother of Melanopos (who had served as a senior city official *[thesmothête]*) and to Melanopos himself.[16] In Aiskhinês 1 a variegated clientele is allegedly serviced by a young prostitute who is a *politês*. At adolescence, Timarkhos had gone down to the Piraeus and sold himself to a motley crowd of customers—"traders, other foreigners, *politai*."[17] A variety of

---

ἡ πρᾶξις γεγένηται. Aiskh. 1.165: Purportedly to avoid animosity, Aiskhinês declines to mention the name of this prominent political figure.

9. Oxyrhynchus Papyri no. 1012 C II 14. More recent discussions of this identification: Jacoby, FGH 324 Introd. n. 64; Harding 1994: 23.

10. Dem. 22.29: Ἀνδροτίων, καὶ σὺ μὴ διὰ ταῦτ' οἴου σοι προσήκειν μὴ δοῦναι δίκην εἰ γφράφεις ἡταιρηκώς. . . .

11. See Aiskhin. passim and esp. 1.70, 111 (Hêgêsandros son of Hêgêsias: Osborne and Byrne 1994: 200–201; Fisher 2001: 188–89).

12. Dem. 19.287: καὶ περὶ πορνείας ἔλεγεν . . . δυοῖν μὲν κηδεσταῖν παρεστηκότοιν . . . Νικίου τε τοῦ βδελυροῦ, ὃς ἑαυτὸν ἐμίσθωσεν εἰς Αἴγυπτον Χαβρίᾳ . . . καὶ τί ταῦτα; ἀλλὰ τὸν ἀδελφὸν ὁρῶν Ἀφόβητον.

13. Lysias explicitly identifies Theodotos as a Plataian (§5), and hence an Athenian *politês* under the decree providing *politeia* to the Plataians (preserved at Dem. 59.104). For efforts to negate the "plain meaning" of the text, see E. Cohen 2000: 169–71.

14. §61: τοῦ δὲ τὸν πατέρ' ἡταιρηκέναι, τοῦ δὲ τὴν μητέρα πεπορνεῦσθαι.

15. See Aristot. *Ath. Pol.* 36.1, 40.2; Lys. 16.3, 30.15; Dem. 59.105. For variant formulations of the requirement, see Mossé [1962] 1979: 141–44. For the application of the "Citizenship Law" in actual practice, see Patterson 1990; E. Cohen 2000: 49–78.

16. σοὶ δὲ τὸ μέχρι μὲν χθὲς καὶ πρώην θεσμοθετοῦντος ἤδη σοῦ προεστάναι τὴν μητέρα .. σὲ δὲ πραθέντα τρισκιλίων δραχμῶν τὴν ἀκμὴν ἡταιρηκέναι . (7.3).

17. § 40: ἐκάθητο ἐν Πειραιεῖ ἐπὶ τοῦ Εὐθυδίκου ἰατρείου, . . . πωλεῖν αὐτὸν προῃρημένος. . . . Ὅσοι μὲν οὖν τῶν ἐμπόρων ἢ τῶν ἄλλων ξένων ἢ τῶν πολιτῶν τῶν ἡμετέρων κατ' ἐκείνους τοὺς χρόνους ἐχρήσαντο τῷ σώματι Τιμάρχου, ἑκὼν καὶ τούτους ὑπερβήσομαι.

alleged clients is specified—Misgolas (apparently a *politês*),[18] Antiklês (who is an "Athenian settler" [*"klêrouch"*] on Samos),[19] the "wild men" Kêdônidês, Autokleidês, and Thersandros (who are connected by an ancient scholion to the Triballoi, a Thracian tribe). Ultimately, the rich slave Pittalakos maintains Timarchos in the slave's own home—along with the slave's treasured fowl and other valued personal possessions—for a prolonged period of sexual exploitation. After Pittalakos refuses a request to cede Timarkhos's services to Hêgêsandros, the wealthy treasurer of the Athenian fleet who has returned to Athens with considerable funds, Hêgêsandros propositions Timarkhos directly and successfully.[20] Disgusted at "having spent huge sums of money in vain" on Timarkhos, the slave ultimately brings a legal action against his Athenian rival.[21] The "status" of the parties involved in these two cases—prostitutes who are *politai*, servicing customers of varied juridical position—directly contradicts the prevailing hierarchical model of sexual labor as an arena in which male citizens are supposedly the purchasers, and other inhabitants of Attika, the providers of sexual services.[22]

Athenian literature also records a number of examples of Athenian citizen-women working as prostitutes.[23] Paralleling the conflict between elite ideology and the reality of actual male vocational pursuits, citizen-women functioning as sex-workers clearly did not embody

---

18. Misgolas is identified in Aiskhinês's text (§41) as Μισγόλας Ναυκράτους Κολλυτεύς, but in the purported text of his deposition (§50) as Μισγόλας Νικίου Πειραιεύς.

19. §53: Ἀντικλῆς Καλλίου Εὐωνυμεύς. οὗτος ἄπεστιν ἐν Σάμῳ μετὰ τῶν κληρούχων.

20. Aiskh. 1.56–57: [Ἡγήσανδρος] ἧκε δεῦρο . . . ἔχων οὐκ ἐλάττους ἢ ὀγδοήκοντα μνᾶς ἀργυρίου . . . καὶ εἰσφοιτῶν ὡς τὸν Πιττάλακον συγκυβετὴν ὄντα, καὶ τοῦτον ἐκεῖ πρῶτον ἰδών, ἥσθη τε καὶ ἐπεθύμησε καὶ ἐβουλήθη ὡς αὐτὸν ἀναλαβεῖν . . . πρῶτον μὲν οὖν τῷ Πιτταλάκῳ διελέχθη δεόμενος παραδοῦναι τοῦτον· ὡς δ᾽ οὐκ ἔπειθεν, αὐτῷ τούτῳ προσβάλλει, καὶ οὐ πολὺν ἀνήλωσε χρόνον, ἀλλ᾽ εὐθὺς ἐπεπείκει. . . .

21. Aiskh. 1.54–64. Aiskhinês emphasizes the monetary resources of both the slave (εὐπορῶν ἀργυρίου [§54], μάτην τοσοῦτον ἀργύριον ἀνηλωκώς [§58]) and the Athenian politician (ἔχων οὐκ ἐλάττους ἢ ὀγδοήκοντα μνᾶς ἀργυρίου [§56] ὧν δ᾽ ἐν τοιαύτῃ ἀφθονίᾳ [§57]).

22. Contemporary scholarship, following Dover ([1978] 1989: 60–68, 81–109) and Foucault (e.g., 1984: 47–62, 98–99), generally views the Greek conceptualization of sexuality as focused not on gender or genital differentiations, but on politicized opposition between activity (inherently masculine) and passivity (demeaned as inherently feminizing). But criticism of this theory as inconsistent with factual evidence is rising: see especially Davidson 2004a, 2007; Hubbard 2014: 142–46; Thornton 1997: 193–202.

23. By 1918, Hirzel had already gathered a portion of the evidence ([1918] 1962: 71, n. 1).

traditional concepts of Athenian femininity.²⁴ Yet the prostitute Naïs is explicitly reported to have had a *kyrios*, a household representative who controlled, at least formally, the affairs of a woman of the citizen class,²⁵ while another Athenian prostitute, identified as a "citizeness" (*astê*), is parodied by Antiphanês as having neither guardian nor kinsmen (and so presumably lacking a dowry).²⁶ In Demosthenes 59, Neaira is accused of having for decades improperly passed as an Athenian *politis* ("citizeness") while functioning as a whore—an improbable (and therefore unpersuasive) accusatory coupling if prostitution were truly incompatible with "citizenship."²⁷ Isaios alludes to the recurring phenomenon of Athenian men, influenced by passionate desire, entering into marriages with prostitutes: because Athenian law prohibited marriage between a male citizen (*astos*) and a foreign woman (*xenê*), these courtesans were necessarily Athenian citizens.²⁸ In Isaios 3, for example, the consort of a *politês* is accused of having been a prostitute, but "her citizen status is never brought into question in the speech" (Roy 1997:16). A well-known prostitute was reportedly the mother of the Athenian general Timotheos (whose father was the preeminent military leader, Konôn),²⁹ and a citizen

---

24. See Glazebrook 2006b, esp. 138, n. 27.

25. Lys. Fr. 82 [Th.]:"Ἔστιν οὖν γυνὴ ἑταίρα, Ναῒς ὄνομα, ἧς Ἀρχίας κύριός ἐστιν. On *kyrieia*, see chapter 4, pp. 107–108; chapter 6, pp. 136–38.

26. Fr. 210 (K.A.) (= Athên. 572a): ἐν γειτόνων αὐτῷ κατοικούσης τινὸς | ἰδὼν ἑταίρας εἰς ἔρωτ' ἀφίκετο, | ἀστῆς, ἐρήμου δ' ἐπιτρόπου καὶ συγγενῶν. . . . On *astai*, see E. Cohen 2000: 50–63.

27. Whether Neaira herself actually was a former prostitute is beyond our knowledge, but the speaker's presupposition (that such a woman could pass for decades as an "Athenian") is significant—see introduction, pp. 10–11, 22–24.

28. Isai. 3.17–18. For the law forbidding Athenian men to marry foreign women, see Dem. 59.16. But many seemingly "foreign" women would actually have been Athenians, since Athenian citizens born abroad constituted a considerable portion of the total Athenian population. During much of the fourth century a quarter or more of *politai* actually lived abroad—as *klêrouchs* in Athenian-sponsored settlements, as aliens resident in other *poleis*, or as military mercenaries. Hansen 1985b: 14. Cf. Sinclair 1988: 224; Beloch 1923: 402–403. Cargill (1995: 77–83 and Appendix B) positively identifies no less than 626 individual Athenians as certain or likely fourth-century settlers in Athenian colonies—a figure that includes very limited representation from the Khersonêsos (which has been little excavated) and other continental areas.

29. Athên. 577b: Τιμόθεος δ' ὁ στρατηγήσας Ἀθηναίων ἐπιφανῶς ἑταίρας ἦν υἱὸς Θράττης τὸ γένος. Foreign birth is ascribed to the mothers of other preeminent Athenian political leaders and generals, including Kleoboulê, mother of Demosthenes. Because these leaders were necessarily Athenian citizens, their mothers must have been accepted as Athenian citizens: see E. Cohen 2000: 77, n. 184.

*hetaira* was allegedly the consort of the wealthy Athenian Olympiôdoros.[30] The prostitute Theodotê (identified in antiquity as an Athenian [*Attikê*]) is queried concerning the real estate that she owns—in a community where only citizens could own landed property.[31]

Because of the partisan nature of Athenian private forensic presentations (see introduction, pp. 14–15) and the Athenian political orators' penchant for slandering opponents,[32] it would be unwise to assume the truthfulness of any of these individual charges of prostitution.[33] Accordingly, some scholars simply dismiss these charges of prostitution as mere vituperative slander endemic in Athenian agonistic presentations.[34] Such conclusions, in my opinion, are overly simplistic: advancing clearly incredible accusations would not have aided a speaker's effort at persuasion and Athenian jurors would have been far more capable than ourselves to evaluate the plausibility of inflammatory charges against their own political leaders.

But what did it actually mean to term a political leader a prostitute? It did not necessarily signify that the man was a "prostitute" in the sense of earning his primary income from selling his body for sexual purposes or of practicing this *tekhnê* as his fundamental occupation. Choice of terminology in English is at best a rough approximation to the Hellenic original: in reality the Athenians had no "courtesans" or "prostitutes" or "sex-workers."[35] McClure has shown that for Athenian males "prostitution is often represented as an activity, but not a state of being" (1983b: 17). A man might appropriately be termed a *hetairos* or a *pornos* not because his métier was personal erotic commerce, but merely because he had at some point accepted something of value in the context of a sexual relationship.

---

30. Dem. 48.53–54. For her status as an Athenian, see McClure 2003:16. See also chapter 4, pp. 112–13.

31. Xen. *Apom*. 3.11.4: ἔστι σοι ἀγρός; . . οἰκία προσόδους ἔχουσα; Characterization as Athenian (Θεοδότην τὴν Ἀττικὴν ἑταίραν): Athên. 535c; see Cox 1998: 175, n. 37. Cf. discussion of Theodotê in chapter 2: pp. 60–62.

32. See Worman 2008: 213–74; Wrenhaven 2012: 158, n. 101.

33. Regarding "*hetaeras* . . . the orators fabricated characteristics or circumstances to serve their rhetorical ends" (McClure 2003b: 41). See also Cooper 1995: 303, nn. 2–3, and Gagarin 2001.

34. Garner, for example, alludes to the "outrageous" accusations "regularly" advanced by speakers in court (1987: 81–82).

35. For fuller exegesis of this point, see "Conventions: *Terminology*" and the discussion in this chapter (pp. 82–83) on the frequent incommensurability in distinct societies of categories used to describe similar-seeming behavior.

Gift-giving—pervasive in the male pederastic culture of Athens—left many male citizens vulnerable to charges of "prostitution."[36]

Furthermore, the enactment of laws targeting the practice of prostitution by male citizens suggests that the phenomenon was significant enough to have engendered a legislative response. Aiskhinês insists that, in proscribing political leadership by those who had prostituted themselves, Athenian legislation was following a historical pattern of dealing with improper behavior that people actually did engage in.[37] Athenian litigants, in fact, frequently insist on a connection between the adoption of particular laws (or the absence thereof) and the prevalence (or absence) of the behavior in question. For example, in the late fourth century, Lykourgos claims that Athenian law made no provision for the punishment of persons abandoning the city in time of war only because such offenses had not occurred in earlier times.[38] Lysias similarly asserts that the Athenians did adopt legislation in response to crimes that actually were taking place but not against offenses whose actual occurrence was implausible.[39] Modern legal scholars have long noted the correlation between the adoption of proscriptive legislation and the prevalence (or perceived prevalence) of the objectionable behavior:[40] recent prohibitions of cyber-bullying and of corporate tax-motivated international "inversions" offer dynamic examples of legal responsiveness to practices not previously occurring—or at least not previously having come to the legislator's attention. In the United Kingdom, Queen Victoria assented to the Criminal

---

36. Lanni 2010: 54; Hubbard 1998: 64; Fisher 2001: 49–50; Hindley 1991: 173 n. 29.

37. Aiskhinês's assertion: text set forth in this chapter (note 1).

38. *Leôk.* 9: παρεῖσθαι δὲ τὴν ὑπὲρ τῶν τοιούτων τιμωρίαν συμβέβηκεν, οὐ διὰ ῥᾳθυμίαν τῶν τότε νομοθετούντων, ἀλλὰ διὰ τὸ μὴ ἐν τοῖς πρότερον χρόνοις γεγενῆσθαι τοιοῦτον μηδέν, μηδ' ἐν τοῖς μέλλουσιν ἐπίδοξον εἶναι γενήσεσθαι. On Lykourgos's argumentation here, see most recently Ober 2008: 183–190; Mossé 2007: 181–88.

39. 31.27: ἀκούω δ' αὐτὸν λέγειν ὡς, εἴ τι ἦν ἀδίκημα τὸ μὴ παραγενέσθαι ἐν ἐκείνῳ τῷ καιρῷ, νόμος ἂν ἔκειτο περὶ αὐτοῦ διαρρήδην, ὥσπερ καὶ περὶ τῶν ἄλλων ἀδικημάτων .. τίς γὰρ ἄν ποτε ῥήτωρ ἐνεθυμήθη ἢ νομοθέτης ἤλπισεν ἁμαρτήσεσθαί τινα τῶν πολιτῶν τοσαύτην ἁμαρτίαν;

40. See, for example, Windlesham 1996: vii, 40, discussing the UK adoption of the Criminal Justice Act 1993 and the US adoption of Public Law 103–322. See also Heinz 1982; Fisher and Sloan, eds., 2013, discussing multiple laws passed in response to perceptions of an "epidemic" of peer-on-peer sexual assaults in American institutions of higher education. McGinn warns against the "attempt to read social practice" from the adoption of legislation even as he cites the U.S. Congress' adoption of the Mann Act in response to perceived widespread trafficking in women (2014: 90).

Law Amendment Act of 1885, which outlawed oral sex between men—but made no mention of similar female behavior. Victoria famously—but undoubtedly apocryphally—insisted that the law need not deal with oral relations among females because women "did not do such things." Had the queen—or popular opinion—believed that "women did do such things," a legislative response might have been forthcoming.

Just as British nineteenth-century legislation suggests the complexity of British perceptions of sexual issues, Athenian reactions to citizens' prostitution in antiquity illustrate the "multiplicity of narratives" circulating in fourth-century Athens, the "ambivalence, ambiguity, and conflict" of a complex culture (introduction, pp. 6–7). A strand of Athenian opinion did laud the self-controlled young men (*sôphrones*) who, in their homoerotic sexual relationships with their lovers (*erastes*), discreetly avoided the direct cash compensation (*misthos*) that would have manifested overt economic dependence. Such behavior and approbation were akin to the indicia of freedom from subservience manifested by female courtesans seeking to comply with Athenian work ethics by differentiating themselves from coerced slaves working in brothels where sex was purchased directly and explicitly for cash (see chapter 2). The dominant centrality in elite Athenian society of *kharis*—the undertaking and dispensing of reciprocal obligations and favors[41]—underlies both the revulsion generated by a male citizen's receipt of "pay" (*misthos*) in return for sexual submission to an *erastês* and the social acceptability of discreet gift-giving by a pursuing *erastês* to his *eromenos*, who is then able appropriately and reciprocally to repay the obligation and impose an equivalent and egalitarian debt on his *erastês*. Yet other considerations—reifying disparate strands of values even in a city where prostitution was tolerated and in some contexts even honored (see chapter 1)—likewise tended to negate the acceptability of citizens exchanging sex for even muted material advantage.

For female citizens (*politides*), prostitution was inherently inconsistent with Athenian women's monopoly on procreating citizen offspring: certainty of paternity was important constitutionally because male citizens, who monopolized political power and the economic and other benefits derived from that predominance,[42] were required to have been born from

---

41. See this chapter, pp. 86–88.

42. Adult males born from citizen stock supposedly held all power, relegating to abject oppression women, children and slaves—and (with rare exceptions) even free men who had

parents both of whom were of the citizen group.⁴³ In fact, the speaker in Demosthenes 59 insists that prostitution by impoverished *politides* (female citizens) was effectively discouraged by the citizenship requirements of double endogamy: if the prohibition against marriage with foreigners (encouraging men to marry even poor *politides* of only middling appearance) should go unenforced, *politides* lacking relatives wealthy enough to provide appropriate dowries will become prostitutes.⁴⁴

Male citizens' prostitution was discouraged by two laws that restricted male prostitutes' participation in the Athenian *polis*. According to Aiskhinês (speaking in the mid-fourth century⁴⁵), any male citizen who had acted as a *hetairos*⁴⁶ was precluded from serving as one of the nine *arkhons* (high city officials), from holding any priesthood, from advocating cooperatively (literally, being a *syndikos*) for the public,⁴⁷ from holding any governmental office whatsoever (either domestically or outside Attika, whether an elective office or one chosen by lot), from serving as herald or ambassador, from judging those serving as ambassadors or from taking pay to act as a "sycophant" (that is, bringing a maliciously extortive action), or from offering any opinion whatsoever in the Council (*Boulê*) or in the Assembly (*Ekklêsia*).⁴⁸ Should any male citizen transgress these prohibitions, a

---

not been born into the narrow circle of privilege (Finley 1981: 26). The dominant male citizen alone, by right of fortunate birth, was a "fully paid-up member of the club, (and) that club was virtually closed to [other] free, adult, male Greeks" (Cartledge 1993: 4). For the view that Athenian civilization was far more complex and multifaceted than this prevailing oversimplification, see E. Cohen 2000.

43. See note 15, this chapter.

44. Dem. 59.112–13: ὥστε καὶ ὑπὲρ τῶν πολιτίδων σκοπεῖτε, τοῦ μὴ ἀνεκδότους γενέσθαι τὰς τῶν πενήτων θυγατέρας. νῦν μὲν γάρ, κἂν ἀπορηθῇ τις, ἱκανὴν προῖκ' αὐτῇ ὁ νόμος συμβάλλεται, ἂν καὶ ὁπωστιοῦν μετρίαν ἡ φύσις ὄψιν ἀποδῷ· προπηλακισθέντος δὲ τοῦ νόμου . . . καὶ ἀκύρου γενομένου, παντελῶς ἤδη ἡ μὲν τῶν πορνῶν ἐργασία ἥξει εἰς τὰς τῶν πολιτῶν θυγατέρας. . . .

45. Attic year 346/5 (see Fisher 2001: 6–8). Provisions limiting prostitutes' participation in political life may have been enacted before 424 (cf. Aristoph. *Hipp*. 876–79), but certainly not in the sixth century, as Lane Fox has argued (1994: 150).

46. The word *hetairos* ("male companion") can mean "male prostitute" but appears relatively rarely in Greek in a sexual context (see, however, Sêmon. 7.49; Aristoph. *Ekklês*. 912; Athên. 571c); men's receipt of compensation for sex is often communicated through *hetairein*, the verbal cognate of *hetairos*. McClure suggests that in contrast to the situation of (female) *hetairai*, selling oneself sexually was perceived as a transient activity for free men (2003b: 17).

47. On *syndikoi*, see Rubinstein 2000: 43–52.

48. ἐάν τις Ἀθηναίων ἑταιρήσῃ, μὴ ἐξέστω αὐτῷ τῶν ἐννέα ἀρχόντων γενέσθαι . . . μηδ' ἱερωσύνην ἱερώσασθαι . . . μηδὲ συνδικῆσαι τῷ δημοσίῳ, μηδὲ ἀρξάτω ἀρχὴν μηδεμίαν

*graphê hetairêseos* (Prosecution for "Companionship") provided for the "harshest penalties" (*megista epitimia*).[49] Separately, Aiskhinês describes a process—*dokimasia rhêtorôn* ("Examination of Speakers")—through which the right to speak in the *Ekklêsia* might be denied to anyone who had acted as a *hetairos* or as a *pornos*.[50] However, in contrast to the *graphê hetairêseos*, which (in Aiskhinês's formulation) carries a multitude of civil disqualifications but only against someone who has acted as a *hetairos*, the *dokimasia rhêtorôn* (in Aiskhinês's formulation) carries no civil disqualifications other than the elimination of the right to speak before the *Ekklêsia*, but is applicable to anyone who has acted either as a *hetairos* or as a *pornos*.

Much academic attention has in recent years been focused on elucidating the consequences, procedures, and interaction of the *dokimasia rhêtorôn* and the *graphê hetairêseos*,[51] resulting in a consensus that posits the two procedures as essentially complementary but of limited application: they both offered alternative procedural routes to limiting a male prostitute's participation in public life, but neither directly nor indirectly outlawed prostitution.[52] Here, too, countervailing historical outcomes and divergent social values have contributed to a complex and inconsistent reality. Although the legislation explicitly purports to apply to any citizen who has acted as a *pornos* or as a *hetairos*, no definition of these terms is offered in the law,[53] and in actual practice considerations of independence/dependence, akin to those differentiating the female *hetaira* from the *pornê* (see chapter 2), influenced the delineation of objectionable male erotic behavior.

---

μηδέποτε, μήτ' ἔνδημον μήτε ὑπερόριον, μήτε κληρωτὴν μήτε χειροτονητήν· μηδὲ κηρυκευσάτω μηδὲ πρεσβευσάτω (μηδὲ τοὺς πρεσβεύσαντας κρινέτω, μηδὲ συκοφαντείτω μισθωθείς) μηδὲ γνώμην εἰπάτω μηδέποτε μήτε ἐν τῇ βουλῇ μήτε ἐν τῷ δήμῳ. . . . Aiskh. 1.19–20.

49. Aiskh. 1.20: ἐὰν δέ τις παρὰ ταῦτα πράττῃ, γραφὰς ἑταιρήσεως πεποίηκε καὶ τὰ μέγιστα ἐπιτίμια ἐπέθηκεν. "Harshest penalties" implies the possibility of execution if a jury accepts a prosecutor's urging of this punishment in a particular case (Lanni 2010: 55).

50. Δοκιμασία ῥητόρων· ἐάν τις λέγῃ ἐν τῷ δήμῳ . . . ἢ πεπορνευμένος ἢ ἡταιρηκώς . . . τούτους ἀπαγορεύει μὴ δημηγορεῖν. ἐὰν δέ τις παρὰ ταῦτα . . . λέγῃ . . . δοκιμασίαν ἐπαγγειλάτω Ἀθηναίων ὁ βουλόμενος, οἷς ἔξεστιν. Aiskh. 1.28–32. Aiskhinês explains ἢ πεπορνευμένος ἢ ἡταιρηκώς as referring to τὸν τὸ σῶμα τὸ ἑαυτοῦ ἐφ' ὕβρει πεπρακότα (Aiskh. 1.29). The fullest exegesis of *dokimasia* at Athens—in all its varied forms—is Feyel 2009.

51. See Todd 2006, 2010; MacDowell 2000, 2005; Gagliardi 2005, 2006, 2010; Lanni 2010; Wallace 2006.

52. See chapter 5, pp. 115–18.

53. Nowak 2010: 183.

From an economic perspective, the legislation was of slight impact, for it had no effect on the vast majority of potential or actual male prostitutes—registered foreigners resident in Athens (*metics*), aliens visiting or unregistered, slaves, citizens who actually earned their living as prostitutes rather than as political leaders and who easily could ensconce themselves among the mass of citizens refraining from political activity (the so-called *apragmones*).[54] Indeed, thousands of Athenian men, literally the majority of citizens, chose not even to attend Assembly meetings[55]— a right of attendance retained by male prostitutes. In any event, few Athenians ever reached the level of public activity targeted by the statute— that of *rhêtôr*, synonymous at Athens with "political leader."[56] And even for *rhêtores*, this potential limitation on political activity seems prima facie to have had little actual effect.[57] Political leaders at Athens were routinely accused of prostitution in the course of political debate, and routinely continued their public careers.[58] The best known invocation of this legislation involves, of course, Timarkhos, a prominent Athenian who had previously participated in Athenian politics notoriously and successfully for decades after his alleged acts of prostitution.[59] (Only after Timarkhos's prosecution of Aiskhinês for his behavior on a controversial embassy to Philip of Macedon was Aiskhinês energized to demand a *dokimasia rhêtorôn* in a preemptive effort to derail Timarkhos's prosecution of himself.)

Still, for the democracy's chieftains, the legislation was not without impact. Although on its terms it targeted only those political leaders who, in the context of a sexual relationship, had—by receipt of inappropriate items of value—violated the ethical imperatives of the homoerotic male love culture of Athenian elites, the difficulty of differentiating appropriate from inappropriate gifts potentially imperiled many of the city's leaders.

---

54. Lanni 2010: 45; D. Cohen 1991b: 222–23; Halperin 1990: 98–99. On the *apragmones*, see Carter 1986: esp. 52–75.

55. Archaeological evidence reveals that the fourth-century Pnyx, even after renovation and slight enlargement from the fifth-century gathering site, could barely contain the 6,000 *politai* needed for a quorum. See Thompson 1982: 138–39. For the possibility that the fourth-century expansion was never completed, see Camp 2001: 153–54. Cf. Forsén and Stanton, eds., 1996: passim.

56. On the significance of *rhêtores* at Athens, see my discussion on pp. 88–89.

57. E. Cohen 2000: 158; McGinn 2014: 90.

58. See this chapter, pp. 70–72.

59. See Fisher 2001: 21; Dover [1978] 1989: 19.

The prosecution of Timarkhos (the subject of Aiskhinês 1) was not a unique event:[60] actual prosecutions potentially targeting political activity by "prostitutes" are relatively well-attested.[61] Already in the fifth century Aristophanês, in the *Knights*, makes allusion to successful actions depriving sexual malefactors (*kinoumenoi*) of citizenship rights, including specifically the capacity to act as *rhêtores*.[62] Fourth-century sources include several explicit references to prosecutions for speaking, or attempting to speak, after engaging in acts of "prostitution." Thus when Androtiôn, a prominent political leader, complains in court that Diodôros has abusively accused him of having been a prostitute but has never brought a *graphê hetairêseos* against him, Diodôros assures Androtiôn that his cavil is unjustified: we will proceed to initiate such a prosecution for prostitution before the tribunal of the Thesmothetes.[63] Aristophôn of Azênia is reported to have gained victory in his personal "war" against Hêgêsandros by threatening to charge him with prostitution under the procedure of *dokimasia rhêtorôn* as employed by Aiskhinês against Timarkhos.[64] In the early fourth century, Andokidês treats the legislation against political leadership by male citizen prostitutes as viably operational, arguing that one of his accusers, Epikharês, far from being in a position to make charges against others, does not—because of his own repeated acts of prostitution—have the right even to address a court in his own defense. Andokidês even claims

---

60. In addition to the cases set forth in the text arising from charges of prostitution, a number of prosecutions are attested relating to other offenses that would have disqualified a would-be speaker, e.g., avoidance of military service (ἀστρατεία, λιποτάξιον: see Hyper. *Athen.*; Lykourg. *Leôkr.*, discussed on pp. 89–90).

61. The number of surviving examples is significant in the context of the extremely small amount of information now extant from the vast universe of individual Athenian legal cases litigated over scores of years. Nonetheless, the absence of statistical material and the chance nature of testimonial survival mean that "it is impossible to say how frequently these laws were formally enforced" (Lanni 2010: 57).

62. Lines 876–80: ΠΑ· ὅστις | ἔπαυσα τοὺς κινουμένους, τὸν Γρῦπον ἐξαλείψας. | ΑΛ· οὔκουν σε δῆτα ταῦτα δεινόν ἐστι πρωκτορηρεῖν | παῦσαί τε τοὺς κινουμένους; κοὐκ ἔσθ᾽ ὅπως ἐκείνους | οὐχὶ φθονῶν ἔπαυσας, ἵνα μὴ ῥήτορες γένοιντο.

63. Dem. 22. 21, 23: (21) Ἔτι τοίνυν ἐπιχειρεῖ λέγειν περὶ τοῦ τῆς ἑταιρήσεως νόμου, ὡς ὑβρίζομεν ἡμεῖς . . . καὶ φησὶ δεῖν ἡμᾶς, εἴπερ ἐπιστεύομεν εἶναι ταῦτ᾽ ἀληθῆ, πρὸς τοὺς θεσμοθέτας ἀπαντᾶν . . . (23) ὅταν (sc. φῇ) δ᾽ ὅτι πρὸς τοὺς θεσμοθέτας προσῆκεν ἐπαγγέλλειν ἡμῖν, ἐκεῖνο ὑπολαμβάνετε, ὅτι καὶ τοῦτο ποιήσομεν καὶ νῦν προσηκόντως περὶ τοῦ νόμου λέγομεν.

64. Aiskhin. 1.64: ὁ Ἡγήσανδρος, ὅτε καὶ προσεπολέμει Ἀριστοφῶντι τῷ Ἀζηνιεῖ πρὶν αὐτῷ τὴν αὐτὴν ταύτην ἐν τῷ δήμῳ ἠπείλησεν ἐπαγγελίαν ἐπαγγελεῖν ἥνπερ ἐγὼ Τιμάρχῳ. . . . Cf. MacDowell 2005: 83–84.

that Epikharês, himself a whore, has had the audacity to bring charges against others for having been prostitutes![65]

In its totality, this legislation offers insight into Athenian prostitution's inherent, inevitable interaction with both money and sex. On the one hand, the statutes provided "expressive" condemnation of male citizens who had exhibited excessive greed—those who had placed or were perceived as likely to place their personal financial advantage over that of the city's institutions (*oikos* [household], army, the *polis* itself): individuals choosing to sell themselves for money in personal dealings might similarly accept money to betray the city's public interests.[66] Yet the legislation simultaneously sought to protect an important aspect of Athenian sexual culture, vividly illustrating the Athenian *imaginaire*, the *polis*'s self-image, "how it sees itself in fantasy, with a large element of idealization and wish fulfillment,"[67] here illuminating the conflict between elite values and the practical realities affecting courtship gifts (deemed ethically unobjectionable) and cash received as payment for sex (deemed ethically unacceptable): ancient Greeks—at times with anguish, at times with amusement—struggled to differentiate the two emoluments, an opacity illuminating Plato's characterization of Athenian sexual conventions as complex, intricate, and many-hued (*Symposium* 182a7–9).

## *In Conflict: Purchased Sex and Elite Homoerotic Culture*

Some males did work as prostitutes providing sex "ensconced in a house" to a succession of individual male purchasers on an ongoing basis,[68] and

---

65. 1.100–101: σὺ (sc. Ἐπίχαρες) περὶ ἑταιρείας ἐμοὶ μνείαν ποιῇ καὶ κακῶς τινας λέγεις; ὃς ἑνὶ μὲν οὐχ ἡταίρησας (καλῶς γὰρ ἄν σοι εἶχε) πραττόμενος δ' οὐ πολὺ ἀργύριον τὸν βουλόμενον ἀνθρώπων... ἐπὶ τοῖς αἰσχίστοις ἔργοις ἔζης, ... (101) Ἀλλ' ὅμως οὗτος ἑταίρων τολμᾷ κατηγορεῖν, ᾧ κατὰ τοὺς νόμους τοὺς ὑμετέρους οὐδ' αὐτῷ ὑπὲρ αὑτοῦ ἔστιν ἀπολογεῖσθαι. In §101 I see no need for Reiske's emendation ἑτέρων.

66. Aiskhin. 1.29: τὸν γὰρ τὸ σῶμα τὸ ἑαυτοῦ ἐφ' ὕβρει πεπρακότα καὶ τὰ κοινὰ τῆς πόλεως ῥᾳδίως ἡγήσατο ἀποδώσεσθαι. Lanni explains the expressive function of law in her brilliant article on "the expressive effect of the Athenian Prostitution Laws" (2010). Cf. Lape 2006: 139–40.

67. Loraux [1984] 1993: 3 (Translator's Note). See introduction, n. 8.

68. See Pl. *Khrm*. 163b5–8 (ἐπ' οἰκήματος καθημένῳ); Xen. *Apom*. 1.6.13 (τήν τε γὰρ ὥραν ἐὰν μέν τις ἀργυρίου πωλῇ τῷ βουλομένῳ, πόρνον αὐτὸν ἀποκαλοῦσιν); Aristoph. *Plout*. 149–59; I.G. 12.3.536. Cf. Aiskh. 1.70.4, 123.2, 130.3. For male sexual service in such *oikêmata*, see introduction, pp. 4–5. There is even a comic reference to a woman's purchase of male sexual

some men did earn their livelihood by providing sex only to a single patron on a long-term basis.[69] But the persons targeted by Athenian legislation against *hetairoi* (and *pornoi*) were quite different: they were not sex-workers per se, but rather those leaders of the state who could be alleged to have violated a male-elite social code that prohibited, in the context of male homosexual courtship, the blatant acceptance of items of value in overly explicit exchange for sexual favors. Athenian legislation, however, does not explicitly target violators of social codes, but rather only those who had "prostituted themselves"—rendered in the *dokimasia rhêtorôn* ("Examination of Speakers") as those who had acted as *hetairoi* or *pornoi* (a verbal formulation).[70] But these are terms that the Athenians themselves did not use clearly or consistently (chapter 1, pp. 31–38). This Greek confusion, however, merely mirrors a tendency throughout human societies to use the single term "prostitution" to cover essentially incommensurate behavior.

Thus today "prostitution", in many societies, inexactly covers a multitude of inconsistent meanings denoting a variety of physical, commercial, and social arrangements. Although scholars have long sought to differentiate commercial sex from other erotic arrangements, emphasizing factors like payment, promiscuity, and emotional attachment (or indifference), the defining line—if any—between prostitution and other forms of sexual exchange remains unclear.[71] Even traditional marriage—in both ancient Greece and in modern societies—has sometimes been characterized as "legal prostitution,"[72] suggesting that within a single society, conflict over

---

services: Eupolis has an Athenian boast of having "laid" two males and a female for "small change" (Fr. 247 [K-A]: ἐν τῆιδε τοίνυν τῆι πόλει φρουρῶν <ἐγώ> ποτ' αὐτὸς | γυναῖκ' ἐκίνουν κολλύβου καὶ παῖδα καὶ γέροντα.)

69. Lysias 3 focuses on such arrangements.

70. But as with the conflation of *hetaira* and *pornê* (chapter 1, pp. 34–35), the verbs *porneuein* and *hetairein* tend to be interchangeable in actual usage (see, for example, Aiskh. 1.29; Dem. 19.233.8). The *graphê hetairêseos* (Prosecution for "Companionship") targeted only someone who has acted as a *hetairos* (this chapter, pp. 77–78).

71. See, for example, Kennedy 2014: 113; McGinn 2004: 7–9, 1998: 17–18: Palmer and Humphrey 1990: 150; Bloch 1912: 7. Cf. Jaggar 1985; Shrage 1994: 99–119.

72. See, for example, Wollstonecraft [1790] 1995: 5–64; Hamilton [1909] 1981: 37; Goldman 1969: 179; Beauvoir 1974: 619. Hesiod assumes marriage to involve—to the male's potential detriment—an exchange of women's sexual services for economic benefits (*Works and Days* 373–75: cf. chapter 1, n. 68. The wife of Olympiôdoros is assailed as a whore (*hetaira, pornê*) merely because of her husband's extravagant gifts to her—extraordinary possessions, extensive gold jewelry, fine clothing, and brilliant outdoor processions, "arrogant extravagances" paid for with funds that might otherwise have been available to adorn the male litigant's own wife and family members (Dem. 48.55).

the meaning of prostitution often may be "merely a surface manifestation of a disagreement over the fundamental categories to be used in describing social activities" (Jagger 1985: 349). Cross-cultural studies have likewise been of limited value, for "prostitution" in one society may describe an activity somewhat or even utterly different from the phenomenon evoked by an equivalent term in another culture (Gilfoyle 1999). Thus studies of "prostitution" in ancient Babylon, colonial Kenya, medieval Occitania, and modern Nepal suggest that "these comparable behavioral forms reflect incommensurable beliefs and values."[73] Ultimately, and in frustration, it is sometimes asserted that in any specific society, "the meaning of 'prostitution' is self-evident" to the persons living in that community (Pateman 1988: 195).

But Aiskhinês finds far from self-evident the difference between male prostitution (which can potentially eliminate a citizen's political rights) and courtship gifts from male lovers to their *eromenoi*[74] (which was not only permitted but also desirable in the homoerotic society applauded by both sides of the only preserved prosecution of an alleged male prostitute active as a *rhêtor*).[75] In lengthy and labored argumentation (1.132–52), Aiskhinês seeks to distinguish between "chaste" male sexual submission to a lover—"admirable" (*kalon*)—and the "contemptible" (*aiskhron*) self-prostitution motivated by compensation for service (*misthos*).[76] In contrast to the wanton sexual excesses of a youth hired for money (financial patronage that is characteristic of monstrously uncivilized men), romantic passion for upstanding and moral youths is the experience (*pathos*) of the "generous" (*philanthropos*) and

---

73. Shrage 1994: 100. See White 1990: 10–21 (colonial Kenya); Karras 1996: 10 (medieval England); Stumpp 1998: 18–24 (ancient Rome), esp. the comparison between Latin *amica* and Greek *hetaira*. Cf. Flemming 1999: 38–39.

74. Plural form of "eromenos," the term used in ancient Greek for the person being courted, for whom the *erastês* ("lover") "has a passionate desire" (Dover 1978 [1989]: 16).

75. Aiskhinês's opponents (1.132) characterized his attack on Timarkhos's behavior as an assault on pederastic culture itself, "the beginning of an appalling ignorant barbarity" (δεινῆς ἀπαιδευσίας ἀρχήν), but Aiskhinês himself insisted on the value of a "righteous" homoerotic love (ἐγὼ δὲ οὔτε ἔρωτα δίκαιον ψέγω) (1.136).

76. Aiskhin. 1.137.5–7: καὶ τὸ μὲν ἀδιαφθόρως ἐρᾶσθαί φημι καλὸν εἶναι, τὸ δ᾽ ἐπαρθέντα μισθῷ πεπορνεῦσθαι αἰσχρόν. "Misthos" is the term applied to cash received in exchange for labor: τοὺς καταισχύνοντας αὑτοὺς μισθοὺς φησι πράττεσθαι τοῦ πράγματος (Aiskhin. 1.94). Receipt of a salary (*misthophoria*) was the hallmark of a slave: when the Athenian state required coin-testers and mint-workers for continuing service, legislation explicitly provided for the payment of *misthophoriai* to the skilled public slaves (*dêmosioi*) who provided these services (SEG 26.72, lines 49–55; Figueira 1998: 536–47).

charitable male soul.⁷⁷ Although the generosity conveyed by the adjective *philanthropos* carries a connotation of benevolence and humaneness, *philanthropos* in common usage often implies material benefit.⁷⁸ Accordingly, the gift-giving prominent in "chaste" male homosexuality was not devoid of tangible gain.⁷⁹ The female "companions" (*hetairai*) prominently present at male parties are paralleled by the young men who (in the phrase of Ephippos) paid with sex for the delicacies they enjoyed at male dinner parties.⁸⁰ Expensive and sometimes even exotic animals—quail, coot, goose, cockerel, even horses and dogs—are conventionally tendered as offerings in the male courtship context.⁸¹ Representations on ceramic material produced in Athens—although not transparently direct illustrations of actual life (see introduction, pp. 20–24)—frequently portray men proffering to youths a broad variety of valuable gifts, including musical instruments, gym apparatus, toys, floral arrangements, and alimentary offerings.⁸² *Eromenoi*, "represented as if they were citizen youths,"⁸³ are even portrayed on Athenian vases as receiving sacks of money: no apparent iconographic differentiation can be discerned between such deliveries of cash and other less explicitly mercenary gifts to youths who have been identified by modern scholars as recipients of presents from lovers.⁸⁴ This phenomenon is explained

---

77. Aiskhin. 1.137.1–5: ὁρίζομαι δ'εἶναι τὸ μὲν ἐρᾶν τῶν καλῶν καὶ σωφρόνων φιλανθρώπου πάθος καὶ εὐγνώμονος ψυχῆς, τὸ δὲ ἀσελγαίνειν ἀργυρίου τινὰ μισθούμενον ὑβριστοῦ καὶ ἀπαιδεύτου ἀνδρὸς ἔργον εἶναι ἡγοῦμαι·

78. The term is frequently used in the context of endowment or gratuity: see, for example, BGU I 202.10; *Mon. Anc. Gr.* 9.10. Cf. UPZ 162.vii.21; OGI 139.20.

79. Although the modalities of gift-giving in male courtship are alluded to in only a few literary passages (all in comedy: Aristoph. *Orn.* 705–7; *Hipp.* 904–9, 1104–99, *Plout.* 153–57), courtship comprises more than half of the pederastic scenes surviving on ceramic representations: Lear and Cantarella 2008: 237, n. 38.

80. ὅταν γὰρ ὢν νέος | ἀλλότριον εἰσελθὼν ὄψον ἐσθίειν μάθηι | ἀσύμβολόν τε χεῖρα προσβάληι βορᾶι, | διδόναι νόμιζ' αὐτὸν σὺ τῆς νυκτὸς λόγον (Fr. 20 [K-A]). Cf. Alexis Fr. 244 (K-A).

81. Dover 1978 [1989]: 92–93. Cf. Aristoph. *Ornith.* 707, *Plout.* 157.

82. Lear 2014: 108; Lear and Cantarella 2008: 39.

83. Von Reden 1995: 198–99. The youths, as pictured, are usually of athletic build, crowned, wearing himations and often carrying spears. Cf. Bazan 1985: 41.

84. See the representations on these vases: Copenhagen Nat. 3634, Bochum Univ. S 507, New York 52.11.4. Cf. Lear and Cantarella 2008: 78–86; Hubbard 2009:11; von Reden 1995: 195–211; Meyer 1988. Even Ferrari, who asks "are there moneybags in these pictures?" recognizes that "current scholarship" uniformly believes that "the identification of the bag with a money pouch is a fact rather than a hypothesis" (2002: 14, 251, n. 21).

perhaps by the assertion of the characters Khremylos and Kariôn in Aristophanês's *Wealth* that there's no real difference between the *pornoi* who deliver sex "for money, and not for love," and the "noble" (*khrêstoi*) *eromenoi* who "being ashamed to demand cash" ask instead for a good steed or a pack of hounds.[85]

To win his case, however, Aiskhinês must, and does, differentiate "males being pursued through modest courtship" from "males working as brothel whores" (*peporneumenous*, the category into which he places Timarkhos, the rival political leader whom he is accusing of having been a prostitute).[86] This Manichean distinction, however, in no way illuminates the line between "generous" benefits that enhance the recipient, and "uncivilized" benefits that prostitute the recipient—the central issue raised by the prosecution of Timarkhos (Aiskhinês 1.137). But like other aspects of Athenian behavior, gift-giving in an erotic context tends to be evaluated on whether it is appropriate to a free person, or suggestive of a servile relationship, a differentiation based on the Athenian concept of *kharis*—a value often seen to lie at the heart of Attic culture.[87] Athenians generally felt an obligation to help their friends and expected in return gratitude (and an entitlement to future reciprocity).[88] Exchange based on money—in sexual contexts, "prostitution"—stood in stark and fundamental opposition to exchange based on reciprocal *kharis*.[89] But just as in the modern world, where commercial services, for monetary payment, increasingly supply personalized labor (caring for children, the elderly, the disabled and the handicapped, and so forth) that was formerly provided at no monetary charge by relatives and friends motivated by personal feeling for and a sense of obligation toward the recipient, so also at Athens in the

---

85. ΚΑ: καὶ τούς γε παῖδάς φασι ταὐτὸ τοῦτο δρᾶν, | οὐ τῶν ἐραστῶν, ἀλλὰ τἀργυρίου χάριν. | ΧΡ. οὐ τούς γε χρηστούς, ἀλλὰ τοὺς πόρνους· ἐπεὶ | αἰτοῦσιν οὐκ ἀργύριον οἱ χρηστοί. ΚΑ. τί δαί; | ΧΡ. ὁ μὲν ἵππον ἀγαθόν, ὁ δὲ κύνας θηρευτικούς. | ΚΑ αἰσχυνόμενοι γὰρ ἀργύριον αἰτεῖν ἴσως | ὀνόματι περιπέττουσι τὴν μοχθηρίαν (ll. 153–59).

86. Aiskh. 1.159: . . . χωρὶς μὲν τοὺς διὰ σωφροσύνης ἐρωμένους, χωρὶς δὲ τοὺς εἰς ἑαυτοὺς ἐξαμαρτάνοντας, ὑμεῖς ἤδη τοῦτ' ἐρωτηθέντες ἀποκρίνασθε πρός ἐμέ, εἰς ὁποτέραν τὴν <τάξιν> Τίμαρχον κατανέμετε, πότερα εἰς τοὺς ἐρωμένους ἢ εἰς τοὺς πεπορνευμένους.

87. *Kharis* defined: Davidson 2007: 523, n. 1; Millett 1991: 58. For the importance of reciprocal relationships at Athens, see Missiou 1998; Herman 1998; Millett 1998.

88. Millett 1991: 24–52 and various essays in Gill et al., eds. 1998.

89. See von Reden 1997: 154; Kurke 1994: 42; Seaford 1994: 199. Cf. Seaford 1998; von Reden 1998; Steiner 1994; Kurke 1989.

fourth century the new "monetised and money-using economy of fourth-century Athens,"[90] a process manifestly coming to supersede a prior system based primarily on familial, social, and political relations,[91] tended to convert every aspect of life—including the sexual—into monetary transactions.[92] And in both the modern world (see introduction, pp. 7–10) and in fourth-century Athens this transformation has generated intense dissonance between persons attached to the older order and those following the new. Traditional male homoerotic society, based on *kharis* rather than purchase, resisted the transformation of sexual courtship into sexual purchase.

Even in the fourth century, as Athens was increasingly becoming an exemplar of a monetary economy, Aristotle is still emphasizing reciprocity in sexual relations as a central distinction between free men and slaves. Through *kharis*, good deeds must be repaid (and bad likewise), and when the free citizen is the recipient of a benefit, he has the presumed opportunity, and the moral obligation, to repay that benefit—and to initiate a fresh contribution to his benefactor in the future. "Otherwise a free man's life would be like that of a slave."[93] Aristotle finds such an example of pure and exalted *kharis* in the *eromenos*' free offer of himself to the burning erotic need of his *erastês*—a gratuitous contribution, without direct recompense.[94] In *The Symposium* (in a discussion attributed to Pausanias) Plato explains that erotic *kharis* is present when an *erastês* is prepared to sacrifice dignity and self-importance in seeking to consummate his longing—to make servile sacrifices that no slave would bear—and when the *eromenos*

---

90. Shipton 2000: 14. Cf. Schaps 2004: 111–21; Shipton 1997; Gofas 1994; Kanellopoulos 1987: 19–22; Theokharês 1983: 100–14.

91. Recent studies have demonstrated the extraordinary impact of the introduction in the sixth and fifth centuries of coined money, a phenomenon that culminated ultimately in the detached monetary transactions of fourth-century Athens. See Schaps 2008; Shipton 2001; Picard 2008b: 147–51. Only in the fourth century were there substantial issuances at Athens of a regular bronze coinage (Camp and Kroll 2001: 144; cf. Kroll 2000: 89) and of fractional commodity money appropriate for retail trade (von Reden 2010: 30–33).

92. Aristot. *Pol.* 1258a10–14: ἀνδρείας γὰρ οὐ χρήματα ποιεῖν ἐστιν ἀλλὰ θάρσος, οὐδὲ στρατηγικῆς καὶ ἰατρικῆς, ἀλλὰ τῆς μὲν νίκην τῆς δ᾿ ὑγίειαν. οἱ δὲ πάσας ποιοῦσι χρηματιστικάς, ὡς τοῦτο τέλος ὄν, πρὸς δὲ τὸ τέλος ἅπαντα δέον ἀπαντᾶν.

93. Aristot. *NE* 1132b–1133a: ἢ γὰρ τὸ κακῶς ζητοῦσιν, εἰ δὲ μή, δουλεία δοκεῖ εἶναι εἰ μὴ ἀντιποιήσει· ἢ τὸ εὖ.

94. *Rhet.* 1385a2–3: ἔστω δὴ χάρις . . . ὑπουργία τῷ δεομένῳ μὴ ἀντί τινος, μηδ᾿ ἵνα τι αὐτῷ τῷ ὑπουργοῦντι ἀλλ᾿ ἵνα τι ἐκείνῳ· μεγάλη δὲ ἂν ᾖ σφόδρα δεόμενος . . . δεήσεις δέ εἰσιν αἱ ὀρέξεις, καὶ τούτων μάλιστα αἱ μετὰ λύπης τοῦ μὴ γιγνομένου. τοιαῦται δὲ αἱ ἐπιθυμίαι, οἷον ἔρως. . . .

in turn in his quest for wisdom and knowledge is likewise willing to be enslaved in every way (*hotioun hypourgôn*).⁹⁵ Ironically, in a society permeated by a profusion of true slavery, the highest amatory relationship of free men would, in this formulation, involve the mutual assumption of interactive servitude. But elite negativity toward cash and commerce remains a leitmotif: such obeisance if undertaken for monetary motivation would be contemptible.⁹⁶

Juridically unfree persons—true slaves who by legal definition were not in a position to receive or to repay *kharis*—accordingly did not belong in the reciprocal world of stylized male courtship conducted in the Greek *gymnasia* and *palaistrai*, venues of exercise and athletic competition, to be sure, but also centers of homoerotic flirtation and activity.⁹⁷ Accordingly, at Athens a law attributed to Solôn forbade slaves to practice gymnastics or to engage in sex with (free) youths, thus coupling (in Plutarch's opinion) exercise and eros, characterizing both as fine and honorable activities, "and in a way encouraging the worthy to those pursuits from which he excluded the unworthy."⁹⁸ The importance of *kharis* in athletically oriented homoeroticism is illustrated by Pindar's *Olympian* 10, where a young boxer is urged to provide *kharis* to Ilas (his trainer, according to ancient commentators), emulating Patroklos and Achilles, and Ganymede (and Zeus)—formulaic male couples who enjoyed reciprocal pleasure and benefit in an erotic context.⁹⁹ In contrast, amplifying Greek high culture's abhorrence of commerce, the actual regulations governing a gymnasium in Beroia

---

95. 183b3–c4, 184d4–d7: τῷ δ'ἐρῶντι πάντα ταῦτα ποιοῦντι χάρις ἔπεστι . . . καὶ τὸ ἐρᾶν καὶ τὸ φίλους γίγνεσθαι τοῖς ἐρασταῖς. (184d4) ὁ μὲν χαρισαμένοις παιδικοῖς ὑπηρετῶν ὁτιοῦν δικαίως ἂν ὑπηρετεῖν, ὁ δὲ τῷ ποιοῦντι αὐτὸν σοφόν τε καὶ ἀγαθὸν δικαίως αὖ ὁτιοῦν ἂν ὑπουργῶν <ὑπουργεῖν>. . . .

96. Pl. *Symp.* 184e5–185a5: γάρ τις ἐραστῇ ὡς πλουσίῳ πλούτου ἕνεκα χαρισάμενος ἐξαπατηθείη . . . οὐδὲν ἧττον αἰσχρόν· . . . ἕνεκα χρημάτων ὁτιοῦν ἂν ὁτῳοῦν ὑπηρετοῖ, τοῦτο δὲ οὐ καλόν. Cf. 183a2–8: εἰ γὰρ χρήματα βουλόμενος παρά του λαβεῖν . . . ἐθέλοι ποιεῖν οἷάπερ οἱ ἐρασταὶ πρὸς τὰ παιδικά, . . . ἐμποδίζοιτο ἂν μὴ πράττειν οὕτω τὴν πρᾶξιν καὶ ὑπὸ φίλων καὶ ὑπὸ ἐχθρῶν . . .

97. *Gymnasia* and *palaistrai* as loci of homoerotic activity: Pl. *Khrm.* 154a–c, *Lys.* 204e; Aiskhin. 1.135 (seducer of numerous youths characterized as ἐν τοῖς γυμνασίοις ὀχληρὸς ὤν). See Fisher 2014: 253–54; Scanlon 2002: 213; Spivey 2012: (in discussion of Boroia).

98. Plut. *Sol.* 1.3: νόμον ἔγραψε διαγορεύοντα δοῦλον μὴ ξηραλοιφεῖν μηδὲ παιδεραστεῖν, εἰς τὴν τῶν καλῶν μερίδα καὶ σεμνῶν ἐπιτηδευμάτων τιθέμενος τὸ πρᾶγμα, καὶ τρόπον τινὰ τοὺς ἀξίους προκαλούμενος ὧν τοὺς ἀναξίους ἀπήλαυνε. Cf. Aiskhin. 1.139: δοῦλον ἐλευθέρου παιδὸς μήτ' ἐρᾶν μήτ' ἐπακολουθεῖν.

99. Lines 16–21, 99–105. Cf. Fisher 2014: 254–55; Provencal 2005.

in Macedonia have survived and are explicit in denying participation in gymnastic activities (literally, the right to "undress") not only to slaves and even freedmen (and their offspring), but also to anyone who has engaged in retail trade, in physical labor for a living,[100] or in prostitution (literally "has acted as a *hetairos*")—and to the insane and the inebriated![101]

Sexual culture, expressed through moral considerations set in a philosophical paradigm, is not, however, the only justification proffered for denying political leadership to those who have prostituted themselves. Some Athenians simply did not wish to entrust public process, in any way, to those excessively self-interested in their own personal acquisition (or retention) of money.

## Protecting the City against Erotic Greed

For the Athenians, management of the right to "address the people" (*dêmêgorein*) was a critical element of governance, not a jejune limitation on a theoretical freedom of speech. This significance reflected the unique importance of "speakers" (*rhêtores*) in the Athenian political process. Unlike conventional modern political arrangements, the Athenian constitution (*politeia*) did not provide for a relatively small number of high officials elected or appointed for a substantial period of time to head a government that would function more or less autonomously of the day-to-day will of the people. Instead ongoing public affairs were administered by large numbers of short-term officers chosen by sortition. Accordingly, the true political leaders of Athens were the prominent *rhêtores* in the Assembly, a gathering of the People (*dêmos*) that met frequently and was the dominant organ of Athens' "pure democracy."[102] And in the Assembly individual speakers were often dominantly influential in the determination (and often in the

---

100. Literally, the "ἀπάλαιστρος" (a word that does not appear elsewhere in ancient Greek, but "probably refers to those [who] lack physical fitness" [Hubbard 2003: 85]). By traditional standards, those engaged in trade and business would have been judged "worst" in body and wealth: aristocratic doctrine insisted that banausic activity deformed the body (Aristot. *Pol.* 1258b37).

101. S.E.G. 27.261: μὴ ἐγδυέσθω δὲ εἰς τὸ γυμνάσιον δοῦλος μηδὲ ἀπελεύθερος μηδὲ οἱ τούτων υἱοὶ μηδὲ ἀπάλαιστρος μηδὲ ἡταιρευκὼς μηδὲ τῶν ἀγοραίαι τέχνῃ κεχρημένων μηδὲ μεθύων μηδὲ μαινόμενος (early second century BCE). See Gauthier and Hatzopoulos 1993: 70–78; Gauthier 2010: 93–96.

102. Ober 1996: 95–96, 1989: 105–112; Hansen 1991: 143–45; Davidson 1997: 252.

implementation) of public policies: Thucydides observes that in the fifth century Periklês's persuasive sway over the Assembly made Athens a democracy in name only, but in fact a society ruled by a single speaker ("the leading man").[103] In the fourth century, private *rhêtores* and the popularly elected "generals" (*stratêgoi*) were frequently equated as the preeminent officers of the state[104] and were dually recognized as the chieftains of the people.[105] In fact, the orators are sometimes explicitly spoken of as if they actually were the elected long-term high officials that Athens in fact did not have.[106] Yet these "speakers"— leading a society where bribery and embezzlement were believed to be commonplace[107]—received no salary or other public compensation. The Athenians not surprisingly were obsessively alert to the danger of destructive monetary influence on speakers' advocacy. "The man who had sold his own body outrageously would also readily vend the public interest of the state."[108]

Such sentiments may well have contributed to a protective legislative response. In discussing the *dokimasia rhêtorôn*, Aiskhinês identifies a variety of offenses—largely involving money-related behavior—that would deprive a citizen of the right to address the *Ekklêsia*: wasting ("consuming") family or inherited assets; receiving improper compensation for sex; not providing nourishment or housing for a [presumably elderly] parent; refusing military service for which a citizen has been conscripted (or acting

---

103. 2.65.9: ἐγίγνετό τε λόγῳ μὲν δημοκρατία, ἔργῳ δὲ ὑπὸ τοῦ πρώτου ἀνδρὸς ἀρχή. Thucydides's leading expounder explains: "Perikles wielded such influence, and for a long period, as has been given to few men to wield over their fellow countrymen; but his constitutional powers were small, and he could only continue to keep his position through his direct influence with the ekklesia" (Gomme 1956: 194). During his ascendancy, Periklês was frequently elected as *stratêgos*.

104. Hyper. 4.27, 5.24; Dein. 1.112, 3.19; Dem. 18.171, 23.184; Aristot. *Rhet.* 1388b17–18. Cf. Hansen 1983; Perlman 1963: 353–54.

105. Dein. 1.71: καὶ τοὺς μὲν νόμους προλέγειν τῷ ῥήτορι καὶ τῷ στρατηγῷ . . . πάσας τὰς δικαίας πίστεις παρακαταθέμνον οὕτως ἀξιοῦν προεστάναι τοῦ δήμου. Cf. Dem. 18.212.

106. See, for example, Lykourg Fr. A.2.1 (Burtt) = V.1a (Conomis): Τρεῖς δοκιμασίαι κατὰ τὸν νόμον γίγνονται· μία μὲν ἦν οἱ ἐννέα ἄρχοντες δοκιμάζονται, ἑτέρα δὲ ἣν οἱ ῥήτορες, τρίτη δὲ ἣν οἱ στρατηγοί.

107. Aiskhin. 3.173; Aristoph. *Hipp.* 438–44, 824–35, 930–33, 991–96, 1141–50, 1218–26, *Plout.* 377–79, 567–70, *Sphêk.* 669–77; Dein. 1.41, 1.77; Dem. 3.29, 19.275, 58.35; Lys. 19.57, 25.9, 25.19, 27.10–11, 28.9, 29.6, 30.25. Cf. Sinclair 1988: 179–86; Davies 1978: 319.

108. τὸν γὰρ τὸ σῶμα τὸ ἑαυτοῦ ἐφ' ὕβρει πεπρακότα καὶ τὰ κοινὰ τῆς πόλεως ἡγήσατο (sc.ὁ νομοθέτης) ἀποδώσεσθαι (Aiskhin. 1.29).

in a cowardly way—"throwing away one's shield"—in combat).[109] Even the act of avoiding military service is not without a peripheral financial dimension: those called up for duty would often suffer monetary disadvantage through their consequent inability to maintain income or to pursue business opportunities. Athênogenês, the target of a law-court presentation written by Hypereidês, is vilified by his opponent for dodging military service by leaving Athens and moving to Troizêne shortly before the war with Philip. While other residents of Attika participated in the ground campaign ending in the disaster at Chaironeia, Athênogenês prospered in exile, "with the intention of returning later to carry on his business when peace was established."[110] Similarly Leôkratês is accused of failing to report for military service when Athens was mobilizing to resist Philip after Chaironeia:[111] instead he allegedly left Athens with the *hetaira* Eirênis in order to pursue business activities—trading in grain with capital that he had brought from Athens and engaging in other substantial financial transactions.[112]

In its battle against personal financial peccadilloes that might signal a propensity toward corruption in public affairs, Athens also deemed as unfit to address the Assembly those individuals who had "consumed" ancestral assets (*patrôia*), including property over which a would-be speaker had become, by inheritance, the titular owner (*klêronomos*).[113] Preservation of

---

109. Aiskhin. 1.28–30: τούτους οὐκ ἐᾷ δημηγορεῖν ... (τις) τὸν πατέρα τύπτων ἢ τὴν μητέρα, ἢ μὴ τρέφων, ἢ μὴ παρέχων οἴκησιν ... ἢ τὰς στρατείας μὴ ἐστρατευμένος, ὅσαι ἂν αὐτῷ προσταχθῶσιν, ἢ τὴν ἀσπίδα ἀποβεβληκώς ... ἢ πεπορνευμένος ἢ ἡταιρηκώς ... ἢ τὰ πατρῷα κατεδηδοκώς, ἢ ὧν ἂν κληρονόμος γένηται.

110. Hyper. *Athên.* 29–31 (ἐν δὲ τῷ πολέμῳ τῷ πρὸς Φίλιππον μικρὸν πρὸ τῆς μάχης ἀπέ[λιπε] τὴν πόλιν· καὶ μεθ' ὑμῶν μὲν οὐ συνεστρατεύσατο εἰς Χαιρώνειαν, ἐξῴκησε δὲ εἰς Τροιζῆνα ... ἐργασόμενος ἐπεὶ εἰρήνη γέγονεν ... εἰς Τροιζῆνα ἐλθὼν καὶ ποιησαμένων αὐτὸν Τροιζηνίων πολίτην, ὑποπεσὼν Μνησίαν τὸν Ἀργεῖον καὶ ὑπ' ἐκείνου κατασταθεὶς ἄρχων. ... Text and Translation: Burtt 1954).

111. Lykourg. *Leôk.* 147: ἔνοχον ὄντα Λεωκράτην .. λιποταξίου δὲ καὶ ἀστρατείας οὐ παρασχὼν τὸ σῶμα τάξαι τοῖς στρατηγοῖς. Cf. §16–17: ἐψηφίσατο ὁ δῆμος .. τοὺς δὲ στρατηγοὺς τάττειν εἰς τὰς φυλακὰς τῶν Ἀθηναίων καὶ τῶν ἄλλων τῶν οἰκούντων Ἀθήνησι, καθ' ὅ τι ἂν αὐτοῖς δοκῇ .τὴν φυλακὴν ἔρημον τὸ καθ' αὑτὸν μέρος κατέλιπεν.

112. Lykourg. *Leôk.* 17, 26–27: μετὰ τῆς ἑταίρας Εἰρηνίδος προσέπλευσε καὶ ᾤχετο φεύγων. ... οἷς παρ' ὑμῶν ἐξεκομίσατο χρήμασιν ἀφορμῇ χρώμενος, ἐκ τῆς Ἠπείρου παρὰ Κλεοπάτρας εἰς Λευκάδα ἐσιτήγει καὶ ἐκεῖθεν εἰς Κόρινθον ... ἔπειτα τὸν προδόντα μὲν ἐν τῷ πολέμῳ, σιτηγήσαντα δὲ παρὰ τοὺς νόμους. ... Cf. §22–23 (sale of slaves and generation of cash from refinancing).

113. ἢ τὰ πατρῷα κατεδηδοκώς, ἢ ὧν ἂν κληρονόμος γένηται (Aiskhin. 1.30).

such assets was critical to preservation of the *oikos*, the "household" that at Athens was the fundamental element of society and the primary repository of wealth.[114] This obligation to preserve ancestral assets—in the language of the *dokimasia* law quoted by Aiskhinês, a duty not to "consume" *patrôia*—explains a passage that has baffled scholars, Deinarkhos's assertion in his speech "Against Demosthenes" that the laws "demand" that a rhêtor or a general (who wants to obtain the confidence of the people) own land in Attika and that he have begotten children in accordance with the laws.[115] Some scholars have dismissed these alleged progenitive and property obligations as a solipsistic statement by Deinarkhos, unsupported by other sources and therefore properly to be disregarded.[116] Others have interpreted Deinarkhos's statement as establishing—in addition to the four disqualifying criteria set forth in Aiskhinês's speech "Against Timarkhos"—two additional transgressions (lack of children and lack of property) that might be the basis for a speaker's debarment through a *dokimasia rhêtorôn*.[117] (Since we do not possess the actual text of the law, but only excerpts quoted by Aiskhinês in a tendentious presentation, there may well have been yet other grounds for denying political leadership to Athenian citizens.) But even Deinarkhos does not explicitly make any reference to the *dokimasia rhêtorôn*, and in fact qualifies the requirements of property and descendants as applicable specifically to a man "who wants to obtain the confidence of the people"—a seemingly hortatory injunction as to how to be a more effective orator or commander. In what way, then, do "the laws demand" of a *rhêtor* the holding of real estate and the production of offspring?

The answer, I suggest, lies in the fact that both legitimate offspring and real estate within Attika were critical to the preservation of an *oikos*, and that the absence of either, in the Athenian context, inherently threatened the destruction of the *oikos* and a consequent "consumption" of the ancestral property. Failure to comply with these "demands" of the law

---

114. For the centrality of the *oikos* at Athens, see chapter 6, pp. 133–34. Cf. Ferrucci 2006; E. Cohen 2000: 32–43; Cox 1998: 132–35.

115. Dein. 1.71: τοὺς μὲν νόμους προλέγειν τῷ ῥήτορι καὶ τῷ στρατηγῷ, <τῷ> παρὰ τοῦ δήμου πίστιν ἀξιοῦντι λαμβάνειν, παιδοποιεῖσθαι κατὰ τοὺς νόμους, γῆν ἐντὸς ὅρων κεκτῆσθαι. . . .

116. MacDowell 2005: 81; Worthington 1992: 235; Ober 1989: 119. Cf. Rhodes 1993: 511; Hansen 1985a: 62.

117. Gagliardi 2010: 104–106, 108. Cf. Caillemer 1892: 325.

could thus be interpreted as a violation of a man's duty to preserve ancestral property—but this failure does not necessarily establish that Athenian society unanimously saw no possible redemptory virtues in any childless or landless citizen.

## Ownership of Land

Although individuals at Athens are sometimes treated as though personally the owners of realty,[118] most wealth—especially ancestral property (*patrôia*)—belonged to the various *oikoi* ("households"), the basic unit of societal organization through which Athens functioned.[119] Real estate was of the essence of the *oikos*: in fact, by metonymy, both ancient Athenians and modern scholars have often equated the physical "house" (*oikia*) with the more extensive "household" (*oikos*), which actually encompassed the physical attributes of the group's house (or houses), the complement of members living in that property, and the wealth belonging to those members.[120] Possession of real estate was so integral to the *oikos* that wealthier households appear to have often acquired extensive land holdings, often in separate parcels within Attika.[121] At the other extreme, depriving one's *oikos* of its real estate was viewed with extreme negativity—and as a basis for deprivation of a citizen's right to address the Assembly. Thus in the *dokimasia rhêtorôn* brought against Timarkhos, Aiskhines identifies the extensive real estate transmitted to Timarkhos by his father: a house in the city adjacent to the Akropolis and worth at least 2,000 *drachmas*, a large country estate abutting on Mount Hymettos, and yet another landed property at Alôpekê (11 or 12 stades south of the city wall). All this family property, according to Aiskhinês, Timarkhos sold at fire-sale prices (Aiskhinês 1.96–98). Incarnating the relationship between the household and its real estate, Timarkhos's mother entreated her son to retain the realty, formally supplicating and imploring him to desist from its sale, asking that the property at Alôpekê at least be kept so that the family would

---

118. See, for example, Dem. 45.28, 36.8; Finley [1951] 1985: 192, no. 175A.

119. See this chapter, note 114, and accompanying text.

120. Confusion between *oikos* and *oikia*: Xen. *Oik.* 1.5; Andok. 1.147; Isai. 3.8, 78. Cf. Pomeroy 1994: 14. For the fullest discussions of the word *oikos* in its various attributes see MacDowell 1989; Karabêlias 1984.

121. Cox 1998: 136–38; Casson 1976.

have land for her interment. Timarkhos refused.[122] For Aiskhinês (and apparently for the jury that ruled against Timarkhos in the *dokimasia rhêtorôn*), Timarkhos's selling of real estate represented a "consuming of his ancestral property." Instead of buying new real estate from the proceeds of the sale of family property, he "ate up and drank up" the proceeds.[123] He thus demonstrated a proclivity to place personal financial advantage over the common good—which was the precise Athenian motivation, through the *dokimasia rhêtorôn*, for denying a citizen access to the Assembly. It is in this sense that Deinarkhos could say that the laws—as embodied in the prohibition against consuming ancestral assets—"demand" that a *rhêtor* own land in Attika: Demosthenes's offense was not that he did not own land (the laws did not "require" this), but rather that he had disposed of "ancestral real estate" and had never replaced it with other real property in Attika,[124] exactly the charge raised against Timarkhos, and clearly a blatant violation of the ban on consuming ancestral property.

## Providing Children for the Oikos

At some time in the past, but perhaps not in the fourth century, Athenian law did require generals to have "begotten children in accordance with the laws,"[125] and the so-called Decree of Themistoklês sets a similar requirement for trierarchs in the early fifth century.[126] There is no independent corroboration of such a requirement for Speakers, and even Deinarkhos's statement at 1.71, in a speech attacking Demosthenes (who at the time had no living legitimate children), can be read as a rhetorically skillful

---

122. Aiskhin. 1.99: τὸ δ' Ἀλωπεκῆσι χωρίον . . . ἱκετευούσης καὶ ἀντιβολούσης τῆς μητρός, ὡς ἐγὼ (sc. ὁ Αἰσχίνης) πυνθάνομαι, ἐᾶσαι καὶ μὴ ἀποδόσθαι, ἀλλ᾽ εἰ μή τι ἄλλο, ἐνταφῆναί < γ᾽ > ὑπολιπεῖν αὐτῇ, οὐκ ἀπέσχετο, ἀλλὰ καὶ τοῦτ᾽ ἀπέδοτο δισχιλίων δραχμῶν.

123. Aiskhin. 1.96–97: ἐτράπετο ἐπὶ τὸ καταφαγεῖν τὴν πατρῴαν οὐσίαν. καὶ οὐ μόνον κατέφαγεν, ἀλλ᾽ εἰ οἷόν τ᾽ ἐστὶν εἰπεῖν, καὶ κατέπιεν. . . . τούτῳ γὰρ κατέλιπεν ὁ πατὴρ οὐσίαν ἀφ᾽ ἧς ἕτερος μὲν κἂν ἐλῃτούργει, οὗτος δὲ οὐδ᾽ αὐτῷ διαφυλάξαι ἐδυνήθη.

124. Dein. 1.70–71: καὶ ποῦ τοῦτ᾽ ἐστὶ δίκαιον . . . μηδὲν δὲ φανερὸν ἐν τῇ πόλει κεκτῆσθαι . . . σὲ δὲ τὴν πατρῴαν γῆν πεπρακέναι. . . .

125. Aristot. *Ath. Pol.* 4.2: ᾑροῦντο . . . στρατηγοὺς δὲ καὶ ἱππάρχους οὐσίαν ἀποφαίνοντας . . . παῖδας ἐκ γαμετῆς γυναικὸς γνησίους ὑπὲρ δέκα ἔτη γεγονότας. Provision as anachronistic: Rhodes 1981: 115–16.

126. On the authenticity and historicity of this text, see most recently Johansson 2004, 2001 (with summary of earlier scholarship).

attribution to *rhêtores* (which Demosthenes was) of a requirement applicable only to generals (which Demosthenes was not). But here, too, an orator's obligation to produce children "in accordance with the laws" can be understood as inherent in the Athenian legal dictate, quoted by Aiskhinês, not to "consume" ancestral assets (1.30). For without children, an *oikos*, on the death of its male *kyrios*, would become an "empty household" (*oikos exerêmoumenos*), its assets "consumed" because, in the absence of offspring, the household's ancestral property would be dissipated to members of an alien *oikos* who had some degree of relationship to the *kyrios* of the vanished *oikos*, in some cases an extremely distant (and sometimes even false) claim to relationship).[127]

Paradigmatically, an *oikos* continued through its male descendants. A male *kyrios* of the household could not dispose of ancestral property, but was obligated to leave it ratably to his sons as continuing stewards, or, if there were no surviving sons, to other male descendants at the same level of descent, if any.[128] (Daughters were provided for through provision of dowry upon marriage.[129]) If the male steward (*kyrios*) of the household had more than a single son,[130] the *oikos* might be preserved through multiple successor households, which divided household property and perpetuated the religious rites of the original *oikos*.[131] In the absence of legitimate (*gnêsioi*) male descendants (natural or adopted[132]), the *oikos* might be preserved through female offspring: a daughter (termed an *epiklêros*) became the means of household survival, utilizing her husband as the *kyrios* of the *oikos* until the couple's adult male offspring could assume this

---

127. See, for example, the distant claimants litigating over the estate of Hagnias II, as described in Demosthenes 43. Cf. Cudjoe and Adam-Magnissali 2010.

128. Dem. 20.102, 44.49, 44.67, 46.14; Isai. 3.1, 6.9, 29.

129. Foxhall 1989: 32–36; Dimakis n. d.: 189; Petropoulos 1939: 211. Dem. 47.53, 57 provides a vivid example of a wife's continuing interest in her dowry.

130. A male functioning as the *kyrios* of an *oikos* should be differentiated from a man who was the *kyrios* of dependent women or minors. Thus an adult son might be married and continue to reside with his wife within the household of which his father was *kyrios*, but the son (and not the father) would be the *kyrios* of the son's own wife.

131. Illustratively, Bouselos's *oikos*, described in Demosthenes 43, was continued through five separate households headed by his five sons, each of whom had a wife and children (§19).

132. Athenian law permitted an *oikos* to be preserved through the *kyrios*' adoption of a son: Isai. 2.13, 3.68, 6.28; Dem. 46.14. See passim Ghiggia 1999; Rubinstein 1993.

responsibility.¹³³ To facilitate the survival of an *oikos*, Athenian law required a female child (of a house without male children) to take as husband her closest living male relative wishing to marry her (apart from those ruled out by strictures against incest). The law encouraged even relatively distant male kinsmen to seek to marry an *epiklêros* by bestowing on her husband control of the income from the household's assets (*patrôia*). Indeed, an *epiklêros* who was already married but childless was required to divorce her existing husband and marry the appropriate male relative¹³⁴—a strong (if to modern observers distasteful) expression of Athenian law's commitment to the preservation of a household's ancestral property and maintenance of its sacred obligations. But all these techniques for preserving the household depended on a male *kyrios'* having produced offspring. This necessity provides the context for a legal provision removing from leadership positions in the *polis* a man who had produced no children—not even through adoption—and had thereby imperiled the continuation of his *oikos* (an institution upon which Athenian society and state depended).

Yet commentators on Athenian sexuality have often seen this provision as having only limited impact—creating "an implicit double standard of behavior, with higher expectations being imposed on political leaders than on other citizens" (Todd 2006: 95). In fact, however, the law's explicit condemnation of specific forms of monetary greed (including male prostitution) would likely and implicitly have affected every inhabitant of Athens, individuals living in a society in which forensic contests and court actions, and the laws, procedures, and transactions underlying these activities, dominated much of everyday life.¹³⁵ A plethora of recent legal studies have explored this "expressive function" of statutory law and have demonstrated the extent to which in modern societies standards of comportment and actual general behavior are impacted by formal legal pronouncements, even when these laws are not widely enforced, or do not target society as a whole, especially in aspects of life that are in flux, and even where competing values may impel some (or many) individuals into noncompliance.¹³⁶ Athenians were aware of this power of law. Lykourgos,

---

133. On the *epiklêros*, see Cudjoe 2010: 191–202; Karabélias 2002; Adam-Magnissali 2008: 19–20; Schaps 1979: 25–42.

134. Isai. 3.64, 10.19.

135. Buis 2014: 321.

136. See Lanni 2006: 46–50; Cooter 2000.

for example, points out to jurors that a primary reason for punishing Leôkratês's unpatriotic behavior is the lesson that would thus be provided both to young Athenians—and to other Greeks who were observing the proceedings.[137]

But the expressive effect of a single law does not alone determine a society's entire response to the phenomenon targeted by that legislation. Athens may not have wanted its political advisers and leaders to include individuals who placed an inappropriate emphasis on their personal financial advantage. But the fact that prostitution remained lawful—operating through formal contractual arrangements (the subject of the next chapter)—may have had a somewhat countervailing positive expressive effect on society's overall attitude toward providers of commercial sex.

---

137. Lykourg. 1: young Athenians (§§9–10); other Greeks (§§14–15).

# 4
## "*Prostitution pursuant to Contract*"

AT ATHENS MALE prostitutes (*hetairoi*) often provided sexual services pursuant to agreements containing reciprocal covenants, frequently of some complexity, often covering extended periods, sometimes in written form. Lysias 3, for example, chronicles how Simôn brought a legal action against a wealthy rival who—through the proffering of foreign travel and other enticements—had induced Simôn's *inamorato*, Theodotos, blatantly to violate a contract (*synthêkai, symbolaion*) to provide future sex for 300 drachmas paid in advance.[1] Such written arrangements for the sale of sex were so commonplace that the phrase "whoring under contract" (*synthêkai, grammateion*)—a usage popularized by a prominent citizen who had worked as a prostitute—had become idiomatic in local discourse.[2] The absence of such a contract strongly implied the nonexistence of an arrangement for the ongoing provision of sexual services for compensation.[3] As a result, requests were routinely anticipated in court proceedings for written contracts (*syngraphai, grammateia*) confirming commercial sexual

---

1. αὐτὸς τριακοσίας δραχμὰς ἔδωκε Θεοδότῳ, συνθήκας πρὸς αὐτὸν ποιησάμενος: Lys. 3.22. For *synthêkai* as "written contract," see note 30.

2. Aiskhin. 1.165: πόθεν οὖν ἴσχυκε καὶ σύνηθες γεγένηται λέγειν, ὡς κατὰ γραμματεῖον ἤδη τινὲς ἡταίρησαν, ἐρῶ. ἀνὴρ εἷς τῶν πολιτῶν . . . λέγεται κατὰ συνθήκας ἡταιρηκέναι τὰς παρ' Ἀντικλεῖ κειμένας· οὐκ ὢν <δ'> ἰδιώτης, ἀλλὰ πρὸς τὰ κοινὰ προσιὼν καὶ λοιδορίαις περιπίπτων, εἰς συνήθειαν ἐποίησε τοῦ λόγου τούτου τὴν πόλιν καταστῆναι, καὶ διὰ τοῦτο ἐρωτῶσί τινες, εἰ κατὰ γραμματεῖον ἡ πρᾶξις γεγένηται. "Under written contract": Loeb translation of κατὰ γραμματεῖον (Adams 1919).

3. Thus Simôn's opponent is said to have falsely claimed the existence of a contract for sexual services so as to provide credibility for his claims of a paid sexual relationship with Theodotos: ἵνα μὴ δοκῇ δεινὰ ποιεῖν, εἰ μηδενὸς αὐτῷ συμβολαίου γεγενημένου τοιαῦτα ἐτόλμα ὑβρίζειν τὸ μειράκιον (Lys. 3.26).

acts.[4] Demosthenes attributes to these written prostitutional documents (*grammateia*) an evidentiary superiority to oral testimony or other possible forms of evidence[5]—a preference akin to the special probative value given in Athenian legal actions to bankers' memoranda.[6] As with written covenants for other kinds of commercial undertakings, agreements providing for sexual services sometimes were deposited for safeguarding with third parties.[7] Again, as with other commercial commitments, prostitutional obligations were undertaken with a panoply of witnesses to confirm the agreements.[8]

Women also are known to have entered into elaborate written commitments providing for sexual labor. In Plautus's *Asinaria*, a Latin adaptation (set in Athens) of a Hellenic original,[9] there is presented, in comic version but at considerable length, a contract in writing (termed *syngraphus*, the Latin rendering of the Greek *syngraphê*[10]), providing for Philaenium, daughter of Cleareta, to spend her time exclusively with the Athenian Diabolus for a period of one year at a price of 2,000 *drachmas*, a "gift"

---

4. Aiskhin. 1.160: Ἐὰν δ' ἐπιχειρῶσι λέγειν ὡς οὐχ ἡταίρηκεν ὅστις μὴ κατὰ συγγραφὰς ἐμισθώθη, καὶ γραμματεῖον καὶ μάρτυρας ἀξιῶσί με τούτων παρασχέσθαι. . . . Cf. § 165: ἐρωτῶσί τινες εἰ κατὰ γραμματεῖον ἡ πρᾶξις γεγένηται.

5. Dem. 22.22–23: Ἔτι τοίνυν ἐπιχειρεῖ λέγειν περὶ τοῦ τῆς ἑταιρήσεως νόμου, ὡς ὑβρίζομεν ἡμεῖς. . . . ἡμεῖς τοίνυν οὐκ ἐκ λόγων εἰκότων οὐδὲ τεκμηρίων, ἀλλὰ παρ' οὗ μάλιστα δίκην ἔστι λαβεῖν τούτῳ, ταῦτ' ἐπιδείκνυμεν—ἄνδρα παρεσχηκότα γραμματεῖον, ἐν ᾧ τὰ τούτῳ βεβιωμέν' ἔνεστιν, ὃς αὐτὸν ὑπεύθυνον ποιήσας μαρτυρεῖ ταῦτα. Cf. de Brauw and Miner 2004 (who argue that prostitutional contracts actually related to noncommercial pederastic sexual relations, "an idea for which there is not a shred of evidence, as they admit" [McGinn 2014: 97, n. 5]). For Demosthenes's charges of prostitution against the political leader Androtiôn, see chapter 3, nn. 9 and 10 and corresponding text.

6. Gernet [1955] 1964: 176, n. 2; Bogaert 1968: 382, n. 461; Harrison 1968–71: 2. 22, n. 7; E. Cohen 1992: 117–18.

7. Aiskhin. 1.165: λέγεται κατὰ συνθήκας ἡταιρηκέναι τὰς παρ' Ἀντικλεῖ κειμένας. For deposit of maritime loan agreements, for example, see Dem. 34.6; Dem. 56.15; for delivery to a third-party of the documentation covering the sale of a business, Hyper. *Athên*. 9.

8. Aiskhin. 1.125: ἀγοραῖα τεκμήρια. For the pervasive use of witnessing in Athenian commercial life, see, for example, Dem. 48.46; Dem. 42.5 and 11; Hyper. *Athên*. 8. See this chapter, nn. 99–103 and corresponding text.

9. Vogt-Spira 1991: 65 unpersuasively argues for Plautus's autonomy from a Greek predecessor. In fact, Plautus testifies that "huic nomen graece Onagost fabulae; Demophilus scripsit, Maccus vortit barbare" (lines 10–11). For the validity of the use of Roman comic material as evidence for Athenian legal and social practices, see introduction, pp. 17–18. Legal material is abundant in Plautus, especially in *Bacch.*, *Curc.*, *Persa*, *Pseud.*, and *Trin*.

10. *Syngraphus* may be "a representation of the Boeotian and Doric inflection of *syngraphê*" (Scafuro 2003/04: 12).

paid in advance.[11] The contract contains extended provisions of humorous paranoia—for example, Philaenium is not even to gaze upon another man and must swear only by female deities. *Asinaria* also offers a vignette (Act 1, Scene 3) in which Diabolus's rival, Argyrippus, proposes a similar contractual arrangement (again denominated *syngraphus*), under which Argyrippus would have exclusive sexual rights to Philaenium for a year (line 230): Philaenium's mother invites Argyrippus to propose any contractual terms he desires, provided that he is able and willing to pay the exorbitant price requested.[12] In *Bacchides*, another Plautine work set in Athens (an adaptation of Menander's *Dis Exapatôn*[13]), a female prostitute has entered into a contract with a soldier to provide sexual services for a year on an exclusive basis and has received a large payment in advance.[14] When she violates her commitment to have no other lover, the soldier demands the return of a portion of his money.[15] The courtesan's inability to make financial amends for her breach of the couple's agreement is the linchpin for the hilariously convoluted plot of the play.[16] (In both *Asinaria* and *Bacchides*, the contracts correspond to agreements that would have been contained

---

11. Lines 751–54: Diabolus Glauci filius Clearetae | lenae dedit dono argenti viginti minas, | Philaenium ut secum esset noctes et dies | hunc annum totum. For an analysis of Athenian prostitution "along the axis of gift- vs. commodity-exchange" (Kurke 1999b: 179), see chapter 1, pp. 32–33. Philaenium's obligations under the comic contract here are actually crafted by her mother, the courtesan (*lena*) Cleareta. On this and other aspects of the contract set forth in *Asinaria*, see James 2006: 228–32. Cf. James 2005.

12. Postremo ut voles nos esse, syngraphum facito adferas; | ut voles, ut tibi lubebit, nobis legem imponito: | modo tecum una argentum adferto (lines 238–40). The dominant role of Philaenium's mother mirrors the leading business position often assumed at Athens by mothers of *hetairai*: see the section "Women as Merchants of Sex" in chapter 6. (With Lowe 1992 and 1999, I follow the transmitted text in attributing to Argyrippus the role of the young lover in this scene.)

13. *Dis Exapatôn* and *Bacchides* are the only surviving plays where a Greek original can be compared directly with its Roman adaptation. The extant texts confirm the essential identity of plot and characterization in the two works (Rosivach 1998: 195, n. 72, contrary to Henry 1985: 99–101).

14. *Bach.* Fr. 10: nec a quóquam acciperes alio mercedem annuam / nisi ab sése, nec cum quiquam limares caput. Cf. line 43. For *mercedem annuam* as "annual contract," here and in other Plautine works, see Rosivach 1998: 171, n. 5 and 176, n. 65. In accord: Barsby 1986: 96.

15. Cf. *Bach.* 590 (ut ducentos Philippos reddat aureos); 868 (nisi ducenti Philippi redduntur mihi); 222–23 (miles . . . qui de amittenda Bacchide aurum hic exigit). Cf. 896 ff.; Fr. 19 (as interpreted by Scafuro 2003/04: 11, n. 36).

16. *Bacch.* 46: nam si haec habeat aurum quod illi renumeret, faciat lubens. The cash required to obtain Bacchis's release from her contractual commitments underlies the slave's deceptions, on which the plot is centered.

in the Athenian plays on which Plautus's works are modeled—although specific covenants were probably adapted to the Roman context and audience.[17]) Similar arrangements are adumbrated in two other Plautine works based on Greek originals and set in Athens. In *Truculentus*, an "annual contract" (*merces annua*) binds Diniarchus and Phronesium,[18] while in *Epidicus* Philippa (and her mother) markedly improve their economic situation through extended arrangements with Periphanes.[19] In Plautus's *Mercator* (derived from the *Emporos* of Menander's contemporary Philemôn), Charinus and the *meretrix* Pasicompsa have been living together for two years pursuant to an agreement of mutual exclusivity.[20] Terence presents similar arrangements. In *Hecyra*, adapted from Apollodôros Karystios's Greek comedy of the same name (and again set in Athens), a courtesan and a soldier appear to have entered into a two-year contract during which the courtesan is forced even to conform the timing and content of her conversations to her lover's dictates.[21] In *Eunuchus* (based on Menander's *Eunoukhos* and set in Athens), "the independent courtesan" Thais enters into a similar contract with her lover Thraso, and possibly with the "foreigner."[22] Contractual arrangements with courtesans are also alluded to in a Latin work of Turpilius (who seems often to have adapted plays from Menander).[23]

In Menander's own *Woman from Samos*, the wealthy Athenian Dêmeas seeks in anger to end his "live-in" relationship with the free *hetaira* Khrysis. But the property settlement that he proposes (through which Khrysis will retain not only "her own property" but additional

---

17. Scafuro 2003/04: 12, 15; Lowe 1992; Webster 1953: 237.

18. Primumdum merces annua, is primus bolust (line 31). Cf. lines 392–93. This agreement seems to have provided Diniarchus with "exclusive access" (Rosivach 1998: 122).

19. Virgini pauperculae tuaeque matri me levare paupertatem (line 556). The relationship (between Athenian citizens) originated in Epidaurus and was continued in Thebes. The couple even begat a child whom the father came to know, albeit briefly (line 600).

20. Lines 533, 536, 536a, 537: ecastor iam bienniumst quom mecum rem coëpit | . . . inter nos coniuravimus ego cum illo et ille mecum: | ego cum viro et ill' cum muliere, nisi cum illo aut ille mecum, | neuter stupri caussa caput limaret.

21. Biennium ibi perpetuom misera illum tuli . . . nam illi haud licebat nisi praefinito loqui quae illi placerent (lines 87–95).

22. See Barsby 1999: 17. For the "foreigner," cf. lines 119–20.

23. Turpilius Com. Fr. 112 Ribbeck *Leuc.* Cf. Schonbeck 1981: 150–51 and 203, n. 73; Herter 1960: 81, nn. 193 and 194.

servants and other valuables) is suggestive of a prior understanding that in real life would likely have been incorporated in a written agreement.[24] Similarly, Loukianos's Philinna refuses to have sex with her lover after he violates their agreement ("contratto": Sirugo 1995: 158, n. 15) on mutual intimate exclusivity.[25] From a court speech we know directly of the complex financial arrangements claimed to have been made by a *hetaira* in Korinth with the Athenian Phryniôn—and with Timanoridas the Korinthian, Eukratês of Leukas, and other of her "lovers" (Demosthenes 59.29–32). The same woman later, acting on her own behalf in a private arbitration proceeding at Athens,[26] allegedly reached agreement with two Athenian patrons requiring mutual consent for any alteration in the terms governing allocations of property and obligations of maintenance undertaken in exchange for her provision of sexual services to both men.[27]

These agreements clearly were of social significance. In the context of Athenian work ethics (see chapter 2), the moral standing of a prostitute depended upon the relative equality of worker and client, a mutuality that might be confirmed by the reciprocal nature of the commitments undertaken by each. Agreements in writing, publicly confirmed by witnesses, helped to establish at least an appearance that commercial sexual labor was appropriately egalitarian, thereby differentiating the work of a *hetairos* or *hetaira* from the dependence inherent in brothel slavery. A "liberal profession" (*eleutherios tekhnê*)[28] so pursued lay far from the furtive provision of shameful evanescent pleasures by a degraded and exploited slave working for the benefit of a master.

---

24. Ἔχεις τὰ σαυτῆς πάντα· προστίθημί σοι ἐγὼ θεραπαίνας, χρυσία (lines 381–82). Robert has suggested emending the text to read Χρυσί (the proper name rather than the Greek for "gold" or "jewels'): see Thomas 1990.

25. See chapter 2, nn. 175 and 176.

26. Dem. 59.45–46: συνῆγον αὐτοὺς οἱ ἐπιτήδειοι καὶ ἔπεισαν δίαιταν ἐπιτρέψαι αὐτοῖς. . . . ἀκούσαντες ἀμφοτέρων καὶ αὐτῆς τῆς ἀνθρώπου τὰ πεπραγμένα, γνώμην ἀπεφήναντο . . . τὴν μὲν ἄνθρωπον ἐλευθέραν εἶναι καὶ αὐτὴν αὑτῆς κυρίαν. . . .

27. Dem. 59.46: ἃ δ᾽ἐξῆλθεν ἔχουσα Νέαιρα παρὰ Φρυνίωνος χωρὶς ἱματίων καὶ χρυσίων καὶ θεραπαινῶν, ἃ αὐτῇ τῇ ἀνθρώπῳ ἠγοράσθη, ἀποδοῦναι Φρυνίωνι πάντα· συνεῖναι δ᾽ ἑκατέρῳ ἡμέραν παρ᾽ ἡμέραν· ἐὰν δὲ καὶ ἄλλως πως ἀλλήλους πείθωσι, ταῦτα κύρια εἶναι· τὰ δ᾽ ἐπιτήδεια τῇ ἀνθρώπῳ τὸν ἔχοντα ἀεὶ παρέχειν. . . .

28. For the Greek conceptualization of a "liberal profession," see chapter 2, esp. n. 1.

But were these arrangements—denominated in our sources as *symbolaia* ("contracts"[29]), *synthêkai* ("contracts" or "written contracts"[30]), *syngraphai* ("written contracts"[31]), *syngraphus* ("written contract"[32]), *grammateia* ("written contracts"[33])—truly "contracts" for juridical purposes? Or were they actually informal arrangements of convenience, giving rise to no legal obligation? Could they be enforced or confirmed by court procedures?[34] Some scholars arbitrarily assume that the "nature of the agreement" precluded law suits to enforce erotic work arrangements (Carey 1989: 103): "To expose his sex life by bringing such an action might make a man a laughing stock" (Ibid.); "Such contracts between men were in practice probably unworkable" (Davidson 1997: 97). Even though "in the world of New Comedy such long-term contracts for a meretrix' services are always treated as enforceable . . . in the real world, a contract of this sort would hardly be enforceable" (Rosivach 1998: 126). Yet despite the paucity of our information on specific cases actually brought at Athens, we do know of at least one reported suit "in the real world" to enforce such a contract—the action of Diophantos in the *archon*'s court to collect 4 *drachmas* promised but not paid for sexual

---

29. "Contract" is by far the dominant English translation of *symbolaion* (Mirhady 2004: 52). Depending on context, however, *symbolaion* is sometimes rendered by words such as "obligation" or "arrangement." (See Kussmaul 1985: 31–32 for a range of German equivalents [including "Vertrag" and "Obligation"].)

30. Although *synthêkai* is generally translated as "covenant" or "contract" (see LSJ; Aristot. *Rhet.* 1367a33–b30; Vélissaropoulos-Karakostas 2002: 131; Todd 2007: 326), Kussmaul has argued that in legal context *synthêkai* always means "written contract" (see 1969 passim).

31. For the difference between *syngraphê* and *synthêkai*, see Paoli's (probably excessively rigid) suggestions: [1930] 1974: 123–24. In Dem. 35, the speaker sometimes seems to use the terms interchangeably: see Dem. 35.14 and 35.43 (and Mirhady's discussion: 2004: 57–58). Cf. E. Cohen 1973: 129–30, n. 68; Scafuro 2003/04: 11, n. 37.

32. See n. 10 and text thereto.

33. For *grammateion* as written contract, see Aiskh. 1.165 (n. 2), Hyper. *Against Athênogenês* 8; Lys. 32.7 ("τὰ γράμματα would include the contracts relating to the loans": Carey 1989: 214). Cf. P. Oxy. 1012, Fr. 9 ii.15.

34. Although "legal significance" is often equated with the right of access to a governmental official or tribunal with decision-making authority, Vélissaropoulos-Karakostas properly observes that in the Greek context, "that is an enormous generalisation which ultimately, on the one hand, disassociates the contractual bond from those who engage in it, and on the other hand, views the lawsuit (*dike*) as the only means to resolve disputes" (2002: 131).

services[35]—a case that was not only actually brought but probably won by the young prostitute.[36] Yet the facts underlying this case are murky,[37] and some legal historians have continued to insist on the legal nullity at Athens of such "consensual" or "executory" contracts, that is, agreements based on mutual promises to be performed in whole or in part in the future. (Athenian prostitutional covenants, precisely because they provide for the sale of future services, are inherently "executory.") I seek therefore to show that (a) substantial evidence establishes that mutual promises, even those merely oral, were legally binding at Athens, (b) even persons ordinarily lacking legal capacity, such as women or slaves, might in business contexts enter into agreements enforceable in Athenian courts,[38] and (c) there were no conceptual or practical barriers at Athens to the enforcement of contracts for the practice of prostitution, a lawful business in a jurisdiction where even contracts for illegal purposes might be enforced through the Athenian courts.

## *Consensual Agreements at Athens*

Athenian sources enunciate, with repetitive consistency, a single fundamental contractual principle: the law upholds as "legally binding (*kyria*[39]) . . . whatever arrangements one party might agree upon with another" (Demosthenes 47.77).[40] Commentators in antiquity consistently

---

35. Aiskh. 1.158: Τίς γὰρ ὑμῶν τὸν ὀρφανὸν καλούμενον Διόφαντον οὐκ οἶδεν, ὅς τὸν ξένον πρὸς τὸν ἄρχοντα ἀπήγαγεν . . . ἐπαιτιασάμενος τέτταρας δραχμὰς αὐτὸν ὑπὲρ τῆς πράξεως ταύτης ἀπεστερηκέναι;

36. After evaluating relevant factors, Fisher finds it "more likely that the case went for Diophantos" (2001: 305). Cf. Loomis 1998: 172.

37. "There are serious difficulties in understanding this case as presented, and serious distortion may be supposed" (Fisher 2001: 304).

38. Of course, as Vélissaropoulos-Karakostas has pointed out (2002: 131, 136), even agreements unenforceable in court are often effectively enforced by means of institutions and compulsions inherent in the business and social communities to which parties to a covenant adhere—and by moral and religious compunctions.

39. For the translation of *kyria* as "legally binding," see Cohen 2006.

40. τὸν (νόμον) ὃς κελεύει κύρια εἶναι ὅσα ἂν ἕτερος ἑτέρῳ ὁμολογήσῃ. In concurrence: Aviles 2011: 26–27; Phillips 2009: 105; Dimopoulou 2014: 265. For the fullest documentation of this paradigm, see Gagliardi 2014. Some scholars believe, however, that such consensual arrangements were legally binding only if buttressed by the presence of witnesses or by the swearing of oaths: see Thür 2013.

report that for the Greeks consensual agreements were legally significant: Aristotle in the *Rhetoric* notes that "the laws" deem "legally binding" (*kyria*) whatever the parties agree upon (provided that these private arrangements are consistent with prevailing law),[41] and Roman savants and jurists expressed a similar view of Greek legal principles.[42] Even Athenian popular discourse recognized the primacy of consensual agreements among willing parties: in a discussion of the demands of erotic love, the acclaimed playwright Agathôn alludes to the city laws sanctifying "that which a willing person should agree upon with another willing person."[43] Hypereidês records that "the law states: whatever arrangements one party might agree upon with another are legally binding."[44] Demosthenes 42 similarly refers to "the law" that "agreements (*homologiai*) are legally binding."[45] Deinarkhos insists that the "law of the *polis*" imposes legal liability on anyone who violates any agreement (*homologêsas*) made with another citizen.[46] Isokratês cites the Athenian rule that agreements between individuals ("private agreements": *homologiai idiai*) be "publicly" enforceable, and insists on the importance of complying with these consensual arrangements (*hômologêmena*).[47] Some texts even

---

41. *Rhet.* 1375b9–10, 1376b8–9: ὁ μὲν κελεύει κύρια εἶναι ἅττ' ἂν συνθῶνται, ὁ δ' ἀπαγορεύει μὴ συντίθεσθαι παρὰ τὸν νόμον ... αἱ μὲν συνθῆκαι οὐ ποιοῦσι τὸν νόμον κύριον, οἱ δὲ νόμοι τὰς κατὰ νόμους συνθήκας. Cf. Dem. 24.117, 46.24. Scholars have assumed, in the absence of evidence to the contrary, that a naked promise by one party was not itself actionable: Wolff 1966a: 322; Vélissaropoulos-Karakostas 1993: 165–66.

42. Asconius, *Commentary on Cic. In Verrem* 2.1.36 (91); Gaius 3.154. Cf. Mitteis 1891: 459–75.

43. Plato, *Symp.* 196c2–3: ἃ δ'ἂν ἑκὼν ἑκόντι ὁμολογήσῃ, φασὶν "οἱ πόλεως βασιλῆς νόμοι" δίκαια εἶναι.

44. *Against Athênogenês* §13: ὁ νόμος λέγει, ὅσα ἂν ἕτερος ἑτέρῳ ὁμολογήσῃ κύρια εἶναι. The speaker does add a condition, otherwise unattested, to this general statement—"but only if they are fair" (τά γε δίκαια). As has been often noted (cf. Whitehead 2000: 267–69; MacDowell 1978: 140; Dorjahn 1935: 279) this is a difficult argument, and Epikratês is unable to cite any explicit Athenian legal precept supporting his assertion. In fact, Athenian purchasers—even consumers—were the beneficiaries of no legally imposed safeguards, such as warranties relating to the quality or usability of the products sold.

45. Dem. 42.12: τὸν (νόμον) κελεύοντα κυρίας εἶναι τὰς πρὸς ἀλλήλους ὁμολογίας.

46. Dein. 3.4: καὶ ὁ μὲν κοινὸς τῆς πόλεως νόμος, ἐάν τις εἰς ἕνα τινὰ τῶν πολιτῶν ὁμολογήσας τι παραβῇ, τοῦτον ἔνοχον εἶναι κελεύει τῷ ἀδικεῖν. The text (Nouhaud 1990) incorporates Lloyd-Jones's emendation (εἰς ἕνα τινα) for manuscripts A and N's ἐναντίον.

47. τὰς μὲν ἰδίας ὁμολογίας δημοσίᾳ κυρίας ἀναγκάζετ'εἶναι (18.24); ἀναγκαῖον εἶναι τοῖς ὡμολογημένοις ἐμμένειν (18.25). On this enforcement of private agreements through public procedures, see Carawan 2006.

emphasize this mutuality of commitment as essential to the creation of a legally enforceable obligation. Thus Demosthenes 56.2 confirms the binding effect of "whatever arrangements a party might willingly agree upon with another,"[48] and Demosthenes 48 cites "the law" governing agreements "which a willing party has agreed upon and covenanted with another willing party."[49]

In contrast to the paucity of evidence supporting many generally accepted modern "reconstructions" of Athenian law,[50] consensual contracts at Athens are attested—as the cases cited show—by a multitude of examples occurring not in a single context, but over a broad range of situations—taxation, personal services, testamentary transmission of wealth, the obtaining of judgments, the transfer and mortgaging of real estate, business transactions, and maritime finance. So pervasive were legally enforceable consensual contracts at Athens—and so useful to sophisticated commercial activity—that proposals for their abolition were advanced by Plato (who was deeply opposed to artful business practices and the profit-seeking business people who engaged in them[51]). For the imagined community set forth in the *Laws*, the philosopher proposed the prohibition of all commercial exchange other than simultaneous "cash for goods and goods for cash" (*nomisma khrêmatôn, khrêmata nomismatos*). Plato's Magnêsia, the state representing not the utopia of the earlier *Republic* but merely a "reformed" Athens,[52] would deny all right of legal action to a seller seeking repayment of monies lent to a buyer to "pay" for goods acquired from the seller. A vendor financing a sale by entering into an executory contract providing for future payment would have to

---

48. τοῖς νόμοις τοῖς ὑμετέροις (sc. οἳ κελεύουσι, ὅσα ἂν τις ἑκὼν ἕτερος ἑτέρῳ ὁμολογήσῃ κύρια εἶναι). For the effect of fraud or improper influence on requisite volition, see Wolff [1957] 1968: 484, n. 3; Maschke 1926: 162; Simônetos 1939: 193 ff.; Jones 1956: 222. Cf. Plato, *Kritôn* 52d9–e3, *Nomoi* 920d.

49. §§ 11, 54: τὸν νόμον . . . καθ' ὃν τὰς συνθήκας ἐγράψαμεν πρὸς ἡμᾶς αὐτούς . . . ἃ μὲν ὡμολόγησε καὶ συνέθετο ἑκὼν πρὸς ἑκόντα.

50. The study of ancient Greek law is notoriously bedeviled by lacunae in our evidentiary sources: scholars often consider the text of a law or the existence of a legal principle to be incontrovertibly well established if it is confirmed by two or three testimonia. The accuracy of a portion of the Law against Hybris, for example, is "assured" because it is quoted in two independent texts (Fisher 1992: 36, n. 1).

51. See chapter 1, p. 25 and n. 3.

52. Kahn 1993: xviii–xxiii. Cf. Morrow [1960] 1993: 592. A good example of Plato's recasting of Athenian practice is his proposal for publishing laws: see Bertrand 1997, esp. 27–29.

"grin and bear it" (*stergetô*) if the purchaser did not honor the agreement. Similarly, a buyer would be denied court access to enforce arrangements permitting delayed delivery of goods.[53] If consensual understandings had not been legally enforceable, Plato's provisions would merely have reproduced existing law. But, as always, "Plato's descriptions must not be taken as simply reproducing actual law" (Pringsheim 1950: 40). Despite Plato's personally favorable attitude toward prostitution,[54] he disliked much, perhaps virtually all, of prevailing Athenian law and legal principles, and Athenian prostitutional contracts—like all reciprocal agreements for future performance—would not have been legally enforceable had Plato in reality enjoyed the power to revise Athenian law at will.

In the actual Athenian court system, however, breach of contractual arrangements was actionable through the *dikê blabês*, a litigational category covering a great variety of "damages" wrongfully sustained.[55] Additional categories of action have been identified that may have been directed specifically to violations of contractual commitments.[56] But could such contracts be legally meaningful only when entered into by free men—who were clearly not the only practitioners of prostitution at Athens—or could legal significance arise from agreements to which women and slaves were parties? Was the underlying purpose (sale of sex) a barrier to the validity or enforceability of a contract of prostitution?

## Contractual Capacity of Women and Slaves

As we have seen, contracts of prostitution were entered into with sexual workers of varied status—including women and slaves. But under

---

53. *Laws* 849e: ἐν τούτοις ἀλλάττεσθαι νόμισμά τε χρημάτων καὶ χρήματα νομίσματος, μὴ προϊέμενον ἄλλον ἑτέρῳ τὴν ἀλλαγήν· ὁ δὲ προέμενος ὡς πιστεύων, ἐάντε κομίσηται καὶ ἂν μή, στεργέτω ὡς οὐκέτι δίκης οὔσης τῶν τοιούτων περὶ συναλλάξεων. ("Here [sc. in Magnêsia] they must exchange money for goods and goods for money, and never hand over anything without getting something in return; anyone who doesn't bother about this and trusts the other party must grin and bear it whether or not he gets what he's owed, because for such transactions there will be no legal remedy" [Translation: Saunders 1951]). Cf. *Laws* 915d6–e2 (no legal action for delayed sale or purchase [μηδ' ἐπὶ ἀναβολῇ πρᾶσιν μηδὲ ὠνὴν ποιεῖσθαι μηδενός·]).

54. He endorsed commercial sex as the least damaging alternative to marriage: see chapter 1, n. 26.

55. Phillips 2009: 90–92.

56. For the putative δίκη συνθηκῶν παραβάσεως (Pollux 8.31), see Katzouros 1981. On the possible δίκη συμβολαίων (Dem. 32.1), see Mirhady 2004: 56.

prevailing modern scholarly tenets (which insist that at Athens slaves and women were legal nullities) such contracts would have been of no juridical significance: at law, slaves supposedly were mere chattels whose masters exercised all legal rights pertaining to them[57]; women were subsumed within the legal personality of their *kyrios*, their "lord and master" (Wolff 1944: 46–47, n. 22), or "sovereign" ("in certain contexts": Todd 1993: 383). Accordingly, it is argued, "an Athenian woman had to be represented in legal transactions by a male relative acting as her guardian (*kyrios*)" (Todd Ibid.), and a slave could not enter into a legal transaction, including contracts of prostitution. However, neither contention is valid. In actual practice, Athenian law made accommodation—albeit only in commercial context—for the legal standing and juridical rights of both women and slaves.

Direct entry by women into contractual arrangements, including agreements of prostitution, was not in fact precluded by *kyrieia*—an Athenian woman's putative need of a male relative to act on her behalf. Although some commentators persist in referring to the *kyrios* as "the head of the household to which (an Athenian woman) was attached" (Just 1985: 173, n. 8), recent studies have established that the senior male in an *oikos* was not the "owner" of family property or (in Wolff's words, Ibid.) "the person who exercises domestic power" over other family members (Wolff Ibid.), but merely the household representative or "steward" in dealing publicly with household assets.[58] In form, "*kyrieia* is a much fuzzier, less formalized institution than social and legal historians have generally thought" (Foxhall 1996: 150). And in practice, the reality of women's extensive involvement in commerce (see chapter 6, pp. 135–36) effectively abrogated *kyrieia* as a barrier to female business operations, implicitly in the many large-scale transactions undertaken by women for their own account,[59] explicitly in retail transactions where the law formally recognized women's

---

57. Slaves' lack of legal rights: Harrison 1968: 163–72; Rihll 2011: 51–52; Klees 1998: 176–217. For slaves' general inability to bring lawsuits, see Plato *Gorg.* 483b; Dem. 53.20. Except for some commercial matters discussed in this chapter (pp. 109–10), their testimony could be used only to the extent that it was extracted under formalized torture, a form of proof that emphasized the general evidentiary incapacity of the *doulos*. See Thür 1977; Humphreys 1985: 356, n. 7.

58. See Ferrucci 2006: 202; Foxhall 1989, 1996: 149–52, 2013: 25. Cf. Schaps 1998a: 163–67.

59. For examples and discussion of this phenomenon, see Hunter 1994: 19–29; Schaps 1979: 52–56. For the mechanisms through which women might avoid the literal limitations of prevailing law, see Foxhall 1989; Harris 1992a.

right to contract, without male representation, in an unlimited number of reasonably significant individual transactions. (Legal authorization for a single commitment was the value of one *medimnos* of barley [often about US $300 in purchasing power equivalence, but at times as much as $1,500–$2,000], an amount more than sufficient to meet the normal requirements for individual sales at retail establishments, or for single commercial sexual encounters).[60] There was even a category of women described as *kyria heautês* ("self-representative," that is, not dependent for legal purposes on a male *kyrios*)[61]—although the parameters and origin of this grouping are unclear.[62] (Strikingly, however, the prominent Neaira, allegedly an Athenian prostitute, is explicitly so denominated.[63])

In the case of a single, exceedingly large transaction involving a woman principal who was not "self-representative," unrelated male citizens were available to act as agents. Binding commitments at Athens could be created through such representatives, who were able to effectuate transactions and undertake obligations that might not be available directly to their principals (provided, of course, that the agents themselves had the requisite capacity). Many citizens accordingly undertook a variety of tasks on behalf of noncitizen and slave business principals.[64]

Contractual arrangements with unfree prostitutes would have been legally enforceable only if slaves could be parties to commercial litigation.[65] In general, however, in the absence of special arrangements

---

60. Isai. 10.10: συμβάλλειν μηδὲ γυναικὶ πέρα μεδίμνον κριθῶν. Cf. Aiskh. 1.18. One *medimnos* of barley often cost about 3 *drachmas*, but at times rose to as much as 18. Cf. Dimakis 1994: 33, 329, n. 77; Hunter 1989a: 294; Foxhall and Forbes 1982: 86; Kuenen-Janssens 1941: 212. On state involvement in the pricing of grain, see chapter 7, pp. 157–60. For prices of sexual encounters, see the section "The Price of Sex" in chapter 7.

61. Men. *Perik.* 497; Xen. *Apom.* 3.11; Dem. 59. 45–46; Antiphanês Fr. 210 (K.A.). Other examples in Bremmer 1985; Hunter 1989b.

62. The number of such "female heads of household" is impossible to determine" (Hunter 1994: 33). But they likely included both wealthy and less advantaged women who for various reasons were not encompassed by the dowry and betrothal system, such as women whose husbands had died on military service. See Modrzejewski 1983: 52–53.

63. Dem. 59.46: γνώμην ἀπεφήναντο . . . τὴν μὲν ἄνθρωπον ἐλευθυέραν εἶναι καὶ αὐτὴν αὐτῆς κυρίαν. . . .

64. See E. Cohen (forthcoming) (a) (LDAS VI); Harris 2013; Gernet [1950] 1955: 159–64; McKechnie 1989: 185. Cf. Cohen 2000: 145–54; Hervagault and Mactoux 1974; Perotti 1974; Partsch 1909: 135 ff.

65. On the business undertakings of *douloi khôris oikountes* ("slaves living independently"), see chapter 7, pp. 172–75.

(such as those arising from interstate treaty or connected with residence rights obtained by free foreigners), the Hellenic cities allowed access to their courts only to their own citizens.[66] But in business matters there is significant evidence that the Athenian courts substantially disregarded incapacity because of personal status—and allowed slaves full court access, as parties and as witnesses. This acceptance is best attested in the important "commercial maritime" cases and courts (*dikai emporikai*), where "standing" was accorded without regard to the personal status of litigants.[67] In the case of slaves, this represented a unique accommodation, for (with the exception of testimony in cases of murder, perhaps only against the alleged murderer of their master) slaves were otherwise absolutely deprived of the right even to be witnesses in legal proceedings.[68] "Commercial maritime" disputes, however, were not the only cases encompassed in the special procedural category of "monthly cases" (*dikai emmênoi*). "Banking cases" (*dikai trapezitikai*) are also denominated by Aristotle as among these "monthly cases" (*Ath. Pol.* 52.2). Although little is known with certainty as to the nature of "banking cases,"[69] there is no reason to assume criteria of standing or evidence substantially different from those of the "allied sphere" (Harrison 1968–71, I: 176) of commercial maritime cases. Strikingly, the clearest example of a slave having the right to testify and participate in an Athenian court, that of Lampis the *nauklêros* in Demosthenes 34, involves a *doulos* who provided credit to a borrower who was the recipient of a number of other loans—some of which may have been provided by bankers.[70] And Pankleôn, engaged in commercial pursuits in a fuller's shop, seeks to avoid a court action (Lysias 23) on the grounds that he is a Plataian, only to be met by the plaintiff's introduction of evidence that he is in fact a slave. Of course, the plaintiff's presentation

---

66. See Cohen 1973: 59–62; Gernet [1938] 1955: 181–82; Gauthier 1972: 149–56. Even the right to reside at Athens may have been granted initially through a procedure in which the foreigner did not directly participate: Levy 1987: 60.

67. Cohen 1973: 69–74, 121; Gernet [1938] 1955: 159–64; McKechnie 1989: 185. Specifically regarding *douloi*, Garlan notes: "Surtout à partir du IV$^e$ siècle, il fallut enfin adapter empiriquement ses capacités juridiques aux fonctions économiques qui lui étaient confiées" (1982: 55). Cf. Paoli [1930] 1974: 106–09.

68. See this chapter, note 57.

69. On the *dikai trapezitikai*, see Gernet [1938] 1955: 176–77.

70. For Lampis's advance of 1,000 *drachmas*, see Dem. 34.6 and Thompson 1980: 144–45. At Dem. 34.5 Lampis is termed the οἰκέτης of Diôn, at 34.10 the "παῖς" of Diôn. For his clear testimonial capacity, see §31.

of proofs of servitude would justify pendency of the case only if slaves actually could be parties to business-oriented lawsuits.

Yet there remained a barrier to slaves' participation in court proceedings: a fundamental Athenian legal principle that a party to an action must personally present his case in court.[71] Since many slaves did not speak Greek as their native language, linguistic ineptitude would often have prevented them from competently representing themselves in litigation, effectively depriving them of access to juridical process. Here too, Athenian law adapted to the needs of commerce and allowed slaves and former slaves (and even free non-Greeks) to be represented by speakers fluent in Greek.[72] Thus the banker (and ex-slave) Phormiôn, whose Greek was poor, was permitted to use Demosthenes to speak for him in an important commercial matter in which he was a defendant.[73] In Demosthenes 34, where the slave Lampis, a ship-owner and financier, is prominently involved as a principal (see above), with the court's acquiescence the plaintiff receives forensic support from at least one, and possibly two "friends."[74] In another commercial maritime case, Demosthenes 56, the court permits Dareios to speak on behalf of Pamphilos, who was unable to present his own case (Blass 1893: 584).

Agents were employed sometimes merely for the principal's convenience.[75] Stephanos was dispatched to represent a banker's interests at Byzantion (Dem. 45.64), and the money-lending Dêmôn sent Aristophôn to Kephallênia to resolve a commercial maritime dispute (Dem. 32.10–12). Timotheos "appointed Philondas as his agent to sail to Macedon" (Moreno 2007: 281) to handle a timber transaction (Dem. 49.26). But because Athenian law sharply restricted the rights and privileges of even free

---

71. "Das attische Recht... verlangte darüber hinaus grundsätzlich, daß jeder Litigant seine Sache auch rednerisch in eigener Person verfocht." Wolff 1968: 111–12. Cf. Rubinstein 2000: 18: "The assumption that an Athenian litigant was expected not only to plead his own case but also to plead it alone, at least in principle, has been fundamental to most recent scholarship on Athenian legal proceedings." In agreement: Bauman 1990: 7; Christ 1998: 37.

72. Blass asserts that in commercial cases Athenian courts commonly permitted presentations by representatives (rather than by parties), since many tradespersons were not Greek by birth (1893: 584).

73. The orator opened his presentation by noting Phormiôn's ἀπειρίαν τοῦ λέγειν, καὶ ὡς ἀδυνάτως ἔχει Φορμίων (Dem. 36.1).

74. Dem. 34.52: καλῶ δὲ καὶ ἄλλον τινὰ τῶν φίλων, ἐὰν κελεύητε.

75. A number of individuals carried out tasks with which their principals did not wish to be openly connected. See Lofberg 1917: 48–59.

noncitizens, slave businessmen would have had frequent need of "representatives" or "agents" in the conduct of their businesses. Thus Pasiôn is attested as retaining the citizen Agyrrhios of Kollytos as a confidential representative in litigational matters (Isokratês 17.31 ff.). Phormiôn, before obtaining his freedom, used the citizen Timosthenês in the conduct of his maritime operations (Dem. 49.31). During his early years of banking activity, before obtaining citizenship, perhaps while still a slave,[76] Pasiôn utilized the citizen Pythodoros "to do and say all things" for him.[77] Similarly, the son of Sopaios (a plutocratic and free, but foreign businessman visiting Athens) used the citizen Menexenos, scion of one of the "wealthiest and most distinguished" Athenian families (Davies 1971: 145), to overcome various legal incapacities: Menexenos deals with the provision of surety required of noncitizens in the polemarch's court (Isokratês 17.12, 14) and appears to have represented this foreigner generally in legal and business matters.[78]

But Athenian law sought to prevent such principals from exploiting free female prostitutes (and free young male sexual workers). The "harshest penalties" (*megista epitimia*, a euphemism at Athens for the possible imposition of the death penalty) were applicable against anyone who engaged in *proagôgeia*—behavior encompassing not only outright control of a sexual enterprise but also any form of criminal compulsion, pimping, or "matchmaking."[79] Although numerous other societies have tolerated, or even encouraged, pimping, for free Athenians a pervasive moral tenet required their avoiding even the appearance of working under the control of another (see the section "Athenian Work Ethics" in chapter 2). In the sale of sexual services, Athenian criminal law and Athenian contractual practices consistently reflected this moral orientation.

---

76. Pasiôn played an important role in the banking business of his masters (Dem. 36.43, 48). J. Jones (1956: 186) has even suggested that Pasiôn, while still a slave, was entirely responsible for the operation of the bank. Although it is often assumed that he was manumitted prior to the events described in Isok. 17 (cf. Davies 1971: 429–30), in fact we do not know when he obtained his freedom.

77. Isok. 17.33: ὑπὲρ Πασίωνος ἅπαντα καὶ λέγει καὶ πράττει.

78. Cf. Isok. 17.9: βουλόμενος εἰδέναι σαφῶς τὸ πρᾶγμα προσπέμπω Φιλόμηλον αὐτῷ καὶ Μενέξενον; 17.12... λέγει... ὡς ἐγὼ καὶ Μενέξενος... ἓξ τάλαντ' ἀργυρίου λάβοιμεν παρ' αὐτοῦ.

79. For full discussion of *proagôgeia*, see chapter 5, pp. 118–24.

## Private Contracts and Public Interests

The "nature of the agreement" did not preclude the legal effectiveness of Athenian private contracts. Some agreements even anticipated a possible conflict between contractual provisions and local law, and affirmatively provided that the terms of the parties' agreement should override any laws or statutes that might purport to nullify provisions contained in the parties' covenant.[80]

Demosthenes 48, a legal case purportedly arising from the excessive wealth showered on a female prostitute, illustrates the apparent willingness of the Athenian courts to enforce even pacts designed to obstruct Athenian legal procedures. Kallistratos alleges that Olympiodôros, the brother of Kallistratos's wife, has breached a contract to divide equally between themselves the assets of a relative who has died intestate, and to jointly oppose any rival claims. According to the plaintiff, Olympiodôros lives with a former brothel slave (*pornê*) who is excoriated as the proximate cause of the defendant's wrongful actions.[81] Kallistratos attacks this woman for intensifying Olympiodôros's irrationality and thus bringing on "the ruin of us all."[82] She is a *hetaira* who causes the plaintiff's own wife and daughter to envy her extensive gold jewelry and fine clothing and the brilliance of her outdoor processions, "arrogant extravagances" paid for with funds that might otherwise have been available to adorn the male litigant's family members.[83] The whore's control over Olympiodôros is supposedly so complete that she incarnates precisely the type of woman against whom the revered lawgiver, Solôn, had provided protection through legislation, rendering ineffective the commitments that a man might make under a woman's improper suasion.[84]

---

80. On classical Greek agreements purporting to override *polis* law(s), see Dimopoulou 2014: 265–73 and Cohen 2014.

81. Ὀλυμπιόδωρος... γυναῖκα μὲν ἀστὴν κατὰ τοὺς νόμους τοὺς ὑμετέρους οὐδεπώποτε ἔγημεν... ἑταίραν δὲ λυσάμενος ἔνδον ἔχει... γυναικὶ πειθόμενος πόρνῃ (§§ 53, 56).

82. αὕτη ἐστὶν ἡ λυμαινομένη ἅπαντας ἡμᾶς καὶ ποιοῦσα τουτονὶ περαιτέρω μαίνεσθαι (§53).

83. §55: Πῶς γὰρ οὐκ ἀδικοῦνται ἢ πῶς οὐ δεινὰ πάσχουσιν, ἐπειδὰν ὁρῶσι τὴν μὲν τούτου ἑταίραν περαιτέρω τοῦ καλῶς ἔχοντος καὶ χρυσία πολλὰ ἔχουσαν καὶ ἱμάτια καλά, καὶ ἐξόδους λαμπρὰς ἐξιοῦσαν, καὶ ὑβρίζουσαν ἐκ τῶν ἡμετέρων αὐταὶ δὲ καταδεεστέρως περὶ ταῦτα ἔχωσιν ἅπαντα; Kallistratos's wife was the sister of Olympiodôros, and Kallistratros's daughter was thus the defendant's niece.

84. §56: Ὀλυμπιόδωρος τοιοῦτός ἐστιν ἄνθρωπος... ὅπερ Σόλων ὁ νομοθέτης λέγει, παραφρονῶν ὡς οὐδεὶς πώποτε παρεφρόνησεν ἀνθρώπων, γυναικὶ πειθόμενος πόρνῃ. Καὶ ἄκυρά γε ταῦτα πάντα ἐνομοθέτησεν εἶναι ὁ Σόλων, ὅ τι ἂν τις γυναικὶ πειθόμενος πράττῃ, ἄλλως τε καὶ τοιαύτῃ. Cf. Dem. 46.14. For a woman's "undue influence," cf. Todd 1993: 62, 225; Karabêlias 1992.

As a result of this woman's influence, Olympiodôros has failed to honor their mutual agreement to work together to nullify the claims of relatives whose standing was equal to or superior to that of the litigants, a contract having a "blatantly illegal" aim (Phillips 2009: 96), namely, the nullification of the rules of estate division set by Athenian law. But Kallistratos, in seeking to enforce this pact, not only explicitly sets forth its unlawful purpose but even explains in detail how plaintiff and defendant together had misled a prior jury in an earlier process that had led to the award to Olympiodôros of the deceased's entire estate (§§43–45). Kallistratos also lays out Olympiodôros's possible defenses, including an anticipated claim that the plaintiff had himself first violated their agreement (§§39–47), but he never even suggests that Kallistratos might proffer as a defense the putative illegality of their compact.

Greek jurisprudential discussions, however, do consider the possibility of conflict between a jurisdiction's grant to individuals of an absolute right to contract as they wish, and the same jurisdiction's contemporaneous prohibition of the very actions that have been agreed upon in a private arrangement. In the fictional city of Magnêsia, sketched in *The Laws*, Plato makes a legal action available for failure to perform any provision of a consensual agreement—except for covenants prohibited by law or statutes.[85] In the real world of fourth-century Greek polities, as Aristotle observes, "sometimes" one law specifically provides that "whatever (the parties) agree upon" is legally binding (*kyria*), while another law categorically prohibits parties from entering into agreements that are contrary to law.[86] To resolve such potential conflicts, an agreement might contain a provision purporting to give priority over *polis* law to the terms contained in the contract. Thus the written contract preserved in Demosthenes 35, the only maritime loan agreement surviving from antiquity, provides explicitly that concerning the matters covered in the document "nothing else be more legally binding than (this) contract."[87] The speaker explicitly interprets this clause as giving the agreement priority even over laws and

---

85. 920d1–5: Ὅσα τις ἂν ὁμολογῶν συνθέσθαι μὴ ποιῇ κατὰ τὰς ὁμολογίας, πλὴν ὧν ἂν νόμοι ἀπείργωσιν ἢ ψήφισμα ... δίκας εἶναι τῶν ἄλλων ἀτελοῦς ὁμολογίας.

86. *Rhet.* 1375b9–10: ἐνίοτε ὁ μὲν κελεύει κύρια εἶναι ἅττ' ἂν συνθῶνται, ὁ δ'ἀπαγορεύει μὴ συντίθεσθαι παρὰ τὸν νόμον.

87. §13: κυριώτερον δὲ περὶ τούτων ἄλλο μηδὲν εἶναι τῆς συγγραφῆς. This document is now generally accepted as genuine: see Purpura 1987: 203 ff.; Todd 1993: 338.

decrees.⁸⁸ A similar covenant was contained in the maritime loan compact that is the subject of litigation in Demosthenes 56.⁸⁹ The inherent mobility of maritime cargoes argues for the reasonableness of provisions establishing the primacy of private contractual arrangements over the law and statutes of any one jurisdiction: the rules of a particular *polis* might have little applicability to financial arrangements made in another jurisdiction covering the transportation of goods to a third locus and involving parties possibly alien to all three areas. Thus in Demosthenes 32, matters relating to maritime loan contracts made in Athens and Syracuse come to be adjudicated in a court on the western Greek island of Kephallênia (§§ 8–9). Similarly, contractual provisions overriding the parochial law of a particular city or cities accord well with the mobility of sex-workers, who might range over "the circuit of the entire (Hellenic) world" (Dem. 59.108) following their employers and their patrons, attending various festivals and other seasonal ceremonies (see introduction, pp. 10–11). Indeed, the promise of foreign travel is among the inducements allegedly offered to entice the sex-worker of Lysias 3 into violating his contract to provide erotic services to Simôn (§10). We cannot, however, confirm that such provisions might have been generally (or occasionally) included in contracts of prostitution, since no actual texts of contracts for erotic services have survived. As a practical matter, moreover, we have no way of knowing whether courts might actually have been willing to favor the parties' consensual arrangements over *polis* law. But agreements for the provision of sexual services were not unlawful at Athens, and no legal barrier would have constrained Athenian courts from enforcing them.

---

88. §39: ἡ μὲν γὰρ συγγραφὴ οὐδὲν κυριώτερον ἐᾷ εἶναι τῶν ἐγγεγραμμένων, οὐδὲ προσφέρειν οὔτε νόμον οὔτε ψήφισμα οὔτ' ἄλλ' οὐδ' ὁτιοῦν πρὸς τὴν συγγραφήν. Cf. IG XII 7.67, 27, and 76.

89. Although the actual text has not been preserved, section 26 of the court presentation confirms the presence of such a clause.

# 5

## *Beyond Legalization*

### LAWS AFFECTING PROSTITUTES

ALTHOUGH ATHENIAN MALE citizens who had prostituted themselves were subject to punishment if they attempted to exercise certain rights of participation in *polis* activity (chapter 3), there is universal agreement that "being a prostitute in itself was not an offense" (MacDowell 2005: 85): there was no legal prohibition against providing sex for cash.[1] Nor was Athens alone in classical antiquity in treating prostitution as a legitimate occupation. Rome, for prime example, "allowed the business of venal sex to proceed virtually unregulated" (McGinn 2004: 1). Almost all modern Western societies, however, have outlawed prostitution, or have "legalized" it only under extensive administrative oversight and/or with ambient criminal strictures.[2] Thus many European countries are said to

---

1. In agreement (among many others): Foxhall 2013: 103; Lanni 2010: 55; Osborne 2004: 14. Gagliardi has suggested, however, that restrictions on male prostitutes' political activity effectively amounted to a criminalization of prostitution (at least for male citizens) since "the penalty, imposed through a *dokimasia rhetoron*, did not depend on anything the individual had done in the assembly, because in fact he had not done anything there, apart from asking to speak" (2005: 93). But this is equivalent to arguing that the US military's refusal to accept recruits who have marked their skin with tattoo(s) effectively criminalizes tattooing, and even Gagliardi denies "that simple prostitution could be prosecuted as an offence, if not followed by the other acts listed in the Solonian law" (2005: 92, n. 15).

2. Canadian law is paradigmatic: while adults' exchange of sex for money has been lawful throughout Canada, federal laws have prohibited the operation of brothels, pimping, and soliciting, effectively criminalizing most exchanges. The Supreme Court of Canada, however, has now struck down these limitations as unconstitutional infringements on prostitutes' rights (12/20/13: appeal of *Bedford v. Canada*, 2010 ONSC 4264 [CanLII]). Proposed federal legislation (intended to withstand court challenge) was adopted in November 2014 (Bill C-36), purportedly leaving prostitution lawful while still inhibiting its actual practice by criminalizing payment for, or advertising of, sexual services.

have "decriminalized" prostitution by eliminating direct prosecution of individual providers of purchased sex,[3] while maintaining prohibitions on soliciting, cohabitating, and/or operating commercial outlets for sex.[4] Because many prostitutes in Western Europe are foreigners (usually illegal immigrants),[5] sex-workers are often arrested (and often deported) for illegal residence, rather than for the commercial sexual activities actually objected to.[6] "Decriminalization" itself is often accompanied by prosecution of customers and by onerous and extensive regulation (physical examinations, bureaucratic rules, complex licensing) that effectively negate, in large measure, the purported authorization of the sale of sex.

Athens likewise had adopted ancillary legislation affecting the practice of prostitution. Criminal penalties were imposed on fathers (and other men) who took money for the erotic services of boys and girls for whom they were responsible.[7] Prostitutes were monitored so closely that tax

---

3. See O'Neill and Barberet 2000: 124–25; Barberet 1995. A number of nations, however, are considering the restoration of direct criminal sanctions, a step taken by Sweden in 1999 (Pisano: 2002: 245–49). For recriminalization efforts in Germany, see *International Conference on Prostitution & Trafficking*- Copenhagen, 5/7–5/8/2011, reported at www.grosse-freiheit.dk/upl/9628/JaniceRaymondtale.pdf; Spain, Newsletter 4/27/2012 at http://takethesquare.net/2012/04/27/barcelona-15m-newsletter-nr-10/.

4. In Germany, for example, prostitution is "legal," but pimping and promoting commercial sex are unlawful. Prostitutional contracts are unenforceable as "sittenwidrig" ("immoral"), and prostitutes are denied rights available to other workers (such as health care, unemployment benefits, collective bargaining). Local municipalities are empowered to impose additional restrictions, and prostitutes are often arrested for illegal residence and other prostitutional-related charges. See www.worldsexguide.org/germany.html. In France, "Trading sex for money is legal (but) soliciting or trafficking in prostitutes is not" (*New York Times*, November 22, 2011). The United Kingdom likewise prohibits soliciting or trafficking (see Sections 19 and 20 of the Policing and Crime Act [2009]).

5. It is estimated that approximately 80 percent of Dutch prostitutes are foreign born (Louis 1999), as are more than half of German prostitutes (Owen 2002). Cf. introduction, n. 41.

6. Brussa 1998; Wijers 1998: 74–75. In 2003, a new French Law on Internal Security (*loi sur la sécurité intérieure*) was adopted, explicitly criminalizing even the appearance of "soliciting" (*racolage* [par] *une attitude meme passive*) (Article 50) and similarly penalizing other aspects of the sale of sex. The Minister of the Interior has insisted that restrictions on commercial sex are part of "la lutte contre les réseaux mafieux" (*Le Monde*, November 16, 2002). Legislation has now cleared the National Assembly, and is awaiting Senate consideration, to levy fines on persons purchasing sex (Assemblée Nationale, loi no. 4057, "visant à responsabiliser les clients de la prostitution," enacted December 2013). As of June 2015, the Senate was still resisting confirmation of the Assembly's action (Le Figaro, June 15, 2015).

7. Aiskhin. 1.13: Διαρρήδην γοῦν λέγει ὁ νόμος, ἐάν τινα ἐκμισθώσῃ ἑταιρεῖν πατὴρ ἢ ἀδελφὸς ἢ θεῖος ἢ ἐπίτροπος ἢ ὅλως τῶν κυρίων τις . . . (ὁ νόμος) ἐᾷ γραφὴν εἶναι, κατὰ δὲ τοῦ μισθώσαντος καὶ τοῦ μισθωσαμένου . . . καὶ ἴσα τὰ ἐπιτίμια ἑκατέρῳ πεποίηκε . . . Plut. *Solôn* 23.2:Ἔτι δ'οὔτε θυγατέρας πωλεῖν οὔτ' ἀδελφὰς δίδωσι, πλὴν ἂν μὴ λάβῃ παρθένον ἀνδρὶ συγγεγενημένην. See

agents collecting the annual impost on prostitution (*pornikon telos*) possessed precise information on individuals "practicing the trade" (*khrômenoi têi ergasiai*).[8] As discussed in chapter 3, male citizens who had taken money for sex were deprived of the opportunity to participate in certain political and civil activities. The *polis* imposed the "harshest penalties" (*megista epitimia*) on anyone acting as a procurer (*progôgeus*) for free women or free youths.[9] Were these laws, then, the Athenian equivalent of today's prevailing European policy of "decriminalizing" prostitution by eliminating direct prosecution of individual prostitutes, while imposing regulatory burdens and punishing tangential aspects of commercial sex, thereby obstructing the supposedly lawful practice of prostitution? Was Athenian prostitution formalistically lawful, but effectively truncated by indirect sanctions?

To the contrary—unlike prevailing European regimes—Athenian law generally touched on commercial sex only as an aspect of broader concerns and treated prostitutes no differently than others in similar situations: some statutes even facilitated the sale of sex by protecting the rights of sex-workers. Thus sanctions on male relatives who prostituted children were merely one element of the extensive legislation protecting children from sexual exploitation—laws that included detailed prohibitions against abuse by caregivers (and others) and safeguards against exploitation of boys by mature males in school or other educational situations (including choral, athletic, and gymnastic training).[10] Taxation of Athenian prostitutes followed the procedures imposed on others, including farmers and merchants: Athens commonly gathered governmental funds not directly through *polis* officials but via third parties who purchased, as highest

---

Glazebrook 2006a, who shows that Solôn 23.2 cannot reasonably be interpreted as providing for the sale into slavery of an unchaste woman (pace Ogden 1996: 141, Blundell 1995: 125, and various other earlier commentators). Cf. the provisions for protection of children under guardianship in the "New Fragments of Hyperides from the Archimedes Palimpsest": Thür (forthcoming); Tchernetska, et al. 2007 (possible protection against sexual abuse: Whitehead 2009: 141–42).

8. Aiskhin. 1.119: καθ' ἕκαστον ἐνιαυτὸν ἡ βουλὴ πωλεῖ τὸ πορνηκὸν τέλος· καὶ τοὺς πριαμένους τὸ τέλος οὐκ εἰκάζειν, ἀλλ' ἀκριβῶς εἰδέναι τοὺς ταύτῃ χρωμένους τῇ ἐργασίᾳ. Cf. Pollux 7.202, 9.29. Diod. Sik. (12.21.1) suggests that such taxation was common throughout Greece. Cf. Polyain. 5.2.13. Similar tax at Kôs: Reinach 1892; Khatzibasileiou 1981: 8.55–56. Cf. chapter 1, n. 37 and accompanying text.

9. See this chapter, section "Prohibition of Pimping (Proagôgeia)."

10. See Aiskhin. 1.9–11, 139; Lysias 1.32. Cf. Davidson 2007: Chapter 3 and Hubbard 2009: 5–6; MacDowell 2000: 15–19; E. Cohen 2000: 159–67; Scanlon 2002: 212–14.

bidder, the right to collect (extort?) certain taxes, seeking to gather sums greater than their obligation to the state, and acting on information and through procedures developed in conjunction with the *Boulê*, the *polêtai*, the *tamias* of the stratiotic fund, and the controllers of the theoric fund, as appropriate.[11] Athens denied political office, at least theoretically,[12] not only to male prostitutes but also to various other persons perceived as excessively motivated by personal financial advantage (see chapter 3, pp. 89–92).

Two other laws actually offered protection for prostitutes at the pinnacle and at the nadir of sexual commerce. The prohibition of *proagôgeia* ("pandering") was especially important to courtesans in the highest rank of the profession (*tekhnê*), the free women popularly known as the "big earners" (*megalomisthoi*).[13] For them, a ban on pandering proffered security from the pimps who, in numerous other societies, have been a major source of sex-workers' oppression. The prohibition of *hybris* ("outrage"), for its part, offered a measure of human-rights protection for even the most vulnerable of whores, the brothel slaves, who were shielded, along with all other residents of Athens, from "gross abuse"—a commitment in a "slave society"[14] that was startling even to many of the free residents of Attika (and has been improperly dismissed as "incomprehensible" by many modern scholars).[15]

## *Prohibition of Pimping (Proagôgeia)*

In many historically attested societies, and in virtually all contemporary communities, the sale of sex has been largely a phenomenon in which

---

11. On "tax farming" at Athens, see Aristot. *Ath. Pol.* 47.2; Andok. 1.73, 133–36; Aristoph. *Sphêk.* 657–59. Cf. Faraguna 2010; Migeotte 2014: 89–102, 2001; Stroud 1998: (esp.) 27–30.

12. For the nuances of partial, potential, and full *atimia* for meretricious and other offenses, see Gagliardi 2005; Fox 1994: 149–51; Wallace 1998; Paoli [1930] 1974: esp. 328–34; Hansen 1976: 55–98. Cf. Wout 2011.

13. *Megalomisthoi*: "the wealthy, famous hetaeras of the law courts and the comic stage" (McClure 2003b: 48). Cf. this chapter, n. 39.

14. For Athens as a "slave economy," see introduction, n. 7. The Athenians believed that the servile population of Attika exceeded that of the free (Isager and Hansen 1975: 16–17). Canfora claims that "according to even the most conservative estimates, there were four slaves for every freeborn Athenian" (1995: 124). In fact, estimates vary widely as to both the total population of Attika and its composition. See introduction, n. 51. Cf. Hyper. Fr. 33; Ath. 272C-D; Xen. *Por.* 4.4, 25, 28.

15. For astonishment, ancient and modern, over the protection of slaves by the *graphê hybreôs*, see nn. 50 and 51, with corresponding text.

female prostitutes, working for men, service male customers—a pattern conforming to the general domination of commerce by men.[16] But at Athens unenslaved prostitutes seem to have been free of outside interference in their sale of sex, and women appear generally to have controlled meretricious businesses (see the section "Women as Merchants of Sex" in chapter 6). In fact, Athenian law imposed the "harshest penalties" (*megista epitimia*, a euphemism at Athens for the death penalty) on anyone who engaged in *proagôgeia* (pimping, prostituting, procuring, pandering) involving the sexual services of a "free youth or free woman."[17]

*Proagôgeia* was a word of protean significations—ranging from pimping to "matchmaking" to outright control of a sexual enterprise. It appears not rarely in classical Greek literature, and in every occurrence "signifies procuring for sexual purposes" (Glazebrook 2006a: 40)—but in varied contexts dealing with the provision of *hetairai*, women and boys.[18] Accordingly, this statute offered a basis for criminal prosecution of anyone who dared to involve himself or herself in *any* aspect of the commercial provision of sex by free women or free youths—other than the self-employment of offering one's own body for sale.

---

16. However, male control of prostitutional enterprises has been far from universal: in a number of postclassical societies, women have controlled, and benefited from, management of prostitutional enterprises. See, for example, Henriot 2001: 238–39 (nineteenth-century China); Corbin 1998: 174–81 (nineteenth-century France); Lentakis 1998: 3.109–110 (Byzantion—contra Leontsini 1989: 169). For the dominance of female entrepreneurs in prostitutional businesses in twenty-first-century Manhattan, see *New York Times*: October 12, 2004.

17. Aiskhin. 1.14: καὶ τίνα ἕτερον νόμον ἔθηκε φύλακα τῶν ὑμετέρων παίδων; τὸν τῆς προαγωγείας, τὰ μέγιστα ἐπιτίμια ἐπιγράψας, ἐάν τις ἐλεύθερον παῖδα ἢ γυναῖκα προαγωγεύῃ. *Megista epitimia* is invoked by Aiskhinês as a fixed penalty but is probably only the orator's interpretation of a statute providing for a procedure (*agôn timêtos*) where the penalty, set by the *dikasts* if they found the defendant guilty, might be execution. (Cf. Aiskhin. 1.184: καὶ τὰς προαγωγοὺς καὶ τοὺς προαγωγοὺς γράφεσθαι κελεύει, κἂν ἁλῶσι, θανάτῳ ζημιοῦν.) But Plutarch reports only a 20 *drachma* penalty for *proagôgeia*: see n. 21.

Because ancient Greek (like English) permits a preceding adjective to refer to either the first or both of two following nouns—with the exact meaning determined by context—some translators of Aiskhin. 1.14 have rendered the Greek text literally as precluding the "proagôgeia" of any woman, including presumably enslaved females (for example, Martin and Budé 1927: I, 25: "un enfant libre ou une femme."). But social and economic context argues strongly that the ban could apply only to free women: slaves were the chattels of their masters. Plutarch understood the protection as applying only to free women (Solôn 1.23), as have most translators (e.g., Adams 1919: 14: "a free-born child or a free-born woman"; Fisher 2001: 74: "free woman or boy.")

18. LSJ definition: to prostitute, to pander. Citations relevant to classical Greece: Xen. *Symp.* 4.62; Aristoph. *Neph.* 980; Diog. Laert. 10.4.7; Athên. 443a, 605c, Epit. 2.2.41; Plut. *Erôt.* 759f9, *Symp. Probl.* 693c9. Its use in Xen. *Symp.* 4.62–64 and in Plato *Theait.* 149–50 is discussed below.

For Aristotle, *proagôgeia* was inherently coercive, akin to *moikheia*. In the *Nicomachean Ethics*, he groups it with other wrongdoing imposed on victims involuntarily: murder by treachery, theft, false adversarial testimony, sexual violation of another man's female relatives (*moikheia*), poisoning, preying on slaves, *proagôgeia*.[19] Likewise for Plutarch, *proagôgeia* is grouped with *moikheia* (and with rape) as a clearly criminal exploitation of a victim. In his *Life of Solôn*, Plutarch notes that legislation attributed to Solôn[20] "permitted the one seizing an adulterer to kill the adulterer. But if someone seizes and forces a free woman, he set a fine of 100 drachmas. And if he procures (*proagôgeuêi*) her for prostitution, 20 drachmas."[21] Plutarch does report, however, that pandering *is* permitted in the case of streeters[22]—prostitutes who at Athens were the embodiment of servile meretricious commerce, sharply distinguished from the *megalomisthoi*, the "courtesans" who incarnate the Athenian conceptualization of free labor ("Selling 'Free' Love," in chapter 2) and who are the prostitutes most likely to benefit from an effective prohibition of procuration. Plutarch's statement is confirmed by a passage in Lysias, who cites another law attributed to Solôn that similarly provided that a man could not be punished as a *moikhos* (a violator of another male's female relatives[23]) if he had had relations with a woman who "sat in a brothel or walked about openly," that is, worked as a

---

19. 1131a2–8: τῶν γὰρ συυναλλαγμάτων τὰ μὲν ἑκούσιά ἐστι τὰ δ' ἀκούσια . . . τῶν δ' ἀκουσίων τὰ μὲν λαθραῖα, οἷον κλοπὴ μοιχεία φαρμακεία προαγωγεία δουλαπατία δολοφονία ψευδομαρτυρία, τὰ δὲ βίαια, οἷον αἰκία κ.τ.λ. Ancient usage of *moikheia* likewise tends to be inexact, generating considerable dispute among modern scholars: see n. 23, this chapter.

20. Although modern scholarship has established that Athenians of the fourth century tended to assign to "Solôn" all laws of indeterminate origin (Fox 1994: 150; MacDowell 2000: 21), Plutarch assumed that the legislation against *proagôgeia* was factually attributable to Solôn.

21. Translation: Glazebrook 2006a: 41. Text: 23.1: Ὅλως δὲ πλείστην ἔχειν ἀτοπίαν οἱ περὶ τῶν γυναικῶν νόμοι τῷ Σόλωνι δοκοῦσι. Μοιχὸν μὲν γὰρ ἀνελεῖν τῷ λαβόντι δέδωκεν· ἐὰν δ' ἁρπάσῃ τις ἐλευθέραν γυναῖκα καὶ βιάσηται, ζημίαν ἑκατὸν δραχμὰς ἔταξε· κἂν προαγωγεύῃ, δραχμὰς εἴκοσι, πλὴν ὅσαι πεφασμένως πωλοῦνται, λέγων δὴ τὰς ἑταίρας. Αὗται γὰρ ἐμφανῶς φοιτῶσι πρὸς τοὺς διδόντας . . . Harrison (1968: 37) explicitly relates Plutarch 23.1 to the Athenian law against procurement, as does Maffi 1984.

22. No pandering πλὴν ὅσαι πεφασμένως πωλοῦνται, λέγων δὴ τὰς ἑταίρας. Αὗται γὰρ ἐμφανῶς φοιτῶσι πρὸς τοὺς διδόντας . . . (23.1). No pandering "except for those who blatantly sell themselves, meaning, to be sure, the *hetairai*. For these women openly are trolling the streets for those who will pay (them), literally 'those giving.'" For Plutarch's conflation of terms for sex-workers (streetwalkers, *hetairai*) a recurring phenomenon in Greek usage, see chapter 1, pp. 34–35.

23. As to the persons protected by legislation against *moikheia*, see Glazebrook and Olson 2014: 72; Cantarella 2005: 240–41, 1991; Foxhall 1991; D. Cohen 1991b: 98–132.

streetwalker, "a calling appropriate to slaves."²⁴ Many female prostitutes *did* work the streets, sometimes in the guise of "musical entertainers": officials responsible for the city's roads (the *astynomoi*) were specifically charged with averting the violence that might arise from customers' competition in public thoroughfares for the music accompaniment (and possible ancillary sexual services) of female players of harps, pipes, and lyres.²⁵

In Athenian juridical contexts, imprecise usage of the term *proagôgeia* was not anomalous.²⁶ At Athens "there was relatively little technical legal vocabulary and the language of the street was itself the language of the law."²⁷ Everyday words, however, often have multiple, and sometimes even inconsistent, meanings determined by context. But context is almost always absent from the texts of laws. In the Athenian legal system, where critical terms were not given definition by code or through judicial precedent, and in which inexact criminal prohibitions were not annullable as "unconstitutionally vague," each court case necessarily evoked a fresh determination of precisely what kind of behavior had been outlawed.²⁸ In this ambience, the very uncertainty of legal definition and the resultant unpredictability of judicial decision itself served as an "effective means of social control,"²⁹ dissuading persons from engaging in behavior that

---

24. Dem. 59.67: τὸν τε νόμον . . . ὃς οὐκ ἐᾶι ἐπὶ ταύτηισι μοιχὸν λαβεῖν ὁπόσαι ἂν ἐπ' ἐργαστηρίου καθῶνται ἢ πωλῶνται ἀποπεφασμένως . . . which is ἡ τῶν πορνῶν ἐργασία (59.113). Lysias (10.19) explains the somewhat archaic wording of this statute: τὸ μὲν πεφασμένως ἐστὶ φανερῶς, πολεῖσθαι δὲ βαδίζειν. See Kapparis 1999: 311–13; Scafuro 1997: 112.

25. Not all street musicians were involved in commercial sex. See chapter 7, pp. 163–64.

26. Variation in usage has resulted, on occasion, in error in translation. Glazebrooke (2006a: 40–41) notes that earlier translators of *proagôgeia* in Plutarch *Solôn* 23.1 tended to (mis)translate the term "as an act of persuasion or seduction," an interpretation contradictory to the other testimonia in which *proagôgeia* appears, illogical in the present context ("with such a translation it is unclear then how the μοιχός differs from the seducer"), and inconsistent with Lysias 1.29 and 1.32 (see Cole 1984: 102). McGinn 2014: 86–87 nonetheless persists in reading *proagôgeia* as "persuasion or seduction."

27. Millett and Todd 1990: 17. Perusal of Todd's Lexicon (appended to Cartledge, Millett and Todd 1990 and to Todd 1993) suggests that this comment is somewhat overstated: Athenian law may have lacked special vocabulary for criminal offenses, but it had developed many technical terms for procedural matters.

28. The entire case against Timarkhos (Aiskhinês 1), for example, depends on interpreting the term *hetairein*, i.e., defining "prostitution"—a word whose definition has generated decades of unresolved academic dispute (see chapter 1, pp. 31–36 chapter 3, pp. 82–83). "Precedent" had little influence at Athens, where panels of hundreds of jurors issued no opinions explaining their decisions, and even the verdicts in cases were not recorded (Lanni 2004: 164 and Gagarin 2008: 195, pace Harris 2013b: 248–49 and 2013c).

29. Cf. Lanni 2006: 115–16; MacCormick 1994: 60.

even conceivably might be confused with the conduct clearly falling within popular conception of the forbidden activity.

The chilling effect of this statute on individual behavior is suggested by Sôkratês's allusion, in Plato's *Theaitêtos*, to midwives' fear of being charged with *proagôgeia*. Claiming to be a midwife (*maia*) (149a1–4)—in the metaphorical role of helping to give birth to an understanding of "knowledge" (*epistêmê*)—Sôkratês insists that midwives, because of their life experience, are best suited to bring together men and women who would make fine parents. "But they flee from this matchmaking (*promnêstikê*) because they're fearful of being charged with that wrongful and unprofessional bringing-together of man and woman which goes by the name of *proagôgeia*."[30]

*Promnêstikê* was not the only activity that might be conflated with *proagôgeia*. In Xenophôn's *Symposion*, Sôkratês equates *proagôgeia* with *mastropeia*. Here Sôkratês claims to be not a midwife but a *mastropos* (3.10)—one who fashions those under his/her control into attractive seducers of customers, teaching his/her charges the enticing sexual skills useful for pleasing clients (4.57–59). But after conducting a detailed analysis of the traits required of a fine *mastropos* (4.56–61), Sôkratês identifies not himself but another participant in the *symposion* (Antisthenês) as surpassingly manifesting these characteristics of the good *mastropos*—which, Sôkratês claims, explains why Antisthenês is an excellent *PROAGÔGOS*![31] Sôkratês does know that the two activities are not absolutely indistinguishable, for he calls *proagôgeia* the "complementary profession" of *mastropeia*: *proagôgeia* is a skilled calling (*tekhnê*) requiring the ability to identify and bring together clients and servicers who would share a mutual attraction and be good for one other.[32] This Antisthenês has done. He has worked successfully in introducing the sophist Prodikos to the wealthy Kallias (after identifying Kallias as yearning for "knowledge" [*philosophia*] and Prodikos as needing money) (4.62).

---

30. 150a1–4: διὰ τὴν ἄδικόν τε καὶ ἄτεχνον συναγωγὴν ἀνδρὸς καὶ γυναικός, ᾗ δὴ προαγωγία ὄνομα, φεύγουσι καὶ τὴν προμνηστικὴν ἅτε σεμναὶ οὖσαι αἱ μαῖαι, φοβούμεναι μὴ εἰς ἐκείνην τὴν αἰτίαν διὰ ταύτην ἐμπέσωσιν· ἐπὶ ταῖς γε ὄντως μαίαις μόναις που προσήκει καὶ προμνήσασθαι ὀρθῶς.

31. 4.64: ταῦτα ὁρῶν δυνάμενόν σε ποιεῖν ἀγαθὸν νομίζω προαγωγὸν εἶναι.

32. ἀγαθὸς προαγωγός: ὁ γὰρ οἷος τε ὢν γιγνώσκειν τε τοὺς ὠφελίμους αὐτοῖς καὶ τούτους δυνάμενος ποιεῖν ἐπιθυμεῖν ἀλλήλων, οὗτος ἄν μοι δοκεῖ . . . πολλοῦ ἂν ἄξιος εἶναι . . . . (4.64). Complementary *tekhnê*: τὴν (τέχνην) ἀκόλουθον ταύτης (4.61).

Antisthenês had also successfully linked Kallias with Hippias of Elis, and had introduced Sôkratês himself to Aiskhylos the Phleiasian and to Zeuxippos of Hêraklea—arousing in Sôkratês enormous passion (and great gratitude to Antisthenês). A *proagôgos* of skill, writes Xenophôn, could make a lot of money—as could a good *mastropos*.³³ But a defendant charged with *proagôgeia* might have had a difficult time separating the two "complementary professions" by establishing that he was in fact teaching the sexual skills that would bring a client and prostitute together (that is, being a *mastropos*) and not functioning as a mere "go-between" (*proagôgos*).

Testifying further to the elasticity of the term *proagôgeia*, Aiskhinês cites the statute against *proagôgeia* in his case against Timarkhos—despite the absence of any contention that the defendant has been acting on behalf of anyone else. But the case against Timarkhos involves prostitution (Timarkhos is charged with years of political activity after years of male prostitution), and the statute is cited in Aiskhinês's narration of various laws dealing with the sale of sex.³⁴ Its relevance is vaguely suggested within the pervasive thought that Timarkhos had "done it to himself"³⁵—although, as Sôkratês claims, the essence of *proagôgeia* is a bringing-together (*synagôgê*) of others. But the language of the law, the language of the street, seems not to have known such fine distinctions—as least when interpreted by a skilled rhetorical wordsmith like Aiskhinês.³⁶ Similarly, a flirtatious youth in Aristophanês's *Clouds* is described as "walking around (*proagôgeuôn*) for himself with his eyes," that is, persuasively inviting

---

33. *Mastropos*: καὶ πάνυ ἂν πολλὰ χρήματα λαμβάνοιμι, εἰ βουλοίμην χρῆσθαι τῇ τέχνῃ (3.10). *Proagôgos*: ἐὰν γὰρ (ἔφη) ταῦτα δύνωμαι, σεσαγμένος δὴ πανητάπασι πλούτου τὴν ψυχὴν ἔσομαι (4.64). Cf. 4.60.

34. Aiskhinês's references to Athenian laws are often problematic. He sometimes purports to be quoting the text of laws verbatim when he is in fact selectively (and sometimes misleadingly) paraphrasing the actual content of the statute. Cf. Fisher 2001: 125; Ford 1999: 242. Furthermore, the manuscripts of Aiskhinês offer paleographical difficulties: they often contain the purported text of laws that Aiskhinês has cited, but these addenda are generally dismissed as illegitimate appendages composed in later antiquity. See MacDowell 1990: 43–47; Harris 1992b: 71–77. But Aiskhines's reference to the statute against *proagôgeia* is straightforward: he does not purport to quote the actual text of the law, nor is purported original language attached to his citation.

35. See, for example, Aiskhin. 1.185–187 (§185: τῷ δὲ παρὰ φύσιν ἑαυτὸν ὑβρίσαντι).

36. Περιττὸς ἐν τοῖς λόγοις (Aiskhin. 1.119, applied to Demosthenes).

sexual attention and at the same time "procuring for himself" in a meretricious way—"streetwalking" being a common manifestation of Athenian prostitution.[37]

The presumed deterrent effect of imprecise interdiction is a familiar feature of contemporary American law. The US Securities and Exchange Commission (SEC), for example, systematically avoids clear and specific descriptions of prohibited behavior, seeking to deny "safe harbor" to persons seeking to devise lawful methods of access to activities proscribed by the Commission.[38] By banning *proagôgeia*, an inexact noun of broad applicability, Athenian law provided maximum protection for free women and free youth in their practice of prostitution. This safeguard appears to have been effective: wealthy female prostitutes were almost invariably free persons.[39] Third-party control of a prostitute's life, and revenues, was effectively lawful only for enslaved women, enslaved youth, and mature free men. But Athenian *philanthrôpia* did not ignore even these victims of coercive exploitation—who were included in the all-encompassing provisions of the law forbidding "outrageous" victimization (the *graphê hybreos*).

## *Protecting Slaves from "Outrageous" Victimization (*Hybris*)*

A fundamental Athenian law purported to protect every inhabitant of Attika—"whether a child or a woman or a man, whether free or slave"— from outrageous abuse (*hybris*). Under a statute preserved in the text of Demosthenes, Athenian law authorized a prosecution for *hybris* "whenever someone intentionally insults the honor (*hybrizei*) of another, whether a child or a woman or a man, whether free or slave, or does something

---

37. 979–80: οὐδ' ἂν μαλακὴν φυρασάμενος τὴν φωνὴν πρὸς τὸν ἐραστὴν | αὐτὸς ἑαυτὸν προαγωγεύων τοῖν ὀφθαλμοῖν ἐβάδιζεν. Cf. Aristoph. *Sphêk.* 1028, *Batr.* 1079, *Thes.* 341. On the equation of "walking" and "whoring," see this chapter, pp. 120–21.

38. For example, by failing to offer a technical definition of "security," the SEC has left unresolved the potential need for provision of detailed offering materials for the sale of Tenant-in-Common interests under the Tax-Deferred Exchange section (§1031) of the US Federal Tax Code. Cf. the continuing absence of a "safe harbor" definition for "insider trading."

39. "Unter der Gruppe der renommierten Hetären, die als Spitzenverdienerinnen galten (*megalomisthoi*) (Athênaios 570b; 558a–e), waren Sklavinnen kaum anzutreffen" (Klees 1998: 147, n. 16). Cf. Lentakis 1999: 146, 165.

improper (*paranomon*) against any such person."⁴⁰ Aiskhinês cites the legislation in language virtually identical with that of Demosthenes.⁴¹ Hypereidês notes the law's explicit protection of slaves from bodily abuse,⁴² and Demosthenes praises the "humane benevolence" (*philanthrôpia*) of the Athenians in forbidding the subjection of slaves to *hybris*.⁴³ This prohibition is so well-attested that there is "general agreement (that) we possess the actual text of the law as it stood in the fourth century" (Fisher 1992: 36), the "genuine law" (MacDowell 1990: 263).⁴⁴

But the behavior actually banned by this legislation is uncertain, for the law contained no definition of *hybris*,⁴⁵ prohibiting instead everything encompassed by a common word having multiple and contradictory significations changing with everyday context. The term *hybris* could describe a broad scope of conduct ranging from mundane "human arrogance, overconfidence or unawareness of the reasons for one's own good fortune" through "behavior seriously injurious" (Fisher 1995: 45–46). However, the meaning of *hybris* in any specific legal context would depend on a decision maker's conclusion in that particular matter. Not surprisingly, scholarly

---

40. 21.47: Ἐάν τις ὑβρίζῃ εἴς τινα, ἢ παῖδα ἢ γυναῖκα ἢ ἄνδρα, τῶν ἐλευθέρων ἢ τῶν δούλων, ἢ παράνομόν τι ποιήσῃ εἰς τούτων τινά . . .

41. Aiskhin. 1.15: Ἐάν τις ὑβρίζῃ εἰς παῖδα (ὑβρίζει δὲ δή που ὁ μισθούμενος) ἢ ἄνδρα ἢ γυναῖκα, ἢ τῶν ἐλευθέρων τινὰ ἢ τῶν δούλων, ἢ ἐὰν παράνομόν τι ποιῇ εἰς τούτων τινά γραφὰς ὕβρεως εἶναι πεποίηκεν. . . . The text of the "law" preserved at Aiskh. 1.16 is patently a forgery: MacDowell 1990: 263–64.

42. Frag. *Mantitheos*: ἔθεσαν οὐ μόνον ὑπὲρ τῶν ἐλευθέρων, ἀλλὰ καὶ ἐάν τις εἰς δούλου σῶμα ὑβρίσῃ, γραφὰς εἶναι κατὰ τοῦ ὑβρίσαντος.

43. 21.48–49: τοῦ νόμου τῆς φιλανθρωπίας, ὃς οὐδὲ τοὺς δούλους ὑβρίζεσθαι ἀξιοῖ . . . . ΄εἰσὶν Ἕλληνές τινες ἄνθρωποι οὕτως ἥμεροι καὶ φιλάνθρωποι τοὺς τρόπους ὥστε . . . οὐδ᾽ ὅσων ἂν τιμὴν καταθέντες δούλους κτήσωνται, οὐδὲ τούτους ὑβρίζειν ἀξιοῦσιν. . . . ΄

44. Harris, appropriating the arguments of Drerup (1898: 297–300), asserts that the text of the law at Dem. 21.47 is a "fake" (1992b: 77; cf. Harris 2008, 2013d: 224–31)—a position that has not won general acceptance (see Fisher 2001: 139–40; Carey 1998; van Wees 2011). Harris's main contention is that the law treats ἢ παράνομόν τι ποιήσῃ εἰς τούτων τινά as "covering every imaginable crime." That clause, however, does nothing more than to ensure that any illegal action taken against a slave (and others)—even in the presence or absence of other relief—is actionable pursuant to the special severities of the *graphê hybreôs*. Harris overlooks the presence of the same clause at Dem. 43.75 (ἐὰν δέ τις ὑβρίζῃ ἢ ποιῇ τι παράνομον)—elaborated upon in 43.77–78 (ὑβριστής, παρανομώτεροι). Finally Harris assumes that Athenian law aimed for exactitude and specificity in the drafting of criminal charges rather than for the deterrence and elasticity inherent in generalized prohibitions subject to interpretation in each individual case.

45. Aiskhinês specifically notes that the statute "summarized all these offenses in a single (term)": τὸν (νόμον) τῆς ὕβρεως, ὃς ἑνὶ κεφαλαίῳ πάντα τὰ τοιαῦτα συλλαβὼν ἔχει (1.15).

efforts to identify a core concept underlying or unifying the various notations of *hybris* have yielded only prolonged scholarly disputation—despite the profusion of surviving evidence. The standard work on *hybris* (Fisher 1992) runs 526 pages and considers hundreds of detailed yet elusive testimonia. Ruschenbusch (1965), for example, sees *hybris* as inclusively covering all offenses against an individual. MacDowell and Cairns insist on arrogance as the defining characteristic of *hybris*.[46] Fisher identifies *hybris* as "the deliberate infliction of serious insult on another human being."[47] Gagarin, in contrast, finds *hybris* distinguished by the use of inordinate force or violence (1979: 232). Others offer still other opinions.[48] *Tot homines, quot sententiae*. Prohibition of behavior so difficult to identify precludes reasonable anticipation of the situations to which the proscription might or would apply.

But because of modern scholarly perception of Athens as a society in which slaves had absolutely no rights (other than perhaps the right not to be murdered),[49] the statute's "plain meaning"—its extension of protection to slaves (and thus even to unfree brothel prostitutes)—has tended to be disregarded, or even arbitrarily dismissed as "incoherent" or theoretically impossible.[50] Even those scholars who do acknowledge the law's explicit statement of protection for slaves and other dependents often assume the provision to have been meaningless in actual practice.[51] Yet Athenian legal protection for persons of inferior status or situation was far from theoretical. Demosthenes notes that harsh punishment had actually been meted out, pursuant to the law against *hybris*, in many cases involving victimization of slaves.[52] Deinarchos reports that at the Eleusinian festival the Athenian *politês* Themistios had been put to death for *hybris* against

---

46. MacDowell 1976, 1978: 129–32; Cairns 1996.

47. 1995: 45. Cf. Fisher 1992: 36–82, 1990: 126.

48. For various other interpretations, see Cairns 1996; Fisher 1992: 2–5.

49. Antiph. 5.47, 6.4. Cf. Isok. 18.52, Dem. 59.9. See Rihll 2011: 49; Harrison 1968: 171–72; Klees 1998: 176–217.

50. The enshrinement of slaves' rights, for example, leaves distinguished scholars grasping (unsuccessfully) for words: "Such a law would have had to envisage a situation involving the treatment of free men as if they were slaves, or citizens as if they were foreigners, or slaves (who are specifically mentioned as within the scope of the law) as if they were—what?" (Murray 1990: 140). "Incoherent": Gernet 1917: 183–97. Cf. Fisher 1992: 59 ff.

51. Todd 1993: 189: "When Demosthenes tells us that it was possible to commit *hybris* against a slave ... we should be careful to place a minimalist interpretation on his words."

52. Dem. 21.48–49: Ἀκούετ', ὦ ἄνδρες Ἀθηναῖοι, τοῦ νόμου τῆς φιλανθρωπίας, ὃς οὐδὲ τοὺς δούλους ὑβρίζεσθαι ἀξιοῖ . . . καὶ πολλοὺς ἤδη παραβάντας τὸν νόμον τοῦτον ἐζημιώκασιν

a Rhodian lyre-girl,[53] and that a certain Euthymakhos was executed for forcing an Olynthian slave woman into a brothel.[54] Legal actions also appear to have been brought over the hybristic treatment of another enslaved Olynthian woman by Athenians at a Macedonian symposium after Philip's destruction of Olynthos,[55] although "we do not know enough about these cases to know in what circumstances they did, or might, reach the courts" (Fisher 1995: 69–70). To mitigate the lengthy legal delays endemic within the Athenian court system,[56] actions charging *hybris* had to be heard within thirty days after the day on which the charges were first brought[57]—a virtually unique acceleration of process.[58] Should the prosecutor prevail, there was to be an immediate determination of penalties.[59] Upon conviction, an offender was held in prison until payment of any fine that had been assessed[60]—an extraordinary remedy in a system where private litigants generally had to enforce court judgments without official assistance[61] and

---

θανάτῳ. The Athenians expressed (feigned?) astonishment at their humane protection of even slaves through the law against *hybris*: see Aiskhin. 1.17; Dem. 21.47–49; Hyper. and Lykurg. cited at Athên. 266e–267a.

53. Dein. 1.23: Θεμίστιον δὲ τὸν Ἀφιδναῖον, διότι τὴν Ῥοδίαν κιθαρίστριαν ὕβρισεν Ἐλευσινίοις, θανάτῳ ἐζημιώσατε. . . . Cf. Worthington 1992: 169. Demosthenes mentions by name a number of other persons executed for misdeeds at such religious gatherings (21.175–181).

54. Dein. 1.23: Εὐθύμαχον δέ < θανάτῳ ἐζημιώσατε > διότι τὴν Ὀλυνθίαν παιδίσκην ἔστησεν ἐπ' οἰκήματος.

55. Dem. 19.196–98; Aiskhin. 2.4, 153–55.

56. For the systemic prevalence and causes of protracted and postponed litigation, see E. Cohen 1973: 10–12; Charles 1938: 9–10.

57. Dem. 21.47. In practice—as anticipated by the statute—state considerations could still sometimes delay prompt resolution of the charges: Dem. 45.4.

58. MacDowell 1990: 266–67 refutes Hansen's claim (1981: 167–70) that requirement of trial within thirty days was not uncommon: no other provision for εἰσαγωγὴ τριάκοντα ἡμερῶν is known at Athens (although we do know of "thirty-day cases" [τριακοσταῖαι δίκαι] from Naupaktos [Meiggs/Lewis 1969: 35–37, #20] and from Hêraklea [Dareste 1892–1904 (1965) I, 194 ff., face II, ll. 26–27]). Cf. Gofas 1979: 180, n. 21. For the δίκαι ἔμμηνοι at Athens, see Lanni 2006: 155; E. Cohen 1973: 23–26; Vélissaropoulos 1980: 242–45.

59. Dem. 21.47: ὅτου δ' ἂν καταγνῷ ἡ ἡλιαία, τιμάτω περὶ αὐτοῦ παραχρῆμα, ὅτου ἂν δοκῇ ἄξιος εἶναι παθεῖν ἢ ἀποτεῖσαι.

60. Dem. 21.47: ἐὰν δὲ ἀργυρίου τιμηθῇ τῆς ὕβρεως, δεδέσθω ἐὰν ἐλεύθερον ὑβρίσῃ, μέχρι ἂν ἐκτείσῃ. Imprisonment thus was not automatically available in cases of transgressions against slaves.

61. See Todd 1993: 144–45; Allen 1997: 34 (contra Harris 2013: 13–14, 50–58). In the case of *hybris*, the fine was paid to the state, not to the victim or prosecutor, thereby giving the *polis* a direct financial interest in extracting payment. See Dem. 21.45.

where even debts owed to the state often were allowed to languish for months before obligors—subject to no restraint—fled.[62]

To avoid the chimera of a protection not practically available to those unable personally to vindicate their rights against a more powerful abuser, prosecution for *hybris* could be pursued by any Athenian *politês*[63]—in contrast to the usual requirement in a private action (*dikê*) of suit by the victim directly or through his or her male representative (*kyrios*).[64] Although Harrison, for example, considers that there was not even a "slender chance" that any outsider would actually prosecute an alleged act of *hybris* by a master against his slave,[65] even our sparse knowledge of actual Athenian litigation provides numerous examples of third parties instituting actions on behalf of women, children, and other dependents. Athenian values encompassed a strong ideological commitment to aid unrelated persons who might be victimized. Solôn reportedly considered the ideal state to be one in which otherwise uninvolved persons came to the aid of those being wronged: a key element in the legislation attributed to him was authorization for volunteers to act on behalf of unrelated victims.[66] Periklês's enunciation of Athenian values in the Funeral Address includes praise of the Athenians' penchant for legally aiding persons being victimized.[67] Even where wrongdoing involved only allegation of financial mismanagement, third parties are known to have come to the victims' defense. In Demosthenes 38, under a statute permitting any willing person to intervene, a certain Nikidas, not otherwise involved, denounced a guardian for

---

62. For the rarity of imprisonment as a procedural or punitive process at Athens, see E. Cohen 1973: 74–83; MacDowell 1990: 268; Hunter 1997. For a variant interpretation, see Allen 1997. On the state's laxity even in situations involving public debtors, note the famous case of Demosthenes's father-in-law, Gylôn (Dem. 28.1–3, Aiskh. 3.171; Davies 1971: 121).

63. Dem. 21.47: γραφέσθω πρὸς τοὺς θεσμοθέτας ὁ βουλόμενος Ἀθηναίων οἷς ἔξεστιν. Some potential cases, however, may have been discouraged by the absence of monetary incentive for a voluntary prosecutor (ὁ βουλόμενος) and by the requirement (see Lipsius [1905–15] 1966: 243–44; Harrison 1968: 195 n. 1) that the prosecutor be an Athenian citizen. For *graphai* open also to prosecution by non-Athenians, see Dem. 59.66 (Epainetos "certainly a foreigner" [Carey 1992: 121]); 59.16; 21.175; 24.105; possibly 59.52.

64. See chapter 4, pp. 108–10.

65. 1968: 172. Cf. Humphreys 1993: 5.

66. τὸ ἐξεῖναι τῷ βουλομένῳ τιμωρεῖν ὑπὲρ τῶν ἀδικουμένων (Aristot. *Ath. Pol.* 9.4). See Plut. *Sol.* 18.3–8; Pl. *Rep.* 462d.

67. οὐ παρανομοῦμεν . . . ἀκροάσει καὶ τῶν νόμων, καὶ μάλιστα αὐτῶν ὅσοι τε ἐπ᾽ ὠφελίᾳ τῶν ἀδικουμένων κεῖνται . . . . (Thouk. 2.37.3).

mismanagement of an estate intended to benefit minor children.[68] When Neaira, an ex-slave staying in Megara, had been subjected to *hybris* by the Athenian *politês* Phryniôn (who claimed to be her master), she sought assistance from the Athenian *politês* Stephanos, whom she had only recently met. He responded to her appeal—for Stephanos the beginning of substantial litigation on her behalf, including defense of her freedom against Phryniôn.[69] Similarly the public slave Pittalakos was able to call on the influential *politês* Glaukôn to vindicate his legal rights against harassment by the prominent Hêgêsandros.[70]

The law against *hybris* clearly affected many aspects of Athenian behavior. Yet its prime impact was felt in sexual context, for eroticized misconduct was a fundamental and frequent manifestation of *hybris*. Of approximately 500 occurrences of *hybris* or its cognates in the principal surviving Athenian prose authors, 82 incidents relate to sexual misconduct—more cases by far than of any other typology.[71] Even an ex-slave's marital bedding of his former mistress generated an action for *hybris* (Demosthenes 45.4). Rape is repeatedly denominated as *hybris*.[72] In fact Aristotle specifically warns rulers that of the various manifestations of *hybris*, sexual abuse of boys and girls and physical violation of individuals are most to be avoided.[73]

But how could one commit *hybris* against a brothel slave? Prostitution was lawful; owners could require slaves to work at such tasks as were assigned.[74] Yet the law against *hybris* could easily be interpreted as

---

68. §23: For *phasis* as a procedure against κάκωσις οἴκου ὀρφανικοῦ, see Harpokr., s.v. φάσις; Aristot. *Ath. Pol.* 56.6.

69. Dem. 59.37–40. The effect on Neaira's *persona* of dependence on male juridical mediation is discussed with considerable insight at Johnstone 1998: 232–33.

70. Aiskhin. 1.62: σκέψασθε μεγάλην ῥώμην Ἡγησάνδρου· ἄνθρωπον . . . ἦγεν εἰς δουλείαν φάσκων ἑαυτοῦ εἶναι. Ἐν παντὶ δὲ κακοῦ γενόμενος ὁ Πιττάλακος προσπίπτει ἀνδρὶ καὶ μάλα χρηστῷ. Ἔστι τις Γλαύκων Χολαργεύς· οὗτος αὐτὸν ἀφαιρεῖται εἰς ἐλευθερίαν.

71. Even physical assault against free persons is reported less frequently. See D. Cohen 1991a: 172–73; MacDowell 1976; Fisher 1976, 1979.

72. See D. Cohen 1991a: 175; Doblhofer 1994, passim; Dover [1978] 1989: 36.

73. *Pol.* 1315a14-16: ἔτι δὲ πάσης μὲν ὕβρεως εἴργεσθαι, παρὰ πάσας δὲ δυεῖν, τῆς τε εἰς τὰ σώματα [κολάσεως] καὶ τῆς εἰς τὴν ἡλικίαν. . . . μὴ χρῆσθαι δεῖ τοῖς τοιούτοις, ἢ . . . φαίνεσθαι ποιούμενον . . . τὰς δὲ πρὸς τὴν ἡλικίαν ὁμιλίας δι' ἐρωτικὰς αἰτίας, ἀλλὰ μὴ δι' ἐξουσίαν.

74. A slave was required to work as his master directed. See Garlan 1988: 60–73; Klees 1998: 109–116. Hence, the master's choice of profession largely determined the slave's future opportunities: οἶμαι γὰρ ἅπαντας ὑμᾶς εἰδέναι, ὅτι τούτον, ἡνίκ' ὤνιος ἦν, εἰ συνέβη μάγειρον ἢ τινος ἄλλης τέχνης δημιουργὸν πρίασθαι, τὴν τοῦ δεσπότου τέχνην ἂν μαθὼν πόρρω τῶν

forbidding outrageous (mis)treatment of even a slave prostitute in his or her sexual labors: the statute was understood to forbid *hybris* "against the body of a slave."[75] Thus Neaira, allegedly a foreign whore born into slavery, charged the Athenian *politês* Phryniôn with *hybris* for forcing her to have sexual intercourse in public places.[76] In homoerotic situations, charges of *hybris* likewise arose from grossly abusive behavior. The public slave Pittalakos brands as *hybris* the actions of the well-connected Athenian *politai* Hêgesandros and Timarchos, who, as the dénouement of a sexual triangle, had sadistically tied Pittalakos to a column and whipped him during a nocturnal revel.[77] The linguistic anarchy inherent in the conceptualization of *hybris* explains the exaggerated conclusion of Montuori—from the varied evidence of Aiskhinês 1—that a charge of *hybris* could be brought against anyone who prostituted a male slave (1976: 12–14). Of course, not every possible accusation would have been made, and a conviction (or other success) would not have resulted from every accusation. Each individual court case involving *hybris* against slaves would have had to resolve anew the inherent conflict between the Athenian commitment to protecting the authority of a slaveowner and Athenian social concepts mandating protection for dependent persons, the *philanthrôpia* on which Athens prided itself.[78] But the law against *hybris might* have protected slave prostitutes in case of extreme abuse. The prevalence of prostitution in Athenian life and the absence of definition in Athenian law preclude any greater predictability.

---

νῦν παρόντων ἦν ἀγαθῶν. ἐπειδὴ δ' ὁ πατὴρ ὁ ἡμέτερος τραπεζίτης ὢν ἐκτήσατ' αὐτὸν . . . εὐδαίμων γέγονεν (Dem. 45.71–72).

75. ἐάν τις εἰς δούλου σῶμα ὑβρίσῃ, γραφὰς εἶναι κατὰ τοῦ ὑβρίσαντος (Hyper. Fr. *Mantitheos*).

76. Dem. 59.33–37: ἐκώμαζέ τ' ἀεὶ μετ' αὐτοῦ, συνῆν τ' ἐμφανῶς ὁπότε βουληθείη πανταχοῦ, φιλοτιμίαν τὴν ἐξουσίαν πρὸς τοὺς ὁρῶντας ποιούμενος. . . . διηγησαμένη πάντα τὰ πεπραγμένα καὶ τὴν ὕβριν τοῦ Φρυνίωνος . . . προΐσταται Στέφανον τουτονὶ αὑτῆς.

77. Although he had the support of *politai* who were prepared to act for him and who might have brought a public action for this *hybris*, the slave instead brought a private suit (*dikê*) on his own behalf against the two *politai*. (Aiskhin. 1.62: βαρέως δὲ φέρων τὴν ὕβριν αὐτῶν ὁ ἄνθρωπος, δίκην ἑκατέρῳ αὐτῶν λαγχάνει. In P. Hamb. 133, a freedwoman's suit against Zoilos for killing her child was later undertaken by her former master. Cf. P. Oxy. 13.1606 (Lys. Fr. 1 [Gernet & Bizos]) where Lysias (or a colleague) defends a *therapaina* who had been sued by Hippothersês for her role in the effort to reclaim property confiscated by the Thirty and sold to Hippothersês.

78. This tension is explored in detail in Fisher 1995.

# 6

## *Mothers and Daughters in a Family Business*

TRADITIONAL ATHENIAN CONCEPTS of manliness (*andreia*)[1] posited only farming as an occupation appropriate for a free man (see chapter 1, pp. 25–26). By relegating household operation and "slavish" business pursuits to foreigners, women, and slaves, this conceptualization of *andreia* tended to deprive Athenian men of economic opportunity and business experience—and contributed to women's control of significant aspects of the Athenian economy, including prostitution. In fact, disdain for commerce was so strong in certain male circles that there persisted in fourth-century Athens a conservative yearning for an earlier period when goods and services were provided, in le's words, "naturally" through the self-sufficiency of farm-based households,[2] not through the "monied mode of acquisition" (*khrêmatistikê ktêtikê*), a relatively recent phenomenon that separated production and exchange from manly "self-sufficiency" (*autarkeia*) and linked them to profit.[3] As mere generators of income

---

1. The prime and literal meaning of *andreia* (see LSJ) is "manliness," that is, "the quality or state of having characteristics suitable for a man" (the American Webster's dictionary definition of "masculinity"). However, extended and figurative uses of *andreia* are frequently encountered in ancient Greek. See E. Cohen 2003: 145.

2. Aristot. *Pol.* 1258a19–b8. "Naturally": κατὰ φύσιν (1258b1). Cf. 1256b10–22; *Rhet.* 1381a21–24; *Oik.* (attributed to Aristot.) 1343a25–b2. See Lewis 1991: 176–83. For the Aristotelian conceptualization of "nature" (φύσις) see Meikle 1995: 85–86, 123.

3. Aristot. *Pol.* 1258b 1–4, 1258a 10–14. Aristotle recognizes the introduction of coinage as the precondition to the development of retail trade (τὸ καπηλικόν), but explicitly differentiates an earlier, "simple" state of this trade from the profit-seeking, complex market activity existing in his own time (*Pol.* 1257b 1–5).

(rather than personally beneficial mechanisms of self-definition),[4] most business pursuits carried slight, if any, prestige (*philotimia*). According to Lykourgos and Hypereidês, real Athenian men had, from ancestral times, preferred a military-oriented and politically involved *andreia* to the acquisition of wealth (*ploutos*).[5] Every aspect of business activity—from selling sex to selling fish, from production or trading of goods to laboring for remuneration—was seen as incompatible with an idealized true masculinity. Consequently, engagement in such "banausic" activities was a barrier to citizenship in many Greek *poleis*, which, like Athens, were structured as closed groups of male farmer-soldiers, "warrior band(s) in Republican form" (Rahe [1992] 1994: 32).[6] Accordingly, male Athenians often disdained business activity, preferring the pursuit of political and/or military careers, or leisurely involvement with cultural and social interests.[7] In the ideal community sketched in *The Laws*, for example, Plato recognizes that both Greek men and women are capable of engaging in business activities, but forbids only the male citizen (*eleutherios Magnêtos*) from engaging in commercial pursuits.[8]

But this idealized notion of masculinity could not be fully realized in the actual lives of most Athenian men. While some Greeks did view labor as essentially the obligation of unfree persons,[9] equating antagonism to "employment" under a master with antipathy to work itself,[10] the majority

---

4. For work as an important catalyst of self-image, see chapter 2, n. 149 and accompanying text.

5. 1.108: οἱ πρόγονοι ... καὶ καταφανῆ ἐποίησαν τὴν ἀνδρείαν τοῦ πλούτου ... περιγιγνομένην. Cf. Hyper. 6.19. In many respects, however, military activity was itself an economic undertaking in classical Greek antiquity, often described in terms common to financial pursuits (e.g., *kerdos, kindynos*): see Thouk. 4.59.2; Isok. *Arkh*. 49; Polyb. 2.2.9, 4.86.4, 5.16.5, 10.17.6, 20.9.4. Cf. Brun and Descat 2000; Migeotte 2000; Garlan 1999: 50–55; Cartledge 1998: 14–16.

6. For opposition, even at Athens, to participation of working men in political decision-making, see chapter 1, pp. 25–26.

7. See Fisher 1998b: 84–86; Stocks 1936; de Ste. Croix 1981: 114–17.

8. γὰρ εἴ τις ... προσαναγκάσειεν ... πανδοκεῦσαι τοὺς πανταχῇ ἀρίστους ἄνδρας ἐπί τινα χρόνον, ἢ καπηλεύειν ἤ τι τῶν τοιούτων πράττειν, ἢ καὶ γυναῖκς (918d8–e3). Μαγνήτων ... ὅσοι τῶν τετταράκοντα καὶ πεντακισχιλίων ἑστιῶν εἰσιν, μήτε κάπηλος ἑκὼν μηδ' ἄκων μηδεὶς γιγνέσθω μηδ' ἔμπορος ... ὅσοι ἐλεύθεροι ἐλευθέρως (919d3–e2). Cf. 846d–847b. See Morrow [1960] 1993: 138–39.

9. See chapter 1, n. 24. Cf. Vernant 1983a.

10. For Athenian disapproval of "employment," see the section "Athenian Work Ethics" in chapter 2.

of Athenians seem to have integrated the economic ideal of autonomous individuality into the reality of personal labor.[11] As a result, the need for income and a commitment to personal accomplishment brought numerous Athenian men into self-employment in craft or trade (see chapter 2, pp. 41–42). But female and servile control of businesses and even, on occasion, of family wealth was a natural consequence of an *andreia* that valorized military, cultural, and political pursuits, but feminized gainful employment. Business was generally dominated not by individual males, but by the "household" (*oikos*, plural *oikoi*), an entity with which virtually all persons at Athens, both free and unfree, were affiliated.[12] Although scholars often dismiss the Athenian *oikos* as "simply 'the private sphere' to which women's activities were relegated,"[13] the *oikos*—and not the male individual[14]—was in reality the basic constituent element of Athenian society. Juridically, "the polis was an aggregation of *oikoi*" (Wolff 1944: 93), with a legal system based on "the rights of families as corporate groups."[15] "Since economic enterprises largely existed and were managed within the structure of households" (Foxhall 1994: 139), the "household" was "the basic economic unit of the polis."[16] Ownership of property effectively came within the control of the *oikos*, and the production of income fell within the scope of its activities.[17] Most wealth—especially ancestral property

---

11. Wood (1988: 126–45) provides context for Athenian recognition of the acceptability of work (if not performed under "servile" [*doulika*] labor conditions).

12. For the nature and ubiquity of the *oikos* at Athens, see chapter 2, pp. 45–46.

13. Foxhall 1994: 138 (who disagrees with this tendency). For Murnaghan, for example, "Outside is the only really desirable place to be" (1988: 13).

14. In ancient Greece "there were no natural rights of the individual" (Morris 1987: 3). Cf. Miller 1974, 1995, passim.

15. Todd 1993: 206. Cf. Roy 1999: 1; Hansen 1997: 10–12. The primacy of the *oikos* is the literal starting point for the two standard treatments of Athenian substantive law (Beauchet [1897] 1969: 1.3 and Harrison 1968–71: 1.1). (Todd sets out [208–11, 225–27] the substantial difficulties inherent in MacDowell's rejection [1989] of the *opinio communis*).

16. Sourvinou-Inwood (1995: 113) who nevertheless finds "some ambiguity as to the extent to which the basic social unit is the oikos or the individual." See Aristot. *Pol.* 1252; Xen. *Oik.*, esp. 1.5, 6.4; Lys. 1 and 32. Cf. Cox 1998: 13; Ogden 1996: 42; Strauss 1993: 35, 43; Todd 1993: 206; Patterson 1990: 43–44, 51, 55–57, 59, 1981: 9–10; Jameson 1990: 179; Foxhall 1989, 1994, and 1996: 140–52; Sissa 1986; Hallett 1984: 72–06; Sealey 1984: 112; Hunter 1981: 15; Lotze 1981: 169; Fisher 1976: 2, 5 ff.; Lacey 1968: 88–90; Ledl 1907–08.

17. See E. Cohen 2000: 40–43. Cf. Harris 2001: 81–83.

(*patrôia*)—belonged to the various households,[18] and as a result, the was seen as the primary repository of wealth.[19] The *oikos* accordingly paid for the expensive "liturgies" about which wealthy Athenians often complained,[20] and the household likewise bore the *eisphorai* and *proeisphorai*, the extraordinary levies that were imposed at intervals to provide funds for a specific undertaking such as a naval campaign.[21]

Within the *oikos*, women generally occupied a central position. According to Xenophon, the wife bore primary responsibility for managing the household (*Oikonomikos* 7.35–43, 9.14–17). Euripides claims that "women order households . . . in the absence of a woman not even the prosperous household is well provided for."[22] Aristotle derides as "absurd" Plato's suggestion that women and men, on the analogy of animal life, can do the same work: human females, unlike their biological counterparts in lower orders, have households to run![23] Hence, the Athenian phenomenon (described by Aiskhinês) of numerous naive young men of wealth whose widowed mothers actively managed the family property.[24] One such widow was Kleoboulê (mother of Demosthenes) who "remained in economic control" of her *oikos* for over a decade, directly "managing four talents" of assets.[25] The widow of the Athenian tycoon Pasiôn, Arkhippê, likewise dominated her *oikos*: she was intimately conversant with all aspects of the

---

18. For the power and limitations of the senior male as household representative, see pp. 136–38. For restrictions on "consumption" of ancestral property, see chapter 3, pp. 90–94.

19. Foxhall 2013: 25. Cf. Xen. *Symp.* 4.34, where a poor man assumes that worldly wealth resides not in the individual but in the *oikos*: νομίζω τοὺς ἀνθρώπους οὐκ ἐν τῷ οἴκῳ τὸν πλοῦτον καὶ τὴν πενίαν ἔχειν ἀλλ᾽ ἐν ταῖς ψυχαῖς.

20. Isaios 7.32, cf. 42. On the liturgical system, see Christ 1990: 148–57; Gabrielson 1994: 43–102; Wilson 2000: 21–28.

21. On *proeisphora*, see Migeotte 2014: 278–82, 524; Wallace 1989. On *eisphora*, see Flament 2007: 88–94, 202–206.

22. Eur. *Mel. Des.* Fr. 660 Mette 1982, lines 9–11 (P. Berol. 9772 and P. Oxy. 1176 Fr. 39, Col. 11) (Fr. 13: Auffret 1987): νέμουσι δ᾽ οἴκους καὶ τὰ ναυστολούμενα | ἔ[σω] δόμων σώιζουσιν, οὐδ᾽ ἐρημίαι | γυναικὸς οἶκος εὐπινὴς ὅ γε ὄλβιος· (οὐδ᾽ ὄλβιος P. Oxy.). Cf. Todd 1993: 204–206.

23. *Republic* 451d ff. *Pol.* 1264b4–6: ἄτοπον δὲ καὶ τὸ ἐκ τῶν θηρίων ποιεῖσθαι τὴν παραβολήν, ὅτι δεῖ τὰ αὐτὰ ἐπιτηδεύειν τὰς γυναῖκας τοῖς ἀνδράσιν, οἷς οἰκονομίας οὐδὲν μέτεστιν.

24. 1.170: Δημοσθένης . . . περιῄει τὴν πόλιν θηρεύων νέους πλουσίους ὀρφανούς, ὧν οἱ μὲν πατέρες ἐτετελευτήκεσαν, αἱ δὲ μητέρες διῴκουν τὰς οὐσίας. πολλοὺς δ᾽ ὑπερβὰς κ. τ. λ.

25. Foxhall 1996: 147. This *oikos* provides perhaps "the best illustration" of a widow's domination of a household functioning as "business enterprise" (Harris 2001: 81). Kleoboulê's dominant role: Dem. 27.40, 53, 55; 28.26, 33, 47–48. Cf. Hunter 1989a: 43–46; Foxhall 1996: 144–47.

family's banking business[26] and had such control over the bank's records that she was even accused of having destroyed them to prevent development of legal claims against Pasiôn's successor, her second husband, Phormiôn.[27] Menander's fictional Krôbylê likewise controls her *oikos*: mistress of land, building, "everything" (Fr. 296–97 [K–A]).

This combination of women's significance within the *oikos*, and that institution's commercial centrality within Athenian society, explains a phenomenon which scholars of ancient Greece have long acknowledged, but whose implications have been seldom explored: women's widespread involvement in business at Athens and their prominence in a broad variety of mercantile and professional métiers.[28] At Athens, women worked as doctors and in other medical callings,[29] and were deeply involved in the functioning of Athenian banks (*trapezai*).[30] They even appear as creditors in real-estate arrangements,[31] and as lenders in other financial transactions.[32] The Eleusinian treasurers are recorded as having dealt directly with at least two women (I.G. II² 1672, lines 64, 71), purchasing from one of them, a certain Artemis of Piraeus, reeds for building materials having

---

26. Dem. 36.14: ἡ πάντ' ἀκριβῶς ταῦτ' εἰδυῖα. . . .

27. Dem. 36.18: τὰ γράμμαθ' ἡ μήτηρ ἡφάνικε πεισθεῖσ' ὑπὸ τούτου, καὶ τούτων ἀπολωλότων οὐκ ἔχει τίνα χρὴ τρόπον ταῦτ' ἐξελέγχειν ἀκριβῶς.

28. For the ubiquity of female commercial activity at Athens, see Lewy 1885; Balabanoff 1905; Herfst 1922 [1980]; D. Cohen 1990: 156–57; Brock 1994; Acton 2014: 19.

29. See I.G. II² 6873 (ἰατρός); Plato, *Theait.* 149a–50b. Cf. Nutton 2012: 112–14; Kennedy 2014: 140–45.

30. For banking as a family business, and women's participation in this métier as members of trapezitic households, see E. Cohen 1992: 101–10. See also Thür 2001: 147–55 (study of a fragmentary Athenian comic papyrus, K-A 8.1152, possibly the work of Menander, identifying Korinthia as a female banker [although this attribution is questioned by Scafuro (forthcoming)]). Women were also customers. In one of the few instances, for example, in which information has survived concerning the circumstances which generated a specific bank deposit, it is a woman, Antigona, who induces a would-be business purchaser to marshal the substantial funds, 40 *mnai*, deposited in a *trapeza* as an apparent "good-faith deposit." Hyper. *Athên.* 4–5.

31. Fine 1951: no. 28. Cf. Finley [1951] 1985: 188.

32. Aristophanes, in the *Thesmophoriazusai* (839–45), for example, describes a woman as engaged in lending money at interest. Although this reference is contained in a comic sally, similar lending by the wife of Polyeuktos is mentioned in a sober court presentation (Dem. 41.7–9, 21). She lent Spoudias 1,800 *drachmas* at interest: on her death, her own records (*grammata*) survived as evidence of the transaction. (Nor does this appear to have been an isolated transaction: the speaker in Demosthenes 41 implies that he himself had borrowed money from the same woman.) Cf. Sealey 1990: 36–40.

a value of at least 70 *drachmas*.³³ A law of Solôn purportedly forbade men to engage in the retail sale of perfume;³⁴ Pherekratês could not even conceive of a man personally involved in the retail offering of fragrances in the *agora* (nor of women working as butchers or fish-cutters).³⁵ In any event, the ubiquity of women in the *agora* market in central Athens—the only retail site for which evidence has survived³⁶—has led one modern scholar to assert that women "seem to have had, if not a monopoly, at least a privileged position in the market-place."³⁷ In fact, female traders held prominent presence as dealers in a broad spectrum of goods, especially foods (like bread, grain, figs, herbs, beans, and salt), and commodities for domestic use such as clothing, garlands, and ribbons.³⁸

Despite this profusion of evidence for women's involvement in commerce, many scholars still have posited *kyrieia*—the requirement that "an Athenian woman had to be represented in legal transactions by a male relative acting as her guardian (*kyrios*)" (Todd 1993: 383)—as a major barrier to women's importance, or even involvement, in Athenian business life. But in reality various direct and indirect mechanisms effectively eliminated the need for a *kyrios* (see chapter 4, pp. 107–108).

In addition, the frequent conduct of business through the *oikos* itself largely ensured the availability, if needed, of a male representative (the *kyrios*, or public agent of the *oikos*)—no matter how unimportant the

---

33. But these same records (I.G. II² 1672–3) reveal scores of transactions in which the named principals are men.

34. ἡ μυρεψικὴ τέχνη ... Σόλωνος δὲ τοῦ νομοθέτου οὐδ' ἐπιτρέποντος ἀνδρὶ τοιαύτης προΐστασθαι τέχνης: Athên. 612a2–6. However, we do know of male involvement in the perfume industry (although not explicitly as sales clerks): see Lys. Fr. 1 Thalheim; I.G. II² 1558.37. The male Athênogenês is described as a perfume seller (Hyper. *Ath.* 26), and Epikratês finds him in the *agora* "at the perfume stalls" (Hyper. *Ath.* 11).

35. Athênogenês explicitly defends such vocational stereotyping: Ἑκάστῳ γὰρ γένει ἁρμόζοντα δεῖν εἶναι καὶ τὰ τῆς τέχνης. 612b2–3, explaining Fr. 70 (K-A) of Pherekratês, a fifth-century comic writer.

36. Substantial retail activity, however, presumably occurred elsewhere, perhaps in the so-called Hippodamian Agora (west of Mounykhia Hill and north of Zea in the Piraeus). See Panagos 1968: 223–24; Garland 1987: 141–42; E. Cohen 2005b: 291, n. 90.

37. Lacey 1968: 171. No ancient evidence, however, supports such a "privileged position," nor Becker's belief (1877–88, 2: 199–202) that a particular section of the *agora*, the *gynaikeia agora*, was reserved for female merchants, rather than for goods intended for women. Cf. Herfst 1922 [1980]: 38–40; Schaps 1979: 136, n. 7.

38. For surveys of women's retail activities, see Brock 1994: 338–40; Schaps 1979: 61–63, 135–37.

man's role might be in the general functioning of a household-related *ergasia*.³⁹ Yet despite this role of the senior male as the "public face" of family business activity, inscriptional evidence still occasionally records both husband and wife as jointly active in a trade or business. Thus Midas and Sotêris work together as sellers of sesame (I.G. II² 1561, at lines 22–30). Artemis the gilder and Dionysios the helmet-maker practice symbiotic trades—apparently in the same shop (S.I.G.³ 1177 = I.G. III¹ App. 69). Euxitheos, the speaker of Demosthenes 57, acknowledges that he works together with his mother selling ribbons.⁴⁰ Stephanos and Neaira function together in the household-oriented prostitutional business described in Demosthenes 59.⁴¹ Although Xenophôn claims that within *oikoi*, men and women make similar economic contributions⁴²—the men "generally" being more responsible for the production of income, and the women for expenditures⁴³—in the most detailed description of an actual business functioning within an *oikos* (the textile operations of Aristarkhos and his female relatives), Xenophôn portrays the senior male as burdened by the knowledge that he is the only member of the family "eating but not contributing."⁴⁴ The often covert economic importance of an otherwise unsung wife is startlingly revealed in a humorous passage of Lysias. Hermaios, the "perfume merchant," retained this epithet only so long as he held his wife's affection: once Aiskhinês the Sokratic won the heart of Hermaios's mature wife, Aiskhines, formerly a peddler, now became the new "perfume merchant" (and the titulary possessor of "Hermaios's"

---

39. Thus Battaros appears in court on behalf of a prostitute in Herôdas's Mimiamb 2 (set in Kôs). A foreigner there, he boasts of his own *prostatês* (citizen "sponsor" or "patron": line 15).

40. Dem. 57.31: ἡμεῖς δ' ὁμολογοῦμεν καὶ ταινίας πωλεῖν.

41. See this chapter, pp. 152–53.

42. Xen. *Oik*. 3.15.1–2: νομίζω δὲ γυναῖκα κοινωνὸν ἀγαθὴν οἴκου οὖσαν πάνυ ἀντίρροπον εἶναι τῷ ἀνδρὶ ἐπὶ τὸ ἀγαθόν.

43. Xen. *Oik*. 3.15.3–5: ἔρχεται μὲν γὰρ εἰς τὴν οἰκίαν διὰ τῶν τοῦ ἀνδρὸς πράξεων τὰ κτήματα ὡς ἐπὶ τὸ πολύ, δαπανᾶται δὲ διὰ τῶν τῆς γυναικὸς ταμιευμάτων τὰ πλεῖστα. But Loukianos's Ioessa assumes that a son, needing money to pay a prostitute, could obtain funds with equal ease from father or mother: (σε) μήτε παραλογισάμενον τὸν πατέρα ἢ ὑφελόμενον τῆς μητρὸς ἠνάγκασα ἐμοί τι κομίσαι (80.12.1). Mousarion's mother posits a similar egalitarian access to funds: Μόνος οὗτος οὐ τέχνην εὕρηκεν ἐπὶ τὸν πατέρα . . . οὐκ ἀπὸ τῆς μητρὸς ᾔτησεν (Louk. 80.7.4).

44. Xen. *Apom*. 2.7.12: αἰτιῶνται αὐτὸν μόνον τῶν ἐν τῇ οἰκίᾳ ἀργὸν ἐσθίειν.

property). The former "perfume merchant," and now-cuckolded husband, entered the ranks of the newly impoverished.⁴⁵

Female control and management of Athenian prostitutional enterprises (and the complex interaction of mothers and daughters in these activities) are thus consonant with the overall organization of Athenian business and family life—just as the interplay of men (and the attention of the male-controlled legal system) are, as one might anticipate, focused on the political, rather than the business, implications of prostitution (see chapter 3, pp. 77–81).

## Women as Merchants of Sex

Despite the frequent scholarly assumption that men generally control erotic enterprises (see chapter 5, pp. 118–19), at Athens females appear to have been dominant in the ownership and operation of businesses offering women's sexual services. As we have seen,⁴⁶ free female prostitutes often were self-employed, living and working without male infringement on their compensation or business activity. Courtesans often, according to Alexis, after achieving some personal success, moved on to acquire younger women, new to the profession, whom they might refashion for maximum profit (*kerdos*).⁴⁷ These female entrepreneurs became, in Athênaios's phrase, "the ladies who run the houses."⁴⁸ Not surprisingly then, when Antigona (allegedly a former *hetaira* now operating her own prostitutional business) receives a commission of 300 *drachmas* for facilitating the sale of a retail operation dealing in fragrances, she earmarks the money for the purchase of yet another female servant.⁴⁹ Theodotê, a

---

45. Lys. Fr. 38.5 (Gernet and Bizos): οὐ τὴν οὐσίαν κέκτηται Ἑρμαίου τοῦ μυροπώλου, τὴν γυναῖκα διαφθείρας ἑβδομήκοντα ἔτη γεγονυῖαν; ἧς ἐρᾶν προσποιησάμενος οὕτω διέθηκεν ὥστε τὸν μὲν ἄνδρα αὐτῆς καὶ τοὺς υἱοὺς πτωχοὺς ἐποίησεν, αὐτὸν δὲ ἀντὶ καπήλου μυροπώλην ἀπέδειξεν· οὕτως ἐρωτικῶς τὸ κόριον μετεχειρίζετο.... (= Fr. 1 Carey).

46. "Selling 'Free' Love," in chapter 2; "Prohibition of Pimping (*Proagôgeia*)," in chapter. 5.

47. Πρῶτα μὲν γὰρ πρὸς τὸ κέρδος ... ῥάπτουσι δὲ | πᾶσιν ἐπιβουλάς. ἐπειδὰν δ᾽ εὐπορήσωσίν ποτε, | ἀνέλαβον καινὰς ἑταίρας, πρωτοπείρους τῆς τέχνης· | εὐθὺς ἀναπλάττουσι ταύτας.... (Fr. 103 [K-A]).

48. τὰς ἐπὶ τῶν οἰκημάτων (568d). Translation: Gulick 1937: 71.

49. ἐκείνη προσπεριέκοψεν αὐτῇ ὡς δὴ εἰς παιδίσκην τριακοσίας δραχμὰς εὐνοίας ἕνεκα.... γυναικὸς ἢ δεινοτάτη μὲν τῶν ἑταιρῶν ἐφ᾽ ἡλικίας ἐγένετο, διατετέλεκε δὲ πορνοβοσκοῦσα (Hyper. *Ath*. 2–3). Cf. §18: τῇ Ἀθηνογένους ἑταίρᾳ ... ἡ ἑ[ταίρα σ]ο[υ].... On this and similar relationships, see Cox 1998: 186–89, especially 187, n. 99.

woman portrayed as having become wealthy because of her penchant for sleeping with "men who are persuasive," commands a stable of comely and provocatively attired young women.[50] Isaios alludes to several women who operated brothels in Athens,[51] and describes with particularity a female entrepreneur who ran a house (*synoikia*) in the Piraeus, where she maintained a number of slave girls.[52] Gyllis, a woman who operates a sexual business employing Myrtalê and Simê and presumably others, all apparently enslaved, is portrayed in Hêrôdas 1 as seeking to persuade the independently established Mêtrikhê to accommodate one of Gyllis's clients.[53] Aspasia, linked to the Athenian political leader Periklês, was allegedly the owner of large numbers of prostitutes.[54] Masurios charges Sôkratês with consorting with Aspasia's sex-workers at her brothels,[55] and Aristophanês asserts, humorously, that the abduction of two of Aspasia's whores was the proximate cause of the Peloponnesian War (*Akharnians* 524–29). Although these particular claims are, of course, not universally accepted,[56] they do illustrate the connection, in popular imagination, between meretricious commerce and female entrepreneurship. Indeed, Aristophanes's portrayal of Lysistrata's erotic guidance of the play's younger women in withholding sex from Athenian men has been likened to the control

---

50. *Apom.* 3.11.4–5: ὁ Σωκράτης ὁρῶν αὐτήν τε πολυτελῶς κεκοσμημένην καὶ μητέρα παροῦσαν αὐτῇ ἐν ἐσθῆτί τε καὶ θεραπείᾳ οὐ τῇ τυχούσῃ, καὶ θεραπαίνας πολλὰς καὶ εὐειδεῖς καὶ οὐδὲ ταύτας ἠμελημένως ἐχούσας, καὶ τοῖς ἄλλοις τὴν οἰκίαν ἀφθόνως κατεσκευασμένην . . . . νὴ τὴν Ἥραν, ἔφη, ὦ Θεοδότη, καλόν γε τὸ κτῆμα.

51. Isai. 6. 21, 6.18. Roussel 1960: 113, n. 1.

52. Ἀπελευθέρα ἦν αὐτοῦ (sc. Εὐκτήμονος) ἣ ναυκληρεῖ συνοικίαν ἐν Πειραιεῖ αὐτοῦ καὶ παιδίσκας ἔτρεφε (Isai. 6.19).

53. Γρύλλος . . . πλουτέων τὸ καλόν . . . καί μευ οὔτε νυκτὸς οὔτ' ἐπ' ἡμέρην λείπει τὸ δῶμα, [τέ]κνον, ἀλλά μευ κατακλαίει καὶ ταταλ[ί]ζει . . . πείσθητί μευ . . . ἐμοὶ δὲ Μυρτάλη τε κ[αὶ] Σίμη νέαι μένοιεν (lines 50–90). (Gyllis's place of residence is left indeterminate in Herôdas's Mimiamb.) On Mêtrikhê, cf. chapter 2, p. 65.

54. Ἀσπασία δὲ ἡ Σωκρατικὴ ἐνεπορεύετο πλήθη καλῶν γυναικῶν, καὶ ἐπλήθυνεν ἀπὸ τῶν ταύτης ἑταιρίδων ἡ Ἑλλάς (Athên.569f7–9). On Aspasia, see chapter 2, pp. 62–63].

55. Athên. 220e: Σωκράτης ὁ μετὰ τῶν Ἀσπασίας αὐλητρίδων ἐπὶ τῶν ἐργαστηρίων συνδιατρίβων. For the commercial sexual connotation of αὐλητρίς (literally "flute-girl"), see Davidson 1997; 80–82; Foxhall 2013: 99. For ἐργαστήριον as brothel, see chapter 1, p. 27, n. 15.

56. MacDowell, however, finds the Aristophanic treatment of the outbreak of the Peloponnesian War "not inconsistent with the account given by Thucydides; it is not illogical or incredible; and I see no reason why it should not be essentially true" (1995: 66; cf. 187–88). Fisher disagrees (1993a: 37, 46, n. 30). Cf. Carey 1993: 252–53; Henderson 2014: 183.

exercised over female sex-workers by senior women operating Athenian sexual businesses.[57]

Although Ancient Greek employs the same terms (*opos*, plural *mastropoi*; *pornoboskos*, plural *pornoboskoi*) for both male and female operators of prostitutional businesses,[58] other linguistic indicia (such as the grammatical gender of accompanying adjectives or articles) and literary context confirm that for Athenians the stereotypical merchant of sex at Athens was female and maternal. According to the lexicon of Phôtios, confirmed by the "Etymologica," a *mastropos* was colloquially referred to as "Mother" (*Mêtêr*)[59]—whether or not the *mastropos* was the literal mother of her sexual workers. Thus the prostitute in Alexis's *Agônis* pleads with her "Mother" not to threaten her with an undesirable customer.[60] In Hêrôdas 1, a visiting *mastropos* is greeted as "Mama Gyllis" by Mêtrikhê, a courtesan not actually related to her by blood.[61] (This maternal sobriquet was even adopted by Mama's wealthy male customer who bewails his passion to "Mama."[62]) Mama in turn addresses Mêtrikhê as "Child,"[63] and speaks in the possessive of the young women who *do* work for her.[64] (Hêrôdas's fifth-century predecessor in mime, Sôphrôn, also testifies to the intimate connection between prostitutes and *mastropoi*—whom he saw as "searching out the natures of courtesans."[65]) In the late fifth century, Aristophanês

---

57. Faraone 2006: 221–22: "In the scenes with the younger women, (Lysistrata) is repeatedly cast as a manipulative and gold-digging madam ... On the other hand, when Aristophanês has Lysistrata interact with the men as their intellectual and political equal, he is clearly drawing on the traditional figure of the elite courtesan. ..." Cf. Henderson 2002.

58. On ancient Greek terminology for occupations, and possible means of differentiating male from female practitioners, see Foxhall 2013: 98–101; Todd 1997:120–24; Harris 2002.

59. Phôtios, s.v. ματρυλλεῖον (the place where *mastropoi* kept their whores and received their customers). Μέγα Ἐτυμολογικόν 574.267 notes that Dorians also called *mastropoi* "mothers" (ματέρας in Peloponnesian dialects).

60. Ἀγωνὶς (ἢ Ἱππίσκος) Fr. 3: ὦ μῆτερ, ἱκετεύω σε, μὴ 'πισειέ μοι | τὸν Μισγόλαν· οὐ γὰρ κιθαρωιδός εἰμ' ἐγώ.

61. ἄμμίη Γυλλίς (line 7).

62. μευ κατακλαίει καὶ ταταλ[ί]ζει (lines 59–60): "He wails at me and calls me mama" (Cunningham 1993: 225).

63. τέκνον (lines 21, 61, 85, and 87). Gyllis is a mature woman: (τὸ γὰρ γῆρας | ἡμέας καθέλκει κἠ σκιὴ παρέστηκεν: lines 15–16; τὰ λευκὰ τῶν τριχῶν: line 67).

64. ἐμοὶ δὲ Μυρτάλη τε κ[αὶ] Σίμη νέαι (lines 89–90).

65. μαστροπός: παρὰ τὸ μαίεσθαι τοὺς τρόπους τῶν πορνευουσῶν γυναικῶν (Fr. 69 [K-A]), a reference preserved only in dubious context.

presents *mastropoi* as quintessential representatives of Athenian womanhood, humorously claiming that women should be damned for stealing the meat used at the Apatourian festival—thefts perpetrated in order to pay their female *mastropoi* (Aristophanês's comical suggestion that the citizen-women of the *Thesmophoriazousai* were all whores, indebted to their procuresses for professional services).⁶⁶ In the *Erôtes*, attributed to Loukianos, a mythical devotée of Aphroditê finds a "daring procuress" for his desires,⁶⁷ while Aristainetos, writing in late antiquity, characterizes both a mother and a female servant as *mastropoi*.⁶⁸ Similarly, in interpreting a fragment from Diphilos, the Liddell-Scott-Jones Lexicon insists that women were the "hardened" panders (*mastropoi*) who provided "love arrangements" for an enormously successful maritime operator (*naukslêros*).⁶⁹ Kynoulkos, in Athênaios's *Deipnosophistai*, assumes that *mastropoi*, as providers of courtesans (*hetairai*), would necessarily be female,⁷⁰ perhaps because, in an Athens not oriented toward casual mixing of the sexes,⁷¹ only other women would have had easy access to the free females who functioned as *hetairai*.⁷² Women are portrayed as *mastropoi* even in the Latin *palliatae*—adaptations from Hellenic originals often set theatrically at Athens.⁷³ In Plautus's *Asinaria*, for example, the domineering mother of the young whore is denominated a *lena* (Latin for *mastropos*): she is in control of the business and of the plot—putting down Argyrippus in Act 1

---

66. εἴπω ... ὥς τ'αὖ τὰ κρέ' ἐξ Ἀπατουρίων ταῖς μαστροποῖς διδοῦσαι . . . . (*Thes.* 553, 558).

67. εὑρέθη δὲ τόλμα τῆς ἐπιθυμίας μαστροπός (49.16).

68. ἡ δὲ (μήτηρ) μαστροπεύουσα πρὸς τὴν κεκτημένην (παιδίσκην ἑαυτῆς) φησί (1.11); ἄβρα δὲ καὶ μαστροπὸς τῆς Γλυκέρας ἡ Δωρίς (1.22). Cf. 2.19.

69. (ναύκληρος) τριταῖος, ἀπαθής, εὐπορηκώς, περιχαρής | εἰς δέκ' ἐπὶ τῇ μνᾷ γεγονέναι καὶ δώδεκα, | λαλῶν τὰ ναῦλα τὰ δάνει· ἐρυγγάνων | ἀφροδίσι' ὑπὸ κόλλοψι μαστροποῖς ποιῶν (Fr. 42 [K-A] lines 19–22). For the gender of the *mastropoi*, cf. LSJ, s.v. and K-A 5.74.

70. σὺ ... ἐν τοῖς καπηλείοις συναναφύρῃ οὐ μετὰ ἑταίρων ἀλλὰ μετὰ ἑταιρῶν, μαστροπευούσας περὶ σαυτὸν οὐκ ὀλίγας ἔχων (567a1–3).

71. The prosperous established Athenian households did seek, at least theoretically, to restrict women's public activity (see, for example, Aristoph. *Thes.* 425, 519, 783 ff.; Aristot. *Oik.* 1343b2–1344a22; Xen. *Oik.* 7.33; Lys. 3.6; Theophr. *Khar.* 28). But, as a practical matter, it was impossible to keep poor women from earning money in the public sphere of commerce (Aristot. *Pol.* 1300a 6–7). As a result, seclusion of women in actual practice in Athens was much attenuated from the normative separation sometimes portrayed in literary sources: see D. Cohen 1989; Hunter 1994: 99–100, 220–21; Just 1989: 105–25; Cantarella 1987: 46, 196–97.

72. Lentakis 1999: 142.

73. See introduction, p. 17.

and entering into the anticipated contract with Diabolus in Act 4. Plautus's *Truculentus* involves two *lenae*, a mother (line 401) and a female servant (line 224). In fact, the *lenae* in these adaptations—such as Philaenium in Plautus's *Asinaria* or the "mother" of Thais in Terence's *Eunuchus* (lines 105–20)—here too are often referred to as "mother" without regard to literal parentage.[74]

In fact, the only clear references in Athenian sources to male *mastropoi* are metaphorical—allegorical passages relating to philosophers unlikely actually to have been engaged in the business of pimping. In Loukianos's *Symposion*, the philosopher Zênothemis (who actually earned his living from teaching) is accused by Kleodêmos of having been "a *mastropos* for his own wife," an insult offered in response to Zênothemis's assertion that Kleodêmos had committed adultery with a pupil's spouse.[75] After several speakers in Xenophôn's *Symposion* have boasted of their wealth or beauty, Sôkratês asserts that he takes pride in functioning as a *mastropos*—a claim treated, not surprisingly, as a joke by his interlocutors. Sôkratês, whose actual trade was stone masonry, insists, however, that he could earn large sums of money should he undertake to practice as a *mastropos* (3.10). Later in the same *Symposion*, Sôkratês offers Antisthenês as a preeminent example of a *mastropos*—not as a result of Antisthenês's finding customers for whores, but because of his skill as a "go-between" (*proagôgos*) among philosophers and people of wealth (4.56–64).[76]

Male involvement in the Athenian sex trade, however, was not limited to the personal provision of erotic services. Both women and men functioned as *proagôgoi* ("pimps," whose activities were highly constrained by Athenian law: see chapter 5).[77] Hêrôdas, recreating at the time of the Roman Empire a fictitious world of stock characters from Hellenic tradition (see introduction, p. 18), opens his series of sketches with dramatic

---

74. Cf. *Satyricon* 7.1 (and the discussion at James 2006: 247, n. 35). Cf. Rosavich 1998: 69–70, 151–52.

75. "Σὺ δὲ τὴν Σωστράτου γυναῖκα τοῦ μαθητοῦ ἐμοίχευες, ὦ Κλεόδημε" . . . "Ἀλλ' οὐ μαστροπὸς ἐγὼ τῆς ἐμαυτοῦ γυναικός," ἡ δ' ὅς ὁ Κλεόδημος, "ὥσπερ σύ" (17.32.9–10). In the same passage, Zênothemis is also charged with improprieties relating to his actual profession—misappropriating student funds and assaulting pupils who failed to make timely payment of their fees.

76. On Antisthenês as figurative *proagôgos* or *mastropos*, see chapter 5, pp. 122–23.

77. τὰς πρωαγωγοὺς καὶ τοὺς προαγωγοὺς: Aiskhin. 1.184.

vignettes first of a female *mastropos* (operating in an indeterminate setting), and then of a male *pornoboskos* living in Kôs. Such *pornoboskoi* were stock characters in New Comedy: Anaxilas, Euboulos, and Poseidippos all are known to have written plays entitled *Pornoboskos*. While virtually nothing is known of the contents of these works, one surviving quotation from Euboulos's work suggests that the *pornoboskos* there was possibly male.[78]

Although scholars often assume that men were the prototypical *pornoboskoi* ("literally 'whore-pasturers,' driving their herds of women around Greece following the seasons and the festivals"[79]), few actual *pornoboskoi* can be positively identified as male. Like *mastropos*, the term *pornoboskos* does not itself identify the gender of its subject. Thus when the owners of a slave prostitute at Korinth seek to prevent her from working in the future under a *pornoboskos*, the sex of the hypothetical "herder" is indeterminate: he/she might be female or male.[80] Likewise, we have no knowledge of the gender of the *pornoboskos* to whom Kharisios makes extravagant payments in Menander's *Epitrepontes*, set in Athens.[81] Yet we do know that some men did work as *pornoboskoi*, flouting traditional proscriptions on male commercial endeavor and evoking (according to Aiskhinês) corresponding animosity from the mass of male citizens.[82] But Athenian references to such males are generally in the abstract, citing them as a class or as a concept or as a type,[83] rather than describing real individuals actually involved in specific business activities. Thus Theophrastos, in his abstruse characterizations of various types of individuals, portrays the "shameless man" as a "market-type" (*agoraios*), ready for every undertaking, including

---

78. Fr. 87 (K-A): τρέφει με Θετταλός τις ἄνθρωπος βαρύς | πλουτῶν, φιλάργυρος δὲ κἀλιτήριος. Kassel and Austin argue that "scortum quod τρέφει leno (Diph. fr. 87) loqui videtur."

79. Davidson 1997: 92. Similarly: McClure 2003: 15. *Pornoboskos* ultimately lost its literal significance, and could be applied simply to the operator of a brothel (as in Hêrôdas 2).

80. Dem. 59.30: οὐ βούλονται αὐτὴν ... ὁρᾶν ἐν Κορίνθῳ ἐργαζομένην οὐδ᾿ ὑπὸ πορνοβοσκῷ οὖσαν . . . .

81. 136–37: πορνοβοσκῶι δώδεκα | τῆς ἡμέρας δραχμὰς δίδωσι.

82. Aiskhin. 1.188: θαυμάζω δ᾿ ὑμῶν ὦ ἄνδρες Ἀθηναῖοι κἀκεῖνο, εἰ τοὺς μὲν πορνοβοσκοὺς μισεῖτε, τοὺς δ᾿ ἑκόντας πεπορνευμένους ἀφήσετε· Aiskhin. 3.246: δίκην τις δέδωκε πονηρὸς καὶ πορνοβοσκός, ὥσπερ Κτησιφῶν· οἱ δέ γε ἄλλοι πεπαίδευνται. Cf. Stoic. 3.36: Fr. 152; Myrt. 4: ὡς ὁ μὲν κλέπτης, ὁ δ᾿ ἅρπαξ, | ὁ δ᾿ ἀνάπηρος, πορνοβοσκός, | καταφαγᾶς.

83. Terence similarly makes reference to the "avaru' leno" at *Heaut*. Prol. 39.

"inn-keeping and whore-herding (*pornoboskêsai*)."[84] Similarly Aristotle, in his *Nicomachean Ethics*, criticizes those who seek excessive gain, "men who work at businesses inappropriate to free males, such as *pornoboskoi* and similar males."[85] In contrast, the fullest-attested and best-known Hellenic "whore-herder" is the married free woman Nikaretê (whose business activity is chronicled at Demosthenes 59.18–23)—originating in Elis, operating in Korinth, shepherding through Greece a band of well-known, high-priced whores whom she owned, and bringing to Athens the young prostitute Neaira, among others.

Theophrastos's juxtaposition of "inn-keeping and whore-herding" is apposite, for erotic commerce at Athens was often ancillary to hospitality businesses—undertakings in which again women frequently played prominent roles. For example, operators of facilities offering drink ("tavern keepers") or lodging ("inn-keepers") sometimes offered sexual services to their customers.[86] Although little information survives concerning the gender of the individuals actually controlling these entities, in general such facilities were effectively owned not by individuals but by "households" (*oikoi*)—households run, as Aristotle observes, by women,[87] such as the female inn-keeper, Khrysis, who appears in Plautus's *Pseudolus*.[88] Entertainers, especially musicians, were popularly seen as available for sexual purchase,[89] but here, too, businesswomen were not absent. While the male owner of the musical entertainers in Xenophôn's *Symposion* seeks to shield his attractive male slave from customers' propositions (4.52–54), the fourth-century medical writer Hippokratês notes matter-of-factly the case of a danseuse owned by a woman who employed her as a prostitute.[90]

---

84. 6.4–5: ὁ δὲ ἀπονενοημένος τοιοῦτός τις . . . τῷ ἤθει ἀγοραῖός τις . . . καὶ παντοποιός . . . δεινὸς δὲ καὶ πανδοκεῦσαι καὶ πορνοβοσκῆσαι.

85. 1121b 40–43: οἱ τὰς ἀνελευθέρους ἐργασίας ἐργαζόμενοι, πορνοβοσκοὶ καὶ πάντες οἱ τοιοῦτοι. . . .

86. For the propinquity of "tavern-keeper" and "brothel-keeper," see Kennedy 2014: 129–30. Cf. Kleberg 1957: 89–91.

87. See this chapter, pp. 133–35.

88. Lines 658–59 (devortor . . . in tabernam . . . apud anum illam . . . Chrysidem).

89. See chapter 7, pp. 163–64.

90. *On Generating Seed and the Nature of the Child* 13 (VII, 490 Littré = Lefkowitz and Fant 232). Cf. Hanson 1990: 322; Halperin 1990; Richlin 1998: 160.

## Mothers and Daughters

As with other Athenian *oikoi*,[91] intergenerational continuity was an important aspect of the functioning of households containing female prostitutes, but in the meretricious ménage it was mother-daughter, not father-son, continuity that mattered. Onomastic practices are illuminating. While Greek women are generally identified in public context by their fathers' names (or in the case of married women, by their husbands'),[92] among female prostitutes matronymic names prevail. Phanô, a daughter residing in a "home that was really a brothel" (Demosthenes 59.67), is referred to consistently as the "daughter of Neaira," her allegedly meretricious mother.[93] Gyllis, the madam (*mastropos*) of Hêrôdas 1, identifies herself as "the mother of Philainis" (line 5), the name of a notorious (*dêmôdês*) prostitute (who was supposedly the author of a treatise on erotica).[94] Virtually all of the prominent *hetairai* of the literary tradition are homonymically shadowed by predecessors or successors of the same name, such as the famous doublets (or triplets) Laïs, Leaina, and Phrynê[95]—a repetition reflective of the many female ascendants and descendants who used the same name "from generation to generation" in their meretricious labors (McClure 2003b: 63).

Inscriptions from the fourth century are confirmatory of this literary evidence. Because of the rarity of daughters bearing their mothers', rather than their fathers', names, "many of the metronymics found on funerary inscriptions can be explained as referring to courtesans" (McClure 2003b: 77). Thus Kallistion is recorded on I.G. II².11793 as the daughter of Nikomakhê. Although Nikomakhê (and its male form Nikomakhos) are exceedingly popular Athenian names (Osborne and Byrne 1994, s.v.), the

---

91. Numerous Athenian *oikoi* extended beyond a single generation: forensic evidence suggests that about three-quarters of newly wed couples resided with parents (Gallant 1991: 21). Cf. E. Cohen 2000: 33–36.

92. For some of the relatively rare exceptions, see Braunstein 1911: 69–81; Christophilopoulos 1946: 130–39; Ogden 1996: 94–96.

93. See Dem. 59.65 (μοιχὸν ἐπὶ τῇ θυγατρὶ τῇ Νεαίρας), 67 (θυγατέρα Νεαίρας), 69 (τῇ τῆς Νεαίρας θυγατρί), 70 (τῇ θυγατρὶ τῇ Νεαίρας). For the treatment of Phanô in Dem. 59, see Hamel 2003: 77–113.

94. See P. Oxy. 2891; Athên. 335c–e, 457e. On the disputed authorship of this book, see Tsantsanoglou 1973: 186 ff. and West 1996: 20–21.

95. On the two "Phrynê"s, see Athên. 583c and 590d. On Laïs and Leaina, see McClure 2003b: 195, nn. 30, 33, 34. Dimakis (1992–93) distinguishes three courtesans who in succession used the name Laïs.

rare Kallistion happens to be the name of a well-known Athenian courtesan of the fourth century whose quarrel with her prostitute mother is reported by Makhôn in an anecdote filled with erotic innuendo.[96] The rarity of matronymic attributions beyond the métier of courtesans argues for the identification of the matronymic Kallistion of the inscription with the anecdotal Kallistion of the courtesan tradition. Similarly Malthakê ("Softie"), a name appropriate for a Greek prostitute,[97] is identified by the matronymic "daughter of Magadis" (I.G. II².12026), and another woman with a similar name, Galênê ("Smoothie"), is identified by the matronymic "daughter of Polykleia" (Osborne and Byrne 1994, s.v. no. 4). I.G. II² 10892 similarly records "Aspasia daughter of Mania" ("Welcome" and "Craziness," two common personal names used by whores).

The interaction between mothers and daughters is a frequent undertone in literary passages touching on female prostitution. Describing the establishment of Theodotê, for example, Xenophôn notes the hovering presence of Theodotê's mother (distinguished by her fashionable clothing and jewelry) and describes the sumptuously adorned, lavishly furnished home in which mother and daughter lived.[98] Nikarkhos, a poet of the Palatine Anthology, explicitly urges the courtesan Philoumenê to "disobey her mother."[99] Daughter frequently followed mother (and even grandmother) as a provider of venal sexual services. Harpalos's famed *hetaira* Glykera was the daughter of the courtesan Thalassis.[100] The *hetaira* Timandra serviced Alkibiadês, the fifth-century Athenian general and bon vivant; her daughter was the renowned courtesan Laïs II (and Laïs III may have been a daughter-successor to Laïs II).[101] The courtesan Leontion, who

---

96. Καλλιστίου δὲ τῆς Ὑὸς καλουμένης | πρὸς τὴν ἑαυτῆς λοιδορουμένης | μητέρα (Κορώνη δ' ἐπεκαλεῖτο τὄυνομα), | διέλυεν ἡ Γνάθαιν'. ἐρωτηθεῖσα δὲ | τί διαφέρονται "τί γάρ," ἔφησεν, "ἄλλο πλὴν | ἄλλ' ἡ Κορώνης, ἕτερ' ἐκείνη μέμφεται." Fr. 18 [Gow] = Athên. 583a1-6.

97. See Athên. 587f = Theophilos Fr. 11.2 (K-A).

98. μητέρα παροῦσαν αὐτῇ ἐν ἐσθῆτί τε καὶ θεραπείᾳ οὐ τῇ τυχούσῃ ... καὶ τοῖς ἄλλοις τὴν οἰκίαν ἀφθόνως κατεσκευασμένην.... νὴ τὴν Ἥραν, ἔφη, ὦ Θεοδότη, καλόν γε τὸ κτῆμα (*Apom.* 3.11.4, 5).

99. *Anth. Pal.* 5.40: τῆς μητρὸς μὴ ἄκουε Φιλουμένα. The scholiast identifies the poem as "πρὸς ἑταίραν Φιλουμένην παραίνεσις."

100. Athên. 586b–c, 595d.

101. Athên. 535c, 574e. A variant tradition identifies Timandra as "Damasandra" (the prostitute mother of the courtesans Laïs and Theodotê: Athên. 574e). On the most famous of the three Laïses, see further chapter 2, n. 167 and related text. For differentiation of the onomastic triplets, see Dimakis 1992–93. On Timandra, see Gilhuly 2009: 93–97.

supposedly combined the pursuit of Epicurean philosophy with the practice of prostitution,[102] was the mother of Danaë, who worked as a *hetaira* in Ephesos (and Athênaios also records a Leontion II and Leontion III).[103] Korônê had acquired the moniker "Grandmother" ("Têthê") apparently because she had followed her mother and her mother's mother in the family trade.[104] Another famed family of prostitutes was begotten by the courtesan Gnathaina, who had even formulated "socializing rules" to be followed by patrons who purchased her daughter's services—and her own.[105] Often accompanied by her younger scion,[106] she wittily marketed filial services by encouraging "impoverished lovers" (*ptôkhoi erastai*) to seek financing (*enekyra*) in order to pay her offspring's charges (Athênaios 585a7–11). Gnathaina's operations also extended to a third generation. In a famous tale, a wealthy customer, coming upon Gnathaina leaving a precinct of Aphroditê with her comely granddaughter, offers Gnathaina 500 *drachmas* instead of the 1,000 *drachmas* she had requested. She accepts the reduced amount—for herself!—and reopens negotiations for the girl (in whom the client is, as the tale goes, not uninterested).[107] Gnathaina may have taken as a role model the mother of the courtesan Dexithea. Apparently at the beginning of her own career, dining with Dexithea, Gnathaina notes how not Dexithea, but Dexithea's mother, received a disproportionate share of delicacies: in mock pique, Gnathaina suggests that she should have chosen to dine with the mother alone![108]

---

102. Athên. 588b. Cf. 585d, 597a, 598e.

103. Δανάην δὲ τὴν Λεοντίου τῆς Ἐπικουρείου θυγατέρα ἑταιριζομένην καὶ αὐτὴν Σώφρων εἴχεν ὁ ἐπὶ τῆς Ἐφέσου (Athên. 593b7–10). For Leontion II and III, see Athên. 585d, 593b, 597a, and McClure 2003b: 188.

104. Athên. 587c1: ἀναφέρουσα ἐκ τριπορνείας ὄνομα. See McClure 2003b: 277, n. 36. Cf. Athên. 583a.

105. ἥτις καὶ νόμον συσσιτικὸν συνέγραψεν, καθ' ὃν δεῖ τοὺς ἐραστὰς ὡς αὐτήν καὶ τὴν θυγατέρα εἰσιέναι (Athên. 585b2–4). On Gnathaina's *Nomos Sussitikos*, and Athênaios's attitude toward it and her, see Hawley 1993: 77. Rules for a *hetaira*'s behavior are set forth in Plautus's comic contract in *Asinaria*, Act 1, Scene 3. Cf. Naevius, Fr. 2 (*Tarentilla*, based on an unknown Greek work).

106. See, for example, Athên. 580e6–f4.

107. μοὶ μὲν δὸς ὅσον ἐπιθυμεῖς, πάτερ· | οἶδα γὰρ ἀκριβῶς καὶ πέποιθα τοῦθ' ὅτι | εἰς νύκτ' ἀποδώσεις τῷ θυγατρίῳ μου διπλοῦν (Athên. 581c1–3). On Gnathaina's charges, see chapter 7, pp. 167–68.

108. παρὰ Δεξιθέα δειπνοῦσα θἠταίρα ποτὲ Γνάθαινα, τοὔψον ἀποτιθείσης πᾶν σχεδὸν τῆς Δεξιθέας τῇ μητρί, "νὴ τὴν Ἄρτεμιν, εἰ, φησίν, ᾔδειν, ἡ Γνάθαινα, τοῦτ' ἐγώ, τῇ μητρὶ συνεδείπνουν ἄν, οὐχὶ σοί, γύναι" (Athên. 580b9–c3).

Ancient comedy confirms the pattern of mother-daughter continuity (and also portrays sisters working as *hetairai*[109]). In Menander's *Synaristosai*, the courtesan Pythias has raised her daughter Plangôn to follow her calling as a *hetaira*.[110] Although little is known in detail of the plot of *Synaristosai* (which survives only in highly fragmentary form), its scenario seems to have been preserved in *Cistellaria*, a Roman comedy modeled closely on Menander's Greek original.[111] In Plautus's version, the *meretrices* Melaenis and Syra have both trained their daughters Gymnasium and Selenium to practice their mothers' trade.[112] Syra expresses her pleasure at, and dependence on, the considerable profit generated for the family from her daughter's ceaseless meretricious labor.[113] Similarly Webster's reconstruction of the plot of Menander's *Messênia*, again necessarily conjectural because of the fragmentary nature of surviving passages, posits the Messênian woman as the mother of the *hetaira* being kept by Psyllos.[114] Prostitutes' mothers are often centrally important to Roman "palliatae," comic adaptations from Hellenic originals.[115] In Terence's *Eunuchus* (based on Menander's *Eunoukhos* and set in Athens), the *meretrix* Thais is presented as the daughter of a courtesan who had benefited from Thais's long-term relationship with a wealthy

---

109. For example, the title of Plautus's *Bacchides* (a close adaptation of Menander's *Dis Exapatôn*: see chapter 4, n. 13) alludes to the two homonymic *hetairai*-sisters at the epicenter of the drama.

110. Frag. 337 (K-A): Διονυσίων . . . ἦν | πομπή | ὁ δ' ἐπηκολούθησεν μέχρι τοῦ πρὸς τὴν θύραν· | ἔπειτα φοιτῶν καὶ κολακεύων <ἐμέ τε καὶ> | τὴν μητέρ' ἔγνω μ'. . . . For the use of ἔγνω in a sexual sense, see Hermogenês, Περὶ εὑρέσεως 4.11, p. 200. For exegesis of this passage, see the fuller Plautine rendition in the next note below. Cf. the illustration from the "House of Menander" at Mytilênê (Charitonidis, Lilly, and Ginouvès 1970: Plate 5).

111. The identity of content is illustrated by Plautus's rendering of Frag. 337 (set forth in Greek in the preceding footnote): per Dionysia/mater pompam me spectatum duxit. Dum redeo domum,/conspicillo consecutust clanculum me usque ad fores./Inde in amicitiam insinuavit cum matre et mecum simul/blanditiis, muneribus, donis (lines 89–93). Cf. Henry 1985: 128.

112. Ego et tua mater, ambae/meretrices fuimus. Illa te, ego hanc mihi educavi/ex patribus conventiciis. Neque ego hanc superbiai/causa pepuli ad meretricium quaestum, nisi ut ne esurirem (lines 36–39).

113. Haec quidem ecastor cottidie viro nubit, nupsitque hodie,/nubet mox noctu: numquam ego hanc viduam cubare sivi./nam si haec non nubat, lugubri fame familia pereat./ . . . multisque damno et mihi lucro sine meo saepe eris sumptu (lines 41–50).

114. Webster 1974: 162. Cf. Meineke 1839–1857, V.1, p. 100.

115. On *palliatae* and their use as evidence for Athenian legal and social practices, see introduction, pp. 17–18.

"foreigner." [116] In Terence's *Heauton Timoroumenos* (set in Athens and based on Menander's play of the same name),[117] Antiphila provides sexual services, under the watchful eye of her prostitute mother. In Plautus's *Miles Gloriosus* (based on the Greek *Alazôn*), the mother of the *meretrix* Philocomasium is her "procurer" (*lena*), and it is the mother—not Philocomasium—who is plied with wine, jewelry, and delicacies in return for the daughter's sexual services.[118] Similarly, the prostitute's mother is dominant in Plautus's *Asinaria* (adapted from Dêmophilos's *Onagos*[119]). It is Cleareta the "procuress" (*lena*)—not her daughter Philaenium the prostitute (*meretrix*)—who negotiates with Argyrippus the price of her daughter's sexual services; it is Cleareta who subsequently ejects him from the house in which mother and daughter live; it is Cleareta who later again offers Argyrripus exclusive access to Philaenium at an exorbitant price, and who finally enters into a contract with Diabolus for Philaenium's erotic labor.[120] Again, in Plautus's *Truculentus*, the mother of the *meretrix* Phronesium appears to have played an important role "as a *lena* exploiting her daughter in the Greek play Plautus used as his model" (Rosivach 1998: 70) (although she is only an object of discussion in *Truculentus*, where she does not actually appear).

In his *Courtesans' Dialogues* (a work of fiction), Loukianos portrays courtesans' households as dual seats of home and of business—replete with servants expediting sales and services,[121] with mothers proffering advice and demands, and sometimes even with children about to be born (80.2). The *hetaira* (or her mother) is clearly in control, securely ensconced behind doors and gates, security features common to Athenian household

---

116. Donatus *Ad Eun.* 107: puduit dicere Thaidem "meretrix mihi mater fuit," quod tamen significat dicendo alicunde civem alibi habitasse. Cf. lines 119–20, 131–36; Rosivach 1998: 177, nn. 72 and 73.

117. Lines 96–98, as interpreted by Rosivach 1998: 61.

118. Insinuat sese ad illam amicam <mei> eri. | Occepit eiius matri subpalparier | vino, ornamentis opiparisque opsoniis, | itaque intumum ibi se miles apud lenam facit (lines 105–108).

119. On this adaptation, and on the legal aspects of the mother's business dealings, see chapter 4, esp. pp. 98–99 and n. 9.

120. For Cleareta's dealing with Argyrippos, see lines 127, 163–65, 171, 195, 229–36.

121. See, for example, 80. 2 (false report from the servant Dôris upsets the *hetaira* Myrtion); 80.4.3 and 80.10.2 (dispatch of servants to investigate disturbing reports); 80.9.1 (Dorkas reports to Pannykhis, her "owner" [κεκτημένη]); 80.13.4 (Hymnis gives direction to Grammis); 80.15.2.13–14 (Parthenis hired by Krokalê to play music at intimate party). Krôbylê dangles before her newly mature daughter, Korinna, a novice prostitute, a future profuse with attendants (and other accoutrements of wealth)—provided she follows Mother's advice (80.6.2–3).

residences, especially those functioning simultaneously as business locations.¹²² In Loukianos's vignettes, mothers (themselves former prostitutes) frequently handle the business aspects of the household. Krôbylê, for example, a former courtesan, is busy arranging assignations and providing instruction for her daughter, Korinna, a novice prostitute.¹²³ She dangles before Korinna a future profuse with the accoutrements of wealth (for herself and her mother¹²⁴) provided she follows Mother's advice in pursuing her career—"when working as a companion at dinner, never speak more than necessary, don't poke fun at any of the guests, and have eyes only for the man who's paying you"; "in bed, maintain focus and pursue a single goal, to make the man happy and a continuing customer."¹²⁵ Krôbylê reminds Korinna of Krôbylê's sacrifices in raising her, and of the eagerness with which she has awaited Korinna's attaining the ability to repay Mommy (*Mannarion*). Family finances had been adequate while Korinna's father (who had worked in the Piraeus in bronze) had been alive, but Mommy's wages as a worker in fabrics had thereafter barely sufficed.¹²⁶ After years of poverty, now Mommy can even buy Korinna lovely jewelry—from Korinna's earnings (80.6.1)! And the household will now be expanded to include servants. . . .¹²⁷

Loukianos describes another mother/daughter *ergasia*: Lyra and her mother Daphnis. Before Lyra matured, Daphnis was in rags: now she goes about in gold, wearing fine clothing, accompanied by four servants.¹²⁸ Another

---

122. See E. Cohen 1992: 68–69; Young 1956: 122–46; Osborne 1985: 31–34, 63–67; Peˆcirka 1973: 123–28.

123. Mother as past courtesan: "cortigiana anziana" (Pellizer and Sirugo 1995: 164), a deduction from her manifest expertise. Assignations: νῦν δ᾽ ἄπιθι λουσομένη, εἰ ἀφίκοιτο καὶ τήμερον τὸ μειράκιον ὁ Εὔκριτος· ὑπισχνεῖτο γάρ (80.6.4).

124. 80.6.2: θρέψεις μὲν ἐμέ, σεαυτὴν δὲ κατακοσμήσεις ῥαδίως καὶ πλουτήσεις καὶ ἐσθῆτας ἕξεις ἀλουργεῖς καὶ θεραπαίνας. 80.6.4: Οὐχ ὁρᾷς τὴν Κόρινναν τὴν τῆς Κρωβύλης θυγατέρα ὡς ὑπερπλουτεῖ καὶ τρισευδαίμονα πεποίηκε τὴν μητέρα;

125. 80.6.3: ἢν δέ ποτε καὶ ἀπέλθῃ ἐπὶ δεῖπνον λαβοῦσα μίσθωμα . . . οὔτε πλέον τοῦ δέοντος φθέγγεται οὔτε ἀποσκώπτει ἐς τινα τῶν παρόντων, ἐς μόνον δὲ τὸν μισθωσάμενον βλέπει. . . . ἐπειδὰν κοιμᾶσθαι δέῃ, ἀσελγὲς «οὐδὲν» οὐδὲ ἀμελὲς ἐκείνη ἄν τι ἐργάσαιτο, ἀλλὰ ἐξ ἅπαντος ἕν τοῦτο θηρᾶται, ὡς ὑπαγάγοιτο καὶ ἐραστὴν ποιήσειεν ἐκεῖνον·

126. 80.6.1: ὅτε δὲ ἐκεῖνος ἔζη, πάντα ἦν ἡμῖν ἱκανά· ἐχάλκευε γάρ . . . νῦν μὲν ὑφαίνουσα, νῦν δὲ κρόκην κατάγουσα ἢ στήμονα κλώθουσα ἐποριζόμην τὰ σιτία μόλις·

127. 80.6.2: ἕξεις θεραπαίνας. . . . σὺ γὰρ πλουτήσεις. . . .

128. 80.6.2: τὴν Δαφνίδα . . . ῥάκη, πρὶν αὐτὴν ἀκμάσαι τὴν ὥραν, περιβεβλημένην· ἀλλὰ νῦν ὁρᾷς οἵα πρόεισι, χρυσὸς καὶ ἐσθῆτες εὐανθεῖς καὶ θεράπαιναι τέτταρες.

of Loukianos's mothers provides her daughter, Gorgona, with an important competitive advantage: aphrodisiacal drugs![129] Mousarion's mother works at building her daughter's clientele[130]—but confronts Mousarion's inclination to favor *amour* over revenue. For the mother, dependent on her daughter's earnings, prostitution is a business, not an amorous bet on future happiness.[131] But when Mother's not looking, Mousarion gives her lover gifts, and turns away paying customers whom her mother favors.[132] Philinna's mother has the opposite problem: equally dependent on selling her daughter's sexual favors, she finds Philinna financially naive about retaining a good lover. After a dinner party at which Philinna has kissed and embraced a male friend of her estranged patron, Diphilos—in the patron's enraged presence—her mother forbids such behavior in the future, reminding her of the family's dependence on Diphilos, offering the proverb "Don't kill the golden goose!"[133]

But the best overview of matrilineality in Athenian female prostitution is provided by the detailed chronicle in Demosthenes 59 of the career, practices, and household of the Greek businesswoman Nikaretê, her daughter Neaira, and Neaira's daughter Phanô, all of whom worked as prostitutes (according to the opposing speaker). The junior women labored under the direction, and for the primary financial benefit, of the senior women (and allegedly, in Neaira's case, of her husband, Stephanos). A former *hetaira* herself,[134] a free person of servile origin married to a cook who appears to have been entirely uninvolved in his wife's sexual business (*tekhnê*), Nikaretê supposedly earned her living (*bios*) from her talent at identifying,

---

129. 80.1.2: φαρμακὶς ἡ Χρυσάριόν ἐστιν ἡ μήτηρ αὐτῆς, Θεσσαλάς τινας ᾠδὰς ἐπισταμένη . . . ἐκείνη ἐξέμηνε τὸν ἄνθρωπον πιεῖν τῶν φαρμάκων ἐγχέασα, καὶ νῦν τρυγῶσιν αὐτόν.

130. 80.7.1: Ἂν δ᾽ ἔτι τοιοῦτον ἐραστὴν εὕρωμεν. . . .

131. (Other prostitutes are) συνετώτεραι καὶ ἴσασιν ἑταιρίζειν (80.7.3). She asks her daughter: σὺ δὲ οἴει ὀκτωκαίδεκα ἐτῶν ἀεὶ ἔσεσθαι; ἢ τὰ αὐτὰ φρονήσειν Χαιρέαν, ὅταν πλουτῇ μὲν αὐτός (80.7.4); ἡλίκα παρὰ τοῦ νεανίσκου λαμβάνομεν (80.7.1). With good customers, mother and daughter will do better financially (τρισευδαίμονες ἐσόμεθα) (80.7.1) But Mousarion is starry-eyed: φησὶν ἡμᾶς γαμήσειν καὶ μεγάλας ἐλπίδας ἔχομεν παρ᾽ αὐτοῦ (80.7.2).

132. 80.7.1: τὸν δάκτυλον δέδωκας ἀγνοούσης ἐμου. 80.7.3: τί καὶ Ἀντιφῶντα μνᾶν ὑπισχνούμενον οὐδὲ τοῦτον ἐδέξω; οὐ καλὸς ἦν καὶ ἀστικὸς καὶ ἡλικιώτης Χαιρέου. . . .

133. 80.3.3: ὅρα μὴ κατὰ τὴν παροιμίαν ἀπορρήξωμεν πάνυ τείνουσαι τὸ καλῴδιον. Literally: "Stretching the string, let's not break it!"

134. Athên. 596e (Νικαρέτη ἡ ἑταίρα). Cf. Kapparis 1999: 207 (who does not rule out a meretricious career for Nikaretê, although he questions the reliability of Athênaios as source).

cultivating, "skillfully" training and then selling the services of attractive young girls.[135] In the conduct of this business, Nikaretê came to Athens with Metaneira and Neaira, purportedly her daughters,[136] whom she hired out as prostitutes at prices extraordinarily profitable for Nikaretê.[137] In fact, elevated financial return is advanced in Demosthenes 59 as the economic rationale for Nikaretê's proffering of her own daughters as whores: the "highest prices" might thus be obtained (see chapter 7, pp. 168–71). Although Neaira's opponent in Demosthenes 59 insists that the seven girls working for Nikaretê (Neaira included) were mere slaves purchased at an early age by Nikaretê, he does concede that each of these "daughters" was ultimately recognized as free[138]—a status seemingly unlikely to be obtained by each and all of seven slave prostitutes if they had truly been mere chattels of Nikaretê. While the text of Demosthenes 59 does contain some evidentiary support for Neaira's actually being the daughter of Nikaretê,[139] resolution of Neaira's true status is today impossible.[140] But more importantly for our purposes—given Athenian court speakers' focus on crafting

---

135. Dem. 59.18: Χαιρισίου μὲν οὖσα τοῦ Ἠλείου ἀπελευθέρα, Ἱππίου δὲ τοῦ μαγείρου τοῦ ἐκείνου γυνή, δεινὰ δὲ [καὶ δυναμένη] φύσιν μικρῶν παιδίων συνιδεῖν εὐπρεπῆ, καὶ ταῦτα ἐπισταμένη θρέψαι καὶ παιδεῦσαι ἐμπείρως, τέχνην ταύτην κατεσκευασμένη καὶ ἀπὸ τούτων τὸν βίον συνειλεγμένη.

136. Dem. 59.21–22: Λυσίας γὰρ ὁ σοφιστὴς Μετανείρας ὢν ἐραστής, ἐβουλήθη πρὸς τοῖς ἄλλοις ἀναλώμασιν οἷς ἀνήλισκεν εἰς αὐτὴν καὶ μυῆσαι . . . ἐδεήθη οὖν τῆς Νικαρέτης ἐλθεῖν εἰς τὰ μυστήρια ἄγουσαν τὴν Μετάνειραν . . . συνηκολούθει δὲ καὶ Νέαιρα αὑτῄ, ἐργαζομένη μὲν ἤδη τῷ σώματι. Dem. 59.19: προειποῦσα δ' αὐτὰς ὀνόματι θυγατέρας.

137. Nikaretê charged for Neaira's ongoing services alone a sum sufficient to meet all of the expenses of her well-populated (Dem. 59.18) and sumptuous (*polytelês*) household: πολυτελὴς ἦν ἡ Νικαρέτη τοῖς ἐπιτάγμασιν, ἀξιοῦσα τὰ καθ' ἡμέραν ἀναλώματα ἅπαντα τῇ οἰκίᾳ παρ' αὐτῶν λαμβάνειν (Dem. 59.29).

138. §§ 18–20: Ἑπτὰ γὰρ ταύτας παιδίσκας ἐκ μικρῶν παιδίων ἐκτήσατο Νικαρέτη . . . Ἄντειαν καὶ Στρατόλαν καὶ Ἀριστόκλειαν καὶ Μετάνειραν καὶ Φίλαν καὶ Ἰσθμιάδα καὶ Νέαιραν ταυτηνί. ἣν μὲν οὖν ἕκαστος αὐτῶν ἐκτήσατο καὶ ὡς ἠλευθερώθησαν ἀπὸ τῶν πριαμένων αὐτὰς παρὰ τῆς Νικαρέτης . . . δηλώσω ὑμῖν. . . .

139. The deposition that follows (believed to be authentic: Carey 1992: 97; Kirschner 1885: 77 ff.) suggests that the deponent believed Neaira actually to have been the daughter of Nikaretê: Φιλόστρατος Διονυσίου Κολωνῆθεν μαρτυρεῖ εἰδέναι Νέαιραν Νικαρέτης οὖσαν, ἧσπερ καὶ Μετάνειρα ἐγένετο. . . . (§23). Because the primary and original meaning of γίγνομαι is "be born," it seems reasonable to treat the genitive form of Neaira here as denoting family relationship.

140. Any judgment is necessarily subjective. Carey, for example, recognizes that details about personal life in Athenian oratory often reflect "only scandalous and unreliable detail," and that "all we know about Neaira derives from this speech." (He nonetheless believes that "the broad outlines of the account are likely to be correct" [1992: 1–2].)

persuasive arguments by offering credible factual patterns[141]—the speech assumes acceptance by an Athenian audience of the plausibility of such mother-daughter arrangements. Here the jury is expected to accept as reasonable the assertion that Neaira worked with her own daughter, Phanô, and her husband, Stephanos, to create "a home that was really a brothel from which they (the family members) earned a good living through prostitution."[142] Neaira accordingly arranged assignations for her daughter.[143] One customer, Epainetos, claimed to have expended huge sums for sex with both the mother and daughter—only to be shaken-down by Stephanos, here playing the professional role of an injured father who had caught Epainetos having sex with his daughter.[144] The affair seems to have been settled by Epainetos's payment of 1,000 *drachmas* for having often "used" Phano.[145]

---

141. See introduction, pp. 14–15 ff.

142. Dem. 59.67: ἐργαστήριον φάσκων καὶ τοῦτο εἶναι, τὴν Στεφάνου οἰκίαν, καὶ τὴν ἐργασίαν ταύτην εἶναι, καὶ ἀπὸ τούτων αὐτοὺς εὐπορεῖν μάλιστα.

143. Ibid.: τήν τε μητέρα αὐτῆς συνειδέναι πλησιάζουσαν αὐτῷ.

144. Dem. 59.64–67: ἐραστὴν ὄντα Νεαίρας ταυτησὶ παλαιὸν καὶ πολλὰ ἀνηλωκότα εἰς αὐτὴν ... (ὁ Στέφανος) λαμβάνει μοιχὸν ἐπὶ τῇ θυγατρὶ τῇ Νεαίρας ταυτησί ... πλησιάζουσαν αὐτῷ, ἀνηλωκέναι τε πολλὰ εἰς αὐτάς. Cf. §68: Στρέφανος ... πορνοβοσκῶν. On the interaction of husband and wife in business, see this chapter, pp. 137–38.

145. Dem. 59.71: Ἐπαίνετον δὲ δοῦναι χιλίας δραχμὰς Φανοῖ εἰς ἔκδοσιν, ἐπειδὴ κέχρηται αὐτῇ πολλάκις. Carey (1992: 121) judges this "settlement document" to be "probably genuine"; Kapparis disagrees (1999: 316–17). On Neaira's opponent's failure to brand Phanô explicitly as a *pornê* or a *hetaira*, see Miner 2003: 24–27.

# 7

# *The Costs, and Rewards, of Sexual Services*

BY THE FOURTH century, Athenian prices—including those for sexual services—were universally expressed not in commodity equivalents but in monetary units (*drachmas* and *obols*).[1] These prices reflected the workings of supply-and-demand factors, almost entirely free of governmental involvement, a process that facilitated the emergence of prostitutes of extraordinary wealth and high income—the so-called "big earners" (*megalomisthoi*).[2] The loss of tax records and other information from the fourth century leaves surviving literary material as the prime source for the pricing of sexual services and for the levels of income and assets attained by prostitutes.[3] Use of such material, however, is not unproblematic. Relevant authors, especially those writing long after the fourth century (like Loukianos and Alkiphrôn), often would have lacked exact, and sometimes even approximate, knowledge of actual prices and other commercial arrangements. Moreover, there is a danger of inaccurate and superficial conclusions if literary material is interpreted without contextualization: close attention

---

1. For the monetization of Athens (and the abandonment of an earlier system of barter and payment in kind), see Schaps 2004, esp. Chapter 8 ("Everything sold in the marketplace was sold for a price, and the price was expressed and expected in coins" [p. 111]). Cf. chapter 3, nn. 90 and 91 (and related text). On the composition and value of Athenian currency, see "Conventions," p. x.

2. Literally, as substantive, "those receiving high pay." See Athên. 569a; Louk. *Apol.* 15, *Herm.* 578. Cf. chapter 5, nn. 13 and 39, and related text.

3. For the contemporary maintenance at Athens of tax records and other information relating to prostitutes and prostitution, and for the failure of this material to survive, see introduction, p. 13.

must be paid to a given work's imaginative, rhetorical, intertextual, and semiotic facets, and to more prosaic historical and philological aspects (see introduction, pp. 12–20).

Consider the corpus of Menander, potentially a prime source of information on Athenian life, especially sexuality, and yet an exemplar of comic humor based on exaggeration.[4] When a character in the ("Flatterer"), a work preserved only in fragments, asserts that a certain prostitute was earning 300 *drachmas* per night (perhaps US$15,000–30,000 in purchasing power equivalence[5]), we have no means of determining whether comic considerations have generated grotesque hyperbole or whether some courtesans actually could command such sums. Gomme and Sandbach find the fee "inflated" but credible (1973: 430–31); Loomis deems it "conceivable but unlikely" (1998: 177). Yet for the purposes of economic history, both judgments are equivalent. Despite the impossibility of determining the truth regarding this specific fee, we can safely conclude that in real life, at least some courtesans did command flagrantly elevated fees, not because Athenian comedy necessarily replicates the factual details of Athenian life ("Old Comedy" certainly does not), but because of Menander's practice of closely aligning his plots and characters with the contextual details of actual life, a Menandrian skill noted and praised in antiquity.[6] Scholars have recurrently demonstrated how Menander's work preserves reliable information about Athenian society, class, and gender, even regarding, for example, specific details of the laws of property and succession.[7] Similar insight is sometimes provided by other literary works, but is often subject to nuanced interpretability.

To facilitate appropriate use of such material, I will proceed first to examine the economic context in which prostitutional fees were set, and only thereafter will examine the evidence that confirms the high sums that appear often to have been expended for erotic services at Athens. More importantly for the prostitute himself or herself was the question, how much, if any, of such elevated compensation (or even of relatively small

---

4. See introduction, pp. 15–16.

5. Lines 117 ff. (see this chapter, n. 72). On "purchasing power equivalence" as a guide to evaluating prices stated in Athenian currency, see convertions, p. 10.

6. ὦ Μένανδρε, καὶ βίε, πότερος ἄρ' ὑμῶν πότερον ἀπεμιμήσατο; Aristoph. Byzant. (*Test. Men.* 83 K.A.). Cf. Quintil. *Inst. Or.* 10.1.69. For further examples of this alignment, see introduction, pp. 16–17.

7. See Buis 2014: 334–37; Cox 2002: 391; Hunter 1994: 85, 217, n. 26; Patterson 1998: 191–205.

fees) might be retained by the sex-worker? Although it is often assumed that slaves' owners appropriated all monies earned by their chattels, various mechanisms had emerged at Athens through which even brothel slaves were able to retain at least a portion of the monies paid for their services. These are described toward the end of this chapter.

## *The Pricing Process at Athens*

At Athens the state was generally uninterested, and uninvolved, in commercial activity, including the pricing of sexual services. Thus the authority of market officials, the *agoranomoi*, was limited to maintaining order and preventing blatant fraud.[8] Except for some modest protection against the making of patently false claims and against the offering of adulterated or defective goods,[9] consumers were not the beneficiaries of warranties relating to the quality or usability of products purchased, nor the recipients of any other governmentally imposed juridical advantages or legal safeguards. The state's lack of involvement in the economy is strikingly illustrated by a complex financial transaction in which a young citizen, Epikratês, was allegedly defrauded in connection with his purchase of a perfume business burdened by substantial (and allegedly undisclosed) debts (Hypereidês, *Against Athênogenês*). The putative victim is left haplessly to seek redress for himself through private legal action: no administrative body is available to protect his rights (Whitehead 2000: 306).

Official intervention in business matters was limited almost entirely to facilitating the availability and affordability of grain,[10] but even here governmental action was constrained. Because of its inability to grow

---

8. Aristot. *Ath. Pol.* 51.1: ἀγορανόμοι . . . τούτοις δὲ ὑπὸ τῶν νόμων προστέτακται τῶν ὠνίων ἐπιμελεῖσθαι πάντων, ὅπως καθαρὰ καὶ ἀκίβδηλα πωλήσεται. Cf. Harp., s.v. κατὰ τὴν ἀγορὰν ἀψευδεῖν, quoting Theophrastos in *The Laws* (Szegedy-Maszak 1981: fr. 20): δυοῖν τούτων ἐπιμελεῖσθαι δεῖν τοὺς ἀγορανόμους, τῆς τε ἐν τῇ ἀγορᾷ εὐκοσμιάς καὶ τοῦ ἀψευδεῖν μὴ μόνον τοὺς πιπράσκοντας ἀλλὰ καὶ τοὺς ὠνουμένους. On the functioning of the *agoranomoi*, see Couilloud-Le Dinahet 1988; Fantasia 2012.

9. False Statements: Dem. 20.9 (κατὰ τὴν ἀγορὰν ἀψευδεῖν νόμον γεγράφθαι); Hyper. *Athên.* 14. Cf. Marzi 1977: 221, n. 37; Ste. Croix 1972: 399. Goods: Hyper. *Athên.* 15 (defective slaves). Cf. Triantyphyllopoulos 1968: 2–7; Stanley 1976: 206–207.

10. The government is known to have involved itself in only one other area of commerce—the avoidance of disorder in the streets by controlling potential disputes over the services of female musicians (see this chapter, pp. 163–64).

sufficient barley and wheat in its own territory,[11] Athens had to import hundreds of ship cargoes of grain annually.[12] Athenian law forbade the shipping of cereals by residents of Attika to any location other than Athens,[13] or the lending of money by residents for transportation of grain to sites outside Attika.[14] Not more than one-third of wheat or barley on board ships arriving in Athens could be re-exported (a restriction applicable even to shippers not domiciled in Attika).[15] The state also made some effort to preclude excessive charges for grain. Thus the Council (*Boulê*) is known on at least one occasion to have been involved in legal action to prevent wholesale purchasers (*sitopôlai*) from banding together to buy grain (and thus possibly impose artificially high, monopolistic prices on Athenian consumers).[16] The grain supply was an obligatory subject for periodic consideration at meetings of the Athenian Assembly (*Ekklêsia*).[17] Such deliberations—at a time of grain shortages caused by endemic piracy and a Spartan naval blockade[18]—led to the appointment of the *nomothetai*, who promulgated the Grain Law of 374/3, discovered in the American excavations of the Agora and published in 1998.[19] This statute provided for the taxation and delivery of barley and wheat from the islands of Lemnos, Imbros, and Skyros (which were under Athenian control), and the sale of this grain at prices set by the Assembly.[20]

---

11. Despite wide variability in the assumptions, methodologies, and conclusions of the large number of scholars who have studied the grain requirements of Athens, virtually all agree on the need for extensive imports: Whitby 1998 (contains full references to primary sources and prior scholarship). Cf. Bissa 2009: 169, 191.

12. Oliver 2007: 15–41; Moreno 2007: 3–33, 323–34; Reed 2003: 18–19. On a single occasion and in a single area, Philip of Macedon in 340 seized between 180 and 230 grain ships bound for Athens (Bresson 1994; Engen 2010: 64, 333 n. 53).

13. Dem. 34.37, 35.50–51. Cf. Lykourg. 1.27.

14. Dem. 35.51. Cf. Dem. 56.11.

15. Aristot. *Ath. Pol.* 51.4. Cf. Harp. and Suidas, s.v. ἐπιμεληταὶ ἐμπορίου.

16. Lysias 22. See Figueira 1986; Gauthier 1981; Seager 1966.

17. Aristot. *Ath. Pol.* 43.4. Cf. Mossé 1996: 37–38.

18. Xen. *Hell.* 5.4.60–61; Dem. 20.77; Diod. 15.34.3–35.2; Plut. *Phôk.* 6, *Camill.* 19.3; Polyainos 3.11.2. For the historical background, see Tuplin 1993: 159; Brun 1983: 39–48.

19. *Editio princeps*: Stroud 1998. For the numerous interpretations of this statute, see Faraguna 2010, 1999b, 2007; Migeotte 2014: 455–56; Bresson 2000a; Osborne 2000; Engels 2001; Fantasia 2004; Jakab 2007; Moreno 2003.

20. πωλόντων ἐν τῆι ἀγ[ορ]ᾶι, ὅταν τῶι δήμωι δοκῆι· πω λεν δὲ μὴ ἐ[ξε]ῖναι ἐπιψηφίσαι πρότερον τοῦ Ἀνθεσ[τ]ηριῶνος μηνός· ὁ δὲ δῆμος ταξάτω τὴν τ[ι]μὴν τῶν πυρῶν καὶ τῶν κριθῶν ὁπόσου χ[ρ]ὴ πωλεν τοὺς αἱρεθέντας (Stroud 1998: lines 41–46).

Migeotte has suggested (2010: 428–30) that the price so set, in the Grain Law and on the occasion of a few other public sales of food, was the *kathestêkuia timê*, an enigmatic term that appears several times in Demosthenes and in surviving epigraphical material.[21] Efforts to explain this expression have generated extensive academic discussion over considerably more than a century.[22] Many scholars render *kathestêkuia timê* as "market price" (i.e., the amount actually being charged, without governmental or similar coercion, in a given place at a given time).[23] Many others prefer "established price" (the amount required under some external standard—be it historical cost, customary charge, or price set officially for a general or specific purpose [as with Migeotte's governmental grain sales]). This "established price" might even look to market prices—"normal" or "prevailing"—as a starting point or as a determinative criterion.[24]

The relevant surviving literary sources provide support for both interpretations. In Demosthenes 56, the speaker reports that at a time of fluctuating grain prices certain Athens-based grain merchants were sending information on a continuing basis concerning the price (*kathestêkuia timê*) of cereals at Athens to confederates who were sailing with a cargo of grain from Egypt. If cereals were expensive at Athens, the grain was to be sent to Athens, but if prices were low, it was to be delivered to another commercial harbor.[25] Here *kathestêkuia timê* seems necessarily to refer to a market price that was fluctuating with variations in supply and demand. Indeed, while the confederates' ship was on its way from Egypt, arrival

---

21. καθεστηκυῖα τιμή: Dem. 34.39, 56.8 and 10. See also a decree of the deme of Rhamnous (Bielman 1994: 95 ff., #24, line 19 = S.E.G 24.154), which refers in ambiguous context to a καθεστηκυῖα τιμή. IG II².400 is sometimes said to refer to a καθεστηκυῖα τιμή, but this reading is merely a restoration by Wilhelm (1889: 148–49, n. 1) of a very fragmentary stone ([τῆς καθισταμ]ένης τιμ[ῆ]ς). Cf. I.G. II ² 499. Ptolemaic papyri from third-century Egypt mention *hestêkuia timê* (PTeb 703, l. 176) and *kathistamenê timê* (PRevLaws, col. 40, 9–16).

22. The earliest discussion of which I know is that of Boeckh 1886 (I: 118, note c; II: 26, n. 63) (written and published earlier). Cf. Wilhelm 1889.

23. Valente 2009; Bers 2003: 96–97; Figueira 1986: 165; Seager 1966; Carey and Reid 1985: 213–14; Bolkestein [1939] 1969: 258, n. 2.

24. Also termed "fixed price": Reger 1993: 312–13; Ampolo 1986: 147; Boeckh [1817] 1886, I, 118, note c; Gernet 1909: 374 ["prix fixé par le commerce international"]; Andreades [1933] 1979: 244, n. 14 ["established price"]; Millett 1990: 193, n. 56 ("customary price").

25. §8: Εἶτα πρὸς τὰς καθεστηκυίας τιμὰς ἔπεμπον γράμματα οἱ ἐπιδημοῦντες τοῖς ἀποδημοῦσιν, ἵνα ἐὰν μὲν παρ' ὑμῖν τίμιος ᾖ ὁ σῖτος, δεῦρο αὐτὸν κομίσωσιν, ἐὰν δ' εὐωνότερος γένηται, εἰς ἄλλο τι καταπλεύσωσιν ἐμπόριον.

of grain supplies from Sicily depressed prices at Athens—whereupon the merchants offloaded their cargo at Rhodes.[26] Yet in Demosthenes 34, the speaker explains that at a time when grain was selling at 16 *drachmas* per *medimnon*, the speaker (and his brother) provided it at the *kathestêkuia timê* of 5 *drachmas*, contrasting the higher market price of 16 *drachmas* with the much lower *kathestêkuia timê*.[27] Because the text of Demosthenes 34 is in conflict with that of Demosthenes 56, efforts have been made (without paleographical justification) to emend the text of the former to state just the opposite of the received text, namely, that when grain was being priced at 16 *drachmas* per *medimnon*, the speaker provided these foodstuffs at 5 *drachmas* per *medimon* <INSTEAD OF> at the *kathestêkuia timê*.[28]

Yet even those scholars interpreting *kathestêkuia timê* as an "established price" have emphasized the importance of supply-and-demand mechanisms in "establishing" this price, and have noted the rarity (and extraordinary nature) of governmental intrusion into market arrangements and pricing even in the case of cereal products. Thus Reger suggests that *kathestêkuia timê* "refer(s) to a price below market set by law or strongly recommended by city officials (like the *agoranomoi*) for the sale of grain during periods of shortage" (1993: 313). The referent for pricing even during this period, however, was still market-determined: the official price was intended to reflect "normal" supply/demand charges—"perhaps prices typical immediately after the harvest served as a guide" (Ibid.). Similarly, Migeotte (2010: 426–30) identifies the *kathestêkuia timê* as the price set by the state for emergency public distributions of grain during those extraordinary periods when normal sources had been disturbed.[29] But because these governmental diffusions occurred irregularly (and even then only citizens were recipients), an autonomous retail market would have continued to exist—whose prices were only indirectly and temporarily affected

---

26. §10: λαβὼν . . . ὁ τουτουὶ κοινωνὸς τὰ γράμματα τὰ παρὰ τούτου ἀποσταλέντα, καὶ πυθόμενος τὰς τιμὰς τὰς ἐνθάδε τοῦ σίτου καθεστηκυίας, ἐξαιρεῖται τὸν σῖτον ἐν τῇ Ῥόδῳ κἀκεῖ ἀποδίδοται.

27. §39: ὅτε δ' ὁ σῖτός ἐπετιμήθη τὸ πρότερον καὶ ἐγένετο ἑκκαίδεκα δραχμῶν, εἰσαγαγόντες πλείους ἢ μυρίους μεδίμνους πυρῶν διεμετρήσαμεν ὑμῖν τῆς καθεστηκυίας τιμῆς, πέντε δραχμῶν τὸν μέδιμνον. . . .

28. Koehler suggested: <ἀντὶ> τῆς καθεστηκυίας τιμῆς. Cf. Marasco 1992: 33–35.

29. Cf. Migeotte 1998; Gallo 1997: 22 ("prezzo vigente in condizioni di regolare disponibilità del prodotto"); Fantasia 1987; Ampolo 1986.

by state action.³⁰ Accordingly, Bresson (2000a: 205–06) has proposed that the *kathestêkuia timê* represents a "fixed wholesale price" (*prix de gros fixé*) that was changed by the *polis* from time to time to reflect the retail market price (which continued to be determined by factors of supply and demand).³¹ Thus the sales mentioned in the Athenian Grain Law took place "in the Agora" (*en têi agorai*) rather than in the retail grain market at Athens (*en tôi sitôi*).³² Since the Grain Law was intended not only to provide cereals to the citizens³³ but also to raise revenue for the state (from the sale to tax-farmers of revenues from the three islands), "in setting the sale price the Athenian people" would have had to choose between "high income or cheap grain" (Osborne 2000: 172). In reality, even in this specialized context, the government was effectively subsidizing the wholesale cost of grain, not controlling the retail price.

All proffered explanations of the *kathestêkuia timê* thus share a recognition that at Athens pricing even of grain was normally determined by market factors. A fortiori, prices for all other items—to which the state paid far less, if any, attention—should have been entirely or essentially free of governmental edict. (In fact, there is no evidence of any official intervention affecting prices of any other foodstuffs at Athens in the classical period.³⁴) Yet scholarly reconstruction of the Athenian economy still tends to portray Athens as a society in which state dictates and other nonmarket considerations determined charges for services.³⁵ Instead of an infinite variety of possible charges established by supply-and-demand pricing,

---

30. "Toutes ces interventions ... n'avaient sur les prix courants que des effets indirects, dont les prix de détail bénéficaient à leur tour ... En dehors des moments de crise, ces interventions perdaient leur raison d'être et les affaires suivaient leur cours normal" (Migeotte 1997: 45).

31. "A Athènes, la fixation du cours du grain importé obéissait à une procédure ... de l'établissement d'une *kathestêkuia timê*: ce prix était réajusté périodiquement en fonction de la loi de l'offre et de la demande" (2000: 205).

32. On the grain market at Athens (ἐν τῶι σίτωι), see Stroud 1974: 180.

33. ὅπως ἂν τῶι δήμωι σι[το]ς ἦι ἐν τῶι κοινῶι (Stroud 1998: 5–6).

34. There is some evidence for governmental involvement in the sale of olive oil, but only during the period of Roman domination: see I.G. II ² 903, sometime in the second century, perhaps 175–170 B.C.E.

35. "La 'Nouvelle Orthodoxie' considère que le marché n'existait pas dans les sociétes anciennes" (Bresson 2000: 272). This "orthodoxy" underlies even such relatively recent studies as Möller 2000; Grenier 1997; Tandy 1997. Cf. Calcagno 2001; Millett 1990, esp. 193; Meikle 1995.

many scholars have insisted on a "standard wage" at Athens of 1 *drachma* per day,[36] perhaps the equivalent of US$50–100 (calculated in terms of purchasing power[37]). This scholarly vision of "standard" rather than market-based pricing reflects the old, orthodox view of Athens as exemplar of an "embedded economy," in which "goods circulated through reciprocity and redistribution rather than through . . . supply and demand."[38] Recent years, however, have brought a multitude of challenges to this view, now largely abandoned among specialists,[39] that Athens entirely lacked a market economy and that economic arrangements were embedded in cultural, social, and political relationships. Loomis, for relevant example, in an exhaustive study of "wages" in Athens has shown that "the frequently repeated statement that the 'standard wage at Athens was one *drachma* per day' is not supported by the evidence" [1998: 257]).

## The Price of Sex

But this change in paradigm has not yet reached the study of Athenian prostitution. Indeed, some modern scholars still seek to impose on Athenian prostitutes stringent administrative regulations,[40] including state control of prices that might be charged for sex.

Assertions are frequently made to the effect that "in Athens, (female) prostitutes were controlled by the clerk of the market (*agoranomos*), who fixed the fee (2 *drachmas*) that they could charge for a single visit,"[41] and that for male

---

36. See, for example, Burford 1972: 138; Himmelman 1979: 139–40; Gallo 1987: 47, 58; Stewart 1990: xii, 65–66.

37. On purchasing-power equivalencies relating to Athens, and for other approaches to exchange ratios, see "Conventions," p. x.

38. Morris 1994: 352. See Polanyi 1957; Weber [1921] 1958, [1909] 1976. For the continuing importance of Polanyi's conceptualizations for students of archaic Greece and of modern Institutional Economics, see Möller 2004; Maucourant 2000.

39. See, for example, Bresson 2007/8: I. 3, 7–36; Morris and Manning 2005: 30 (listing recent criticisms of earlier dogma); Christesen 2004; Schaps 2004: 32–33, 1998; Silver 2004, 2003; Harris 2001; Kron 1996. Resistance to "market" approaches to ancient Greece is not, however, extinct: see Mattingly and Salmon 2001: 3; Millett 2001: 24, 40 (n. 26).

40. See chapter 5.

41. Krenkel 1988: 1294. (*Agoranomos* is an erroneous reference to the *astynomos* of *Ath. Pol.* 50.2 (n. 43, this chapter). Similarly: Henderson 2014: 186 ("By law, a prostitute's fee was limited to two drachmas.") Herter [1960] 2003: 71–72: two *drachmas* "officially established as the maximum" for "the simplest form of love"; Keuls 1985: 208 ("the finances of prostitutes were controlled by the city magistrates [astynomoi]"). Cf. Reinsberg 1993: 144.

prostitutes there was a standard fee of 4 *drachmas* "that was higher than the fee charged by female prostitutes" (Krenkel 1978, 1988: 1294, 1296). These claims have no factual basis. The "standard" male fee of 4 *drachmas* is merely the amount sued for by a certain Diophantos, who claimed that he had not been paid for the performance of a sex act (*praxis*).[42] Even in this case, our sources provide no indication whether 4 *drachmas* was Diophantos's entire fee (or merely the portion left unpaid). The alleged government-imposed limit of 2 *drachmas* for a single encounter with a woman is derived from a provision in Aristotle's *Constitution of the Athenians* describing the jurisdiction of the *astynomoi* ("city commissioners") over the streets, including such matters as discharges by drainpipes into public roadways, encroachments on thoroughfares by buildings and balconies, and the maintenance of an orderly process for the hiring of female musicians (who apparently congregated in certain street location[s]). If bidding for the services of these performers exceeded 2 *drachmas*, the *astynomoi* were authorized to allocate the musician(s) through a lottery process to one of the parties seeking their services.[43] Because of the popular ascription to musicians of sexual availability,[44] scholars have interpreted this provision as a limit on compensation for female sexual services—not merely for musically inclined prostitutes, but for all women. This arrangement, however, is better interpreted, in my opinion, as precisely what it purports to be—a limit, presumably for each engagement, on the maximum price to be paid for musical accompaniment—a ceiling intended to avoid brawls on public thoroughfares from competing revelers: "On the street the flute-girls really came into their element, in the *kômos*, a conga of revelers" (Rhodes [1981] 1993: 81), in which "Woman is present as musician, dancer, flutist, or parasol-bearer, not as hetaira" (Frontisi-Ducroux and Lissarrague 1990: 228). In fact, literary sources and surviving illustrative material suggest that many performers were skilled artists who had no involvement in commercial sex.[45] If musicians "might

---

42. Aiskh. 1.158: Τίς γὰρ ὑμῶν τὸν ὀρφανὸν καλούμενον Διόφαντον οὐκ οἶδεν, ὅς τὸν ξένον πρὸς τὸν ἄρχοντα ἀπήγαγεν . . . ἐπαιτιασάμενος τέτταρας δραχμὰς αὐτὸν ὑπὲρ τῆς πράξεως ταύτης ἀπεστερηκέναι; The term *praxis* implies a transaction for commercial consideration: see Xen. *Anab*. 1.3.16, *Kyn*. 2.2; Pind. *Ol*. 1.85; PMag. Par. 1.2366.

43. 50.2: ἀστυνόμοι . . . καὶ τάς τε αὐλητρίδας καὶ τὰς ψαλτρίας καὶ τὰς κιθαριστρίας οὗτοι σκοποῦσιν ὅπως μὴ πλείονος ἢ δυεῖν δραχμαῖς μισθωθήσονται, κἂν πλείους τὴν αὐτὴν σπουδάσωσι λαβεῖν οὗτοι διακληροῦσι καὶ τῷ λαχόντι μισθοῦσιν. Cf. Hyper. *Eux*. 3.

44. See Coccagna 2011: 119, n. 3; Davidson 1997: 80–82; McClure 2003a: 21.

45. See, for example, Pl. *Symp*. 176e. Cf. Kennedy 2014: 127–29; Goldman (forthcoming); Lewis 2002: 95–97.

also be called on to provide sexual entertainment,"[46] these erotic services "would be a matter of separate negotiation" (Loomis 1998: 94)—and there is no reason why the charges ultimately agreed upon might not have far exceeded the putative limitation imposed by modern scholars.

In fact, substantial evidence indicates a wide range of prices for both male and female sex, a spectrum reflective not of governmental edict but of the parties' situation, needs, desires, and capacity.[47] Prices actually varied so greatly that Lykôn, the Peripatetic philosopher, achieved notoriety for having determined precisely what each female prostitute in Athens sought to charge.[48] Much surviving information, to be sure, appears in comic texts (where exaggeration, especially in sexual situations, is inherently endemic); some quotations relate to long-term relationships and hence are uninformative concerning charges for single acts; still other citations lack context. But from the remaining relevant material, it seems clear that even the lowest charges for an individual sexual act far exceeded the amounts that might be earned in other pursuits by relatively well-compensated, self-employed males, and far exceeded the 2 *obols* per day needed for daily sustenance.[49] In a city where important *polis*-officials and skilled construction workers typically received slightly more or less than 1 *drachma* per day (equivalent to 6 *obols*)[50]—and compensation beyond 2 1/2 *drachmas* per day is essentially unknown[51]—the lowest price mentioned for a single *praxis*

---

46. Rhodes 1981: 574; Omitowoju 1997:21–22, n. 46. On the "fluidity" of female prostitutional "discursive categories," see Henry 1986: 147; Kurke 1997: 109; on the diversity and complexity of the sexual market for women in Athens, Davidson 1997: 74–76.

47. Ancient testimonia on prostitutional charges at Athens have been studied by Schneider 1913; Halperin 1990; Loomis 1998: 166–85.

48. Athên. 547d: Λύκων κατ' ἀρχὰς ἐπιδημήσας παιδείας ἕνεκα ταῖς Ἀθήναις . . . πόσον ἑκάστη τῶν ἑταιρουσῶν ἐπράττετο μίσθωμα ἀκριβῶς ἠπίστατο.

49. Men. *Epitrep.* 137–41: δώδεκα δραχμὰς . . . μηνὸς διατροφὴν ἀνδρὶ καὶ πρὸς ἡμερῶν | ἕξ . . . . δύ' ὀβολοὺς τῆς ἡμέρας, | [ἱκανό]ν τι τῶι πεινῶντι πρὸς πτισάνην ποτέ. For nutritional requirements at Athens (approximately 0.839 kilos of wheat per day per adult male, supplemented by modest intake of olives and wine), see Whitby 1998: 114–17; Sallares 1991: 301. For the cost of this sustenance, and additional limited expenses of subsistence, see Gallo 1987: 24–29; Loomis 1998: 220–31.

50. Compensation for construction work on the Erekhtheion between 409 and 407: I. G. I³ 474–76. See Randall 1953; Paton 1927: 338–39, 380, 382, 398, 416. In the period before 322, "magistrates" (*archons*) received 4 *obols* per day. *Politai* serving on juries received 3 *obols*; councillors (*bouleutai*), 5 to 6 *obols*; assembly members (*ekklêsiastai*), 6 to 9 *obols*. See Aristot. *Ath. Pol.* 62.2. Cf. Loomis 1998: 23–25.

51. A sampling of wages at Eleusis in 329/8 and 327/6: workers carrying construction materials (such as bricks or wood), sifting plaster, mixing mortar, breaking clods, 1 *dr.*, 3

by a female prostitute is 1 *obol* (for a woman, presumably a slave, working in a brothel).[52] In contrast, a "high-class and socially acceptable *hetaira*" was paid a minimum of 2 *drachmas* for a single encounter—and possibly much more—"depending on her age, attractions, mood at the moment, and the resources and urgency of the customer" (Loomis 1998: 185).[53] One woman even earned the sobriquet "Two-Drachmas" because of the consistency with which she obtained this sum.[54] The comic poet Theopompos observes that female prostitutes "of middling rank" commanded 4 *drachmas*.[55] The elder Laïs, even in advanced years, reportedly received as much as 4 *drachmas* per *praxis* (but sometimes as little as 3 *obols*)—both sums considerably less than she had commanded in her youth.[56] In Menander's *Epitrepontes*, Kharisios is portrayed as spending 12 *drachmas* a day on the *hetaira* Habrotonon.[57] Loukianos, recreating fourth-century Athens in his *Hetairikoi Dialogoi* ("Courtesans' Dialogues"), sets highly variant fees for the relationships he describes in a series of comic vignettes. Ampelis is unhappy with the 5 *drachmas* or so paid to her over an extended period by Dêmophantos, but she has no objection to the 10 *drachmas* that Kallidês has given her for services of unspecified duration.[58] Kharmidês, indifferent to Typhaina, pays her 5 *drachmas* as compensation (*misthôma*) for one evening, but he is unable, he says, easily to pay the 1,000 *drachmas* that his inamorata Philêmation is demanding for an extended relationship.[59]

---

*obols* per day (I. G. II²1672-73.28-30, 32-34, 44-46, 60-62); two sawyers, 3 dr. (perhaps aggregate pay for both: I. G. II²1672.159-60); workers laying bricks and working on wood, 2 and 1/2 dr. (I. G. II²1672.26-28); workers laying roof tiles, 2 dr. (I. G. II²1672.110-111); architect, 2 dr. (I. G. II²1672.12); mason finishing stone and plasterer, 1 dr., 1 and 1/2 *obols* each (I. G. II²1672.31-32).

52. Philêmôn, Fr. 3 (K-A): εἷς ὀβολός· εἰσπήδησον.

53. Similarly: Kilmer 1993: 167; Skinner 2005: 98.

54. Athên. 596f (Gorgias, FGrH 351 F1).

55. Poll. 9.59 (= Theopomp. Com. Fr. 22 [K-A]): οὔ φησιν εἶναι τῶν ἑταιρῶν τὰς μέσας | στατηριαίας.

56. Epikratês, Fr. 3 (K-A), lines 11-12, 16-18: αὕτη γὰρ οὖν ὁπότ' ἦν νεοττὸς καὶ νέα, | ὑπὸ τῶν στατήρων ἦν ἀπηγριωμένη, . . . ἤδη . . . δέχεται δὲ καὶ στατῆρα καὶ τριώβολον.

57. Fr. 1 (Sandbach): ὁ νῦν ἔχων <τὴν> Ἀβρότονον τὴν ψάλτριαν . . . Lines 136-37: πορνοβοσκῶι δώδεκα | τῆς ἡμέρας δραχμὰς δίδωσι.

58. 80.8.2-3: οὗτος οὐδεπώποτε πλέον πέντε δραχμῶν δεδώκει καὶ . . . συνεκάθευδέ μοι ἐνίοτε . . . (Καλλίδης) ἔνδον ἦν δέκα δραχμὰς πεπομφώς.

59. 80.11.1, 3: Ἑταίραν δὲ τίς παραλαβὼν πέντε δραχμὰς τὸ μίσθωμα δοὺς καθεύδει . . . χιλίας αἰτούσῃ οὐκ εἶχον διδόναι ῥᾳδίως.

Krokalê demands even more from Deinomakhos—2 talents (12,000 drachmas) as the price for an extended, exclusive relationship, twice the sum ultimately proffered by Dêmophantos for an exclusive liaison of eight months with Ampelis.[60] Philostratos, for his part, gave Pannykhis 1 talent and promised another, again for a continuing relationship.[61] Myrtalê finds contemptible Dôriôn's alleged payment of 2 *drachmas* for two nights (a fee paid not in cash but by a gift of footwear of indeterminate value) and is not thrilled by a potpourri of additional gifts worth in all perhaps some 5 *drachmas*.[62] By contrast, a businessman supposedly paid Myrtalê 200 *drachmas* in cash for an extended relationship—and further showered her with gifts, even mundanely covering her obligation for rent.[63]

Compensation for male prostitutes appears to have been similarly flexible. Andokidês, for example, speaking at the beginning of the fourth century, attacks Epikharês for charging "not much money" for providing male sex to anyone willing to pay.[64] An Athenian (stationed in Kyzikos) boasts of having purchased sex from both a young man and an older man (and a woman) for "small change."[65] How low might such fees be? Makhôn tells of a request by a man for 3 *obols* for servicing the female Gnathaina.[66] In contrast, early in the fourth century,[67] Simôn received from Theodotos 300 *drachmas* (paid in advance) for an ongoing male sexual liaison—a

---

60. 80.15.2: ἡ Κροκάλη δύο τάλαντα αἰτήσασα, εἰ βούλεται μόνος ἔχειν αὐτήν, 80.8.3: τάλαντον δοὺς μόνος εἶχεν ὀκτὼ ὅλους μῆνας.

61. 80.9.3–4: ΠΑΝ· οὔτε γὰρ τοῦτον ἀποπέμψαι καλὸν τάλαντον ἔναγχος δεδωκότα . . . καὶ πολλὰ ὑπισχνούμενον . . . ΦΙΛ. Παννυχὶς ἐμή ἐστι, καὶ τάλαντον εἴληφε, λήψεται δὲ ἤδη καὶ ἕτερον.

62. 80.14.2: . . . ΔΩΡ· ὑποδήματα ἐκ Σικυῶνος τὸ πρῶτον δύο δραχμῶν. ΜΥΡ· ἀλλ᾽ ἐκοιμήθης νύκτας δύο. ΔΩΡ· . . . ἀλάβαστρον μύρου ἐκ Φοινίκης, κ.τ.λ. ΜΥΡ· Πέντε ἴσως δραχμῶν πάντα ταῦτα.

63. 80.14.3: καὶ ἐλλόβια ταυτὶ καὶ δάπιδα, καὶ πρώην δύο μνᾶς, καὶ τὸ ἐνοίκιον κατέβαλεν ὑπὲρ ἡμῶν.

64. Andok. 1.100: εἶτα σὺ (sc. ὁ Ἐπιχάρης) περὶ ἑταιρείας ἐμοὶ μνείαν ποιῇ καὶ κακῶς τινας λέγεις; ὃς ἑνὶ μὲν οὐχ ἡταίρησας (καλῶς γὰρ ἄν σοι εἶχε), πραττόμενος δ᾽ οὐ πολὺ ἀργύριον τὸν βουλόμενον ἀνθρώπων, ὡς οὗτοι ἴσασιν, ἐπὶ τοῖς αἰσχίστοις ἔργοις ἔζης.

65. Eupolis Fr. 247 (K-A): ἐν τῇδε τοίνυν τῇ πόλει φρουρῶν <ἐγώ> ποτ᾽ αὐτὸς | γυναῖκ᾽ ἐκίνουν κολλύβου καὶ παῖδα καὶ γέροντα.

66. ὦ μειράκιον . . . φησι, πῶς ἴστης φράσον. | ὁ δὲ μειδάσας, Κύβδ᾽, ἔφη, τριωβόλου (lines 306–308 [Gow]).

67. Lysias's speech, chronicling these events, was delivered some time after 394 (see §45, which alludes to the Battles of Korinth and Korôneia in that year).

huge sum that was still insufficient to match the foreign travel and other enticements offered by Simôn's wealthy rival, who induced Simôn to abandon his relationship with Theodotos.[68] A much higher payment was supposedly received by a certain Melanopos in the 320s—3,000 *drachmas* for "the flower of his youth" (*akmê*).[69] More typically, perhaps, Loukianos writes of Kleodêmos's offer of 2 *drachmas* for sex with a male waiter,[70] while the male transvestite in Aristophanês's *Thesmophoriazousai* accepts a payment of 1 *drachma* for a sex act (lines 1193-96).

In practice, prices for sexual services largely reflected market factors—especially consumer preference—that were sometimes modified by the personal feelings of individual prostitutes or their associates. The workings of supply and demand are illustrated by anecdotes and theater scenes describing the enormous sums requested, and often received, from men of wealth by courtesans in high demand. As mentioned earlier,[71] the prostitute at the center of Menander's *Kolax* was supposedly receiving 300 *drachmas* per night from a "foreign" client—a sum that a brothel-operator (*pornoboskos*) describes as ten times the usual fee of other high-priced women, a payment so daunting that the *pornoboskos* fears even to suggest it to clients desirous of her services.[72] By contrast, the glorious Gnathainion, at the peak of her attractions in the early third century, is said generally to have demanded only 100 *drachmas* a night from her suitors but her mother (grandmother?[73]) Gnathaina is said to have demanded ten times that amount from a Persian satrap (his "handsome" counter-offer [Gow 1965: 120] was 500 *drachmas*).[74]

---

68. Lys. 3.22: αὐτὸς τριακοσίας δρασχμὰς ἔδωκε Θεοδότῳ, συνθήκας πρὸς αὐτὸν ποιησάμενος, ἐγὼ δ' ἐπιβουλεύσας, ἀπέστησα αὐτοῦ τὸ μειράκιον... σκέψασθε δὲ ὡς ἄπιστα εἴρηκε. τὴν γὰρ οὐσίαν τὴν ἑαυτοῦ ἄπασαν πεντήκοντα καὶ διακοσίων δραχμῶν ἐτιμήσατο. Cf. chapter 2, p. 68; chapter 4, n. 1 and accompanying text.

69. Letter attributed (falsely) to Aiskhinês (7.3): σὲ δὲ πραθέντα τρισκιλίων δραχμῶν τὴν ἀκμὴν ἡταιρηκέναι.

70. *Symp.* 15: μετὰ μικρὸν ὁ μὲν προσῆλθεν ὡς ἀποληψόμενος παρὰ τοῦ Κλεοδήμου τὴν φιάλην, ὁ δὲ τόν τε δάκτυλον ἀπέθλιεν αὐτοῦ καὶ δραχμὰς δύο, οἶμαι, συνανέδωκε μετὰ τῆς φιάλης·

71. This chapter, p. 156.

72. Lines 117 ff. (Koerte): ἢ μι' ἐλάμβανεν | [ὅσον οὐχ]ὶ δέκα, τρεῖς μνᾶς ἑκάστης ἡμέρας | [παρὰ τοῦ] ξένου. δέδοικα δ' οὕτω λαμβάνειν· For the meaning of the term *pornoboskos* (literally "whore-pasturer"), see chapter 6, n. 79 and related text.

73. On the family's business operations and relationships, see chapter 6, p. 147.

74. On 100 *drachmas* as Gnathainion's general fee, see Gow's interpretation (1965: 120) of Athên. 584c: ὡς δ' ὁ τὴν μνᾶν τῇ θυγατρὶ δοὺς αὐτῆς οὐδὲν ἔτι ἔφερεν κ.τ.λ. On Gnathaina's demand from the satrap, see Makhôn 338–41 (Gow): ἐπυνθάνετο μίσθωμα πράττεται πόσον |

Similarly the peerless Phrynê, when in ardor, was supposedly willing to reduce her fee of 100 *drachmas* to 40.[75]

Psychological factors—emotional "fetishes"—sometimes affected pricing. The procuress Nikaretê, herself free, supposedly presented as her own offspring the child prostitutes whom she owned, including Neaira, who allegedly came whoring to Attika before reaching puberty. Nikaretê's motivation: the "highest prices" might be obtained from customers desiring to have sex with young girls whom they believed to be the free offspring of the woman providing the children's services.[76] Was such trafficking in children and relatives an isolated anomaly, preserved for modern posterity by the vagaries of chance, or was it—like modern exploitation of dependents—a widespread (although difficult to quantify) phenomenon? We might dismiss as xenophobic travesty Aristophanês's *Akharnians*, in which much of the action (lines 730–835) concerns the effort of a Megarian to sell his young daughters to Dikaiopolis for sexual exploitation.[77] But in Isaios 3, the speaker matter-of-factly charges that Nikodêmos had frequently and recurrently sold the sexual services of his sister.[78] In fact, the provision of female relatives for paid sexual use was common enough to evoke legislative action seeking to restrict this phenomenon:[79] an Athenian law attributed to Solôn forebade the selling of "daughters

---

τῆς νυκτός, ἡ Γνάθαινα δ᾽ εἰς τὴν πορφύραν | καὶ τὰ δόρατ᾽ ἀποβλέψασα δραχμὰς χιλίας | ἔταξεν.

75. Makhôn 450–55: Φρύνην ἐπείρα Μοίριχος τὴν Θεσπικήν· | κἄπειτεν αἰτήσασαν αὐτὸν μνᾶν μίαν | ὁ Μοίριχος, Μέγ᾽, εἶπεν. οὐ πρῴην δύο | χρυσοῦς λαβοῦσα παραγένου ξένῳ τινί; | Περίμενε τοίνυν καὶ σύ, φησ᾽, ἕως ἂν οὗ | βινητιάσω καὶ τοσοῦτον λήψομαι. On Phrynê, see Cooper 1995; Lentakis 1999: 224–38.

76. Dem. 59.18–22: Ἑπτὰ γὰρ ταύτας παιδίσκας ἐκ μικρῶν παιδίων ἐκτήσατο Νικαρέτη . . . προειποῦσα δ᾽ αὐτὰς ὀνόματι θυγατέρας, ἵν᾽ ὡς μεγίστους μισθοὺς πράττοιτο τοὺς βουλομένους πλησιάζειν αὐταῖς ὡς ἐλευθέραις οὔσαις. . . . Νέαιρα αὑτηί, ἐργαζομένη μὲν ἤδη τῷ σώματι, νεωτέρα δὲ οὖσα διὰ τὸ μήπω τὴν ἡλικίαν αὐτῇ παρεῖναι . . . .

77. See Henderson 1991: 60–61. Glazebrook 2006a: 40, however, cites this as one of several items of evidence that "suggest that free sisters and daughters in Greece were sold for prostitution" on occasion by their *kyrioi*, and that the law cited at Plut. *Sol*. 23.1–2 (this chapter, n. 80) legalized such sales in the case of unchaste daughters or sisters.

78. §§10–11: ὁ ἀδελφὸς αὐτὴν ἅπασι τοῖς πλησιάζουσιν ἐκδέδωκεν. περὶ ὧν εἰ δεήσειε καθ᾽ ἕκαστον διελθεῖν, οὐκ ἂν πάνυ μικρὸν ἔργον γένοιτο . . . κοινὴν αὐτοὶ ὡμολογήκασιν εἶναι τοῦ βουλομένου τὴν γυναῖκα . . . .

79. For the Athenian practice of promulgating legislation "to deal with improper behavior that people actually do engage in" (Aiskhin. 1.13), see chapter 3, pp. 70–81.

and sisters"—except for females who had already experienced heterosexual intercourse.⁸⁰

Customers would also pay higher fees for sexual relations with women of seemingly bourgeois pretension (*epi proskhêmatos tinos*) living in a stable marital relationship⁸¹—a market phenomenon (also encountered in modern sexual commerce) of enhanced payment for denigration.⁸² Thus, according to the Athenian author Xenophôn, the coveted "sublime courtesans" (*hetairai semnotatai*) invited to consort at the Aphrodisia with high-ranking Theban military leaders (*polemarchs*) appear to have been married women of elite status.⁸³ Scenes on Athenian pottery showing men making monetary approaches to women busy with domestic pursuits have long been interpreted as mere "affectation on the part of prostitutes or their owners: by equipping themselves with the symbols of respectability, they could wring higher fees out of their customers."⁸⁴ A high-living Athenian,

---

80. Plut. *Solôn* 23.2: Ἔτι δ᾽ οὔτε θυγατέρας πωλεῖν οὔτ᾽ ἀδελφὰς δίδωσι, πλὴν ἂν μὴ λάβῃ παρθένον ἀνδρὶ συγγεγενημένην. On the authenticity of the laws cited by Plutarch in *Solôn* 23.1–2, see Ruschenbusch 1966, who judges this provision clearly attributable to Solôn (pp. 13, 46). In agreement on the law's authenticity: Manfredini and Piccirilli 1977: 244; Lape 2002/3: 126; Glazebrook 2006a. For methodological considerations in evaluating allegedly Solonian laws, see Scafuro 2006: 177–80.

81. Dem. 59.41: διεγγυηθεῖσα δ᾽ ὑπὸ Στεφάνου καὶ οὖσα παρὰ τούτῳ τὴν μὲν αὐτὴν ἐργασίαν οὐδὲν ἧττον ἢ πρότερον ἠργάζετο, τοὺς δὲ μισθοὺς μείζους ἐπράττετο τοὺς βουλομένους αὐτῇ πλησιάζειν, ὡς ἐπὶ προσχήματος ἤδη τινὸς οὖσα καὶ ἀνδρὶ συνοικοῦσα.

82. Psychological elements—especially of debasement and abuse—not directly related to genital sexuality are an important determinant of modern prostitutional compensation (Rosen 1982: 97; Pateman 1988: 259, n. 33). According to some observers, denigration is the essence of purchased eroticism: "Prostitution and pornography are acts of dominance expressed through sexuality" (Kitzinger 1994: 197); "Prostitution occurs within multiple power relations of domination, degradation, and subservience" (MacKinnon 2005: 157). Cf. Dines and Jensen 2004: 371–77. But purchased debasement does not lack ideological defense: sadomasochistic lesbian groups valorize what others consider to be the "dehumanization of sexual relations" involved in customers' frequent choice of "abusive" satisfactions. See Barry 1995: 69–73, 79–90; Leidholdt 1990: ix; Goode 1978: 72. The continued erotic centrality of power within ostensibly egalitarian female relationships has evoked considerable analytical concern (see Kitzinger 1991, 1994; Hoagland 1988; Lobel 1986).

83. *Hell.* 5.4.4: ὁ μὲν οὖν Φιλλίδας τά τε ἄλλα ἐπεμελεῖτο τοῖς πολεμάρχοις, ὡς Ἀφροδίσια ἄγουσιν ἐπ᾽ ἐξόδῳ τῆς ἀρχῆς, καὶ δὴ καὶ γυναῖκας πάλαι ὑπισχνούμενος ἄξειν αὐτοῖς τὰς σεμνοτάτας καὶ καλλίστας τῶν ἐν Θήβαις, τότε ἔφη ἄξειν. . . . ἐκ δὲ τούτου εἰσήγαγε τὰς ἑταίρας δή. . . . For the marital status of the courtesans, see Davidson 2004b: 172. Cf. Pirenne-Delforge 1994: 283, n. 49.

84. Keuls 1985: 258. The phenomenon appears first to have been recognized by Robert in 1919. See Meyer 1988; Sutton 2004; Rodenwaldt 1932; Ferrari 2002: 12–17 (skeptically). Lewis concludes that in Athenian ceramic iconography, "wool-work as symbolic of both female virtue and sexual appeal is very powerful" (2002: 65).

Phryniôn, is explicitly described in Demosthenes 59 as taking pleasure in publicly degrading the prostitute under his control, a free woman, herself given to luxury, who was allegedly paid exceptionally well—with money, jewels, clothing, and servant-girls—for enduring sexual humiliation.[85] Indeed, in the agonistic environment of Athens, with its valorization of "zero-sum competition," some purchasers' self-esteem and perceived self-worth might be enhanced only to the extent that sexual submission was felt to dishonor and humiliate a person or his/her "household" (*oikos*).[86] The resultant willingness of customers to lavish huge sums on "citizen" prostitutes is exemplified by Simôn, who supposedly contracted to pay the *politês* Theodotos 300 *drachmas*—when his own possessions amounted to only 250 *drachmas*![87] But this desire to prevail—to enhance oneself by debasing another—could easily lead to the would-be predators' victimization. Neaira supposedly would entice a "wealthy but unknowledgeable foreigner" into a sexual relationship—after which her "husband" Stephanos, as an outraged cuckold, would extract a considerable cash settlement from the victim.[88] Similarly in Hypereidês's *Against Athênogenês*, Antigona (a former prostitute, now a brothel-operator) and her Egyptian confederate, Athênogenês, sell an entire perfumery operation to Epikratês, who claims to have had no interest in the business but only to have lusted after the son of the slave who operated the enterprise. By purchasing the business and freeing the slaves, Epikratês hoped to gain the slave boy's gratitude and good will (*kharis*: §6).[89] But the proceeds of the sale

---

85. §§30–35: Φρυνίωνα τὸν Παιανιέα . . . πολυτελῶς διάγοντα τὸν βίον . . . προσθέντα τὸ ἐπίλοιπον (sc. ἀργύριον) . . . ἐκώμαζέ τ᾽ἀεὶ μετ᾽αὐτῆς, συνῆν τ᾽ἐμφανῶς ὁπότε βουληθείη πανταχοῦ, φιλοτιμίαν τὴν ἐξουσίαν πρὸς τοὺς ὁρῶντας ποιούμενος . . . συσκευασαμένη . . . ὅσα ἦν αὐτῇ ὑπ᾽ἐκείνου περὶ τὸ σῶμα κατεσκευασμένα ἱμάτια καὶ χρυσία, καὶ θεραπαίνας δύο. . . .

86. On the importance of "zero-sum" competition in Athenian culture, see Gouldner 1965: 49; Dover 1964: 31; Winkler 1990a: 178; D. Cohen 1995: 63. But prostitution aside, Davidson argues that "the picture of ancient sex and sexual morality as a plus-minus 'zero-sum game,' where one party can only 'win' at the expense of the other, is not only unsubstantiated but contradicts what evidence there is" (2004a: 81).

87. Lys. 3.22–24: αὐτὸς μὲν τριακοσίας δραχμὰς ἔδωκε Θεοδότῳ, συνθήκας πρὸς αὐτὸν ποιηάμενος . . . σκέψασθε δὲ ὡς ἄπιστα εἴρηκεν. τὴν γὰρ οὐσίαν τὴν ἑαυτοῦ ἅπασαν πεντήκοντα καὶ διακοσίων δραχμῶν ἐτιμήσατο. καίτοι θαυμαστὸν εἰ τὸν ἑταιρήσοντα πλειόνων ἐμισθώσατο ὧν αὐτὸς τυγχάνει κεκτημένος. For Simôn's valuation of his own property, see Todd 2007: 328.

88. Dem. 59.41: συνεσυκοφάντει δὲ καὶ οὗτος, εἴ τινα ξένον ἀγνῶτα πλούσιον λάβοι ἐραστὴν αὐτῆς, ὡς μοιχὸν ἐπ᾽ αὐτῇ ἔνδον ἀποκλείων καὶ ἀργύριον πραττόμενος πολύ.

89. Contrary to Meyer 2010: 24, n. 55, enslaved families at Athens are often attested as remaining together, especially *douloi khôris oikountes* (Men. *Epitrep.* 50–52, 85–86, 191; Dem. 34.37). A fragment of Hypereidês proclaims slave-dealers' respect for family ties: Jones 2008.

(4,000 *drachmas*, equivalent to perhaps US$200,000–$400,000 in purchasing power parity) would in this case have gone to the slaves' owner—not to the slave boy who would actually have provided the erotic pleasures and emotional satisfaction sought by Epikratês (§§ 4–5). Yet even in this transaction the slave was able to extract for himself the compensation that he really desired: in connection with entering into a sexual relationship (*syneinai*) with the love-smitten purchaser, he persuaded Epikratês to alter the form of transaction to one in which his father and brother would also attain their freedom.⁹⁰

Epikratês's experience is paradigmatic—both as to "how sex could drive and complicate interactions between slave and free families and households at Athens" (Golden 2011: 146) and as to how a practical (and explicit) division of a slave's earnings between master and servant often superseded the seemingly clear strictures of the law assigning all proceeds of a slave's labor to his owner. In contrast, free prostitutes would have been entitled, as a matter of law, to retain for themselves all of the revenues generated by their services. But in practice, in many societies, even free sex-workers have been compelled to surrender much or most or all of their income to third parties—to pimps and procurers, or other owners and operators of sexual businesses. At Athens, however, as we saw in chapter 5, free prostitutes received at least some legal protection from such exploitation.

## *The Rewards of Sexual Services*

In Menander's *Epitrepontes*, Kharisios is portrayed as spending a startlingly high 12 *drachmas* per day for sex with Habratonon, a brothel slave—money paid to her apparent master, a *pornoboskos* ("operator of a sex business," usually, and inadequately, translated as "pimp" or "procurer").⁹¹ This *pornoboskos*, if the prostitute's owner,⁹² would have been legally entitled to

---

90. §24: τὸν μὲν γὰρ παῖδα ἔπεμπέ μοι λέγοντα ὅτι οὐκ [ἂν συ]νείη μ[οι, εἰ μὴ λ]ύσομαι αὐτοῦ τὸν πατέρα καὶ τὸν [ἀδελφ]όν (Colin). Kenyon's text is not significantly different: ἂν μὴ ὠνῶμαι αὐτοῦ τὸν κ.τ.λ. rather than εἰ μὴ λύσομαι αὐτοῦ τὸν κ.τ.λ.

91. οὐχ ὁ τρόφιμός σου . . . ὁ νῦν ἔχων <τὴν> Ἀβρότονον τὴν ψάλτριαν | ἔγημ' ἔναγχος; (Fr. 1 [Sandbach]), πορνοβοσκῶι δώδεκα | τῆς ἡμέρας δραχμὰς δίδωσι (ll. 136–37), (to Habratonon) ἐκεῖνο δ' οὐ λέγεις, ὅτι | ἐλευθέρα γίνηι σύ· τοῦ γὰρ παιδίου | μητέρα σε νομίσας λύσετ' εὐθὺς δηλαδή (538–40), καταφθαρεὶς τ' ἐν ματρυλείωι τὸν βίον | μετὰ τῆς καλῆς γυναικὸς ἦν ἐπεισάγει | βιώσεθ' (692–94). *Pornoboskoi* might be male or female: for their role in Athenian prostitution; see the section "Mothers and Daughters" in chapter 6.

92. The *pornoboskos* may merely have leased the slave or have otherwise been acting as agent or pledgee for the slave's actual master. On the hiring-out of slaves, see Xen. *Por.* 4.14ff.

all sums paid for her sexual services;[93] stricto sensu, a master was legally the owner of any personal property informally "belonging" to his or her slave.[94] Thus, the Attic Stêlai record the simultaneous confiscation of a slave-owner's property, and of the belongings of his slave: since the unfree person's possessions were juridically treated as "owned" by his master, they too went to the state.[95]

But, in practice, an enslaved *pornê* like Habranaton still was able to benefit personally from at least a portion of the large sums paid for her erotic labor. Customers sometimes made expenditures in a form that would benefit the prostitute individually and that did not lend itself to appropriation by a slave-prostitute's owner. Lysias, for example, paid for Metaneira's enjoyment of the festivities at Eleusis and for her initiation into the Mysteries—knowing that her owner could not deprive her of this personal emolument.[96] More importantly, the institution of *apophora*—a sharing between master and slave of the *doulos*'s earnings—was highly developed and broadly practiced at Athens. Slaves often paid their owners a fixed sum while working and living on their own: these *douloi khôris oikountes* kept for themselves all revenues beyond the portion owed to their masters.[97] Thus, in Menander's *Epitrepontes*, a charcoal-burner,

---

(Nikias providing *douloi* for labor in the mines); Dem. 27.20, 53.20 ff.; Lys. 12.19; Isai. 8.35. For the loan of slaves, see Antiph. 6.23; for pledge, Dem. 27.9; I.G. II² 2747–49, 2751.

93. See, for example, Dem. 59.21 (see text below, n. 96). Cf. Todd 1993: 184–200, esp. 188; Harrison 1968–71: I.174–76.

94. For slaves' acquisition ("ownership") of assets see chapter 2, n. 31.

95. Stêlê 6, 31–46 (Pritchett, Amyx, and Pippin 1953). Cf. Lewis 1966 [1997]: 182, n. 32; Langdon 1991: 70.

96. Dem. 59.21–22: Λυσίας . . . Μετανείρας ὢν ἐραστής, ἠβουλήθη πρὸς τοῖς ἄλλοις ἀναλώμασιν οἷς ἀνήλισκεν εἰς αὐτὴν καὶ μυῆσαι, ἡγούμενος τὰ μὲν ἄλλα ἀναλώματα τὴν κεκτημένην αὐτὴν λαμβάνειν.

97. The overwhelming majority of scholars identify the *khôris oikountes* as slaves (Kamen 2011: 44), but a few (most recently Zelnick-Abramovitz 2005 and Fisher 2006 and 2008) believe that the term (depending on context) can refer to both present slaves (*douloi*) and freed slaves (*apeleutheroi*). Cf. Klees 2000: 15–17. For references to and examples of "slaves living (and/or working) on their own," see (in addition to the testimonia cited in the text) Theophr. *Khar.* 30.15; Dem. 34.37; Xen. *Ath. Pol.* 1.10–11("sans doute": Perotti [1974: 50, n. 15]); Telês fr. 4b (pp. 46–47 Hense); and the activities of slaves identified as μισθοφοροῦντα, many of whom may have maintained their own *oikoi* (Xen. *Ath. Pol.* 1.17; Xen. *Poroi* 4.14–15, 19, 23; Isai. 8.35; Dem. 27.20–21, 28.12, 53.21; Theophr. *Khar.* 30.17. Modern treatments of the *douloi khôris oikountes* are rare. In 1981, Ste. Croix had lamented (563, n. 9) the absence of even a single "satisfactory treatment" of the *khôris oikountes*. See now, however, Klees 1998: 143–54; E. Cohen 2000: 130–54. See also Biezunska-Malowist 1966; Kazakévich 2008 [1960].

living outside the city with his wife, pays to his owner only a portion of his earnings.⁹⁸ Similarly a group of "nine or ten" slave leather-workers are reported (Aiskhinês 1.97) to have operated a workshop: the slave in charge (*hêgemôn tou ergastêriou*) paid their master a fixed sum of 3 obols per day, and the other slaves, 2. Slave craftsmen employed in the construction trades are known to have received monetary compensation; when living outside the master's quarters, these unfree laborers paid a portion of their compensation to their owners and kept the remainder.⁹⁹ *Apophora* arrangements also were entered into by *douloi* skilled in the production of pottery.¹⁰⁰ Even individual slaves working in the mines are known to have shared their revenue with their masters (Andokidês 1.38). At a vastly more elevated level, the *douloi* Xenôn, Euphrôn, Euphraios, and Kallistratos—while still enslaved—as principals operated the largest bank in Athens, that of Pasiôn.¹⁰¹ Their only involvement with their owners appears to have been an annual payment of fixed lease obligations: they retained excess revenues (if any) for themselves.¹⁰² Pasiôn himself—while still unfree—had played a major role in his owners' bank,¹⁰³ and thereafter in his own *trapeza* (Isokratês 17). Phormiôn (who ultimately succeeded Pasiôn as Athens' most important financier)¹⁰⁴—while still a slave—had

---

98. σὺ δὲ ταυτί, γύναι, | λαβοῦσα πρὸς τὸν τρόφιμον ἐνθάδ᾽ εἴσφερε | Χαιρέστρατον. νῦν γὰρ μενοῦμεν ἐνθάδε, | εἰς αὔριον δ᾽ ἐπ᾽ ἔργον ἐξορμήσομεν | τὴν ἀποφορὰν ἀποδόντες (ll. 376–80).

99. See Randell 1953; Burford 1963.

100. See Webster 1973. For analogous Roman practices, see Gamauf 2009; Wiedemann 1987: 33; Prachner 1980; Harris 1980; Tapio 1975.

101. The scale of this bank's operation—and the financial capacity of the four slaves operating it—is suggested by the rental paid annually to their masters (Dem. 36.37); 1 talent a year. Over the ten-year term of the lease, they would have paid to the bank's owners, Pasiôn's grown children, some 10 talents (between US$3,000,000 and $6,000,000, calculated on the basis of purchasing power parity).

102. They functioned pursuant to a leasing arrangement (*misthôsis*), described in the preceding note, that provided for a fixed rent: see Dem. 36.43, 46, 48; E. Cohen 1992: 76. Only on expiration of the lease did their owners καὶ ἐλευθέρους ἀφεῖσαν (Dem. 36.14) ("enfranchised them," see Harrison 1968–71: I.175, n. 2).

103. Dem. 36.43: παρὰ τοῖς αὑτοῦ κυρίοις Ἀντισθένει καὶ Ἀρχεστράτῳ τραπεζιτεύουσι πεῖραν δοὺς ὅτι χρηστός ἐστι καὶ δίκαιος, ἐπιστεύθη. Cf. Dem. 36.46, 48.

104. Dem. 36.4, 11, 37; 45. 31–32. Phormiôn's lease of Pasiôn's bank was entered into with Phormiôn ἤδη καθ᾽ ἑαυτὸν ὄντι (§4). In thus noting explicitly that Phormiôn had already obtained his freedom when he entered into operating leases, giving him complete control of the bank and of a shield-workshop, the speaker necessarily implies that slave status would

been a partner in a maritime trading business.[105] We know of a *doulos* who operated his master's business for a fixed payment and was free to retain any additional income after expenses;[106] a slave who ran a substantial perfume business,[107] again subject only to a fixed payment to his owner (Meidas in Hypereidês, *Against Athênogenês* 9); and unfree persons operating their own businesses in the *agora* and personally liable for legal transgressions without reference to their masters (Stroud 1974: 181–82, lines 30–32).

Neaira's life, as presented in Demosthenes 59, illustrates how individual slave prostitutes might accumulate cash savings by retaining a share of the revenues generated by their services. When Neaira has the opportunity to purchase her freedom from Timanoridas and Eukratês for the enormous price of 3,000 *drachmas* (perhaps US$150,000–$300,000, at purchasing price parity) she covers most of this cost with cash contributions from various past patrons—and provides the rest from her savings![108] Although all of these monies technically belonged to her masters—who were legally entitled to everything that she possessed or obtained—they "gladly" (*hêdeôs*) accepted the monies as payment from her, and in return freed her. In fact, one-third of the 3,000 *drachmas* required was paid by her masters—perhaps a reflection of

---

not have been a bar to entering into these substantial obligations: otherwise the mere fact of his being lessee of the businesses would have established his status as free.

105. See Dem. 49.31, where Timosthenês, active in overseas commerce ("ἀφικνεῖται κατ' ἐμπορίαν ἰδίαν ἀποδημῶν"), is characterized as Phormiôn's κοινωνός at a time when Phormiôn was still a *doulos*. (Κοινωνός is difficult to translate: see E. Cohen 1992: 76, n. 71.) Davies 1971: 432 sees "Phormiôn's later activity as a shipowner" as having its "roots" in this earlier business involvement in maritime trade.

106. Milyas in Demosthenes 27. See Francotte [1900] 1979: 12; Bolkestein 1958: 63. Demosthenes, many years later, refers to Milyas as "our freedman" (ὁ ἀπελεύθερος ὁ ἡμέρερος) (Dem. 27.19), but there is no indication that Milyas was not still a slave when he was operating Demosthenes's father's workshops.

107. The considerable scale of the business is suggested by the colossal amount of debts incurred in its operation: 5 talents composed of both conventional (*khrea*) and *eranos* loans (§§ 7, 14, 19).

108. Τιμανορίδας τε ὁ Κορίνθιος καὶ Εὐκράτης ὁ Λευκάδιος . . . ἀφιέναι αὐτῇ ἔφασαν εἰς ἐλευθερίαν . . . τὰς δ' εἴκοσι μνᾶς ἐκέλευον αὐτὴν ἐξευροῦσαν αὐτοῖς ἀποδοῦναι . . . καὶ δίδωσι αὐτῷ (sc. τὸν Φρυνίωνα) τὸ ἀργύριον ὃ παρὰ τῶν ἄλλων ἐραστῶν ἐδασμολόγησεν ἔρανον εἰς τὴν ἐλευθερίαν συλλέγουσα, καὶ εἴ τι ἄρα αὐτὴ περιεποιήσατο, καὶ δεῖται αὐτοῦ προσθέντα τὸ ἐπίλοιπον, οὗ προσέδει εἰς τὰς εἴκοσι μνᾶς, καταθεῖναι αὐτῆς τῷ τε Εὐκράτει καὶ τῷ Τιμανορίδᾳ ὥστε ἐλευθέραν εἶναι (§§ 29–31).

a previously established ratio of revenue sharing between slave and owners.[109]

Timanoridas and Eukratês made no profit on this sale. Neaira's prior mistress, Nikaretê, herself a former slave and prostitute,[110] had maintained a lavish household—entirely paid for by Timanoridas and Eukratês as a condition to continued access to the slave-prostitute. As a result, the two clients had found it advantageous to purchase Neaira outright for 3,000 *drachmas* rather than to continue to cover Nikaretê's domestic expenses.[111] As a member of Nikaretê's household and thereafter as the property of two men who had come into emotional relationships with her, Neaira as a slave had been exposed to an affluence that made her situation after liberation intolerable: she was used to luxury, but her new clients (in Megara) were stingy.[112]

Prostitutes of slave origin frequently enjoyed considerable prosperity after gaining their freedom, in some cases eventually operating their own sex businesses, which often used several or more prostitutes whom they had purchased. Again, the career of Neaira's first owner, Nikaretê, illustrates this. Herself originally a prostitute who was the property of an Elisian, Nikaretê obtained her freedom and came to own women whom she provided at high prices at festivals and *symposia* throughout Greece, to "wealthy and distinguished men, poets, foreign aristocrats and masters of (literary) composition" (Davidson 1997: 92). When not traveling, she maintained a residence in Korinth, enjoying an "extravagant" (*polytelês*) life (Demosthenes 59.29).

The material prosperity of free Athenian prostitutes, individually and as a group, is a recurrent theme in ancient literature. Indeed, a Greek aphorism envisioned the god "Wealth" *(Ploutos)* as permanently encamped in

---

109. ἡδέως ἂν αὑτοῖς εἴη ἔλαττόν τ' ἀργύριον κομίσασθαι παρ' αὐτῆς ἢ κατέθεσαν... ἀφιέναι οὖν αὐτῇ ἔφασαν εἰς ἐλευθερίαν χιλίας δραχμάς, πεντακοσίας ἑκάτερος (§30).

110. Νικαρέτη, Χαρισίου μὲν οὖσα τοῦ Ἠλείου ἀπελευθέρα... τέχνην ταύτην κατεσκευασμένη καὶ ἀπὸ τούτων τὸν βίον συνειλεγμένη (Dem. 59.18). Cf. Athên. 596e (Νικαρέτη ἡ ἑταίρα).

111. §29: ἐπειδήπερ πολυτελὴς ἦν ἡ Νικαρέτη τοῖς ἐπιτάγμασιν, ἀξιοῦσα τὰ καθ' ἡμέραν ἀναλώματα ἅπαντα τῇ οἰκίᾳ παρ' αὐτῶν λαμβάνειν, κατατιθέασιν αὐτῆς τιμὴν τριάκοντα μνᾶς τοῦ σώματος τῇ Νικαρέτῃ....

112. διατρίψασα δ' ἐν τοῖς Μεγάροις δυ' ἔτη... ὡς αὐτῇ ἡ ἀπὸ τοῦ σώματος ἐργασία οὐχ ἱκανὴν εὐπορίαν παρεῖχεν ὥστε διοικεῖν τὴν οἰκίαν (πολυτελὴς δ' ἦν, οἱ Μεγαρῆς δ' ἀνελεύθεροι καὶ μικρολόγοι... (Dem. 59.36).

the homes of noted *hetairai*.¹¹³ The elevated compensation commanded by many free *hetairai* paid for the sumptuous life enjoyed by the high-earning (*megalomisthoi*) courtesans described in chapter 2 (see the section "Selling 'Free' Love"). For patrons, *hetairai* were the incarnations of luxurious living, the embodiments of a sumptious style of life.¹¹⁴ But they were notoriously so expensive that the mere act of maintaining a courtesan (or two) itself suggested that the patron possessed considerable wealth.¹¹⁵ Indeed, the destruction of sizeable estates is often attributed to involvement with male or female courtesans.¹¹⁶ Prostitutes' control of erotic businesses—and of their profits—in many cases provided a further source of affluence (see chapter 6).

Sex-workers' prosperity attracted the attention of the Athenian state, which in the fourth century had a desperate need of money. The long-term decline in income from the silver mines, which were state-owned, had exacerbated the loss in the Peloponnesian War of the empire and the revenues derived from tribute-paying dependencies.¹¹⁷ A prostitutional tax (*pornikon telos*), a per capita charge, was levied on all persons "practicing the trade" (*khrômenoi têi ergasiai*). This impost is attested only for the fourth century but mirrors the relatively modest taxes long imposed on farm properties and on mercantile trade and parallels the head tax on

---

113. Amphis, Fr. 23 (K-A): τυφλὸς ὁ Πλοῦτος εἶναί μοι δοκεῖ | ὅστις γε παρὰ ταύτην μὲν οὐκ εἰσέρχεται, | παρὰ δὲ Σινώπηι καὶ Λύκαι καὶ Ναννίωι | ἑτέραις τε τοιαύταισι παγίσι τοῦ βίου |ἔνδον κάθητ'. . . .

114. Pl. *Rep.* 373a: οὐδὲ αὕτη ἡ δίαιτα, ἀλλὰ κλῖναί τε προσέσονται καὶ τράπεζαι καὶ τἆλλα σκεύη, καὶ ὄψα δὴ καὶ μύρα καὶ θυμιάματα καὶ ἑταῖραι καὶ πέμματα, καὶ ἕκαστα τούτων παντοδαπά. . . . καὶ χρυσὸν καὶ ἐλέφαντα καὶ πάντα τὰ τοιαῦτα κτητέον.

115. Dem. *Epist.* 3.30: (sc. Πυθέαν) εὐποροῦντα μὲν οὕτως ὥστε δύ' ἔχειν ἑταίρας, αἳ μέχρι φθόης καλῶς ποιοῦσαι προπεπόμφασιν αὐτόν, πέντε τάλαντα δ' ὀφλόντα ῥᾷον ἐκτεῖσαι ἢ πέντε δραχμὰς ἂν ἔδειξεν πρότερον. See Dem. 36.45; Aiskhin. 1.42, 75, 115. Cf. Post 1940: 445.

116. Excessive expenditures on sex and other vices supposedly consumed the vast estate of the enormously wealthy Kallias, aristocratic general and "whore-crazy' (*pornomanês*) patron of boys and women (see Eupolis's *Kolakes* and *Autolykos*). (Davies, however, suggests that an ancillary cause of his financial difficulties, "ignored by the ancient tradition," was the loss of mining revenues after 413: 1971: 261). Cf. Xen. *Apom.* 1.2.22, 1.3.11–12; *Oik.* 1.13; Pl. *Rep.* 573d, 574b–c; Schol. Aristoph. *Neph.* 109d; Eupolis Fr. 50 (K-A); Antiphanês Fr. 2 (K-A); Isok. 8.103, 10.25. See Dem. *Epist.* 3.30 (prior note).

117. On the fall in silver production (which had been entirely disrupted by the war), see Hopper 1953: 215–16, 250–52; Ober 1985: 28–29. For the resultant adverse effect on state revenues, see Hopper 1968. During some periods of the fourth century Athens did receive some revenue from outlying areas: for the 1/12 tax on grain production from Lemnos, Imbros, and Skyros, see this chapter, n. 19.

aliens resident in Athens (the *metoikion*).¹¹⁸ But in a city where only the extremely (and conspicuously) rich were forced to pay the recurrent "liturgical" and "special" taxes¹¹⁹—whose confiscatory impact evoked anguished complaints from its prosperous victims¹²⁰—some wealthy courtesans even found themselves obligated to pay the *eisphora*, a recurring "extraordinary" tax on property that was imposed only on the several hundred persons who were (or appeared to be) the richest inhabitants of Attika.¹²¹ Many well-to-do Athenians endeavored to avoid Athens' harsh taxation by eschewing indicia of affluence and by operating through the "clandestine economy" (*aphanês ousia*).¹²² But because the Athenian Council (*Boulê*) had to deliver to tax-farmers annual lists of persons working at prostitution

---

118. On the *pornikon telos*, see chapter 1, n. 37; chapter 5, n. 8, and text on pp. 116–17. For the *metoikion*, see Meyer 2010: 28–32, 40–41, and 78–79; Whitehead 1977: 9–10; Gauthier 1972: 122, 1988: 28–29; and Lévy 1988: 53–61. For the *egktêtikon* levy (a tax on real property within a deme), see I.G. II² 1214; Jones 1999; 64–66; Langdon 1985: 8. On mercantile levies, essentially harbor taxes, see Migeotte 2014: 509–12; Stroud 1998: 27–28; Harris 1999: 270–72; Gofas 1994: 59–62.

119. Because fiscal obligations were imposed exclusively on the wealthy, the term "taxpayers" (λειτουργοῦντες) became in popular usage interchangeable with "the rich" or "the well-off" (Aristot. *Pol.* 1291a33–34; Xen. *Ath. Pol.* 1.13; Dem. 21.151, 153, 208; Isok. 8.128; Lysias 27.9–10). The rest of the population, characterized as "poor" (πένητες, ἄποροι) were generally exempt from the payment of taxes (ἀτελεῖς). See Dem. 18.102, 108: cf. Hemelrijk 1925: 140–42. For much of the fourth century, from a resident population of some 300,000, less than 1,000 were subject to these special taxes, but at extremely high rates. See E. Cohen 2005a; Gabrielsen 1994: 176–80; Ruschenbusch 1990, 1985, 1978. Migeotte insists that "ces contributions n'étaient pas des taxes à proprement parler" (2014: 521, n. 439), but the compulsory nature of the exactions argues otherwise.

120. Xenophôn pities a youth thinking that his wealth would free him of financial worries: the state will oppress him with ordinary and extraordinary taxes—and if his resources prove at all inadequate for meeting these public burdens it will punish him "just as though he were caught robbing it of its own property" (*Oikon.* 2. 6–7). Cf. Dem. 1. 8–9, 24.197–98, 38.26, 47.54; 50.8–9; 52.26; Isaios 4.27, 6.60–61, 7.40; Isok. 8.128, 12.145; Lys. 7.31–32, 12.20, 18.7, 18.21, 19.9, 19.29, 19.57–59, 20.23, 28.3, 29.4, 30.26; Xen. *Hell.* 6.2.1, *Symp.* 4.30–32; Hyper. F. 134; Aristot. *Pol.* 1309a15 ff.; Antiphanês Fr. 202 (K-A); Dêmêtr. Fr. 136 Wehrli = Plut. *Mor.* 349a; Diod. 13.47.7, 52.5, 64.4; Anax. 2 (p. 22, lines 5 ff. ed. Hammer). See Davies 1981: 82–84; Christ 1990: 150–57; Wyse [1904] 1967: 396.

121. Dem. 22.56: Σινώπην προσηνεχύραζεν καὶ Φανοστράτην, ἀνθρώπους πόρνας, οὐ μέντοι ὀφειλούσας εἰσφοράς. For *eisphora* as an expropriatory tax on wealth, see Gabrielsen 1994, esp. 184 ff.; E. Cohen 1992: 195–97. On the *eisphora* generally, see Flament 2007: 88–94, 191–92, 202–206 and 222–23.

122. The Athenian economy was effectively divided into "disclosed" (*phanera*) and "clandestine" (*aphanês*) markets. In the disclosed market, real-estate loans were attested by boundary-stones placed openly on property, and estates were transferred with full confirmation of already-known holdings, principally real-estate. In the *aphanês* market, investments and ownership were cloaked in secrecy, protected from tax-collectors and creditors. On the

(chapter 5, n. 8), the authorities already were aware of the business activities of courtesans. Moreover, the conspicuous ostentation of many prostitutes would have made them especially vulnerable to inclusion among the apparently wealthiest Athenians. The grandeur of Theodotê's establishment, for example, is awesome to a visiting Athenian of moderate means (see chapter 2, pp. 60–62). In Menander's *Woman from Samos*, the free *hetraira* Khrysis enjoys sumptuous personal possessions,[123] and in Terence's *Heauton Timoroumenos*, based on Menander's play of the same name, the *meretrix* Bacchis, flouting her gold and jewelry, is accompanied on stage by at least ten servants.[124] Elite Athenian women haplessly envied the visible luxury, extensive gold jewelry, and fine clothing of the *hetaira* supported by Olympiodôros (Demosthenes 48.55). The famed Athenian courtesan Phrynê was perceived as wealthy even for a *hetaira*. Wags reported her jocular willingness to rebuild the walls of Thebes—provided that she received proper donor recognition: "Alexander the Great had destroyed the walls, but Phrynê the Courtesan (*hetaira*) rebuilt them!"[125] In their turn, male prostitutes like Timarkhos and Hêgêsandros were notorious for the excessive luxuries—gambling, debauchery, and conspicuous consumption—on which they squandered the large sums that they earned.[126] Indeed, the sumptious life style maintained by male prostitutes is a recurrent *tropos* in Greek comedic theater.[127]

Athenian law sought to shield *hetairoi* and *hetairai* from the coercion and fear inflicted on whores by predators in many historical societies, explicitly protecting young male and free female prostitutes, and their income and

---

economic effects of this dichotomy, see E. Cohen 1992: 191–94, 201–207. On its legal implications, see Gernet 1981: 347–48.

123. See especially lines 373 and 381.

124. Lines 245–48, 451–52, 739, 751.

125. Kallistratos in Περὶ Ἑταιρῶν (Athên. 591d): ἐπλούτει δὲ σφόδρα ἡ Φρύνη καὶ ὑπισχνεῖτο τειχιεῖν τὰς Θήβας, ἐὰν ἐπιγράψωσιν Θηβαῖοι ὅτι "Ἀλέξανδρος μὲν κατέσκαψεν, ἀνέστησεν δὲ Φρύνη ἡ ἑταίρα."

126. Aiskhinês 1.42, 62, 75, 115. Before gaining access to his family fortune (which he allegedly squandered) Timarkhos supported his exorbitant life style (ἀφθονία) by prostitution: only later ἐπειδὴ δὲ ταῦτα μὲν ἀπωλώλει καὶ κατεκεκύβευτο καὶ κατωψοφάγητο, οὑτοσὶ δ' ἔξωρος ἐγένετο, ἐδίδου δ' εἰκότως οὐδεὶς ἔτι . . . ἐνταῦθα ἤδη ἐτράπετο ἐπὶ τὸ καταφαγεῖν τὴν πατρῴαν οὐσίαν (Aiskhin. 1.95–96).

127. See Ephippos, Fr. 20 (K-A): ὅταν γὰρ ὢν νέος | ἀλλότριον εἰσελθὼν ὄψον ἐσθίειν μάθῃ . . . | διδόναι νομίζ' αὐτὸν σὺ τῆς νυκτὸς λόγον. Cf. Alexis, Fr. 244 (K-A); Aristoph. *Hipp.* 424, *Neph.* 690–92.

possessions, from the "assistance" of pimps and panderers (see chapter 5). As a result, far from being hapless victims of wealthy men and exploitative male pimp-oppressors, female prostitutes at Athens are known to have provided financial support to mature male dependents. Neaira's husband, Stephanos, for example, allegedly had no assets of his own: Neaira, accustomed to luxury at the expense of others, found herself supporting not only him, but also her three children, her two personal servants, and a butler—and all from the proceeds of her prostitutional services.[128] Tales abound of such largesse. Theodotê supposedly paid for the burial of her client Alkibiadês of the aristocratic Alkmeonid family (Athênaios 574e). Gryllion, a member of the elite Areopagos Council at Athens, is said to have lived parasitically from the largess of Phrynê; Satyros was supported by Pamphila, another high-earning prostitute (Athênaios 591d–e). Makhôn and Lygkeus even fashion humor from this role reversal: the bellies of parasitic women are filled with babies; those of parasitic men, with food.[129]

---

128. Dem. 59.42: οὐσία μὲν γὰρ οὐχ ὑπῆρχεν Στεφάνῳ οὐδὲ Νεαίρᾳ, ὥστε τὰ καθ' ἡμέραν ἀναλώματα δύνασθαι ὑποφέρειν, ἡ δὲ διοίκησις συχνή, ὁπότε δέοι τοῦτόν τε καὶ αὐτὴν τρέφειν καὶ παιδάρια τρία, ἃ ἦλθεν ἔχουσα ὡς αὐτόν, καὶ θεραπαίνας δύο καὶ οἰκέτην διάκονον, ἄλλως τε καὶ μεμαθηκυῖα μὴ κακῶς ἔχειν τὰ ἐπιτήδεια ἑτέρων ἀναλισκόντων αὐτῇ τὸ πρότερον. Cf. Dem. 59.36, 46.

129. Athên. 246b, 584b–c; Makhôn Frs. 6, 7 (Gow).

# Works Cited

Acton, P. 2014. *Poiesis: Manufacturing in Classical Athens*. Oxford.
Adam-Magnissali, S. 2008. *Η Απονομή της Δικαιοσύνης στην αρχαία Αθήνα*. Athens.
Adams, C. 1919. *The Speeches of Aeschines*. Cambridge, MA.
Adams, J. 1983. "Words for 'Prostitute' in Latin." *Rheinisches Museum* 126: 321–58.
Alessandri, S. 1984. "Il significato storico della legge di Nicofonte sul dokimastes monetario." *Annali della Scuola Normale Superiore di Pisa* (3rd Ser.) 14: 369–93.
Allen, D. 1997. "Imprisonment in Classical Athens." *Classical Quarterly* 47: 121–35.
———. 2000. *The World of Prometheus: The Politics of Punishing in Democratic Athens*. Princeton.
Ampolo, C. 1986. "Il Pane quotidiano delle città antiche fra economia e anthropologia." *Opus* 5: 143–51.
Anderson, G. 1976. "Lucian's Classics: Some Short Cuts to Culture." *Bulletin of the Institute of Classical Studies* (London) 23: 59–68.
———. 1978. "Patterns in Lucian's Quotations." *Bulletin of the Institute of Classical Studies* (London) 25: 97–110.
Andreades, A. 1933. *A History of Greek Public Finance*, I. Translated by C. Brown. Cambridge. (Reprinted in 1979 as *Ιστορία της ελληνικής δημοσίας οικονομίας*, Vol. 1. Rev. ed. Athens 1992.)
Arafat, K. 2000. "The Recalcitrant Mass: Athenaeus and Pausanias." In Braund and Wilkins, eds., pp. 191–202.
Askola, H. 2007. *Legal Responses to Trafficking in Women for Sexual Exploitation in the European Union* (Modern Studies in European Law). Portland, OR.
Attalah, W. 1966. *Adonis dans la littérature et l'art grecs*. Paris.
Aviles, D. 2011. "'Arguing against the Law.' Non-Literal Interpretation in Attic Forensic Oratory." *Dike* 14: 19–42.
Azize, Y., K. Kempadoo, and T. Cordero. 1996. *Trafficking in Women: Latin American and Caribbean Region*. Utrecht.
Bäbler, B. 1998. *Fleissige Thrakerinnen und wehrhafte Skythen. Nichtgriechen im klassischen Athen und ihre Archäologische Hinterlassenschaft*. Stuttgart.

Bäbler, B. 2001. Review of E. Cohen 2000. *Bryn Mawr Classical Review* 2001.05.19.
Bain, K., and P. Howells. 2003. *Monetary Economics: Policy and Its Theoretical Basis.* New York.
Balabanoff, A. 1905. *Untersuchungen zur Geschäftsfähigkeit der griechischen Frau.* Leipzig.
Balot, R. 2001. *Greed and Injustice in Classical Athens.* Princeton.
Barbalet, J., ed. 2002. *Emotions and Sociology.* Oxford.
Barberet, R. 1995. *Victimologia y Prostitucion: Informe de Resultados.* Madrid.
Barry, K. 1984. *Female Sexual Slavery.* New York.
———. 1995. *The Prostitution of Sexuality.* New York.
Barsby, J. 1986. *Plautus: Bacchides.* Warminster.
Bauman, R. 1990. *Political Trials in Ancient Greece.* London.
Beard, M. 1991. "Adopting an Approach II." In *Looking at Greek Vases,* edited by T. Rasmussen and N. Spivey, pp. 12–35. Cambridge.
Beard, M., and J. Henderson. 1997. "With This Body I Thee Worship: Sacred Prostitution in Antiquity." *Gender and History* 9: 480–523.
Beasley, J. 1947. "Some Attic Vases in the Cyprus Museum." *Proceedings of the British Academy* 33: 195–244.
Beauchet, L. [1897] 1969. *Histoire du droit privé de la république athénienne.* 4 Vols. Amsterdam.
Beauvoir, S. de. 1974. *The Second Sex.* Translated by H. Parshley. NewYork.
Becker, W. 1877–88. *Charikles.* Revised by H. Göll. Berlin.
Bell, L., ed. 1987. *Good Girls, Bad Girls: Feminists and Sex Trade Workers Face to Face.* Toronto.
— Bell, S. 1994. *Reading, Writing and Rewriting the Prostitute Body.* Bloomington, IN.
Beloch, K. 1912–27. *Griechische Geschichte.* 4 vols. 2nd ed. Strassburg.
Benner, A. and F. Fobes. 1949. *The Letters of Alciphron, Aelian and Philostratus.* Cambridge, MA.
Benveniste, E. 1973. *Indo-European Language and Society.* London.
Bérard, C. and C. Bron. 1989. *A City of Images: Iconography and Society in Ancient Greece.* Princeton. (Translation of *La cité des images; Religion et société en Grèce antique.* Lausanne 1984.).
— Berezin, M. 2005. "Emotions and the Economy." In *The Handbook of Economic Sociology,* edited by N. Smelser and R. Swedberg, pp. 109–27. Princeton.
Bers, V. 2003. *Demosthenes, Speeches 50–59.* Austin, TX.
Bertrand, J.-M. 2003. "De la fiction en droit grec. Quelques réflexions." In *Symposion 1999,* edited by G. Thür and F. Fernández Nieto, pp. 387–411. Köln.
Beschi, L. 1967–68. "Contributi di topografia ateniese." *Annuario della Scuola archeologica di Atene* 45/46: 520–26.
Bettalli, M. 1982. "Note sulla produzione tessile ad Atene in età classica." *Opus* 1: 261–78.

Bettalli, M. 1985. "Case, Botteghe, Ergasteria: Note sui luoghi di produzione e di vendita nell' Atene classica." *Opus* 4: 29–41.

Bielman, A. 1994. *Retour à la liberté. Libération et sauvetage des prisonniers en Grèce ancienne*. École française d'Athènes. Études épigraphiques 1. Paris.

Biezunska-Malowist, I. 1966. "The χωρὶς οἰκοῦντες in Demosthenes' First Philippic." *Eos* 56: 66–72. In Polish with Latin summary.

Bindman, J. 1997. *Redefining Prostitution as Sex Work*. WWW.walnet.org/csis/papers/redefining/htm.

Biscardi, A. 1989. "Contratto di lavoro e 'misthosis' nella civiltà greca del diritto." *Revue Internationale des Droits de l'Antiquité* 36: 75–97.

———. 1991. *Αρχαίο ελληνικό δίκαιο*. Translated by P. Dimakis. Athens. (Originally published as *Diritto greco antico* [Milan 1982]).

Bishop, R., and L. Robinson. 1998. *Night Market: Sexual Cultures and the Thai Economic Miracle*. London.

Bissa, E. 2009. *Governmental Intervention in Foreign Trade in Archaic and Classical Greece*. Leiden.

Blass, F. 1893. *Die attische Beredsamkeit* III.1: *Demosthenes*. Leipzig.

Blavatskaja, T. 1972. "Zur Geschichte der Sklavenhaltung in den nordwestlichen Gebieten Griechenlands." In *Die Sklaverei in hellenistischen Staaten im 3.–1. Jh. v. Chr.*, edited by T. Blavatskaja, V. Tatiana, E. Golubcova, and A. Pavlovskaja, pp. 3–105. Wiesbaden.

Bloch, I. 1912. *Die Prostitution*. Vol. 1. Berlin.

Blümner, H. 1912. *Technologie und Terminologie der Gewerbe und Künste bei Griechen und Römern*. Vol. 1. Leipzig.

Blundell, S. 1995. *Women in Ancient Greece*. Cambridge, MA.

Boeckh, A. 1817. *Die Staatshaushaltung der Athener*. Berlin. 3rd ed. 1886. (Translated as *The Public Economy of Athens*. London 1842. Repr. 1976.)

Bogaert, R. 1968. *Banques et banquiers dans les cités grecques*. Leiden.

Bolkestein, H. [1939] 1969. *Wohltätigkeit und Armenpflege im vorchristlichen Altertum*. Utrecht.

Bolles, L. 1992. "Sand, Sea and the Forbidden." *Transforming Anthropology* 3: 30–34.

Bompaire, J. 1958. *Lucien écrivain: Imitation et création*. Paris.

Bongenaar, J. 1933. *Isocrates' trapeziticus vertaald en toegelicht*. Utrecht.

Bourdieu, P. 1977. *Outline of a Theory of Practice*. Translated by Richard Nice. Cambridge.

Bradley, K. etc., eds. 2011. *The Cambridge World History of Slavery: Vol. 1, The Ancient Mediterranean World*. Cambridge.

Branham, R. 1989. *Unruly Eloquence: Lucian and the Comedy of Traditions*. Cambridge, MA.

Braund, D., and J. Wilkins, eds. 2000. *Athenaeus and His World: Reading Greek Culture in the Roman Empire*. Exeter.

Braunstein, O. 1911. *Die politische Wirksamkeit der griechischen Frau: Eine Nachwirkung vorgriechischen Mutterrechtes*. Diss. Leipzig.

Bremmer, J. 1985. "La donna anziana: Libertà e indipendenza." In *Le donne in Grecia*, edited by G. Arrigoni, pp. 275–98. Rome.

Bresson, A. 1994. "L'attentat d'Hiéron et le commerce grec." In *Économie antique. Les échanges dans l'Antiquité: Le rôle de l'État*, edited by J. Andreau, P. Briant and R. Descat, pp. 47–68. Saint-Bertrand-de-Comminges. (Reprinted in, and quoted from, Bresson, 2000b, pp. 131–49.)

———. 2000a. "Prix officiels et commerce de gros à Athènes." In Bresson, 2000b, pp. 183–210.

———. 2000b. *La cité marchande*. Bordeaux.

———. 2007/8. *L'économie de la Grèce des cités*. Paris.
  Vol. 1. Les structures et la production. 2007.
  Vol. 2: Les espaces de l'échange. 2008.

Brewis, J., and S. Linstead. 2004. "'The Worst Thing is the Screwing.' Consumption and the Management of Identity in Sex Work." In *Sexualities: Identities, Behaviors, and Society*, edited by M. Kimmel and R. Plante, pp. 317–30. Oxford.

Brock, R. 1994. "The Labour of Women in Classical Athens." *Classical Quarterly* 44: 336–46.

Bromberg, S. 1998. "Feminist Issues in Prostitution." In *Prostitution*, edited by J. Elias, pp. 294–320. Amherst, NY.

Brown, P. 1990. "Plots and Prostitutes in Greek New Comedy." *Papers of the Leeds International Latin Seminar*. Volume 6: 241–66.

Brun, P. 1983. *Eisphora, syntaxis, stratiotika: Recherches sur les finances militaires d'Athènes au IVe siècle av. J. C.* Paris.

Brun, P., and R. Descat. 2000. "Le profit de la guerre dans la Grèce des cités." In *La guerre dans les économies antiques*, edited by J. Andreau, P. Briant, and R. Descat, pp. 211–30. Saint-Bertrand-de-Comminges.

Brussa, L. 1998. "The TAMPEP Project in Western Europe." In Kempadoo and Doezema, eds., pp. 246–59.

Budin, S. 2003a. "*Pallakai*, Prostitutes, and Prophetesses." *Classical Philology* 98: 148–59.

———. 2003b. *The Origin of Aphrodite*. Bethesda, MD.

———. 2004. "A Reconsideration of the Aphrodite-Ashtart Syncretism." *Numen* 51: 95–145.

———. 2006. "Sacred Prostitution in the First Person." In Faraone and McClure, eds., pp. 77–92.

———. 2008. *The Myth of Sacred Prostitution in Antiquity*. Cambridge.

Buis, E. 2014. "Law and Greek Comedy." In *The Oxford Handbook on Greek and Roman Comedy*, edited by M. Fontaine and A. Scafuro, pp. 181–98. Oxford.

Bundrick, S. 2008. "The Fabric of the City: Imaging Textile Production in Classical Athens." *Hesperia* 77: 283–334.

Burtt, J. 1954. *Minor Attic Orators*. Vol. 2. Cambridge, MA.

Burford, A. 1972. *Craftsmen in Greek and Roman Society*. London.
Burke, E. 1992. "The Economy of Athens in the Classical Era." *Transactions of the American Philological Association* 122: 199–226.
Butler, J. 2002. *Undoing Gender*. New York.
Caillemer, E. 1892. "Dokimasia." In *Dictionnaire des antiquités grecques et romaines*, edited by C. Daremberg, E. Saglio, E. Pottier, and G. Lafaye. Paris.
Cairns, D. 1996. "*Hybris*, Dishonour, and Thinking Big." *Journal of Hellenic Studies* 116: 1–32.
Calame, C. 1977. *Les choeurs de jeunes filles en Grèce archaïque*. 2 Vols. Rome.
———. 1989. "Entre rapports de parenté et relations civiques: Aphrodite l'hétaïre au banquet politique des *hetaîroi*." In *Aux Sources de la Puissance: Sociabilité et Parenté*, edited by F. Thélamon, pp. 101–11. Rouen.
———. 1996. *L'Éros dans la Grèce antique*. Paris. (English translation: Princeton 1999.)
Calcagno, C. 2001. Review of Möller 2000. *Business History Review* 75: 913–16.
Calderini, A. [1908] 1965. *La manomissione e la condizione dei liberti in Grecia*. Rome.
Camp, J. 2001. *The Archaeology of Athens*. New Haven, CT.
Camp, J. and J. Kroll. 2001. "The Agora Mint and Athenian Bronze Coinage." *Hesperia* 70: 127–62.
Canfora, L. 1995. "The Citizen." In *The Greeks*, edited by J.-P. Vernant, pp. 120–52. (Translation of *L'uomo greco* [1991]). Chicago.
Cantarella, E. 1987. *Pandora's Daughters: The Role and Status of Women in Greek and Roman Antiquity*. Translated, with revisions, by M. Fant. Baltimore, MD. (Originally published as *L'ambiguo malanno* [1981]).
———. 1991. "Moicheia. Reconsidering a Problem." In *Symposion 1990*, edited by M. Gagarin, pp. 289–96. Köln.
———. 2005. "Gender, Sexuality and Law." In *The Cambridge Companion to Greek Law*, edited by M. Gagarin and D. Cohen, pp. 236–53. Cambridge.
Carawan, E. 2006. "The Athenian Law of Agreement." *Greek, Roman and Byzantine Studies* 46: 339–74.
Carey, C. ed. 1992. *Apollodoros against Neaira [Demosthenes] 59*. Warminster.
———. 1993. "The Purpose of Aristophanes' Acharnians." *Rheinisches Museum* 136: 254–63.
———. 1998. "The Shape of Athenian Laws." *Classical Quarterly* 48: 93–109.
———. ed. 1989. *Lysias: Selected Speeches*. Cambridge.
Carey, C., and R. Reid. 1985. *Demosthenes: Selected Private Speeches*. Cambridge.
Cargill, J. 1995. *Athenian Settlements of the Fourth Century B.C.* Leiden.
Carmen, A., and H. Moody. 1985. *Working Women: The Subterranean World of Street Prostitution*. New York.
Carter, L. 1986. *The Quiet Athenian*. Oxford.
Carter, V., and E. Giobbe. 2006. "Duet: Prostitution, Racism, and Feminist Discourse." In *Prostitution and Pornography: Philosophical Debate about the Sex Industry*, edited by J. Spector, 17–39. Stanford.
Cartledge, P. 1993. *The Greeks: A Portrait of Self and Others*. Oxford.

Cartledge, P. 1998. "The Economy (Economies) of Ancient Greece." *Dialogos* 5: 4–24.
———. 2001. "The Political Economy of Greek Slavery." In Cartledge, Cohen, and Foxhall, eds., pp. 156–66.
———. 2002. "The Economy (Economies) of Ancient Greece." In *The Ancient Economy*, edited by W. Scheidel and S. von Reden, pp. 11–32. Cambridge.
Cartledge, P., E. Cohen, and L. Foxhall, eds. 2001. *Money, Labour and Land: Approaches to the Economies of Ancient Greece*. London.
Casson, L. 1976. "The Athenian Upper Class and New Comedy." *Transactions of the American Philological Association* 106: 29–59. (Reprinted in *Athenian Trade and Society*. Detroit 1984.)
Castoriadis, C. 1975. *L'Institution imaginaire de la société*. Paris.
———. 2002. *Sujet et vérité dans le monde social-historique*. Paris.
Chancer, L. 1998. *Reconcilable Differences: Confronting Beauty, Pornography and the Future of Feminism* (including "Toward a Sociological Feminist Theory of Prostitutes and Prostitution," pp. 188–99). Berkeley.
Chantraine, P. 1968–70. *Dictionnaire étymologique de la langue grecque*. 2 Vols. Paris.
Chapkis, W. 1997. *Live Sex Acts: Women Performing Erotic Labor*. New York.
———. 2000. "Power and Control in the Commercial Sex Trade." In Weitzer, ed., pp. 181–201.
Charitonidis, S., L. Kahil, and R. Ginouvès. 1970. *Les Mosaïques de la Maison du Ménandre à Mytiléne*. Berlin.
Charles, J. 1938. *Statutes of Limitations at Athens*. Chicago.
Christ, M. 1990. "Liturgical Avoidance and *Antidosis* in Classical Athens." *Transactions of the American Philological Association* 120: 147–69.
———. 1998. *The Litigious Athenian*. Baltimore.
Christesen, P. 2004. Review of Reed 2003. *Bryn Mawr Classical Review* 2004.07.22.
Christophilopoulos, A. 1946. "Σχέσεις γονέων καὶ τέκνων κατὰ τὸ βυζαντικὸν δίκαιον." Συμβολαὶ τοῦ ἑλληνικοῦ καὶ τοῦ ῥωμαϊκοῦ δικαίου 4: 130–39.
Citti, V. 1997. "Una coppia nominale in Lisia." In *Schiavi e dipendenti nell'ambito dell' "oikos" e della "familia,"* edited by M. Moggi and G. Cordiano, pp. 91–96. Pisa.
Coccagna, H. 2011. "Embodying Sympotic Pleasure: A Visual Pun on the Body of an *Aulêtristria*." In Glazebrook and Henry, eds., pp. 106–21.
Cohen, D. 1987. "Law, Society and Homosexuality in Classical Athens." *Past and Present* 117: 1–21.
———. 1989. "Seclusion, Separation, and the Status of Women." *Greece & Rome* (2nd Ser.) 36: 1–15.
———. 1990. "The Social Context of Adultery at Athens." In *Nomos: Essays in Athenian Law, Politics and Society*, edited by P. Cartledge, P. Millett, and S. Todd, pp. 147–65. Cambridge.
———. 1991a. "Sexuality, Violence, and the Athenian Law of *Hubris*. *Greece & Rome* 38: 171–88.

———. 1991b. *Law, Sexuality and Society: The Enforcement of Morals in Classical Athens*. Cambridge.

Cohen, D. 1995. *Law, Violence and Community in Classical Athens*. Cambridge.

———. 1996. "Seclusion, Separation, and the Status of Women in Classical Athens." In *Women in Antiquity*, edited by I. McAuslan and P. Walcott, pp. 134–45. Oxford.

Cohen, E. 1973. *Ancient Athenian Maritime Courts*. Princeton.

———. 1990a. "A Study in Contrast: 'Maritime Loans' and 'Landed Loans' at Athens." In *Symposion 1988*, edited by A. Biscardi, J. Mélèze-Modrzejewski, and G. Thür, pp. 57–79. Köln.

———. 1990b. "Commercial Lending by Athenian Banks: Cliometric Fallacies and Forensic Methodology." *Classical Philology* 85: 177–90.

———. 1992. *Athenian Economy and Society: A Banking Perspective*. Princeton.

———. 1993. "The Athenian Economy." In *Nomodeiktes: Greek Studies in Honor of Martin Ostwald*, edited by R. Rosen and J. Farrell, pp. 197–206. Ann Arbor.

———. 1994. "Status and Contract at Athens." In *Symposion 1993*, edited by G. Thür, pp. 141–52. Köln.

———. 1998. "The Wealthy Slaves of Athens: Legal Rights, Economic Obligations." In *Le monde antique et les droits de l'homme*, edited by H. Jones, pp. 105–29. Brussels. Actes de la 50$^e$ session de la société Fernand de Visscher pour l'histoire des droits de l'antiquité. Brussels, September 16–19, 1996.

———. 2000. *The Athenian Nation*. Princeton.

———. 2001. "Introduction." In Cartledge, Cohen and Foxhall, eds., pp. 1–7. London.

———. 2003. "The High Cost of *Andreia* at Athens." In *'Andreia' and Ancient Constructs of 'Manly Courage,'* edited by I. Sluiter and R. Rosen, pp. 145–65. Leiden.

———. 2005a. "Unintended Consequences? The Economic Effect of Athenian Tax Laws." In *Symposion 2001*, edited by M. Gagarin and R. Wallace, pp. 283–91. Vienna.

———. 2005b. "Commercial Law." In *A Companion to Ancient Greek Law*, edited by M. Gagarin and D. Cohen, pp. 290–302. Cambridge.

———. 2006. "Consensual Contracts at Athens." In *Symposion 2003*, edited by H.-A. Rupprecht, pp. 73–84. Vienna.

———. 2014. "Private Agreements Purporting to Override Polis Law." In *Symposion 2013*, edited by M. Gagarin and A. Lanni, pp. 277–86. Vienna.

———. (forthcoming) (a). "Overcoming Legal Incapacity at Athens: Juridical Adaptations Facilitating the Business Activity of Slaves." *Legal Documents in Ancient Society* VI (Jerusalem Conference: 2013).

———. (forthcoming) (b). "Slaves' Commercial Activity: Legal Ramifications for Ancient Athens—and for Modern Scholarship." (Conference in honor of Michael Gagarin: 2011.)

Cole, S. 1984. "Greek Sanctions Against Sexual Assault." *Classical Philology* 79: 97–113.

Collins, P. 1990. *Black Feminist Thought: Knowledge, Consciousness and the Politics of Empowerment*. New York.

Cooper, C. 1995. "Hyperides and the Trial of Phryne." *Phoenix* 49: 303–18.

Cooter, R. 2000. "Three Effects of Social Norms on Law: Expression, Deterrence, and Internalization." *Oregon Law Review* 79: 1–22.

Corbin, A. 1998. *Women for Hire: Prostitution and Sexuality in France after 1850.* (Translation of *Les filles de noce: Misére sexuelle et prostitution aux 19ᵉ et 20ᵉ siècles.* Paris 1978.) Cambridge, MA.

Couilloud-Le Dinahet, M.-Th. 1988. "Les magistrats grecs et l'approvisionnement des cités." *Cahiers d'Histoire* 33: 321–32.

Cox, C. 1998. *Household Interests: Property, Marriage Strategies, and Family Dynamics in Ancient Athens.* Princeton.

———. 2002. "Crossing Boundaries through Marriage in Menander's *Dyskolos*." *Classical Quarterly* 52 (n.s.): 391–94.

———. 2003. "Women and Property in Ancient Athens: A Discussion of the Private Orations and Menander." Paper presented at the Center for Hellenic Studies, Conference on Women and Property in Ancient Near Eastern and Mediterranean Societies. www.chs.harvard.edu/activities_events.sec/conferences.ssp/conference_women_property.pg.

Cudjoe, R. 2010. *The Social and Legal Position of Widows and Orphans in Classical Athens.* Athens.

Cudjoe, R., and S. Adam-Magnissali. 2010. "Family Law in [Demosthenes] 43: *Against Makartatos*, 75." Ἐπετηρὶς τοῦ Ἀρχείου τῆς Ἱστορίας τοῦ Ἑλληνικοῦ Δικαίου 42: 67–93.

Cunningham, I. 1971. *Herodas Mimiambi.* Oxford.

———. 1993. Translation of Herodas. In *Theophrastus, Herodas, Cercidas and the Choliambic Poets*, edited and translated by J. Rusten, I. Cunningham, and A. Knox. Cambridge, MA.

Dahl, K. 1976. *Thesmophoria: En graesk kvindefest.* Copenhagen.

Dalby, A. 1996. *Siren Feasts: A History of Food and Gastronomy in Greece.* London.

———. 2002. "Levels of Concealment: The Dress of '*Hetairai*' and '*Pornai*' in Greek Texts." In Llewellyn-Jones, ed., 2002, pp. 111–24.

Davidson, J. 1994. "Consuming Passions: Appetite, Addiction and Spending in Classical Athens." Diss. Oxford.

———. 1997. *Courtesans and Fishcakes: The Consuming Passions of Classical Athens.* London.

———. 2004a. "Dover, Foucault, and Greek Homosexuality: Penetration and the Truth of Sex." In *Studies in Ancient Greek and Roman Society*, edited by R. Osborne, pp. 78–118. Cambridge. (Reprint of *Past and Present* 170: 3–51.)

———. 2004b. "Liaisons dangereuses: Aphrodite and the Hetaira." *Journal of Hellenic Studies* 124: 169–73.

———. 2005. Review of Llewellyn-Jones, ed., 2002 and Llewellyn-Jones 2003. *Journal of Hellenic Studies* 125: 181–83.

———. 2007. *The Greeks and Greek Love.* London.

Davidson, J., and J. Taylor. 2004. "Fantasy Islands: Exploring the Demand for Sex Tourism." In *Sexualities: Identities, Behaviors, and Society*, edited by M. Kimmel and R. Plante, pp. 331–41. Oxford.

Davies, G. 1994. "The Language of Gesture in Greek Art: Gender and Status on Grave Stelai." *Apollo* 140, no. 389: 6–11.

Davies, J. 1971. *Athenian Propertied Families, 600–300 B.C.* Oxford.

———. 1978. *Democracy and Classical Greece*. Stanford.

———. 1981. *Wealth and the Power of Wealth in Classical Athens*. Salem, NH.

———. 2001. "Temples, Credit, and the Circulation of Money." In Meadows and Shipton, eds., pp. 117–28.

Davis, N., and C. Stasz. 1990. *Social Control of Deviance: A Critical Perspective*. New York.

De Brauw, M., and J. Miner. 2004. "Androtion's Alleged Prostitution Contract: Aes. 1.165 and Dem. 22.23 in Light of P. Oxy. VII 1012." *Zeitschrift der Savigny-Stiftung für Rechtsgeschichte* (Romanist. Abt.) 121: 301–13.

Delacoste, F., and P. Alexander. 1998. *Sex Work: Writings by Women in the Sex Industry*. 2nd ed. San Francisco.

Delavaud-Roux, M. 1993. *Les Danses armées en Grèce antique*. Aix-en-Provence.

Delz, J. 1950. *Lukians Kenntnis der athenischen Antiquitäten*. Diss. Freiburg in der Schweiz. (non vidi).

———. 1960. Review of Bompaire 1958. *Gnomon* 32: 756–61.

———. 2001. "Monnaie multiple et monnaie frappée en Grèce archaïque." *Revue Numismatique* 157: 69–81.

Detienne, M. 1977. *The Gardens of Adonis. Spices in Greek Mythology*. Sussex. (First published in French as *Les Jardins d'Adonis*. Paris 1971.)

Dillon, M. 2002. *Girls and Women in Classical Greek Religion*. London.

Dilts, M. 1986. *Scholia Demosthenica*. Vol. 2. Leipzig.

Dimakis, P. n.d. *Ὁ θεσμὸς τῆς προικὸς κατὰ τὸ ἀρχαῖον ἑλληνικόν δίκαιον*. Athens.

———. 1988. "Orateurs et hetaïres dans l'Athènes classique." In *Éros et droit en Grèce classique*, edited by P. Dimakis, pp. 43–54. Paris.

———. 1992–93. "Οι Τρεις Λα·ι·δες." In *Πρακτικά του Δ' Διεθνούς Συνεδρίου Πελοποννησιακών Σπουδών*. Athens.

———. 1994. "Η θέση των γυναικών στην Αθήνα της κλασικής εποχής." In *Πρόσωπα και θεσμοί της αρχαίας Ελλάδας*, pp. 17–34. Athens.

Dimopoulou, A. 2014. "Ἄκυρον ἔστω: Legal Invalidity in Greek Inscriptions." In *Symposion 2013*, edited by M. Gagarin and A. Lanni, pp. 249–75. Vienna.

Dines, G., and R. Jensen. 2004. "Pornography and Media: Toward a More Critical Analysis." In *Sexualities: Identities, Behaviors, and Society*, edited by M. Kimmel and R. Plante, pp. 369–80. Oxford.

Doblhofer, G. 1994. *Vergewaltigung in der Antike*. Beiträge zur Altertumskunde 46. Stuttgart.

Doezma, J. 2001. "Ouch! Western Feminists' 'Wounded Attachment' to the 'Third World Prostitute.'" *Feminist Review* 67: 16–38.

Dorjahn, A. 1935. "Anticipation of Arguments in Athenian Courts." *Transactions of the American Philological Association* 55: 274–95.

Dougherty, C. 1996. "Democratic Contradictions and the Synoptic Illusion of Euripides' *Ion*." In Ober and Hedrick, eds., pp. 249–70.

Dover, K. 1964. "Eros and Nomos." *Bulletin of the Institute of Classical Studies* 9: 31–42.

———. [1974] 1984. *Greek Popular Morality in the Time of Plato and Aristotle*. Berkeley.

———. 1978 [1989]. *Greek Homosexuality*. London.

———. 1984. "Classical Greek Attitudes to Sexual Behavior." In *Women in the Ancient World*, edited by J. Peradotto and J. Sullivan, pp. 143–57. Albany, N.Y.

———. 1988. *The Greeks and Their Legacy*. Vol. 2 of *Collected Papers*. Oxford.

Dubois, P. 2003. *Slaves and Other Objects*. Chicago.

Edlund, L., and E. Korn. 2002. "A Theory of Prostitution." *Journal of Political Economy* 110, no. 1: 181–214.

Ehrenberg, V. 1962. *The People of Aristophanes: A Sociology of Old Attic Comedy*. New York.

———. 1969. *The Greek State*. 2nd ed. London.

Elster, J. 1998. "Economics and Economic Theory." *Journal of Economic Literature* 36: 47–74.

Engels, J. 2001. "Das athenische Getreidesteuer-Gesetz des Agyrrhios." *Zeitschrift für Papyrologie und Epigraphik* 134: 97–124.

Engen, D. 2010. *Honor and Profit: Athenian Trade Policy and the Economy and Society of Greece, 415–307 B.C.E.* Ann Arbor.

Fantasia, U. 1987. "Il grano di Leucone e le finanze di Atene: Nota a Demostene, 20, 33." *Annali della Scuola Normale Superiore di Pisa* (3rd Ser.) 17: 89–117.

———. 2004. "Appaltatori, grano pubblico, e finanze cittadine: Ancora sul *nomos* di Agirrio." *Mediterraneo Antico. Economie, società, culture* 7: 513–40.

———. 2012. "Gli agoranomi e l'approvvigionamento granario delle città greche in età ellenistica." In *Agoranomes et édiles: Institutions des marchés antiques*, edited by L. Capdetrey and C. Hasenohr, pp. 35–45. Paris.

Fantham, E., H. Foley, N. Kampen, S. Pomeroy, and H. Shapiro. 1994. *Women in the Classical World*. Oxford.

Faraguna, M. 1999a. "Aspetti della schiavitù domestica femminile in Attica tra oratoria ed epigrafia." In *Femmes-esclaves: modèles d'interprétation anthropologique, économique, juridique (Atti del XXI Colloquio internazionale del G.I.R.E.A.)*, edited by F. Merola and A. Storchi Marino, pp. 57–79. Naples.

———. 1999b. "Intorno alla nuova legge ateniese sulla tassazione del grano." *Dike* 2:63–79.

———. 2007. "Risposta a Éva Jakab." In *Symposion 2005*, edited by E. Cantarella, pp. 123–30. Vienna.

Faraguna, M. 2010. "Il sistema degli appalti pubblici ad Atene nel IV sec. a.C. e la legge di Agirrio." In *Nuove ricerche sulla legge granaria ateniese del 374/3 a.C.*, edited by A. Magnetto, D. Erdas, and C. Carusi, pp. 129–48. Pisa.

Faraone, C. 1999. *Ancient Greek Love Magic*. Cambridge, MA.

———. 2006. "Priestess and Courtesan: The Ambivalence of Female Leadership in Aristophanes' *Lysistrata*." In Faraone and McClure, eds., pp. 207–23.

Faraone, C. and L. McClure, eds. 2006. *Prostitutes and Courtesans in the Ancient World*. Madison, WI.

Fauth, W. 1967. *Aphrodite Parakyptusa*. (Abhand. Mainz. Akad. der geistes- und sozialwissenschaftlichen Klasse 1966, no. 6). Wiesbaden.

Ferrari G. 1911. Review of C. Freundt, *Wertpapiere im antiken und frühmittelalterlichen Rechte*. *Byzantinische Zeitschrift* 20: 532–44.

———. 2002. *Figures of Speech: Men and Maidens in Ancient Greece*. Chicago.

Ferrucci, S. 2005. "La ricchezza nascosta: Osservazioni su aphanes e phanera ousia." *Mediterraneo Antico. Economie, società, culture* VIII/1: 145–70.

———. 2006. "L 'oikos' nel diritto attico." *Dike* 9: 183–210.

Feyel, C. 2009. *Dokimasia. La place et le rôle de l'examen préliminaire dans les institutions des cités grecques*. Nancy.

Figueira, T. 1986. "*Sitopolai* and *Sitophylakes* in Lysias' 'Against the Graindealers': Governmental Intervention in the Athenian Economy." *Phoenix* 40:149–71.

———. 1998. *The Power of Money: Coinage and Politics in the Athenian Empire*. Philadelphia.

Fine, J. 1951. *Horoi. Studies in Mortgage, Real Security, and Land Tenure in Ancient Athens*. Hesperia, Suppl. 9. Princeton.

Finley, M. 1951 [1985]. *Studies in Land and Credit in Ancient Athens*. With a new introduction by P. Millett. New Brunswick, NJ.

———. [1953] 1981. "Land, Debt and the Man of Property in Classical Athens." *Political Science Quarterly* 68: 249–68. (Reprinted as and quoted here from Chapter 4 in Finley, 1981, pp. 62–76.)

———. 1981. *Economy and Society in Ancient Greece*. Edited by B. Shaw and R. Saller. London.

———. 1982. "Le Document et l'histoire économique de l'antiquité." *Annales (Economies, Société, Civilisations)* 37: 697–713.

———. ed. 1979. *The Bücher-Meyer Controversy*. New York.

Fischer, M. 2013. "Ancient Greek Prostitutes and the Textile Industry in Attic Vase-Painting ca. 550–450 B.C.E." *Classical World* 106: 219–59.

Fisher, B., and J. Sloan, eds. *Campus Crime: Legal, Social and Policy Perspectives*. 3rd ed. Springfield, IL.

Fisher, N. 1976, 1979. "*Hubris* and Dishononour." *Greece & Rome* 23: 177–93 and 26: 32–47.

———. 1976. *Social Values in Classical Athens*. London.

Fisher, N. 1990. "The Law of *hubris* in Athens." In *Nomos: Essays in Athenian Law, Politics and Society*, edited by P. Cartledge, P. Millett, and S. Todd, pp. 123–45. Cambridge.

———. 1992. *Hybris*. Westminster.

———. 1993a. "Multiple Personalities and Dionysiac Festivals: Dicaeopolis in Aristophanes' *Acharnians*." *Greece and Rome* 41: 31–47.

———. 1993b. *Slavery in Classical Greece*. London.

———. 1995. "*Hybris*, Status and Slavery." In *The Greek World*, edited by A. Powell, pp. 44–84. London.

———. 1998a. "Violence, Masculinity and the Law in Athens." In *When Men Were Men: Masculinity, Power and Identity in Classical Antiquity*, edited by L. Foxhall and J. Salmon, pp. 68–97. London.

———. 1998b. "Gymnasia and the Democratic Values of Leisure." In *Kosmos: Essays in Order, Conflict and Community in Classical Athens*, edited by P. Cartledge, P. Millett, and S. von Reden, pp. 84–104. Cambridge.

———. 2001. *Aeschines against Timarchos*. Oxford.

———. 2006. "Citizens, Foreigners, Slaves." In *Companion to the Classical Greek World*, edited by K. Kinzl, pp. 327–49. Malden, MA.

———. 2008. "'Independent' Slaves in Classical Athens and the Ideology of Slavery." In *From Captivity to Freedom*, edited by C. Katsari and E. Dal Lago, pp. 121–46. Leicester.

———. 2014. "Athletics and Sexuality." In Hubbard, ed., pp. 244–64.

Flament, C. 2007. *Une économie monétarisée: Athènes à l'époque classique (440–338): Contribution à l'étude du phénomène monétaire en Grèce ancienne*. Louvain.

Flashar, H. 1969. "Der Epitaphios des Perikles." *Sitzungsberichte der Heidelberger Akademie der Wissenschaften*. I. 56 ff.

Flemming, R. 1999. "*Quae corpore quaestum facit*: The Sexual Economy of Female Prostitution in the Roman Empire." *Journal of Roman Studies* 89: 38–61.

Flower, M. 1994. *Theopompus of Chios: History and Rhetoric in the Fourth Century BC*. Oxford.

Ford, A. 1999. "Reading Homer from the Rostrum: Poems and Laws in Aeschines' *Against Timarchus*." In *Performance Culture and Athenian Democracy*, edited by S. Goldhill and R. Osborne, pp. 231–56. Cambridge.

Forsén, B., and G. Stanton, eds. 1996. *The Pnyx in the History of Athens*. Helsinki.

Foucault, M. 1984. *The Foucault Reader*. Edited by P. Rabinow. New York.

Fox, R. Lane. 1994. "Aeschines and Athenian Democracy." In *Ritual, Finance, Politics: Athenian Democratic Accounts Presented to David Lewis*, edited by R. Osborne and S. Hornblower, pp. 135–55. Oxford.

Foxhall, L. 1989. "Household, Gender and Property in Classical Athens." *Classical Quarterly* 39: 22–44.

———. 1991. "Response to Eva Cantarella." In *Symposion 1990*, edited by M. Gagarin, pp. 297–303. Köln.

Foxhall, L. 1994. "Pandora Unbound: A Feminist Critique of Foucault's *History of Sexuality*." In *Dislocating Masculinity: Comparative Ethnographies*, edited by A. Cornwall and N. Lindisturre, pp. 133–46. London.

———. 1996. "The Law and the Lady." In *Greek Law in Its Political Setting*, edited by L. Foxhall and A. Lewis, pp. 133–152. Oxford.

———. 2013. *Studying Gender in Classical Antiquity*. Cambridge.

Foxhall, L., and H. Forbes. 1982. "*Sitometreia*: The Role of Grain as a Staple Food in Classical Antiquity." *Chiron* 12: 41–90.

Foxhall, L., and A. Lewis. 1996. "Introduction." In *Greek Law in its Political Setting*, edited by L. Foxhall and A. Lewis, pp. 1–8. Oxford.

Frier, B., and D. Kehoe. 2007. "Law and Economic Institutions." In Scheidel, Morris, and Saller, eds., pp. 113–43.

Frontisi-Ducrous, F., and F. Lissarrague. 1990. "From Ambiguity to Ambivalence: A Dionysiac Excursion through the 'Anakreontic' Vases." In Halperin, Winkler, Zeitlin, eds., pp. 211–56.

Frost, F. 2002. "Solon *Pornoboskos* and Aphrodite Pandemos." *Syllecta Classica* 13: 34–46.

Fuks, A. 1951. "*Kolonos misthios*: Labour Exchange in Classical Athens." *Eranos* 49: 171–73.

Gabrielsen, V. 1986. "Φανερά and ἀφανὴς οὐσία in Classical Athens." *Classica et Mediaevalia* 37: 99–114.

———. 1994. *Financing the Athenian Fleet: Public Taxation and Social Relations*. Baltimore.

Gagarin, M. 1979. "The Athenian Law against *Hybris*." In *Arktouros: Hellenic Studies presented to Bernard Knox*, edited by G. Bowersock, W. Burkert, and M. Putnam, pp. 229–36. Berlin and New York.

———. 1996. "The Torture of Slaves in Athenian Law." *Classical Philology* 91: 1–18.

———. 2001. Review of *Law and Social Status in Classical Athens*, edited by V. Hunter and J. Edmonson, pp. 53–74. 2000. *Bryn Mawr Classical Review* 2001.10.3.

———. 2005. "The Unity of Greek Law." In *The Cambridge Companion to Greek Law*, edited by M. Gagarin and D. Cohen, pp. 29–40. Cambridge.

———. 2008. *Writing Greek Law*. Cambridge.

Gagliardi, L. 2005. "The Athenian Procedure of Dokimasia of Orators." In *Symposion 2001*, edited by R. Wallace and M. Gagarin, pp. 89–97. Vienna.

———. 2006. "Risposta a Stephen Todd." In *Symposion 2003*, edited by H.-A. Rupprecht, pp. 113–20. Vienna.

———. 2010. "Athenian *Dokimasiai*. A Response to Stephen Todd." In *Symposion 2009*, edited by G. Thür, pp. 99–118. Vienna.

———. 2014. "La legge sulla ὁμολογία e i vizi della volontà nei contratti in diritto ateniese." In *Symposion 2013*, edited by M. Gagarin and A. Lanni, pp. 177–214. Vienna.

Gallant, T. 1991. *Risk and Survival in Ancient Greece: Reconstructing the Rural Domestic Economy*. Stanford.

Gallo, L. 1987. "Salari e inflazione: Atene tra V e IV sec. A. C." *Annali della Scuola Normale Superiore di Pisa* (3rd ser.) 17.1: 19–63.

———. 1997. "I prezzi nelle stele attiche: Un' indagine campione." In *Prix et formation des prix dans les économies antiques*, edited by J. Andreau, P. Briant, and R. Descat, pp. 21–32. Entretiens d'archéologie et d'histoire. Saint-Bertrand-de-Comminges.

Gamauf, R. 2009. "Slaves Doing Business: The Role of Roman Law in the Economy of a Roman Household." *European Review of History* 16.3: 331–46.

Garlan, Y. 1975. *War in the Ancient World: A Social History*. London. (Translation of *La guerre dans l'Antiquité*, Paris 1972.)

———. 1980. "Le Travail libre en Grèce ancienne." In Garnsey, ed., pp. 6–22.

———. 1982. *Les esclaves en Grèce ancienne*. Paris. (Translated as "Slavery in Ancient Greece" [Ithaca, NY. 1988]).

———. 1988. *Slavery in Ancient Greece*. Ithaca, NY. (Originally published as *Les esclaves en Grèce ancienne*. Paris 1982.)

Garland, R. 1987. *The Piraeus*. Ithaca, NY.

Garner, R. 1987. *Law and Society in Classical Athens*. London.

Garnsey, P. 1985. "Grain for Athens." In *Crux: Essays in Greek History Presented to G.E.M. de Ste. Croix*, edited by P. Cartledge and F. Harvey, pp. 62–75. London.

———, ed. 1980. *Non-Slave Labour in the Greco-Roman World*. Cambridge.

Garrison, D. 2000. *Sexual Culture in Ancient Greece*. Norman, OK.

Gauthier, Ph. 1972. *Symbola. Les étrangers et la justice dans les cités grecques*. Nancy.

———. 1981. "De Lysias à Aristote (*Ath. Pol.* 51.4): Le commerce du grain à Athènes et les fonctions des sitophylaques." *Revue historique de droit français et étranger* 59: 5–28.

———. 1988. "Métèques, périèques et *paroikoi*: Bilan et points d'interrogation." In *L'Etranger dans le monde grec*, edited by R. Lonis, pp. 24–46. Etudes anciennes 4. Nancy.

Gauthier, Ph., and M. Hatzopoulos. 1993. *La Loi gymnasiarchique de Beroia*. Athens.

Gauthier, Philippe. 2010. "Notes on the Role of the Gymnasion in the Hellenistic City." In Koenig, ed., pp. 87–101.

Gerdes L., ed. 2006. *Prostitution and Sex Trafficking*. Farmington Hills, MI.

Gernet, L. 1907. Review of "Salvioli, *Capitalisme*." *Notes critiques* n.s. 7: 203–05. (Reprinted *in Les Grecs sans miracle* [Paris 1983], pp. 87–88).

———. 1909. "L'approvisionement d'Athènes en blé au Ve et au IVe siècle." *Mélanges d'histoire ancienne* 25, no. 3 (Paris 1909): 171–385. Reprint 1979.

———. 1917. *Recherches sur le développement de la pensée juridique et morale en Grèce. Étude sémantique*. Paris.

———. [1950] 1955. "Aspects du droit athénien de l'esclavage." *Archives d'histoire du droit oriental* 1950: 159–87. (Reprinted in Gernet, [1955] 1964, pp. 151–72).

———. [1951] 1964. "Le droit de la vente et la notion du contrat en Grèce d'après M. Pringsheim." *Revue historique de droit français et étranger* 29: 560–84 (Reprinted in [1955] 1964, pp. 201–24).

Gernet, L. [1955] 1964. *Droit et société dans la Grèce ancienne*. Paris.

———. 1981. "Choses visibles et invisibles." *Revue Philosophique* 146: 79–86 (Chapter 16 of *The Anthropology of Ancient Greece*, pp. 343–51. Baltimore 1981.)

———. ed. 1926. *Lysias*. Paris.

Gilfoyle, T. 1999. "Prostitutes in History: From Parables of Pornography to Metaphors of Modernity." *American Historical Review* 104, no. 1: 117–41.

Gilhuly, C. 1999. "Representations of the *Hetaira*." Diss. Berkeley.

———. 2006. "The Lesbian Phallus in Lucian's *Dialogues of the Courtesans*." In Faraone and McClure, eds., pp. 274–91.

———. 2009. *The Feminine Matrix of Sex and Gender in Classical Athens*. Cambridge.

Gill, C., N. Postlethwaite, and R. Seaford, eds. 1998. *Reciprocity in Ancient Greece*. Oxford.

Glazebrook, A. 2006a. "Prostituting Female Kin (Plut. Solon 23.1–2)." *Dike* 8: 33–53.

———. 2006b. "The Bad Girls of Athens: The Image and Function of Hetairai in Judicial Oratory." In Faraone and McClure, eds., pp. 125–38.

———. 2011. "*Porneion*: Prostitution in Athenian Civic Space." In Glazebrook and Henry, eds., pp. 34–59.

———. 2012. "Prostitutes, Plonk, and Play: Female Banqueters on a Red-Figure Psykter from the Hermitage." *Classical World* 105: 497–524.

Glazebrook, A., and M. Henry. 2011. "Introduction: Why Prostitutes? Why Greek? Why Now?" In Glazebrook and Henry, eds., pp. 3–13.

Glazebrook, A., and M. Henry, eds. 2011. *Greek Prostitutes in the Ancient Mediterranean, 800 BCE–200 CE*. Madison, WI.

Glinster, F. 2000. "The Rapino Bronze, the Touta Marouca, and Sacred Prostitution in Early Central Italy." In *The Epigraphic Landscape of Roman Italy*, edited by A. Cooley, pp. 19–38. London.

Gofas, D. 1979. "Les 'emmenoi dikai' à Thasos." In *Symposion 1974*, edited by A. Biscardi, pp. 175–88 (Reprint: Gofas 1993: 71–77). Köln.

———. 1993. Μελέτες ἱστορίας τοῦ ἑλληνικοῦ δικαίου τῶν συναλλαγῶν. Athens.

———. 1994. θάλασσα καὶ συναλλαγὲς στὴν ἀρχαία Ἑλλάδα. Athens.

Golden, M. 1990. *Children and Childhood in Classical Athens*. Baltimore.

———. 1992. "Slavery and Homosexuality at Athens." In *Homosexuality in the Ancient World*, edited by W. Dynes and S. Donaldson, pp. 162–78. New York. (Reprint from *Phoenix* 38 [1984]: 308–24.)

———. 2003. "Introduction." In *Sex and Difference in Ancient Greece and Rome*, edited by M. Golden and P. Toohey, pp. 1–20. Edinburgh.

———. 2011. "Slavery and the Greek Family." In K. Bradley and P. Cartledge, eds., pp. 134–52.

Goldhill, S. 1998. "The Seductions of the Gaze: Socrates and His Girlfriends." In Cartledge, Millett, and von Reden, eds., pp. 105–24.

Goldman, E. 1969. "The Traffic in Women." In *Anarchism and Other Essays*, pp. 183–200. New York.

Goldman, M. 2015. "Associating the *Auletris*: Flute Girls and Prostitutes in the Classical Greek Symposium." Helios 42.1: 29–60.

Gomme, A. 1933. *The Population of Athens in the Fifth and Fourth Centuries B.C.* Oxford.

———. 1956. *A Historical Commentary on Thucydides*, Volume 2. Oxford.

Gomme, A., and F. Sandbach. 1973. *Menander: A Commentary*. Oxford.

Goode, E. 1978. *Deviant Behavior: An Interactionist Approach*. New York.

Goody, J. 1980. "Slavery in Time and Space." In *Asian and African Systems of Slavery*, edited by J. Watson, pp. 16–42. Berkeley.

———. 1986. *The Logic of Writing and the Organization of Society*. Cambridge.

Gouldner, A. 1965. *Enter Plato: Classical Greece and the Origins of Social Theory*. New York.

Gow, A. 1965. *Machon: The Fragments*. Cambridge.

Graham, A. 1992. "Thucydides 7.13.2 and the Crews of Athenian Triremes." *Transactions of the American Philological Association* 122: 257–70.

———. 1998a. "The Woman at the Window: Observations on the 'Stele from the Harbour' of Thasos." *Journal of Hellenic Studies* 118: 22–40.

———. 1998b. "Thucydides 7.13.2 and the Crews of Athenian Triremes: An Addendum." *Transactions of the American Philological Association* 128: 89–114.

Grenier, J.-Y. 1997. "Économie du surplus, économie du circuit. Les prix et les échanges dans l'Antiquité gréco-romaine et dans l'Ancient régime." In *Prix et formation des prix dans les économies antiques*, edited by J. Andreau, P. Briant and R. Descat, pp. 385–404. Entretiens d'archéologie et d'histoire. Saint-Bertrand-de-Comminges.

Griffin, S. 2001. *The Book of the Courtesans*. New York.

Gulick, C. ed. 1937. *Athenaeus*. Vol. 6. Cambridge, MA.

Haley, S. 2002. "Lucian's 'Leaena and Clonarium': Voyeurism or a Challenge to Assumptions?" In *Among Women: From the Homosocial to the Homoerotic in the Ancient World*, edited by N. Rabinowitz and L. Auanger, pp. 286–303. Austin, TX.

Hallett, J. 1984. *Fathers and Daughters in Roman Society: Women and the Elite Family*. Princeton.

Halperin, D. 1990. *One Hundred Years of Homosexuality and Other Essays on Greek Love*. New York.

———. 1995. *Saint-Foucault: Towards a Gay Hagiography*. Oxford.

———. 2002. *How to Do the History of Homosexuality*. Chicago.

Halperin, D., J. Winkler, and F. Zeitlin, eds. 1990. *Before Sexuality: The Construction of Erotic Experience in the Ancient Greek World*. Princeton.

Halporn, J. 1993. "Roman Comedy and Greek Models." In *Theater and Society in the Classical World*, edited by R. Scodel, pp. 191–213. Ann Arbor.

Hamel, D. 2003. *Trying Neaira: The True Story of a Courtesan's Scandalous Life in Ancient Greece*. New Haven, CT.

Hamilton, C. [1909] 1981. *Marriage as a Trade*. London.

Handa, J. 2000. *Monetary Economics*. London.
Hansen, M. 1976. *"Apagoge," "Endeixis" and "Ephegesis" against "Kakourgoi," "Atimoi" and "Pheugontes."* Odense.
———. 1981. "Two Notes on the Athenian *Dikai Emporikai*." In *Symposion 1979*, edited by P. Dimakis, pp. 167–75. Köln.
———. 1983. "*Rhetores* and *Strategoi* in Fourth-Century Athens." *Greek, Roman and Byzantine Studies* 24: 151–80.
———. 1985a. "The History of the Athenian Constitution." *Classical Philology* 80: 51–66.
———. 1985b. *Demography and Democracy*. Copenhagen.
———. 1991. *The Athenian Democracy in the Age of Demosthenes*. Oxford.
———. 1997. *The Polis as an Urban Centre and as a Political Community*. (Acts of the Copenhagen Polis Centre 4). Copenhagen.
Hanson, A. 1990. "The Medical Writers' Woman." In Halperin, Winkler, and Zeitlin, eds., pp. 309–37.
Hanson, V. 1995. *The Other Greeks: The Family Farm and the Agrarian Roots of Western Civilization*. New York.
Harding, P. 1994. *Androtion and the Attis: The Fragments Translated with an Introduction and Commentary*. Oxford.
Harris, D. 1995. *The Treasures of the Parthenon and Erechtheion*. Oxford.
Harris, E. 1988. "When is a Sale not a Sale? The Riddle of Athenian Terminology for Real Security Revisited." *Classical Quarterly* (n.s.) 38: 351–81.
———. 1992a. "Women and Lending in Athenian Society: A *Horos* Re-Examined." *Phoenix* 46: 309–21.
———. 1992b. Review of D. MacDowell, *Demosthenes against Meidias*. *Classical Philology* 87: 71–80.
———. 1995. *Aeschines and Athenian Politics*. New York.
———. 2001. Review of A. Bresson, *La cité marchande*. *Bryn Mawr Classical Review* 2001.09.40.
———. 2002. "Workshop, Marketplace and Household: The Nature of Technical Specialization in Classical Athens and Its Influence on Economy and Society." In Cartledge, Cohen, and Foxhall, eds., pp. 67–99. London.
———. 2006. *Democracy and the Rule of Law in Classical Athens: Essays on Law, Society, and Politics*. Cambridge.
———. 2008. *Demosthenes: Speeches 20–22*. Austin, TX.
———. 2013a. "Were There Business Agents in Classical Greece? The Evidence of Some Lead Letters." *The Letter: Law, State, Society and the Epistolary Format in the Ancient World*, edited by U. Yiftach-Firanko, pp. 105–24. Wiesbaden.
———. 2013b. *The Rule of Law in Action in Democratic Athens*. Oxford.
———. 2013c. "The Plaint in Athenian Law and Legal Procedure." *In Archives and Archival Documents in Ancient Societies (Legal Documents in Ancient Societies IV)*, edited by M. Faraguna, pp. 143–62. Trieste.

Harris, E. 2013d. "The Against Meidias (Dem. 21)." A Chapter in *The Documents in the Attic Orators*, edited by M. Canevaro, pp. 209–36. Oxford.

Harrison, A. 1968, 1971. *The Law of Athens*. 2 Vols. Oxford.

Harsin, J. 1985. *Policing Prostitution in Nineteenth-Century Paris*. Princeton.

Hartmann, E. 2002. *Heirat, Hetärentum und Konkubinat im klassischen Athen*. Frankfurt.

Harvey, D. 1988. "Painted Ladies: Fact, Fiction, and Fantasy." In *Proceedings of the 3rd Symposium on Ancient Greek and Related Pottery*, edited by J. Christiansen and T. Melander, pp. 242–54. Copenhagen.

Hauschild, H. 1933. *Die Gestalt der Hetäre in der griechischen Komödie*. Leipzig.

Havelock, C. 1995. *The Aphrodite of Knidos and Her Successors*. Ann Arbor.

Hawley, R. 1993. "'Pretty, Witty and Wise:' Courtesans in Athenaeus' *Deipnosophistae* Book 13." *International Journal of Moral and Social Studies* 8.1: 73–89.

Heinz, A. 1982. *Governmental Responses to Crime: Legislative Responses to Crime: The Changing Content of Criminal Law*. Washington, DC.

Heitsch, E. 1984. *Antiphon aus Rhamnus*. Mainz.

Helbig, W. 1873. *Untersuchungen über die campanische Wandmalerei*. Leipzig.

Helm, R. 1927. *Lukianos*. In Pauly-Wissowa, ed., 13, cols. 1725–77.

Hemelrijk, J. [1925] 1979. Πενία en πλοῦτος. Amsterdam.

Henderson, J. 2002. "Strumpets on Stage: The Early Comic Hetaera." *Dionisio* 1: 78–87.

———. 2014. "Comedy in the Fourth Century II: Politics and Domesticity." In *The Oxford Handbook on Greek and Roman Comedy*, edited by M. Fontaine and A. Scafuro, pp. 181–98. Oxford.

Henriot, C. 2001. *Prostitution and Sexuality in Shanghai: A Social History, 1849–1949*. (Translation of *Belles de Shanghai: Prostitution et sexualité en Chine aux XIXe-XXe siècles* [Paris 1997]). Cambridge.

Henry, M. 1985. *Menander's Courtesans and the Greek Comic Tradition*. (Studien zur klassischen Philologie 20.) Frankfurt.

———. 1986. "*Ethos, Mythos, Praxis:* Women in Menander's Comedy." *Helios* n.s. 13.2: 141–50.

———. 1992. "The Edible Woman: Athenaeus' Concept of the Pornographic." In *Pornography and Representation in Greece and Rome*, edited by A. Richlin, pp. 250–68. New York.

———. 1995. *Prisoner of History: Aspasia of Miletus and Her Biographical Tradition*. Oxford.

———. 2000. "Athenaeus the Ur-Pornographer." In Braund and Wilkins, eds., pp. 503–10.

Henry, M. 2011. "The Traffic in Women: From Homer to Hipponax, from War to Commerce." In Glazebrook and Henry, eds., pp. 14–33.

Herfst, P. 1922 [1980]. *Le travail de la femme dans la Grèce ancienne*. Utrecht.

Herman, G. 1998. "Reciprocity, Altruism and the Prisoner's Dilemma: The Special Case of Classical Athens." In C. Gill, N. Postlethwaite, and R. Seaford, eds., pp. 199–225.

Herter, H. 1957. "Dirne." *Reallexikon für Antike und Christentum* 3: 1149–1257. Stuttgart.

———. 1960 [2003]. "The Sociology of Prostitution in Antiquity." In *Sex and Difference in Ancient Greece and Rome*, edited by M. Golden and P. Toohey, pp. 57–113. Edinburgh 2003. (Translation of "Die Soziologie der antiken Prostitution im Lichte der heidnischen und christlichen Schriftum." *Jahrbuch für Antike und Christentum* 3 [1960]: 70–111.)

Hervagault, M.-P., and M.-M. Mactoux. 1974. "Esclaves et société d'après Démosthène." In *Actes du colloque 1972 sur l'esclavage*, pp. 57–102. Annales Littéraires de l'Université de Besançon. Paris.

Herzig, O. 1940. *Lukian als Quelle für die antike Zauberei*. Diss. Tübingen.

Heyl, B. 1979a. *The Madam as Entrepreneur: Career Management in House Prostitution.* New Brunswick, NJ.

———. 1979b. "Prostitution: An Extreme Case of Sexual Stratification." In *The Criminology of Deviant Women*, edited by F. Adler and R. Simon, pp. 198–210. Boston.

Highleyman, L. 1997. "Professional Dominance: Power, Money and Identity." In Nagle, ed., pp. 145–55.

Hindley, C. 1991. "Law, Society and Homosexuality in Classical Athens." *Past and Present* 133: 167–83.

Hirzel, R. [1918] 1962. *Der Name. Ein Beitrag zu seiner Geschichte im Altertum und besonders bei den Griechen.* Amsterdam.

Hoagland, S. 1988. *Lesbian Ethics: Toward New Value.* Palo Alto.

Hoffmann, G. 1986. "L'espace théâtral et social du *Dyskolos* de Ménandre." *Métis* 1: 269–90.

Hoigard, C., and Z. Finstad. 1992. *Backstreets: Prostitution, Money and Love.* University Park, PA.

Holmwood, J. 2005. "Functionalism and its Critics." In *Modern Social Theory: An Introduction*, edited by A. Harrington, pp. 87–109. Oxford.

Hopper, R. 1953. "The Attic Silver Mines in the Fourth Century B.C." *Annual of the British School at Athens* 48: 200–54.

———. 1968. "The Laurion Mines: A Reconsideration." *Annual of the British School at Athens* 63: 293–326.

———. 1979. *Trade and Industry in Classical Greece.* London.

Householder, F. 1941. *Literary Quotation and Allusion in Lucian.* New York.

Hubbard, T. 1998. "Popular Perceptions of Elite Homosexuality in Classical Athens." *Arion* 6 (Ser. 3): 48–78.

———. 2000. "Pederasty and Democracy: The Marginalization of a Social Practice." In *Greek Love Reconsidered*, edited by T. Hubbard, pp. 1–11. New York.

———. 2003. *Homosexuality in Greece and Rome: A Sourcebook of Basic Documents.* Berkeley.

———. 2009. Review of Davidson 2007 and Lear and Cantarella 2008. H-Net Book Review (published by H-Histsex, February 2009).

———. 2014. "Peer Homosexuality." In Hubbard, ed., pp. 127–49.

———. ed. 2014. *A Companion to Greek and Roman Sexualities.* Oxford.

Humphreys, S. 1978. *Anthropology and the Greeks.* London.

———. [1983] 1993. *The Family, Women and Death.* 2nd ed. Ann Arbor.

———. 2007. "Social Relations on Stage: Witnesses in Classical Athens." In *Oxford Readings in the Attic Orators*, edited by E. Carawan, pp. 140–213. Oxford.

Hunter, V. 1981. "Classics and Anthropology." *Phoenix* 35: 144–55.

———. 1989a. "Women's Authority in Classical Athens." *Echos du Monde Classique/ Classical Views* 33 (n.s. 8): 39–48.

———. 1989b. "The Athenian Widow and Her Kin." *Journal of Family History* 14: 291–311.

———. 1994. *Policing Athens: Social Control in the Attic Lawsuits, 420–320 B.C.* Princeton.

———. 1997. "The Prison of Athens: A Comparative Perspective." *Phoenix* 51.3–4: 296–326.

Hussey, E. 1985. "Thucydidean History and Democritean Theory." In *Crux: Essays in Greek History Presented to G.E.M. de Ste. Croix*, edited by P. Cartledge and F. Harvey, pp. 118–38. London.

Immerwahr, H. 1984. "An Inscribed Cup by the Ambrosios Painter." *Antike Kunst* 27: 10–13.

Isager S. and M. Hansen. 1975. *Aspects of Athenian Society in the Fourth Century B.C.* Odense.

Jacquemin, A. 1999. *Offrandes monumentales à Delphes.* Paris.

Jagger, A. 1985. "Prostitution." In *Philosophy of Sex*, edited by A. Soble, pp. 348–68. Totowa, NJ.

Jakab, E. 2006. "Antwort auf Edward Cohen." In *Symposion 2003*, edited by H.-A. Rupprecht, pp. 85–91. Vienna.

———. 2007. "SEG XLVIII.96: Steuergesetz oder Frachtvertrag?" In *Symposion 2005*, edited by E. Cantarella, pp. 105–21. Vienna.

James, S. 2005. "A Courtesan's Choreography: Female Liberty and Male Anxiety at the Roman Dinner Party." In *Defining Genre and Gender in Roman Literature: Essays Presented to William S. Anderson*, edited by W. Batstone and G. Tissol, pp. 269–301. New York.

———. 2006. "A Courtesan's Choreography: Female Liberty and Male Anxiety at the Roman Dinner Party." In Faraone and McClure, eds., pp. 224–51.

Jameson, M. 1977–78. "Agriculture and Slavery in Classical Athens." *Classical Journal* 73: 122–45.

———. 1990. "Private Space and the Greek City." In *The Greek City from Homer to Alexander*, edited by O. Murray and S. Price, pp. 171–95. Oxford.

———. 1997. "Women and Democracy in Fourth-Century Athens." In *Esclavage, guerre, économie en Grèce ancienne: Hommages à Yvon Garlan*, edited by P. Brulé and J. Oulhen, pp. 95–107. Rennes.

———. 2002. "On Paul Cartledge, 'The Political Economy of Greek Slavery.'" In Cartledge, Cohen, and Foxhall, eds., pp. 156–66.

Jeffreys, S. 1997. *The Idea of Prostitution*. Melbourne.

Jenness, V. 1993. *Making It Work: The Prostitutes' Rights Movement in Perspective*. Hawthorne, NY.

Johansson, M. 2001. "The Inscription from Troizen: A Decree of Themistokles?" *Zeitschrift für Papyrologie und Epigraphik* 137: 69–92.

———. 2004. "Plutarch, Aelius Aristides and the Inscription from Troizen." *Rheinisches Museum* 147: 343–54.

Johnstone, S. 1998. "Cracking the Code of Silence: Athenian Legal Oratory and the Histories of Slaves and Women." In *Women and Slaves in Greco-Roman Culture*, edited by S. Murnaghan and S. Joshel, pp. 221–35. London.

———. 2002. "Apology for the Manuscript of Demosthenes 59.67." *American Journal of Philology* 123: 229–56.

Joly, R. 1969. "Esclaves et médecins dans la Grèce antique." *Sudhoffs Archiv* 53: 1–14.

Jones, A. 1948. *Inaugural Lecture: Ancient Economic History*. London.

———. [1957] 1978. *Athenian Democracy*. Oxford.

Jones, C. 1986. *Culture and Society in Lucian*. Cambridge MA.

———. 2008. "Hypereides and the Sale of Slave Families." *Zeitschrift für Papyrologie und Epigraphik* 164: 19–20.

Jones, H., ed. 1998. *Le monde antique et les droits de l'homme*. Actes de la 50ᵉ session de la société Fernand de Visscher pour l'histoire des droits de l'antiquité. Brussels, September 16–19, 1996. Brussels.

Jones, J. 1956. *The Law and Legal Theory of the Greeks*. Oxford.

Jones, N. 2008. *Politics and Society in Ancient Greece*. Westport, CT.

Jordan, D. 1985. "A Survey of Greek Defixiones Not Included in the Special Corpora." *Greek Roman and Byzantine Studies* 26: 151–97.

Joshel S., and S. Murnaghan. 1998. "Introduction: Differential Equations." In *Women and Slaves in Greco-Roman Culture*, edited by S. Murnaghan and S. Joshel, pp. 1–21. London.

Judeich, W. 1896. "Aspasia." In Pauly-Wissowa, ed., II: 1716–21.

Just, R. 1985. "Freedom, Slavery and the Female Psyche." In *Essays in Greek History Presented to G.E.M. de Ste. Croix*, edited by P. Cartledge and F. Harvey, pp. 169–88. London.

———. 1989. *Women in Athenian Law and Life*. London.

Kahn, C. 1993. "Foreword." In Morrow, pp. xvii–xxxi.

Kakavoyianni, O., and I. Dovinou. 2003. "Ιερό Αφροδίτης." In *Αρχαιολογικές Έρευνες στην Μερέντα Μαρκοπούλου· I. Άφροδίτης* pp. 34–35. Athens.

Kamen, D. 2011. "Reconsidering the Status of *Khôris Oikountes.*" *Dike* 14: 43–53.

———. 2013. *Status in Classical Athens.* Princeton.

Kane, S. 1993. "Prostitution and the Military: Planning AIDS Intervention in Belize." *Social Science and Medicine* 36: 956–79.

Kanellopoulos, A. 1987. *Ἀρχαιοελληνικὰ πρότυπα τῆς Κοινῆς Ἀγορᾶς.* Athens.

Kapparis, K. 1999. *Apollodoros "Against Neaira" [D.59].* Berlin.

Kapparis, K. 2011. "The Terminology of Prostitution in the Ancient Greek World." In Glazebrook and Henry, eds., pp. 222–55.

Kara, S. 2009. *Sex Trafficking: Inside the Business of Modern Slavery.* New York.

Karabêlias, E. 1984. "Le contenu de l'oikos en droit grec ancien." In *Μνήμη Γεωργίου Α. Πετροπούλου*, edited by P. Dimakis, I: 441–54. Athens.

———. 1992. "L'acte à cause de mort (diathéke dans le droit attique)." In *Actes à cause de mort* I, pp. 47–121. (Recueils de la société Jean Bodin pour l'histoire comparative des institutions 59.) Brussels.

———. 2002. *L'épiclérat attique.* Athens.

Karras, R. 1996. *Common Women: Prostitution and Sexuality in Medieval England.* Oxford.

Katzouros, Ph. 1981. "Pollux et la 'Δίκη Συνθηκῶν Παραβάσεως'." In *Symposion 1979*, edited by P. Dimakis, pp. 197–216. Köln.

Kazakévich, E. 2008 [1960]. "Were the χωρὶς οἰκοῦντες Slaves?" *Greek Roman and Byzantine Studies* 48: 343–80. (Originally Published in Russian in *Vestnik Drevnej Istorii* 73.3 [1960]: 23–42.)

Keesling, C. 2006. "Heavenly Bodies: Monuments to Prostitutes in Greek Sanctuaries." In Faraone and McClure, eds., pp. 59–76.

Keiser, R. 1986. "Death Enmity in Thull: Organized Vengeance and Social Change in a Kohistani Community." *American Ethnologist* 13: 489–505.

Kempadoo, K. 1998. "Globalizing Sex Workers' Rights." In Kempadoo and Doezema, eds, pp. 1–28.

Kempadoo, K., and J. Doezema, eds. 1998. *Global Sex Workers: Rights, Resistance, and Redefinition.* New York.

Kennedy, R. 2014. *Immigrant Women in Athens: Gender, Ethnicity, and Citizenship in the Classical City.* New York.

Keuls, E. 1983. "'The Hetaera and the Housewife': The Splitting of the Female Psyche in Greek Art." *Mededelingen van het Nederlands Historisch Instituut te Rome* 44–45: 23–40.

———. 1985. *The Reign of the Phallus: Sexual Politics in Ancient Athens.* New York.

———. 1989. "Archaeology and the Classics: A Rumination." In *Classics: A Discipline and Profession in Crisis?*, edited by P. Culham and L. Edmonds, pp. 225–29. Lanham, MD.

Khatzibasileiou, B. 1981. Τα δημοσιονομικά της Κω από μαρτυρίες αρχαίων επιγραφών = Vol. 8 of *Κωακά.*

Kilmer, M. 1993. *Greek Erotica on Red-figure Vases.* London.

———. 1997. "Painters and Pederasts: Ancient Art, Sexuality and Social History." In *Inventing Ancient Culture: Historicism, Periodization, and the Ancient World,* edited by M. Golden and P. Toohey, pp. 36–49. London.

Kirschenbaum, A. 1987. *Sons, Slaves and Freedmen in Roman Commerce.* Jerusalem.

Kitzinger, C. 1991. "Feminism, Psychology and the Paradox of Power." *Feminism and Psychology: An International Journal* 1(1): 111–29.

———. 1994. "Problematizing Pleasure: Radical Feminist Deconstructions of Sexuality and Power." In *Power/Gender: Social Relations in Theory and Practice,* edited by H. Radtke and H. Stam, pp. 194–209. London.

Kleberg, T. 1957. *Hôtels, restaurants et cabarets dans l'antiquité romaine: Études historiques et philologiques.* Uppsala.

Klees, H. 1998. *Sklavenleben im klassischen Griechenland* (= Vol. 30 of *Forschungen zur antiken Sklaverei,* edited by H. Bellen). Stuttgart.

———. 2000. "Die rechtliche und gesellschaftliche Stellung der Freigelassenen im klassischen Griechenland." *Laverna* 11: 1–43.

Knigge, U. [1988] 1991. *The Athenian Kerameikos* (tr. of *Der Kerameikos von Athens,* 1988). Berlin.

———. 2005. *Der Bau Z. Kerameikos* 17, pts. 1–2. Munich.

Kofler, D. 1949. *Aberglaube und Zauberei in Lukians Schriften.* Diss. Innsbruck.

Korver, J. 1934. *De Terminologie van het Creditwesen in het Grieksch.* Amsterdam.

Kosmopoulou, A. 2001. "Female Professionals on Classical Attic Gravestones." *Annual of the British School at Athens* 96: 281–319.

Koutorga, M. de. 1859. *Essai sur les trapezites ou banquiers d'Athènes.* Paris.

Kränzlein, A. 1975. "Die attischen Aufzeichnungen über die Einleiferung von phialai exeleutherikai." In *Symposion 1971,* edited by H. Wolff, pp. 255–64. Köln.

Krenkel, W. 1978. "Männliche Prostitution in der Antike." *Das Altertum* 24: 49–55.

———. 1988. "Prostitution." In *Civilization of the Ancient Mediterranean: Greece and Rome,* edited by M. Grant and R. Kitzinger, pp. 1291–97. New York.

Kroll, J. 2000. Review of Kurke 1999b. *Classical Journal* 96: 85–90.

Kron, J. 1996. "Landed and Commercial Wealth at Classical Athens." Diss. Toronto.

Kruger, K. 2001. *Weaving the Word: The Metaphorics of Weaving and Textile Production.* London.

Kudlien, F. 1968. *Die Sklaven in der griechischen Medezin der klassischen und hellenistischen Zeit* (= Vol. 2 of *Forschungen zur antiken Sklaverei,* edited by J. Vogt). Stuttgart.

Kuenen-Janssens, L. 1941. "Some Notes on the Competence of the Athenian Woman to Conduct a Transaction." *Mnemosyne* (3rd Ser.) 9: 199–214.

Kurke, L. 1989. "*Kapêlia* and Deceit." *American Journal of Philology* 110: 535–44.

———. 1994. "Herodotus and the Language of Metals." *Helios* 22: 36–64.

———. 1997. "Inventing the *Hetaira*: Sex, Politics, and Discursive Conflict in Archaic Greece." *Classical Antiquity* 16: 106–50.

———. 1999a. "Pindar and the Prostitutes, or Reading Ancient 'Pornography.'" In *Constructions of the Classical Body,* edited by J. Porter, pp. 101–25. Ann Arbor.

Kurke, L. 1999b. *Coins, Bodies, Games, and Gold: The Politics of Meaning in Archaic Greece*. Princeton.

———. 2002. "Gender, Politics, and Subversion in the *Chreiai* of Machon." *Proceedings of the Cambridge Philological Society* 48: 20–65.

Kussmaul, P. 1969. *Synthekai. Beiträge zur Geschichte des attischen Obligationsrechtes*. Diss. Basel.

———. 1985. "Zur Bedeutung von συμβόλαιον bei den attischen Rednern." In *Catalepton: Festschrift für Bernhard Wyss*, edited by C. Schäublin, pp. 31–44. Basel.

Labarre, G. 1998. "Les métiers du textile en Grèce ancienne." *Topoi* 8: 791–814.

Lacey, W. 1968. *The Family in Classical Greece*. London.

Lane, R. 1991. *The Market Experience*. Cambridge.

Lanni, A. 2004. "Arguing from Precedent: Modern Perspectives on Athenian Practice." In *The Law and the Courts in Ancient Greece*, edited by E. Harris and L. Rubinstein, pp. 156–71. London.

———. 2010. "The Expressive Effect of the Athenian Prostitution Laws." *Classical Antiquity* 29: 45–67.

Lape, S. 2002/3. "Solon and the Institution of the 'Democratic' Family Form." *Classical Journal* 98.2: 117–39.

———. 2004. *Reproducing Athens: Menander's Comedy, Democratic Culture, and the Hellenistic City*. Princeton.

———. 2006. "The Psychology of Prostitution in Aeschines' Speech against Timarchus." In Faraone and McClure, eds., pp. 139–60. Madison.

Larmour, D., P. Miller, and C. Platter, eds. 1998. *Rethinking Sexuality: Foucault and Classical Antiquity*. Princeton.

Leach, E. 1965. *Political Systems of Highland Burma*. 2nd ed. Boston.

Lear, A. 2014. "Ancient Pederasty." In Hubbard, ed., pp. 102–27.

Lear, A., and E. Cantarella. 2008. *Images of Ancient Greek Pederasty: Boys Were Their Gods*. London.

Lefkowitz, M., and M. Fant, eds. 1992. *Women's Life in Greece and Rome*. 2nd ed. Baltimore.

Legras, B. 1997. "La prostitution féminine dans l'Égypte ptolémaïque." In *Symposion 1995*, edited by G. Thür and J. Vélissaropoulos-Karakostas, pp. 249–64. Köln.

Leidholdt, D. 1990. "Introduction." In *Sexual Liberals and the Attack on Feminism*, edited by D. Leidholdt and J. Raymond. New York.

———. 2003. "Prostitution and Trafficking in Women." In *Prostitution, Trafficking, and Traumatic Stress*, edited by M. Farley, pp. 167–83. Binghampton, NY.

Leigh, C. 1997. "Inventing Sex Work." In Nagle, ed., pp. 223–31.

Lentakis, A. 1998. *Η πορνεία*. Vol. 3 of Ο έρωτας στην αρχαία Ελλάδα. Athens.

———. 1999. *Οι εταίρες*. Vol. 4 of Π έρωτας στην αρχαία Ελλάδα. Athens.

Leontsini, S. 1989. *Die Prostitution im frühen Byzanz*. Diss. Vienna.

Lévy, E. 1988. "Métèques et droit de résidence." In *L'Etranger dans le monde grec*, edited by R. Lonis, pp. 47–67. Etudes anciennes 4. Nancy.

Lewis, D. 1959. "Attic Manumissions." *Hesperia* 28: 208–38.

———. 1966 [1997]. "After the Profanation of the Mysteries." In *Ancient Society and Institutions: Studies Presented to Victor Ehrenberg*, edited by E. Badian, pp. 177–91. Oxford. (Reprinted in *Selected Papers in Greek and Near Eastern History*, edited by D. Lewis and P. Rhodes, pp. 258–72. Cambridge 1997.)

———. 1968. "Dedications of Phialai at Athens." *Hesperia* 37: 368–80.

Lewis, S. 2002. *The Athenian Woman: An Iconographic Handbook*. London.

Lewis, T. 1991. "Acquisition and Anxiety: Aristotle's Case against the Market." In *Pioneers in Economics 2*, edited by M. Blaug, pp. 173–94. Aldershot, England. (Reprinted from *Canadian Journal of Economics* 11[1]: 69–90. 1978.)

Lewy, H. 1885. *De civili condicione mulierum graecarum*. Breslau.

Lind, H. 1988. "Ein Hetärentum am Heiligen Tor?" *Museum Helveticum* 45: 158–69.

Lipsius, J. [1905–15] 1966. *Das attische Recht und Rechtsverfahren*. 3 Vols. Hildesheim.

Lissarrague, F. 1990. *L'autre guerrier: Archers, peltastes, cavaliers dans l'imagerie attique*. Paris.

Llewellyn-Jones, L., ed. 2002. *Women's Dress in the Ancient Greek World*. Swansea.

———. 2003. *Aphrodite's Tortoise: The Veiled Woman of Ancient Greece*. Swansea.

Lloyd, G. [1966] 1987. *Polarity and Analogy: Two Types of Argumentation in Early Greek Thought*. Bristol.

Lobel, K. 1986. *Naming the Violence: Speaking Out about Lesbian Violence*. Washington, DC.

Loewenstein, G. 2000. "Emotions in Economic Theory and Economic Behavior." *American Economic Review* 90: 426–32.

Lofberg, J. 1917. *Sycophancy in Athens*. Chicago.

Longo, P. and R. Parker. 1992. *Male Prostitution and the Risk of HIV Transmission*. Final Report. Global Program on AIDS. Geneva.

Loomis, W. 1998. *Wages, Welfare Costs and Inflation in Classical Athens*. Ann Arbor.

Loraux, N. [1981] 1986. *The Invention of Athens: The Funeral Oration in the Classical City*. Cambridge, MA. (Originally published as *L'invention d'Athènes: Histoire de l'oraison funèbre dans la "cité classique."* Paris.)

———. [1984] 1993. *The Children of Athena: Athenian Ideas about Citizenship and the Division between the Sexes*. Translated by C. Levine. Princeton. (Originally published as *Les enfants d'Athéna: Idées athéniennes sur la citoyenneté et la division des sexes*. Paris.)

———. 1995. *The Experiences of Tiresias: The Feminine and the Greek Man*. Princeton. (Originally published as *Les Expériences de Tirésias. Le féminin et l'homme grec*. Paris 1990.)

Lord, C. trans. 1984. *Aristotle: The Politics*. Chicago.

Lotze, D. 1981. "Zwischen Politen und Metöken: Pasivbürger im klassischen Athen?" *Klio* 63: 159–78.

Louis, M. 1999. "Legalizing Pimping, Dutch Style." In *Making the Harm Visible: Global Sexual Exploitation of Women and Girls*, edited by D. Hughes and C. Roches, pp. 192–96. Kingston, RI.

Love, J. 1991. *Antiquity and Capitalism*. London.
Lowe, J. 1992. "Aspects of Plautus' Originality in the *Asinaria*." *Classical Quarterly* 42: 152–75.
———. 1999. 'L' *Asinaria* e il suo modello greco." In *Lecturae Plautinae Sarsinates II Asinaria*, edited by R. Raffaelli and A. Tontini, pp. 13–24. Urbino.
MacDowell, D. 1962. *Andokides: "On the Mysteries."* Oxford.
———. 1976. "*Hybris* in Athens." *Greece & Rome* 23: 14–31.
———. 1978. *The Law in Classical Athens*. London.
———. 1989. "The *Oikos* in Athenian Law." *Classical Quarterly* 39: 10–21.
———, ed. 1990. *Demosthenes against Meidias*. Oxford.
———. 1995. *Aristophanes and Athens*. Oxford.
———. 2000. "Athenian Laws about Homosexuality." *Revue internationale des droits de l'antiquité*. 3rd Ser. 47: 14–27.
———. 2005. "The Athenian Procedure of Dokimasia of Orators." In *Symposion 2001*, edited by R. Wallace and M. Gagarin, pp. 79–87. Vienna.
MacIntyre, A. 1981. *After Virtue: A Study in Moral Theory*. Notre Dame, IN.
MacKinnon, C. 1987. *Feminism Unmodified: Discourses on Life and Law*. Cambridge, MA.
———. 2005. *Women's Lives: Men's Laws*. Cambridge, MA.
Maffi, A. 1984. "Le «Leggi sulle donne». IC. 4, 72. II. 16–20, Plut., Sol. 23.1–2." In *«Sodalitas». Scritti in onore di Antonio Guarino*, IV, pp. 1553–67. Naples.
———. 2005. "Family and Property Law." In *The Cambridge Companion to Greek Law*, edited by M. Gagarin and D. Cohen, pp. 254–66. Cambridge.
Mahaffy, J. 1896. *Greek Life and Thought from the Death of Alexander to the Roman Conquest*. London.
Manfredini, M., and L. Piccirilli. 1977. *Plutarco. "La Vita di Solone."* Milan.
Marasco, G. 1992. *Economia e Storia*. Viterbe.
Martin, V. and G. de Budé. 1927. *Eschine* (Collection des Universités de France). Vol. I. Paris.
Martini, R. 1997. "Sul contratto d'opera nell'Atene classica." In *Symposion 1995*, edited by G. Thür and J. Vélissaropoulos-Karakostas, pp. 49–55. Köln.
Marx, K. 1970–72. *Capital*. 3 Vols. London. (English translation of *Das Kapital*.)
Marzi, M. 1977. "Iperide." In *Oratori Attici Minori I: Iperide, Eschine, Licurgo*, edited by M. Marzi, P. Leone, and E. Malcovati, pp. 7–328. Turin.
———, ed. 1979. *Lisia. Per ferimento premeditato*. Città di Castello.
Maschke, R. 1926. *Die Willenslehre im griechischen Recht*. Berlin.
Mattingly, D., and J. Salmon. 2001. "The Productive Past: Economies beyond Agriculture." In *Economies beyond Agriculture in the Classical World*, edited by D. Mattingly and J. Salmon, pp. 3–14. London.
Mazza, M. 1978. "Marx sulla schiavitù antica. Note di lettura." In *Analisi marxista e società antiche*, edited by L. Capogrossi, A. Giardina, and A. Schiavone, pp. 107–45. Rome.

McAleer, P. 2006. "The Problem of Eastern European Sex Slavery Is Exaggerated." In Gerdes, ed., pp. 42–47.

McCarthy, M. 2000. *Slaves, Masters and the Art of Authority in Plautine Comedy.* Princeton.

McClintock, A. 1993. "Sex Workers and Sex Work: Introduction." *Social Text* 37: 1–10.

———, ed. 1993. "Sex Work Issues." *Social Text* 37 (special edition devoted to sexual workers' issues).

McClure, L. 2003a. "Subversive Laughter: The Sayings of Courtesans in Book 13 of Athenaeus' *Deipnosophistae*." *American Journal of Philology* 124: 259–94.

———. 2003b. *Courtesans at Table: Gender and Greek Literary Culture in Athenaeus.* London.

———. 2006. "Introduction." In Faraone and McClure, eds., pp. 3–18.

McGinn, T. 1998. *Prostitution, Sexuality and the Law in Ancient Rome.* Oxford.

———. 2004. *The Economy of Prostitution in the Roman World: A Study of Social History and the Brothel.* Ann Arbor.

———. 2011. "Conclusion: Greek Brothels and More." In Glazebrook and Henry, eds., pp. 256–68. Madison.

———. 2014. "Prostitution: Controversies and New Approaches." In Hubbard, ed., pp. 83–101.

McKechnie, P. 1989. *Outsiders in the Greek Cities in the Fourth Century BC.* London.

Meikle, S. 1995. "Modernism, Economics, and the Ancient Economy." *Proceedings of the Cambridge Philological Society* 41: 174–91.

———. 1996. "Aristotle on Business." *Classical Quarterly* 46: 138–51.

Meineke, A. 1839–57. *Fragmenta Comicorum Graecorum.* Berlin.

Meyer, E. 1895. "Die wirtschaftliche Entwicklung des Altertums." *Jahrbücher für Nationalökonomie und Statistik* 9(64): 1–70. Reprinted in Finley, ed., 1979.

Meyer, E. 2010. *Metics and the Athenian Phialai-Inscriptions.* Stuttgart.

Meyer, M. 1988. "Männer mit Geld. Zu einer rotfigurigen Vase mit 'Alltagsszene.'" *Jahrbuch des Deutschen Archäologischen Instituts* 103: 87–125.

Miers, S., and I. Kopytoff, eds. 1977. *Slavery in Africa.* Madison, WI.

Migeotte, L. 1998. "Les ventes de grain public dans les cités grecques aux périodes classique et hellénistique." In *La mémoire perdue. Recherches sur l'administration romaine,* pp. 229–46. Coll. de l'École française de Rome 243. Rome.

———. 2000. "Les dépenses militaires des cités grecques: essai de typologie." In *La guerre dans les économies antiques,* edited by J. Andreau, P. Briant and R. Descat, pp. 145–76. Saint-Bertrand-de-Comminges.

———. 2001. "Quelques aspects légaux et juridiques de l'affermage des taxes en Grèce ancienne." In *Symposion 1997,* edited by E. Cantarella and G. Thür, pp. 165–74. Köln.

———. 2009. *The Economy of the Greek Cities.* Berkeley. (Translation of *L'économie des cités grecques de l'archaïsme au Haut-Empire romain.* Paris 2002.)

Migeotte, L. 2010. "Le contrôle des prix dans les cités grecques." In L. Migeotte, *Économie et finances publiques des cités grecques*, pp. 419–38. Lyon.

———. 2014. *Les finances des cités grecques*. Paris.

Miller, E. 1986. *Street Woman*. Philadelphia.

Miller, F. 1974. "The State and the Community in Aristotle's *Politics*." *Reason Papers* 1: 61–69.

———. 1995. *Nature, Justice, and Rights in Aristotle's "Politics."* Oxford.

Miller, M. 1997. *Athens and Persia: A Study in Cultural Receptivity*. Cambridge.

Millett P. 1982. "The Attic *Horoi* Reconsidered in the Light of Recent Discoveries." *Opus* 1: 219–49.

———. 1990. "Sale, Credit and Exchange in Athenian Law and Society." In *Nomos: Essays in Athenian Law, Politics and Society*, edited by P. Cartledge, P. Millett, and S. Todd, pp. 167–94. Cambridge.

———. 1991. *Lending and Borrowing in Ancient Athens*. Cambridge.

———. 1998. "The Rhetoric of Reciprocity in Classical Athens." In C. Gill, N. Postlethwaite, and R. Seaford, eds. pp. 227–53.

———. 2000. "The Economy." In *Classical Greece*, edited by R. Osborne, pp. 23–51. Oxford.

———. 2001. "Productive to Some Purpose? The Problem of Ancient Economic Growth." In *Economies beyond Agriculture in the Classical World*, edited by D. Mattingly and J. Salmon, pp. 17–48. London.

Millett, P., and S. Todd. 1990. "Law, Society and Athens." In *Nomos: Essays in Athenian Law, Politics and Society*, edited by P. Cartledge, P. Millett, and S. Todd, pp. 1–18. Cambridge.

Miner, J. 2003. "Courtesan, Concubine, Whore: Apollodorus' Deliberate Use of Terms for Prostitutes." *American Journal of Philology* 124: 19–37.

Mirhady, D. 1996. "Torture and Rhetoric in Athens." *Journal of Hellenic Studies* 116: 119–31.

———. 2000. "The Athenian Rationale for Torture." In *Law and Social Status in Classical Athens*, edited by V. Hunter and J. Edmonson, pp. 53–74. Oxford.

———. 2004. "Contracts in Athens." In *Law, Rhetoric, and Comedy in Classical Athens: Essays in Honour of Douglas M. MacDowell*, edited by D. Cairns and R. Knox, pp. 51–63. Swansea.

Missiou, A. 1992. *The Subversive Oratory of Andokides*. Cambridge.

———. 1998. "Reciprocal Generosity in the Foreign Affairs of fifth-century Athens and Sparta." In C. Gill, N. Postlethwaite, and R. Seaford, eds., pp. 181–98.

Mitteis, L. 1891. *Reichsrecht und Volksrecht in den östlichen Provinzen des römischen Kaiserreichs mit Beiträgen zur Kenntnis des griechischen Rechts und des spätrömischen Rechtsentwicklung*. Leipzig.

Modrzejewski, J. 1983. "La structure juridique du mariage grec." In *Symposion 1979*, edited by P. Dimakis, pp. 39–71. Köln.

Mohanty, C. 1991. "Under Western Eyes: Feminist Scholarship and Colonial Discourses." In *Third World Women and the Politics of Feminism*, edited by C. Mohanty, A. Russo, and L. Torres, pp. 51–80. Bloomington, Indiana.

———. 1997. "Women Workers and Capitalist Scripts: Ideologies of Domination, Common Interest and the Politics of Solidarity." In *Feminist Geneologies, Colonial Legacies, Democratic Futures*, edited by M. Alexander and C. Mohanty, pp. 3–29. New York.

Mohr, R. 1992. *Gay Ideas: Outing and Other Controversies*. Boston.

Möller, A. 2000. *Naukratis*. Oxford.

Momigliano, A. 1952. *George Grote and the Study of Greek History*. London.

Montgomery, H. 1998. "Children, Prostitution, and Identity: A Case Study from a Tourist Resort in Thailand." In Kempadoo and Doezema, eds., pp. 139–50.

Moreno, A. 2003. "Athenian Bread-Baskets: The Grain-Tax Law of 374/3 BC Re-Interpreted." *Zeitschrift für Papyrologie und Epigraphik* 145: 97–106.

———. 2007. *Feeding the Democracy: The Athenian Grain Supply in the Fifth and Fourth Centuries BC*. Oxford.

Morris, I. 1987. *Burial and Ancient Society: The Rise of the Greek City-State*. Cambridge.

———. 1994. "The Athenian Economy Twenty Years after *the Ancient Economy*." *Classical Philology* 89: 351–66.

———. 2001. "Hard Surfaces." In Cartledge, Cohen, and Foxhall, eds., pp. 8–43.

Morris, I., and J. Manning. 2005. "Introduction." In *The Ancient Economy: Evidence and Models*, edited by I. Morris and J. Manning, pp. 1–44. Stanford.

Morris, I., R. Saller, and W. Scheidel. 2007. "Introduction." In Scheidel, Morris, and Saller, eds., pp. 1–12.

Morrow, G. [1960] 1993. *Plato's Cretan City. A Historical Interpretation of the Laws*. Princeton.

Mossé, C. [1962] 1979. *La Fin de la démocratie athénienne*. Paris.

———. 1973. *Athens in Decline: 404–86*. London.

———. 1983. *La Femme dans la Grèce antique*. Paris.

———. 1996. *Les institutions grecques*. Paris.

———. 2007. *D'Homère à Plutarque: Itinéraires historiques*. Paris.

Murray, O. 1990. "The Solonian Law of Hubris." In *Nomos: Essays in Athenian Law, Politics and Society*, edited by P. Cartledge, P. Millett, and S. Todd, pp. 139–45. Cambridge.

Nafissi, M. 2004. "Class, Embeddedness, and the Primitive Modernity of Ancient Athens." *Comparative Studies in Society and History*: 378–410.

———. 2005. *Ancient Athens and Modern Ideology*. London.

Neils, J. 2000. "Others within the Other: An Intimate Look at Hetairai and Maenads." In *Not the Classical Ideal: Athens and the Construction of the Other in Greek Art*, edited by B. Cohen, pp. 203–26. Leiden.

Nesselrath, H.-G. 2014. "Later Greek Comedy in Late Antiquity." In *The Oxford Handbook on Greek and Roman Comedy*, edited by M. Fontaine and A. Scafuro, pp. 667–679. Oxford.

Network of Sex Work Projects. 2002. http://www.nswp.org.
Nevett, L. 1999. *House and Society in the Ancient Greek World*. Cambridge.
Nouhaud, M. 1990. *Dinarque: Discours*. Paris.
Nowak, M. 2010. "Defining Prostitution in Athenian Legal Rhetorics." *Tijdschrift voor Rechtsgeschiedenis* 78: 183–197.
Nussbaum, M. 1998. " 'Whether from Reason or Prejudice': Taking Money for Bodily Services." *Journal of Legal Studies* 27(2)(pt. 2): 693–724.
———. 1999. *Sex and Social Justice*. Oxford.
Nutton, V. 2012. *Ancient Medicine*. Oxford.
Ober, J. 1985. *Fortress Attica: Defense of the Athenian Land Frontier 404–322 B.C.* Leiden.
———. 1989. *Mass and Elite in Democratic Athens*. Princeton.
———. 1991. "Aristotle's Political Sociology: Class, Status, and Order in the *Politics*." In *Essays on the Foundations of Aristotelian Political Science*, edited by C. Lord and D. O'Connor, pp. 112–35. Berkeley.
———. 1996. *The Athenian Revolution: Essays on Ancient Greek Democracy and Political Thought*. Princeton.
———. 2008. *Democracy and Knowledge: Innovation and Learning in Classical Athens*. Princeton.
Ober J., and C. Hedrick, eds. 1996. *Dêmokratia: A Conversation on Democracies, Ancient and Modern*. Princeton.
Ogden, D. 1996. *Greek Bastardy in the Classical and the Hellenistic Periods*. Oxford.
Oliver, G. 1995. "The Athenian State under Threat: Politics and Food Supply, 307 to 229 B.C." Diss. Oxford.
———. 2007. *War, Food, and Politics in Early Hellenistic Athens*. Oxford.
Omitowoju, R. 1997. "Regulating Rape: Soap Operas and Self-interest in the Athenian Courts." In *Rape in Antiquity: Sexual Violence in the Greek and Roman Worlds*, edited by S. Deacy and K. Pierce, pp. 1–24. London.
O'Neill, M., and R. Barberet. 2000. "Victimization and the Social Organization of Prostitution in England and Spain." In Weitzer, ed., pp. 123–37.
Osborne, M. and S. Byrne, eds. 1994. *A Lexicon of Greek Personal Names. II. Attica*. Oxford.
Osborne, R. 1985. *Demos: The Discovery of Classical Attika*. Cambridge.
———. 1995. "The Economics and Politics of Slavery at Athens." In *The Greek World*, edited by A. Powell, pp. 27–43. London.
———. 2000. Review of Stroud 1998. *Classical Review* 50: 172–73.
———. 2004. *Greek History*. London.
Overall, C. 1992. "What's Wrong with Prostitution? Evaluating Sex Work." *Signs: Journal of Women in Culture and Society* 17 (4): 705–24.
Owen, R. 2002. "Italy Divided over Plan to Bring Back Brothels." May 9, 2002. http://www.timesonline.co.uk/article/0,,3-290855,00.html.
Palmer, S., and J. Humphrey. 1990. *Deviant Behavior: Patterns, Sources and Control*. New York.

Panagos, C. 1968. *Le Pirée*. Athens.
Paoli, U. [1930] 1974. *Studi di diritto attico*. Milan.
———. 1951. "La *in ius vocatio* dans les comédies de Plaute." *Studi Senesi* 63: 283–304.
———. 1976. *Altri Studi di Diritto Greco e Romano*. Milan.
Papazarkadas, N. 2012. Review of Meyer 2010. *Classical Review* 62: 553–55.
Parker, R. 1996. *Athenian Religion: A History*. Oxford.
Partsch, J. 1909. *Griechisches Bürgschaftsrecht*. Leipzig.
Pateman, C. 1988. *The Sexual Contract*. Cambridge.
———. 2006. "What's Wrong with Prostitution?" In *Prostitution and Pornography: Philosophical Debate about the Sex Industry*, edited by J. Spector, pp. 50–79. Stanford.
Paton, J., ed. 1927. *The Erechtheum*. Cambridge, MA.
Patterson, C. 1990. "Those Athenian Bastards." *Classical Antiquity* 9: 40–73.
———. 1998. *The Family in Greek History*. Cambridge, MA.
Pecîrka, J. 1973. "Homestead Farms in Classical and Hellenistic Hellas." In *Problèmes de la terre en Grèce ancienne*, edited by M. Finley, pp. 113–47. Paris.
———. 1976. "The Crisis of the Athenian Polis in the Fourth Century B.C." *Eirene* 14: 5–29.
Pellizer, E., and A. Sirugo, ed. 1995. *Luciano: Dialoghi delle cortigiane*. Venice.
Perlman, S. 1963. "The Politicians in the Athenian Democracy of the Fourth Century B.C." *Athenaeum* 41: 327–55.
Perotti, E. 1974. "Esclaves ΧΩΡΙΣ ΟΙΚΟΥΝΤΕΣ." In *Actes du colloque 1972 sur l'esclavage*. Annales Littéraires de l'Université de Besançon, pp. 47–56. Paris. (Translation of "Una categoria particolare di schiavi attici, i χωρὶς οἰκοῦντες." *Rendiconti del'reale Istituto Lombardo di Scienze e Lettere* 106 [1972]: 375–88.)
Pesando, F. 1987. *Oikos e ktesis. La casa greca in età classica*. Perugia.
Peschel, I. 1987. *Die Hetäre bei Symposium und Komos in der attisch-rotfigurigen Vasenmalerei des 6-4 Jahrh. v. Chr*. Frankfurt.
Petropoulos, G. 1939. *Πάπυροι τῆς ἐν Ἀθήναις Ἀρχαιολογικῆς Ἑταιρείας*. Athens.
Pheterson, G. 1996. *The Prostitution Prism*. Amsterdam.
———, ed. 1989. *A Vindication of the Rights of Whores*. Seattle.
Phillips, D. 2009. "Hypereides 3 and the Athenian Law of Contracts." *Transactions of the American Philological Association* 139: 89–122.
Picard, O. 2008a. "L'économie grecque: sources, méthodes et problématique." In *Économies et sociétés en Grèce ancienne (478–88 av. J.-C.)*, edited by O. Picard, pp. 10–44. Paris.
———. 2008b. "Le système athénien." In *Économies et sociétés en Grèce ancienne (478–88 av. J.-C.)*, edited by O. Picard, pp. 111–59. Paris.
Piccirili, L. 1978. "La legge di Solone sulla dote (Plut. Sol. 20, 6)." *Scritti storico-epigrafici in memoria di Marcello Zambelli*, edited by L. Gasperini, pp. 320–24. Rome.
Pierce, K. 1997. "The Portrayal of Rape in New Comedy." In *Rape in Antiquity: Sexual Violence in the Greek and Roman Worlds*, edited by S. Deacy and K. Pierce, pp. 163–84. London.

Pirenne-Delforge, V. 1994. *L'Aphrodite grecque. Kernos* Supp. 4. Liège-Athens.
Pisano, I. 2002. *Io puttana: Parlano le prostitute.* Milan.
Polanyi, K. 1957. "Aristotle Discovers the Market." In *Trade and Markets in the Early Empires,* edited by K. Polanyi, M. Arensberg, and H. Pearson, pp. 64–97. Glencoe, IL.
Pomeroy, S. 1975. *Goddesses, Whores, Wives and Slaves: Women in Classical Antiquity.* New York.
———. 1984. "Suggested Undergraduate Syllabus." In *Women in the Ancient World: The Arethusa Papers,* edited by J. Peradotto and J. Sullivan, pp. 373–77. (Originally published in *Arethusa* 6: 59–73.)
———. 1994. *Xenophon Oeconomicus: A Social and Historical Commentary.* Oxford.
Popper, K. 1950. *The Open Society and Its Enemies.* Princeton.
Porter, J. and L. Bonilla. 2000. "Drug Use, HIV, and the Ecology of Street Prostitution." In Weitzer, ed., pp. 103–21.
Préaux, C. 1961. "De la Grèce classique à l'Égypte hellénistique: les formes de la vente d'immeuble." *Chronique d'Égypte* 36: 187–95.
Pringsheim, F. 1950. *The Greek Law of Sale.* Weimar.
Pritchett, W., D. Amyx, and A. Pippin. 1953. "The Attic *Stelai*. Part 1." *Hesperia* 22: 225–99.
Provencal, V. 2005. "*Glukus himeros*: Pederastic Influence on the Myth of Ganymede." In *Same Sex Desire and Love in Greco-Roman Antiquity and in the Classical Tradition of the West,* edited by B. Verstaete and V. Provencal, pp. 87–136. New York.
Pruit, D., and S. LaFont. 1995. "For Love and Money: Romance Tourism in Jamaica." *Annals of Tourism Research* 22.2: 422–40.
Purpura, G. 1987. "Ricerche in tema di prestito marittimo." *Annali del Seminario Giuridico dell' Università di Palermo* 39: 189–337.
Rabinowitz, N. 2002. "Excavating Women's Homoeroticism in Ancient Greece: The Evidence from Attic Vase Painting." In *Among Women: From the Homosocial to the Homoerotic in the Ancient World,* edited by N. Rabinowitz and L. Auanger, pp. 106–66. Austin.
———. 2011. "Sex for Sale? Interpreting Erotica in the Havana Collection." In Glazebrook and Henry, eds., pp. 122–46.
Rahe, P. [1992] 1994. *Republics Ancient and Modern: Classical Republicanism and American Revolution.* Chapel Hill.
Randall, R. 1953. "The Erechtheum Workmen." *American Journal of Archaeology* 57: 199–210.
Raubitschek, A. 1941. "Phryne." In Pauly-Wissowa, ed., 20.1: 893–901.
Reardon, B. 1971. *Courants littéraires grecs des IIe et IIIe siècles après J.-C.* Paris.
Reden, S. von. 1992. "Arbeit und Zivilisation. Kriterien der Selbstdefinition im antiken Athen." *Münstersche Beiträge z. antiken Handelsgeschichte* 11: 1–31.
———. 1995. *Exchange in Ancient Greece.* London.

Reden, S. von. 1997. "Money, Law and Exchange: Coinage in the Greek Polis." *Journal of Hellenic Studies* 117: 154–76.

———. 1998. "The Commodification of Symbols: Reciprocity and its Perversions in Menander." In Gill, Postlethwaite, and Seaford, eds., pp. 255–78.

———. 2010. *Money in Classical Antiquity*. Cambridge.

Reed, C. 2003. *Maritime Traders in the Ancient Greek World*. Cambridge.

Reeder, E., ed. 1995. *Pandora: Women in Classical Greece*. Princeton.

Reger, G. 1993. "The Public Purchase of Grain on Independent Delos." *Classical Antiquity* 12: 300–34.

Reinach, T. 1892. "L'impôt sur les courtisanes à Cos." *Revue des Etudes Grecques* 5: 99–102.

Reinsberg, C. 1989. *Ehe, Hetärentum und Knabenliebe im antiken Griechenland*. Munich. (2nd ed.: 1993.)

Reynolds, H. 1986. *The Economics of Prostitution*. Springfield, IL.

Rhodes, P. [1981] 1993. *A Commentary on the Aristotelian Athenaion Politeia*. Oxford.

Richlin, A. 1998. "Foucault's *History of Sexuality*: A Useful Theory for Women?" In *Rethinking Sexuality: Foucault and Clasical Antiquity*, edited by D. Larmour, P. Miller, and C. Platter, pp. 138–70. Princeton.

Rihll, E. 2011. "Classical Athens." In Bradley and Cartledge, eds., pp. 48–73.

Robert, C. 1892. "Ὄνοι πήλινοι." Ἀρχαιολογικὴ Ἐφημερίς: 247–56.

———. 1919. *Archaeologische Hermeneutik*. Berlin.

Robinson, C. 1979. *Lucian and His Influence in Europe*. Chapel Hill.

Rodenwaldt, G. 1932. "Spinnene Hetären." *Archäologischer Anzeiger*: 7–22.

Rosen, R. 1982. *The Lost Sisterhood: Prostitution in America, 1900–1918*. Baltimore.

Rosivach, V. 1989. "*Talasiourgoi* and *Paidia* in IG II 1553–78: A Note on Athenian Social History." *Historia* 38: 365–70.

———. 1995. "Solon's Brothels." *Liverpool Classical Monthly* 20.1–2: 2–3.

———. 1998. *When a Young Man Falls in Love: The Sexual Exploitation of Women in New Comedy*. London.

———. 2001. "Class Matters in the *Dyskolos* of Menander." *Classical Quarterly* 51 (n.s.): 127–34.

Roussel, P. *Isée*. Paris.

Roy, J. 1997. "An Alternative Sexual Morality for Classical Athens." *Greece & Rome* 44: 11–22.

———. 1999. "*Polis* and *Oikos* in Classical Athens." *Greece and Rome* 46: 1–18.

Rubin, G. 1975. "The Traffic in Women: Notes on the 'Political Economy' of Sex." In *Toward an Anthropology of Women*, edited by R. Reiter, pp. 157–210. New York.

Rubinstein, L. 2000. *Litigation and Cooperation: Supporting Speakers in the Courts of Classical Athens*. Stuttgart.

Rueschemeyer, D. 1984. "Theoretical Generalization and Historical Perspective in the Comparative Sociology of Reinhard Bendix." In *Vision and Method in Historical Sociology*, edited by T. Skocpol, pp. 129–69. Cambridge.

Ruschenbusch, E. 1965. "*Hybreos Graphe*: ein Fremdkörper in athenischen Recht des 4. Jahrhunderts v. Chr." *Zeitschrift der Savigny-Stiftung für Rechtsgeschichte. Romanist. Abt.* 82: 302–309.

———. 1966. *Solônos Nomoi*. Wiesbaden.

———. 1979. *Athenische Innenpolitik im 5 Jahrhundert v. Chr.: Ideologie oder Pragmatismus?* Bamberg.

Russell, D. 1993. *Against Pornography. The Evidence of Harm.* Berkeley.

Rusten, J. 1985. "Two Lives or Three? Pericles on the Athenian Character (Thucydides 2.40.1–2)." *Classical Quarterly* 35: 14–19.

Ste. Croix, G. de. 1972. *Origins of the Peloponnesian War.* London.

Sakurai, M. 2008. "The Thesmophoria and Marital Institutions in Democratic Athens." In *ΜΙΚΟΠΣ ΙΕΡΟΜΝΗΜΩΝ: μελέτες εις μνήμην Michael H. Jameson*, edited by A. Matthaiou and I. Polinskaya, pp. 41–51. Athens.

Saller, R., I. Morris, and W. Scheidel, eds. 2007. "Introduction." *The Cambridge Economic History of the Graeco-Roman World*, pp. 1–12. Cambridge.

Saunders, T. 1951. *Plato: The Laws.* Middlesex.

Scafuro, A. 1997. *The Forensic Stage: Settling Disputes in Graeco-Roman New Comedy.* Cambridge.

———. 2003/04. "The Rigmarole of the Parasite's Contract for a Prostitute in *Asinaria*: Legal Documents in Plautus and His Predecessors." *Leeds International Classical Studies* 3.4 (http://www.leeds.ac.uk/classics/lics/).

———. 2006. "Identifying Solonian Laws." In *Solon of Athens: New Historical and Philological Approaches*, edited by J. Blok and A. Lardinois, pp. 175–96. Leiden.

———. (forthcoming). *re Thür 2001*.

Scanlon, T. 2002. *Eros and Greek Athletics.* Oxford.

Schaps, D. 1979. *Economic Rights of Women in Ancient Greece.* Edinburgh.

———. 1998. "What Was Free about a Free Athenian Woman?" *Transactions of the American Philological Association* 128: 161–88.

———. 1998. Review of D. Tandy: *Warriors into Traders: The Power of the Market in Early Greece. Bryn Mawr Classical Review* 98.11.1: 1–13.

———. 2004. *The Invention of Coinage and the Monetization of Ancient Greece.* Ann Arbor.

———. 2008. "What Was Money in Ancient Greece?" In *The Monetary Systems of the Greeks and Romans*, edited by W. Harris, pp. 38–48. Oxford.

Scheidel, W. 1998. "Addendum." In P. Garnsey, *Cities, Peasants and Food in Classical Antiquity*, pp. 195–200. Cambridge.

———. 2007. "Demography." In Scheidel, Morris, and Saller, eds., pp. 38–86.

———. 2008. "The Divergent Evolution of Coinage in Eastern and Western Eurasia." In *The Monetary Systems of the Greeks and Romans*, edited by W. Harris, pp. 267–86. New York.

Scheidel W., I. Morris, and R. Saller eds. 2007. *The Cambridge Economic History of the Greco-Roman World.* Cambridge.

Schmid, W. 1959. "Menanders Dyscolos und die Timonlegende." *Rheinisches Museum* 102: 157–82.

Schmitt Pantel, P., and F. Thelamon. 1983. "Image et histoire: Illustration ou document?" In *Images et céramique grecque. Actes du colloque de Rouen, 25–26 novembre 1982*, edited by F. Lissarrague and F. Thelamon, pp. 9–20. Rouen.

Schnapp, A. 1986. "Comment déclarer sa flamme, ou les archéologues au spectacle." *Le Genre humain* 14: 147–159.

Schneider, K. 1913. "Hetairai." In Pauly-Wissowa, ed., 8: 1331–1372.

Schodorf, K. 1905. *Beiträge zur genaueren Kentnis der attischen Gerichtssprache aus den Zehn Redners, Beiträge zur historischen Syntax der griechischen Sprache*. Vol. 17. Würzburg.

Schonbeck, H.-P. 1981. *Beiträge zur Interpretation der plautinischen "Bacchides."* Düsseldorf.

Schuhl, P. 1953. "Adêla." *Annales publiées par la Faculté des Lettres de Toulouse, Homo: Etudes philosophiques*, I (May): 86–93.

Schumacher, L. 2001. *Sklaverei in der Antike: Alltag und Schicksal der Unfreien*. Munich.

Schwimmer, E. 1979. "The Self and the Product: Concepts of Work in Comparative Perspective." In *Social Anthropology of Work*, edited by S. Wallmann, pp. 287–315. London.

Seaford, R. 1994. *Reciprocity and Ritual*. Oxford.

———. 1998. "Introduction." In Gill, Postlethwaite, and Seaford, eds. 1998, pp. 1–11.

———. 1966. "Lysias and the Corn-Dealers." *Historia* 15: 172–84.

———. 1984. "On Lawful Concubinage in Athens." *Classical Antiquity* 3: 111–33.

———. 1990. *Women and Law in Classical Greece*. Chapel Hill.

Sebesta, J. 2002. "Visions of Gleaming Textiles and a Clay Core: Textiles, Greek Women, and Pandora." In Llewellyn-Jones, ed., pp. 125–42.

Senior, O. 1992. *Working Miracles: Women's Lives in the English-Speaking Caribbean*. Bloomington, IN.

Shafer, J. 2006. "The Problem of Sex Trafficking in the United States Is Overstated." In Gerdes, ed., pp. 29–33.

Shapiro, H. 1992. "Eros in Love: Pederasty and Pornography in Greece." In *Pornography and Representation in Greece and Rome*, edited by A. Richlin, pp. 53–72. New York.

———. 2000. "Leagros and Euphronios: Painting Pederasty in Athens." In *Greek Love Reconsidered*, edited by T. Hubbard, pp. 12–32. New York.

Shipton, K. 1997. "The Private Banks in Fourth-Century B.C. Athens: A Reappraisal." *Classical Quarterly* 47: 396–422.

———. 2000. *Leasing and Lending: The Cash Economy in Fourth-Century B.C. Athens*. London.

———. "Money and the Elite in Classical Athens." In *Money and its Uses in the Ancient Greek World*, edited by A. Meadows and K. Shipton, pp. 129–44. Oxford.

Shrage, L. 1989. "Should Feminists Oppose Prostitution?" *Ethics* 99: 347–61.

———. 1994. *Moral Dilemmas of Feminism: Prostitution, Adultery, and Abortion.* New York.

Sickinger, J. 1999. *Public Records and Archives in Classical Athens.* Chapel Hill.

———. 2013. Review of Meyer 2010. *Journal of Hellenic Studies* 133: 205–06.

Sidwell, K. 2000. "Athenaeus, Lucian, and Fifth-Century Comedy." In Braund and Wilkins, eds., pp. 136–52.

Sigerist, H. 1970. *Der Arzt in der griechischen Kultur.* Esslingen.

Silver, M. 1995. *Economic Structures of Antiquity.* Westport, CT.

———. 2003. Review of *The Ancient Economy*, edited by W. Scheidel and S. von Reden. At *Ancient Economies* (Economic History Services), January 3, 2003, http://www.eh.net/bookreviews/library/0570.shtml.

———. 2004. "Modern Ancients." In *Commerce and Monetary Systems in the Ancient World: Means of Transmission and Cultural Interaction*, edited by R. Rollinger and C. Ulf, pp. 65–87. Wiesbaden.

Simônetos, G. 1939. "Das Verhältnis von Kauf und Übereignung im altgriechischen Recht." In *Festschrift für Paul Koschaker*, edited by M. Kaser, H. Kreller, and W. Kunkel, 3: 172–98. Weimar.

———. 1943. "Τὰ ἐλαττώματα τῆς βουλήσεως εἰς τὰς δικαιοπραξίας." *Ἀρχεῖον ἰδιωτικοῦ δικαίου* 14: 290–313.

Sinclair, R. 1988. *Democracy and Participation in Athens.* Cambridge.

Sissa, G. 1986. "La famille dans la cité grecque (V-IV siècle avant J.-C.)." In *Histoire de la famille*, edited by A. Burguière et al., pp. 163–94. Paris.

———. 1999. "Sexual Bodybuilding: Aeschines against Timarchus." In *Constructions of the Classical Body*, edited by J. Porter, pp. 147–68. Ann Arbor.

Skinner, M. 1996. "Zeus and Leda: The Sexuality Wars in Contemporary Classical Scholarship." *Thamyris* 3.1: 103–23.

———. 2005. *Sexuality in Greek and Roman Culture.* Oxford.

Sommerstein, A. 2009. *Talking about Laughter and Other Studies in Greek Comedy.* Oxford.

Sourlas, D. 2014. "Praise for a *Hetaira*: A New Graffito from Fifth-Century B.C. Athens." In *ΑΘΗΝΑΙΩΝ ΕΠΙΣΚΟΠΟΣ: Studies in Honour of Harold B. Mattingly*, edited by A. Matthaiou and R. Pitt, pp. 241–57. Athens.

Sourvinou-Inwood, C. 1995. "Male and Female, Public and Private, Ancient and Modern." In *Pandora: Women in Classical Greece*, edited by E. Reeder, pp. 111–20. Princeton.

Spector, J. 2006. "Obscene Division: Feminist Liberal Assessments of Prostitution versus Feminist Liberal Defenses of Pornography." In *Prostitution and Pornography: Philosophical Debate about the Sex Industry*, edited by J. Spector, 50–79. Stanford.

Spivey, N. 2012. *The Ancient Olympics.* Oxford.

Stadter, P. 1989. *A Commentary on Plutarch's Pericles.* Chapel Hill.

Stanley, P. 1976. *Ancient Greek Market Regulations and Controls.* Diss. Berkeley.

———. 1999. "The Economic Reforms of Solon." *Pharos (Studien zur griechische-römischen Antike)* 11: 174–203.

Ste. Croix, G. de. 1972. *Origins of the Peloponnesian War.* London.

———. 1981. *The Class Struggle in the Ancient Greek World.* London.

Stears, K. 2001. "Spinning Women: Iconography and Status in Athenian Funerary Sculpture." In *Les pierres de l'offrande: Autour de l'oeuvre de Christoph W. Clairmont. Actes,* edited by G. Hoffmann and A. Lezzi-Hafter, pp. 107–14. Zurich.

Stefanizzi, S. 2010. "Measuring the Non-Measurable: Towards the Development of Indicators for Measuring Human Trafficking." In *Measuring Human Trafficking: Complexities and Pitfalls,* edited by E. Savona and S. Stefanizzi, pp. 45–54. New York.

Steiner, D. 1994. *The Tyrant's Writ.* Princeton.

Steinhauer, G. 1994. "Inscription agoranomique du Pirée." *Bulletin de Correspondance Hellénique* 118: 51–68.

———. 2003. *Η οχύρωση και η πύλη της Λετιοινείας.* Piraeus.

Stewart, A. 1990. *Greek Sculpture.* New Haven.

———. 1997. *Art, Desire and the Body in Ancient Greece.* Cambridge.

Stocks, J. 1936. "Scholê." *Classical Quarterly* 30: 177–87.

Strauss, B. 1987. *Athens after the Peloponnesian War: Class, Faction, and Policy, 403–386 B.C.* Ithaca, NY.

———. 1993. *Fathers and Sons in Athens: Ideology and Society in the Era of the Peloponnesian War.* Princeton.

Stroud, R. 1974. "An Athenian Law on Silver Coinage." *Hesperia* 43: 157–88.

———. 1998. *The Athenian Grain-Tax Law of 374/3 B.C. Hesperia* Supplement 29. Princeton.

Stumpf, G. 1986. "Ein athenisches Münzgesetz des 4. Jh. V. Chr." *Jahrbuch für Numismatik und Geldgeschichte* 36: 23–40.

Stumpp, B. 1998. *Prostitution in der römischen Antike.* Berlin.

Sullivan, B. 1994. "Feminism and Female Prostitution." In *Sex Work and Sex Workers in Australia,* edited by R. Perkins, R. Garrett, and F. Lovejoy, pp. 253–68. Sydney.

Sutton, R. 1981. *The Interaction between Men and Women portrayed on Attic Red-Figure Pottery.* Diss. Chapel Hill.

———. 1992. "Pornography and Persuasion on Attic Pottery." In *Pornography and Representation in Greece and Rome,* edited by A. Richlin, pp. 3–35. New York.

———. 2004. "Family Portraits: Recognizing the *Oikos* on Attic Red-Figure Pottery." In *XARIS: Essays in Honor of S. A. Immerwahr (Hesperia,* Supplement 33), edited by A. Chapin, pp. 327–50.

Tandy, D. 1997. *Warriors into Traders: The Power of the Market in Early Greece.* Berkeley.

Tarn, W. [1927] 1952. *Hellenistic Civilization.* London.

Tchernetska, N., E. Handley, C. Austin, and L. Horváth. 2007. "New Readings in the Fragment of Hyperides' Against Timandros from the Archimedes Palimpsest." *Zeitschrift für Papyrologie und Epigraphik* 162: 1–4.

Theokharês, R. 1983. *Αρχαία και Βυζαντινή Οικονομική Ιστορία*. Athens.

Thomas, R. 1989. *Oral Tradition and Written Record in Classical Athens*. Cambridge.

———. 1992. *Literacy and Orality in Ancient Greece*. Cambridge.

Thompson, W. 1980. "An Athenian Commercial Case: Demosthenes 34." *Tidjschrift voor Rechtsgeschiedenis* 48: 137–49.

———. 1983. "The Athenian Entrepreneur." *L'Antiquité Classique* 51: 53–85.

Thornton, B. 1997. *Eros: The Myth of Ancient Greek Sexuality*. Boulder, CO.

Thür, G. 1977. *Beweisführung vor den Schwurgerichtshöfen Athens: die Proklesis zur Basanon*. Vienna.

———. 2001. "Recht im hellenistischen Athen (Ephebie. Kassel/Austin, Adespota 1152. Basanos)." In *Symposion 1997*, edited by E. Cantarella and G. Thür, pp. 141–64. Köln.

———. 2013. "The Statute on *Homologein* in Hyperides' Speech against Athenogenes." *Dike* 16: 1–10.

———. (forthcoming) "Guardianship in Athenian Law: New Evidence." *Legal Documents in Ancient Society* VI (Jerusalem Conference: 2013). Trieste.

Tod, M. 1901–02. "Some Unpublished 'Catalogi Paterarum Argentearum.'" *Annual of the British School at Athens* 8: 197–230.

———. 1950. "Epigraphical Notes on Freedmen's Professions." *Epigraphica* 12: 3–26.

Todd, S. 1990. "The Purpose of Evidence in Athenian Courts." In *Nomos: Essays in Athenian Law, Politics and Society*, edited by P. Cartledge, P. Millett, and S. Todd, pp. 19–39. Cambridge.

———. 1993. *The Shape of Athenian Law*. Oxford.

———. 1994. "Status and Contract in Fourth-Century Athens." In *Symposion 1993*, edited by G. Thür, pp. 125–40. Köln.

———. 1997. "Status and Gender in Athenian Public Records." In *Symposion 1995*, edited by G. Thür and J. Vélissaropoulos-Karakostas, pp. 113–24. Köln.

———. 2006. "Some Notes on the Regulation of Sexuality in Athenian Law." In *Symposion 2003*, edited by H.-A. Rupprecht, pp. 93–111. Vienna.

———. 2007. *A Commentary on Lysias: Speeches 1–11*. New York.

———. 2010. "The Athenian Procedure(s) of *Dokimasia*." In *Symposion 2009*, edited by G. Thür, pp. 73–98. Vienna.

———. 2011. "Introduction to Against Pancleon." In *The Oratory of Classical Greece: Volume 16*, edited by M. Gagarin, pp. 137–39. Austin.

Trapp, M. 1996. "Alciphron." In *Oxford Classical Dictionary*, 3rd ed., edited by S. Hornblower and A. Spawforth, p. 54. Oxford.

Travlos, J. 1937. "Ἀνασκαφαὶ Ἱερᾶς Ὁδοῦ." *Praktika*: 25–41.

Trevett, J. 1992. *Apollodoros the Son of Pasion*. Oxford.

Triantyphyllopoulos, I. 1968. "Τὰ πραγματικὰ ἐλαττώματα τοῦ πωληθέντος κατὰ τὰ ἀρχαῖα Ἑλληνικὰ δίκαια ἐξαιρέσει τῶν παπύρων." *Ἐφημερὶς τῶν Ἑλλήνων Νομικῶν* 35: 1–10.

Troung, T. 1990. *Sex, Money and Morality: The Political Economy of Prostitution and Tourism in South East Asia*. London.

Tsantsanoglou, K. 1973. "The Memoirs of a Lady from Samos." *Zeitschrift für Papyrologie und Epigraphik* 12: 183–95.

Tuplin, C. 1993. *The Failings of Empire*. Stuttgart.

Turner, J. 2000. *On the Origins of Human Emotions*. Stanford.

Valente, M. 2009. "Kathestekuia time: prezzo politico o prezzo di mercato?" *Rivista storica dell' Antichità* 39: 51–58.

Vanoyeke, V. 1990. *La prostitution en Grèce et a Rome*. Paris.

Vélissaropoulos, J. 1980. *Les nauclères grecs*. Geneva.

Vélissaropoulos-Karakostas, J. 1993. Λόγοι Ευθήνης. Athens.

———. 2002. "Merchants, Prostitutes and the 'New Poor.'" In Cartledge, Cohen, and Foxhall, pp. 130–39.

Vermeulen, G. 2010. "The Long Road from Rhetoric to Evidence on Trafficking in Human Beings: About Research Efforts to Prepare Proper EU Monitoring on the Matter." In *Measuring Human Trafficking: Complexities and Pitfalls*, edited by E. Savona and S. Stefanizzi, pp. 107–24. New York.

Vernant, J.-P. 1971. *Mythe et pensée chez les Grecs*. 2 vols. 4th ed. Paris.

———. 1983. "Hestia-Hermes, the Religious Expression of Space and Movement in Ancient Greece." In *Myth and Thought among the Greeks*. London.

———. 1989. *L'individu, la mort, l'amour. Soi-même et l'autre en Grèce ancienne*. Paris.

Vlassopoulos, K. 2011. Review of Meyer 2010. *Bryn Mawr Classical Review* 2011.02.48.

Vogt-Sprira, G. 1991. "*Asinaria* oder Maccus vortit Attice." In *Plautus Barbarus. Sechs Kapitel zur Originalität des Plautus*, edited by E. Lefèvre, E. Stärk, and G. Vogt-Sprira, pp. 11–68. Tübingen.

Walbank, M. 1996. "Greek Inscriptions from the Athenian Agora: Financial Documents." *Hesperia* 65: 433–65.

Wallace, R. 1989. "The Athenian *Proeispherontes*." *Hesperia* 58: 473–90.

———. 1993. "Personal Conduct and Legal Sanction in the Democracy of Classical Athens." In *Questions de responsabilité*, edited by J. Zlinzsky, pp. 397–413. Miskolc (Hungary).

———. 1994a. "Private Lives and Public Enemies: Freedom of Thought in Classical Athens." In *Athenian Identity and Civic Ideology*, edited by A. Scafuro and A. Boegehold, pp. 205–38. Baltimore.

———. 1994b. "The Athenian Laws of Slander." In *Symposion 1993*, edited by G. Thür, pp. 109–24. Köln.

———. 1997. "On Not Legislating Sexual Conduct in Fourth-Century Athens." In *Symposion 1995*, edited by G. Thür and J. Vélissaropoulos-Karakostas, pp. 151–66. Köln.

———. 1998. "Unconvicted or Potential 'Atimoi' in Ancient Athens." *Dike* 1: 63–78.

———. 2006. "The Legal Regulation of Private Conduct at Athens. Two Controversies on Freedom." *Dike* 9: 107–28.

Walsh, C. 2003. *Monetary Theory and Policy*. Cambridge, MA.
Watson, A. 1987. *Roman Slave Law*. Baltimore, MD.
Weber, M. [1921] 1958. "Die Stadt." *Archiv für Sozialwissenschaft* 47: 621–772. (Reprinted in, *Wirtschaft und Gesellschaft* [Tübingen 1922]; English translation, *The City*, Glencoe, IL. 1958.)
Webster, T. 1953. *Studies in Later Greek Comedy*. Manchester.
———. 1973. *Potter and Patron in Classical Athens*. London.
———. 1974. *An Introduction to Menander*. Manchester.
———. 1995. *Monuments Illustrating New Comedy*. London.
Wees, H. van. 2011. "The Law of Hybris and Solon's Reform of Justice." In *Sociable Man: Essays on Ancient Greek Social Behaviour in Honour of Nick Fisher*, edited by S. Lambert, pp. 117–43. Swansea.
Wehrli, F. 1969. *Die Schule des Aristoteles* VII. 2nd ed. Basel.
Weisberg, D. 1996. *Applications of Feminist Legal Theory to Women's Lives: Sex, Violence, Work, and Reproduction*. Philadelphia.
Weiss, C. 1989. "Phintias in Malibu und Karlsruhe." In *Greek Vases in the J. Paul Getty Museum*. Volume 4, pp. 83–94. Malibu, CA.
Weiss, E. 1923. *Griechisches Privatrecht auf rechtsvergleichender Grundlage*. Leipzig.
Weitzer, R. 2000a. "Why We Need More Research on Sex Work." In Weitzer, ed., pp. 1–16.
———. 2000b. "The Politics of Prostitution in America." In Weitzer, ed., pp. 159–80.
———, ed. 2000. *Sex for Sale: Prostitution, Pornography and the Sex Industry*. New York.
Welskopf, E. 1980. "Free Labor in the City of Athens." In *Non-Slave Labour in the Greco-Roman World*, edited by P. Garnsey, pp. 23–25. Cambridge.
Welwei, K.-W. 1974. *Unfreie im Antiken Kriegsdienst*. Vol. I. Stuttgart.
West, M. 1996. *Die griechische Dichterin: Bild und Rolle*. Stuttgart.
Whitaker, R. 1999. *Assuming the Position: A Memoir of Hustling*. New York.
Whitby, M. 1998. "Athenian Grain Trade in the Fourth Century B.C." In *Trade, Traders, and the Ancient City*, edited by H. Parkins and C. Smith, pp. 102–28. London.
White, H. 1999. "Afterword." In *Beyond the Cultural Turn: New Directions in the Study of Society and Culture*, edited by V. Bonnell and L. Hunt, pp. 315–24. Berkeley.
White, L. 1990. *The Comforts of Home: Prostitution in Colonial Nairobi*. Chicago.
Whitehead, D. 1977. *The Ideology of the Athenian Metic*. Cambridge.
———. 1984. "Immigrant Communities in the Classical Polis: Some Principles for a Synoptic Treatment." *L'Antiquité Classique* 53: 47–59.
———. 2000. *Hypereides: The Forensic Speeches*. Oxford.
———. 2009. *Hypereides'* Timandros: Observations and Suggestions." *Bulletin of the Institute of Classical Studies* (London) 52: 135–48.
Wiedemann, T. 1985. "The Regularity of Manumission at Rome." *Classical Quarterly* 35: 162–75.
———. 1987. *Slavery*. Oxford.

Wijers, M. 1998. "Women, Labor, and Migration: The Position of Trafficked Women and Strategies for Support." In Kempadoo and Doezema, eds., pp. 69–78.
Wilhelm, A. 1889. "Attische Psephismen." *Hermes* 24: 108–152.
Will, E. 1954. "Trois quarts de siècle de recherches sur l'économie grecque antique." *Annales (Economies, Société, Civilisations)* 9: 7–22.
Williams, D. 1983. "Women on Athenian Vases: Problems of Interpretation." In *Images of Women in Antiquity*, edited by A. Cameron and A. Kuhrt, pp. 92–106. London.
Wilson, P. 2000. *The Athenian Institution of the Khoregia: The Chorus, the City and the Stage*. Cambridge.
Windlesham, L. 1996. *Responses to Crime: Legislating with the Tide*. Oxford.
Winkler, J. 1990a. "Laying Down the Law: The Oversight of Men's Sexual Behavior in Classical Athens." In *Before Sexuality: The Construction of Erotic Experience in the Ancient Greek World*, edited by D. Halperin, J. Winkler, and F. Zeitlin, pp. 171–209. Princeton.

———. 1990b. *The Constraints of Desire: The Anthropology of Sex and Gender in Ancient Greece*. New York.

Wolff, H. 1944. "Marriage Law and Family Organization in Ancient Athens." *Traditio* 2: 43–95. (Reprinted in *Beiträge zur Rechtsgeschichte Altgriechenlands und des hellenistisch-römischen Ägypten* [Weimar 1961], pp. 155–242.)

———. 1957 [1968]. "Die Grundlagen des griechischen Vertragsrechts." *Zeitschrift der Savigny-Stiftung für Rechtsgeschichte, Romanist. Abt*. 74: 26–72. (Reprinted in *Zur griechischen Rechtsgeschichte*, edited by E. Berneker, pp. 483–533. Darmstadt 1968.)

———. 1966a. "Debt and Assumpsit in the Light of Comparative Legal History." *The Irish Jurist* 3: 316–27 (Reprinted in *Opuscula Dispersa*, edited by J. Wolf and F. Wieacker, pp. 123–34. Amsterdam 1974.)

———. 1968. *Demosthenes als Advokat. Funktionem und Methoden des Prozeßpraktikers im klassischen Athen*. Berlin.

———. 1975. "Juristische Graezistik—Aufgaben, Probleme, Möglichkeiten." In *Symposion 1971*, edited by H. Wolff, J. Modrzejewski, and D. Nörr, pp. 1–22. Köln.

Wollstonecraft, M. [1790] 1995. *A Vindication of the Rights of Men and a Vindication of the Rights of Woman and Hints*. Cambridge.
Wood, E. 1988. *Peasant-Citizen and Slave: The Foundations of Athenian Democracy*. London.
Worman, N. 2008. *Abusive Mouths in Classical Athens*. Cambridge.
Worthington, I. 1992. *A Historical Commentary on Dinarchus: Rhetoric and Conspiracy in Later Fourth-Century Athens*. Ann Arbor.
Wout, E. van't. 2011. "From Oath-Swearing to Entrenchment Clause: The Introduction of *Atimia*-Terminology in Legal Inscriptions." In *Sacred Words: Orality, Literacy and Religion*, edited by A. Lardinois et al., pp. 143–60. Leiden.

Wrenhaven, K. 2009. "The Identity of the 'Wool-Workers' in the Attic Manumissions." *Hesperia* 78: 367–86.

———. 2012. *Reconstructing the Slave: The Image of the Slave in Ancient Greece.* London.

Wycherley, R. 1957. *The Athenian Agora III: Literary and Epigraphical Testimonia.* Princeton.

Wynter, S. 1998. "WHISPER: Women Hurt in Systems of Prostitution Engaged in Revolt." In *Sex Work: Writings by Women in the Sex Industry*, edited by P. Alexander and F. Delacoste, pp. 266–70. 2nd ed. San Francisco.

Wyse, W. [1904] 1967. *The Speeches of Isaeus.* Cambridge.

Young, J. 1956. "Studies in South Attica: Country Estates at Sounion." *Hesperia* 25: 122–46.

Zagagi, N. 1995. *The Comedy of Menander: Convention, Variation and Originality.* Bloomington, IN.

Zecchini, G. 1939. *La cultura storica di Ateneo.* Milan.

Zelnick-Abramovitz, R. 2005. *Not Wholly Free: The Concept of Manumission and the Status of Manumitted Slaves in the Ancient Greek World.* Mnemosyne Supplement 266. Leiden.

———. 2013. *Taxing Freedom in Thessalian Manumission Inscriptions.* Mnemosyne Supplement 361. Leiden.

Zinserling, V. 1977. "Zum Problem von Alltagsdarstellungen auf attischen Vasen." In *Beiträge zum antiken Realismus*, edited by M. Kunze, pp. 38–56. Berlin.

Zoticus, L. von. 1997. "Butch Gigolette." In Nagle, ed., pp. 170–76.

# *General Index*

Adônia 30, 34. *See also* festivals and prostitution
agora 25, 28, 53n99, 136
*agoranomoi* 157, 160, 162–63
*andreia. See* masculinity
Androtiôn 70–71, 80
Aphroditê 29–30, 31, 51
    Ourania 52n98
    Pandêmos 30
Aspasia 62, 139
Assembly 77–79, 88–90
*astynomoi* 121, 162n41, 163
Athêna 30, 51, 56–57
attitudes towards prostitution
    positive 29, 106
    negative 26–28

*banausia* 25–26, 39–40, 88
brothels 3–4, 5, 20–21, 31, 44, 52
    definition of 27
    inns as 144

Chrysippus 41n11
citizenship, Athenian 26, 46–47, 69, 71, 73, 76–77
clients 71–72
clothing of prostitutes 23–24, 61, 63, 64
comedic sources 15–20, 148–49
    New Comedy 15–17, 19, 100–102, 143, 156
    Roman 17, 98–100, 141–42

commerce
    elite attitudes towards 6–7, 25–28, 44–45, 70, 85–86, 88n100, 89 (*see also* liberal profession)
    comparisons, cross-cultural 82–83, 115–16, 119n16, 124
contracts (of prostitution) 97–114
    in comedy 98–101, 102
    enforcement of 103, 104–106, 108–109
    legal significance of 102–104
    and private agreements 112–14
    for sexual services 28, 60, 68, 70–71, 97–103, 114
    and slaves 106–107, 108–111
    and women 106–108
courtesans. See *hetairai, hetairoi*

Decree of Themistoklês 93
decriminalization of prostitution 115–17
definition of prostitution 7–10, 82–83, 121n28
democracy 30, 88–89
demographics 13, 118n14
*dikê blabês* 106
dinner-parties 60, 63, 84, 160
*dokimasia rhêtorôn. See* Examination of Speakers

Eirênis 90
Ekklêsia. *See* Assembly

Examination of Speakers 78–81, 82, 115n1. *See also rhêtores*, Assembly

*fabulae palliatae*. *See* comedic sources, Roman
feminism and prostitution 7–10
festivals and prostitution 11, 30, 114, 141, 143
forensic sources 14–15, 20

gift-giving 75, 79, 81, 83–86
Gnathaina 65, 147, 166, 167
Gnathainion 65, 167
*grammateia*. *See* contracts (of prostitution)
*graphê hetairêseos*. *See* prosecution
gymnasia 87–88, 130

Hêgêsandros 67n183, 71, 72, 80, 129, 130, 178
Hêrakleidês Pontikos 28
*hetairai* 5, 16n77, 17, 22–23, 32–38, 46–47, 59–68
 income of 64, 65–67, 165–66, 167–68, 169–70, 175–76, 177–79
 independence of 59–60, 62–67, 100, 138–39
 statues of 63 (*see also* Pythionikê)
*hetairoi* 33, 34, 46, 74–75, 77, 78, 82, 88, 89, 101, 178–79. *See also hetairai*; male prostitutes
homosexuality 3, 21
 as aristocratic social code 81–82, 83–88
*hybris* 24, 64, 65, 124–30
Hypereidês 63

iconography of
 prostitutes 21–24, 84–85
 as *hetairai* 63
 as textile laborers 51–52, 169
inheritance 93–96

*kathestêkuia timê* 159–61. *See also* pricing
*kharis*. *See* reciprocal gratitude
Kolonôs Agoraios 45
Khrysis 17, 63, 100–101
*kyrioi* 73, 94–95, 106–108, 110–111, 128–29, 136–37

Laïs 65, 145, 146, 165
Leaina 145
laws
 against excessive greed 80–96
 on prostitution 28, 34, 69, 75, 77–78, 115–30
liberal profession 39–68, 131–33
 prostitution as 37–38, 39–40, 59–62, 101
 work ethics 41–42
 (see also *hetairai*)

male prostitutes 7–8, 13, 21, 33, 34, 36, 50, 81–85. *See also hetairoi*
 involvement in politics 74–75, 77–81, 88 (see also *rhêtores*)
 juridical status 79, 87–88
 pricing of 162–63, 166–67, 178
marriage 73
masculinity 70, 72n22, 131–33
*mastropoi* 40n4, 49, 65, 140–43, 145. *See also* pimping
*megalomisthoi* 22, 59n132, 118, 120, 124n37, 155. *See also hetairai*; prostitutes, income of
*megista epitimia* 77–78, 111, 117, 119
Mêtrikhê 65, 139, 140
*moikheia* 120
monetization 85–86, 155
moral criticism of prostitution
 Athenian 27, 28
 modern 7–11, 28, 115–16
multiple tasking 49–52

Naïs 73
Neaira 11, 34, 56, 64–65, 73, 108, 129, 130, 144, 145, 151–53, 168, 170, 174–75, 179
New Institutional Economics 2
Nikaretê 15, 144, 151–53, 168, 175

oikos 45–46, 90–92
   as brothel 145, 149–50, 153
   economic and political significance of 133–35, 136–38
Olympiôdoros 73–74, 112–13, 178

patrôia 90–91, 133–34. See also property ownership
Periklês 62, 89, 128
philanthrôpia 83–84, 124, 125, 130
Phrynê 62–63, 145, 168, 178, 179
pimping 65, 111, 118–24, 171–72
   matrilineal 138–53, 168
politai, politides. See citizenship, Athenian
pornai 31–38; 46–48. See also prostitutes; prostitutes, nomenclature of
porneion. See brothels
pornikon telos. See taxes on prostitution
pornoboskoi 140, 143–44, 167, 171–72. See also pimping
pornoi 33, 34, 46, 50, 82, 84–85. See also hetairoi; male prostitutes
Praxitelês 63
pricing
   as determined by market 157–62
   of grain 108, 157–61
   of sex 15, 56, 155–57, 162–71
proagôgeia. See pimping
promnêstikê. See pimping
property ownership 92–93, 133–34
prosecution
   for hybris 124–30
   for prostitution 77–78, 80–81 (see also decriminalization; laws; megista epitimia; pimping)
prostitutes. see also hetairai; hetairoi; pornai; pornoi
   citizens as 69–74, 76–79
   commercial interests of 27–28, 31–33, 35, 37–38, 131
   education of 48–49
   as entertainers 49, 121, 139n54, 144, 163–64
   foreigners as 70
   income of 36, 55–56, 59n132, 60n139, 147, 156, 171–79 (see also pricing)
   juridical status 22–24 (see also slaves)
   onomastic practices of 58, 145–46
   political participation of 34, 36
   protection of 116, 117, 124–30
   social status of 22–24, 33
   as wool-workers 49–54, 55–59
purchasing power parity x, 64, 108, 156, 170–71, 174
Pythionikê 10, 11, 31, 43n31, 48

reciprocal gratitude 38, 76, 85–87. See also gift-giving
regulation. See decriminalization of prostitution; laws; taxes on prostitution
rhêtores 78, 79, 80, 88–91, 93–94

self-employment 42, 44
sexuality, active and passive 72
Sinôpê 11, 43n31
slaves 2, 41–42, 43–45. See also liberal profession
   in business 108–111
   manumission of 53–56, 57–58
   as prostitutes 4–5, 11–12, 46–48, 86–87, 106–107, 118, 120–21, 126–27, 175 (see also pornai)
   rights of 124–30

Sôkratês 60–62, 122–23, 142
Solôn 30, 87, 112, 120–21, 128, 135
*symbolaia* 97, 102. *See also* contracts (of prostitution)
*symposia*. *See* dinner-parties
*syngraphai* 97, 98, 99, 102. *See also* contracts (of prostitution)
*synthêkai* 97, 102. *See also* contracts (of prostitution)

*talasiourgoi*. *See* prostitutes, as wool-workers
taxes on prostitution 13, 30, 116–17, 117–18, 155, 176–78
terminology ix, 2n5, 17–18, 31–38, 58, 62n153, 121n28
Theodotê 60–62, 74, 138–39, 146, 179

Theodotos 68, 97, 166–67, 170
Thesmophoria 30. *See also* festivals and prostitution
Timarkhos 34, 71–72, 79, 80, 85, 92–93, 122, 130, 178
Timotheos 73
trafficking, human 10–11

vase-painting. *See* iconography of prostitutes
Victorian England 74–75

women
  in commerce 106–108, 135–38
  in the household 134–35
  as merchants of sex 119, 138–53
    (*see also* pimping)

# Index of Passages Cited

**Literary Citations**

Aiskhinês
  *Speeches*
    1: 14, 70, 121n28
    1.9–11: 117n10
    1.13: 69, 75, 116n7, 168
    1.14: 119
    1.15: 125
    1.16: 125n41
    1.17: 125n52
    1.19–20: 77–78
    1.28–30: 89–90
    1.28–32: 78
    1.29: 81, 82n70
    1.30: 90, 94
    1.37–38: 34n62
    1.40: 49, 71–72
    1.40–41: 34n62
    1.41: 55n109, 72n18
    1.42: 176n115, 178
    1.45: 34n62
    1.50: 72n18
    1.50–51: 34
    1.51–52: 34n62
    1.53: 72
    1.54–64: 67n183, 72
    1.62: 129, 130, 178
    1.64: 80
    1.70: 71
    1.70.4: 81n68
    1.74: 4
    1.74–76: 34n62
    1.75: 176n115, 178
    1.94: 83n76
    1.95–96: 178n126
    1.96–98: 92–93
    1.97: 50n85, 56n114, 173
    1.99: 93
    1.111: 71
    1.115: 176n115, 178
    1.119: 13, 30n37, 117, 123
    1.123: 46
    1.123.2: 81n68
    1.124: 21, 27n15, 46
    1.125: 98n8
    1.130.3: 81n68
    1.132: 83n75
    1.132–52: 83
    1.135: 87n97
    1.136: 83n75
    1.137.1–5: 83–84
    1.137.5–7: 83
    1.139: 87n98, 117n10
    1.158: 102–103, 163
    1.159: 85
    1.160: 97–98
    1.165: 71–72, 97, 98n4, 98n7, 102n33
    1.170: 134
    1.184: 119n17, 142

Aiskhinês (cont.)
  1.185–87: 123
  1.188: 143
  2.4: 127
  2.153–55: 127
  3.171: 128n62
  3.173: 89n107
  3.246: 143
  *Letters*
    7.3: 71, 167

Alexis
  Fr. 3 (Kassel—Austin): 140
  Fr. 36: 50n85
  Fr. 103: 138
  Fr. 244: 84n80, 178n127

Alkiphrôn
  3.27: 27n15
  4: 49n73
  4.5.2: 63n156
  4.14.8: 30n40
  4.17.5: 64n163
  4.19: 36n70
  Fr. 4: 27n15

Amphis
  *Kouris*
    Fr. 23 (Kassel—Austin): 63n155, 175–76

Anaxilas
  *Neottis*
    Fr. 21 (Kassel—Austin): 38
    Fr. 22.1: 34
    Fr. 22.22: 34
  *Hôrai*
    Fr. 31.22: 34

Anaximenês
  Fr. 2 (Hammer): 177n120

Andokidês
  1.38: 173
  1.73: 13n66, 118n11
  1.100: 70, 166
  1.100–101: 80–81
  1.133–36: 13n66, 118n11
  1.147: 92n120

Anthologia Palatina
  5.40: 146
  6.48: 56n114, 57
  6.283: 56n114, 57
  6.284: 56n114, 57, 59
  6.285: 56n114
  6.285.5–6: 57n120
  6.285.7–10: 57n121

Antiphanês
  *Agroikos*
    Fr. 2 (Kassel—Austin): 176n116
  *Akestria*
    Fr. 21–24: 50n85
  *Misoponêros*
    Fr. 157: 27n18
  *Stratiôtês ê Tykhôn*
    Fr. 202: 177n120
  *Hydria*
    Fr. 210: 37, 73, 108n61

Antiphôn
  1: 5
  2d.8: 45n44
  5.47: 126n49
  6.4: 126n49
  6.23: 171n92

Aristainetos
  1.11: 141
  1.22: 141
  2.19: 141n68

Aristophanês
  *Akharneis*
    32–36: 25n1
    524–29: 138
    730–835: 168
  *Batrakhoi*
    1079: 124n37
    1349–51: 50n84

## Index of Passages Cited

*Eirênê* 25n1
*Ekklêsiazousai*
  215: 50n85
  717–24: 46
  878–82: 4n14
  912: 77
*Hippeis*
  424: 178n127
  438–44: 89n107
  824–35: 89n107
  876–79: 77
  876–80: 80
  904–9: 84n79
  930–33: 89n107
  991–96: 89n107
  1104–99: 84n79
  1141–50: 89n107
  1218–26: 89n107
*Lysistrata* 139–40
  519–20: 50n84
  536–37: 50n84
  641–47: 51n91
  728–30: 50n84
*Nephelai*
  53–55: 50n84
  109d: 176n116
  690–92: 178n127
  979–80: 123–24
  980: 119n18
*Ornithes*
  705–7: 84n79
  707: 84n81
*Ploutos*
  149–55: 34
  153–57: 84n79
  153–59: 84–85
  157: 84n81
  377–79: 89n107
  567–70: 89n107
  768: 45n41
*Sphêkes*
  657–59: 13n66, 118n11
  669–77: 89n107
  1028: 124n37
*Thesmophoriazousai*
  293–94: 30n38
  329–31: 30n39
  341: 124n37
  425: 141n71
  519: 141n71
  553: 140–41
  558: 140–41
  783: 141n71
  797–99: 4n14
  839–45: 135
  1177–98: 49n74
  1193–96: 167

Scholiast to Aristoph.
  *Neph.* 109d: 176n116
  *Plout.* 768: 45n41

Aristophanês
  of Byzantion 156

Aristotle
  *Athênaiôn Politeia*
    2.2: 40n11
    4.2: 93
    9.4: 128
    29.5: 26n11
    36.1: 71n15
    40.2: 71n15
    43.4: 158
    47.2: 13n66, 118n11
    49.4: 44n34
    50.2: 39n3, 163
    51.1: 157
    51.4: 158
    52.2: 109
    56.6: 129n68
    58.3: 53n100
    62.2: 164n50
  *Metaphysics*
    982b25–26: 40n7

Aristotle (cont.)
  Nicomachean Ethics
    1121b40–43: 144
    1124b26–1125a1: 40
    1131a2–8: 120
    1132b–1133a: 86
    1160a16: 44n35
  Oikonomika
    1343a25–b2: 131n2
    1343b2–1344a22: 141n71
    1344a26–27: 41n13
    1344a27–29: 48n69
  Poetics
    1454a21–2: 53n102
  Politics
    1252: 133n16
    1252b12–14: 45
    1253b4–7: 45
    1253b33–1254a1: 50
    1256b10–22: 131n2
    1257b1–5: 131n3
    1258a10–14: 86n92, 131
    1258a19–b8: 131
    1258b1–4: 131
    1258b25–27: 26n7
    1258b33–39: 26n7
    1258b37: 26n12, 88n100
    1260a41–b2: 26n7
    1264b4–6: 134
    1277a32–b7: 26n7
    1277b33–1278a13: 26n7
    1278a8: 26
    1289b26–34: 25
    1291a33–34: 177n119
    1291b14–30: 25
    1300a6–7: 141n71
    1309a15: 177n120
    1315a14–16: 129
    1316b1–5: 26
    1334b29–1335b37: 28n26
    1335b38–1336a2: 28n26
    1337b18–22: 26n7
    1337b20–21: 40n11
    1338a32: 39n1
    1341b8–18: 26n7
    1341b10–15: 40n11
  Rhetoric
    1367a30–32: 41n9
    1367a33: 40
    1367a33–b30: 102n30
    1375b9–10: 104, 113
    1376b8–9: 104
    1381a21–24: 131n2
    1385a2–3: 86
    1388b17–18: 89n104

Asconius
  Commentary on
    Cicero In Verrem
    2.1.36 (91): 104n42

Athênaios 18–20
  Deipnosophistai
    219c–d: 62n151
    220d: 4
    220e: 139
    246b: 179
    272c–d: 118n14
    335c–e: 145n94
    443a: 119n18
    457e: 145n94
    512b4–6: 28n24
    516b: 51n88
    535c: 74n31, 146
    547d: 164
    555–612: 36n70
    558a–e: 59n132, 124n37
    567–73b: 7n29
    567a1–3: 141
    567e: 63n155
    568d: 138
    569a: 155
    569d–f: 30n36
    569f7–9: 139
    569f–570a: 34

570b: 59n132, 124n137
571c: 38n79, 77
572f: 10n49
573c: 29n33
574c–d: 31n41
574e: 146, 179
577b: 73
580b9–c3: 147
580e6–f4: 147
581c1–3: 147
581c2–e6: 65n169
583a: 147n104
583a1–6: 146
583c: 145n95
584b–c: 179
584c: 167
585a7–11: 147
585b2–4: 147
585d: 147
586b–c: 146
587c1: 147
587f: 146
588b: 147
588c: 29n34
588e4–6: 65
588e8–10: 65
590b–c: 63n157
590d: 145n95
590d–592f: 63n156
591d: 63n155
591d–e: 179
593b: 147
593b7–10: 147
594f–595a: 31n42
595a: 11n55, 43n31
595d: 146, 178
596e: 151, 175n110
596f: 165
597a: 147
598e: 147
605c: 119n18
612a2–6: 136

612b2–3: 136n35
621c5–7: 18n87

Deinarkhos
  1.112: 89n104
  1.23: 5n20, 126–27
  1.41: 89n107
  1.70–71: 93
  1.71: 89, 91
  1.77: 89n107
  3.4: 104
  3.19: 89n104

Demosthenes
  *Speeches*
    1.8–9: 177n120
    3.29: 89n107
    5.8: 32n50
    18.102: 177n119
    18.108: 177n119
    18.129: 27n16, 44n35
    18.171: 89n104
    19.70: 27n21
    19.196–98: 127
    19.233: 34n59
    19.233.8: 82n70
    19.246: 27n21
    19.249: 27n21
    19.275: 89n107
    19.287: 71
    20.9: 157
    20.77: 158
    20.102: 94n128
    21.45: 127n61
    21.47: 124–25, 127, 128
    21.47–49: 125n52
    21.48–49: 125
    21.151: 177n119
    21.153: 177n119
    21.175: 128n63
    21.208: 177n119
    22.21: 80
    22.22–23: 98

Demosthenes (*cont.*)
    22.23: 80
    22.29: 71
    22.56: 34n60, 177n121
    22.61: 71
    23.184: 89n104
    24.105: 128n63
    24.197–98: 177n120
    24.117: 104n41
    27.9: 171n92
    27.19: 174n106
    27.20: 171n92
    27.20–21: 172n97
    27.40: 134n25
    27.53: 134n25
    27.55: 134n25
    28.1–3: 128n62
    28.12: 172n97
    28.26: 134n25
    28.33: 134n25
    28.47–48: 134n25
    32.1: 106n56
    32.8–9: 114
    32.10–12: 110
    33.7: 43n30
    34: 160
    34.5: 109n70
    34.6: 98n7, 109
    34.10: 109n70
    34.31: 109n70
    34.37: 158, 170, 172n97
    34.39: 159, 160
    34.52: 110
    35.13: 113
    35.14: 102n31
    35.39: 113–14
    35.43: 102n31
    35.47–49: 53n100
    35.50–51: 158
    35.51: 158
    36.1: 110
    36.4: 173
    36.6: 44n35
    36.11: 44n35, 173
    36.13: 44n35
    36.14: 134–35, 173n102
    36.18: 135
    36.29: 44n35
    36.37: 173
    36.43: 111n76, 173
    36.45: 55n108, 176n115
    36.46: 173
    36.48: 111n76, 173
    38.23: 128–29
    38.26: 177n120
    41.7–9: 135n32
    41.21: 135n32
    42.5: 98n8
    42.11: 98n8
    42.12: 104
    43: 94n127
    43.19: 94n131
    43.75: 125n44
    43.77–78: 125n44
    44.49: 94n128
    44.67: 94n128
    45.4: 127n57
    45.4: 129
    45.28: 92n118
    45.31–32: 173
    45.64: 43n30, 110
    45.71: 48n69
    45.71–72: 129n74
    45.72: 49n71
    45.74: 45n41
    46.14: 94n128, 94n132, 112n84
    46.24: 104n41
    47.53: 94n129
    47.54: 177n120
    47.56: 46n45
    47.57: 94n129
    47.58–59: 24
    47.61: 23
    47.77: 103
    48.11: 104

# Index of Passages Cited

48.39–47: 113
48.43–45: 113
48.46: 98n8
48.53: 34n60, 55n107, 112
48.53–54: 73–74
48.54: 104
48.55: 55n107, 64n163,
    82n72, 112, 178
48.56: 34n60, 112
49.22: 46n46
49.26: 110
49.31: 111, 173
50.8–9: 177n120
52.8: 46n46
52.14: 46n46
52.26: 177n120
53.16: 24
53.20: 106n56, 171n92
53.21: 172n97
56: 110, 114, 159–60
56.2: 105
56.8: 159
56.10: 159–60
56.11: 158n14
56.15: 98n7
57: 43n28
57.29, 35: 27n19
57.31: 137
57.32: 42
57.45: 26n13, 37–38, 41
58.35: 89n107
59: 14, 43n28,
    64–65, 73, 137, 151–53, 174–75
59.9: 126n49
59.16: 73n28, 128n63
59.18: 27n17, 48n68, 49n73,
    152, 175
59.18–20: 152
59.18–22: 15n73, 168
59.18–23: 144
59.19: 152
59.21: 172n93
59.21–22: 152, 172

59.23: 152
59.29: 56n118, 152, 175
59.29–31: 174
59.29–32: 101
59.30: 143, 174–75
59.30–35: 169–70
59.32–35: 64
59.33–37: 130
59.36: 175, 179n128
59.37: 64n165
59.37–40: 129
59.38: 64–65
59.41: 169, 170
59.42: 179
59.45–46: 101, 108n61
59.46: 108, 179n128
59.52: 128n63
59.64–67: 153
59.65: 145
59.66: 128n63
59.67: 27n15,
    120–21, 145, 153
59.68: 153n144
59.69: 145
59.70: 145
59.71: 60n137, 153
59.104: 71
59.108: 11n54, 114
59.113: 39n1, 46–47, 120–21
*Letters*
3.30: 176

Scholiast to Demosthenes
    69: 48

Dêmêtrios of Phalêron
    Fr. 136 (Wehrli): 177n120

Diodôros of Sicily
    2.23: 51n88
    12.21.1: 117n8
    13.47.7: 177n120
    13.52.5: 177n120
    13.64.4: 177n120

Diodôros of Sicily (*cont.*)
15.34.3–35.2: 158
32.11: 51n88

Diogenês Laertios
2.105: 4n17
10.40.7: 119n18

Dionysios of Halikarnassos
*Antiquitates Romanae*
1.84.4: 37

Diphilos
Fr. 42.19–22
(Kassel—Austin): 141
Fr. 42.39: 30n40
Fr. 42.39–40: 34
Fr. 49: 30n40

Donatus
*Ad Eunuchum*: 148–49

Ephippos
Fr. 20 (Kassel—Austin): 84, 178

Epikratês
Fr. 3.11–12 (Kassel—Austin): 165
Fr. 3.16–18: 165

Euboulos
Fr. 67 (Kassel—Austin):
3n13, 29n31
Fr. 82: 3n13, 29n31
Fr. 87: 143

Eupolis
Fr. 50 (44) (Kassel—Austin):
55n106, 176n116
Fr. 247: 81n68, 166
Fr. 434: 50n85

Euripides
*Hippolytos*
522: 63n156

*Hiketidês*
881–87: 25n1
*Melanippê Desmôtês*
Fr. 660.9–11 (Mette): 134
*Orestês*
917–22: 25n1

Gaius
*Institutiones*
3.154: 104n41

Harpokratiôn
s.v. ἀποστασίου: 53n100
s.v. ἀρρηφορεῖν: 51n91
s.v. ἀφανὴς οὐσία καὶ φανερά: 32n50
s.v. ἐπιμεληταὶ ἐμπορίου: 158n15
s.v. κατὰ τὴν ἀγορὰν ἀψευδεῖν: 157
s.v. καταχύσματα: 45n41
s.v. φάσις: 129n68

Herodotus
2.121e2: 3n12
2.126: 3n12
2.135: 27n16, 44n35

Hermogenês
*Peri Heureseôs*
4.11: 148n110

Hêrôdas: 142–43
*Mimiambi*
1: 18
1.5: 145
1.7: 140
1.21: 140
1.50–90: 139
1.59–60: 140
1.61: 140
1.64–65: 65
1.67: 140
1.76–77: 65
1.85: 140
1.87: 140
2: 18, 137n39, 143n79

2.30: 47
2.36: 46n49
2.36–37: 47
2.46–48: 47

Hesiod
  Works and Days
    373–75: 82n72

Hippokratês
  On the Nature of the Child
    13: 144

Hyperidês
  3.3: 163n42
  4: 80n60
  4.2–3: 138
  4.4–5: 135n30, 170–71
  4.6: 170
  4.8: 98n8, 102n33
  4.9: 98n7, 174
  4.11: 136n34
  4.13: 104
  4.14: 157
  4.15: 1574.18: 138n49
  4.22: 44n35
  4.24: 171
  4.26: 136n34
  4.27: 89n104
  4.29–31: 90
  5.24: 89n104
  6.19: 132
  fr. 33: 118n14
  fr. 120–24: 125, 130
  fr. 134: 177n120

Isaios
  2.13: 94n132
  3.1: 94n128
  3.8: 92n120
  3.10–11: 168
  3.17–18: 73
  3.64: 95n134

3.68: 94n132
3.78: 92n120
3.80: 30n38
4.27: 177n120
5.39: 26n13, 41
6.9: 94n128
6.18: 139
6.19: 139
6.19–21: 4–5
6.21: 139
6.28: 94n132
6.29: 94n128
6.49–50: 30n39
6.60–61: 177n120
7.32: 134
7.40: 177n120
7.42: 134n20
8.35: 171n92, 172n97
10.10: 108
10.19: 95n134

Isokratês
  Speeches
    8.48: 43n27
    8.103: 176n116
    8.128: 177
    10.25: 176n116
    12.145: 177n120
    14.48: 40–41
    17: 173
    17.9: 111n78
    17.12: 111
    17.14: 111
    17.31: 111
    17.31–32: 43n30
    17.33: 111
    17.43: 43n30
    18.24: 104
    18.25: 104
    18.52: 126n49
  Letters
    9.49: 132n5

John Chrysostom
  In Joannem
    PG 59.165.23: 48n66
  de Mansuetudine
    PG 63.554.12: 48n66

Kallimakhos
  Fr. 433 (Pfeiffer): 60n134

Libanios
  8.301–302: 48

Loukianos
  Apologia
    15: 155
  Erôtes
    49.16: 141
  Hermotimos
    578: 155
  Hetairikoi Dialogoi: 18–19,
      20, 65–68
    80.1.1: 66n172
    80.1.2: 151
    80.2: 66n172, 149
    80.2.1: 30n38
    80.3.1: 66
    80.3.3: 66, 151
    80.4: 66n173
    80.4.1: 160n133
    80.4.3: 49n73, 149
    80.5.4: 64n163
    80.6: 56n115
    80.6.1: 150
    80.6.2: 64n163, 150
    80.6.2–3: 149n121
    80.6.3: 150
    80.6.4: 150
    80.7.1: 151
    80.7.1–3: 67
    80.7.2: 151
    80.7.3: 151
    80.7.4: 137n43, 151
    80.8.1: 66n172
    80.8.2–3: 165
    80.9.1: 149
    80.9.3: 67
    80.9.3–4: 166
    80.9.5: 67n183
    80.10.2: 149
    80.10.4: 49n73
    80.11: 66
    80.11.1: 165
    80.11.3: 66, 165
    80.12.1: 137n43
    80.13.4: 67, 149
    80.14: 66n172
    80.14.1: 67n183
    80.14.2: 166
    80.14.3: 166
    80.15.2: 67–68, 149, 166
  Symposion
    15: 167
    17.32.9–10: 142

Lykourgos
  Fragments
    A.2.1 (Burtt): 89n106
  Kata Leôkratous: 80n60
    1.9–10: 95–96
    1.14–15: 95–96
    1.27: 158n13
    1.108: 132
    9: 75
    16–17: 90n111
    17: 90
    22–23: 90n112
    26–27: 90
    147: 90

Lysias
  Speeches
    1: 133n16
    1.29: 121n26
    1.32: 117n10, 121n26
    3: 14, 68, 70, 82n69
    3.6: 68, 141n71

Index of Passages Cited

3.10: 114
3.12: 68
3.5: 71
3.22: 14–15, 97, 166–67
3.22–24: 170
3.26: 97
3.31: 68
3.45: 166n67
4: 14, 47–48
4.1: 60n137
4.12: 48n62, 55
4.16: 55
4.19: 47n61, 55
7.31–32: 177n120
10.19: 27n15, 120–21
12.19: 171n92
12.20: 177n120
16.3: 71n15
18.7: 177n120
18.21: 177n120
19.9: 177n120
19.29: 177n120
19.57: 89n107
19.57–59: 177n120
20.23: 177n120
22: 158
23: 109–110
24.6: 44n34
25.9: 89n107
25.19: 89n107
27.9–10: 177n119
27.10–11: 89n107
28.3: 177n120
28.9: 89n107
29.4: 177n120
29.6: 89n107
30.15: 71n15
30.25: 89n107
30.26: 177n120
31.27: 75
32: 133n16
32.7: 102n33

*Fragments*
Fr. 1 (Carey): 136n34
Fr. 1 (Gernet—Bizos): 130n77
Fr. 38.5 (Gernet—Bizos): 137–38
Fr. 11 (Gernet—Bizos): 42n20
Fr. 79 (Thalheim): 32n50
Fr. 82 (Thalheim): 73
Fr. 246 (Carey): 42n20

Makhôn
Fr. 6 (Gow): 179
Fr. 7: 179
Fr. 15.252: 60n134
Fr. 16.258: 60n134
Fr. 16.262–84: 60n134
Fr. 16.306–308: 166
Fr. 17.338–41: 167
Fr. 18.433–38: 146
Fr. 18.450–55: 168

Menander
*Dyskolos* 16
*Epitrepontes* 47
  50–52: 170n89
  85–86: 170n89
  136–37: 47n55, 143
  137–41: 164
  191: 170n89
  376–80: 172–73
  430–31: 47n55
  646: 47n55
  749–50: 30n38
  Fr. 1.136–37 (Sandbach): 165, 171
  Fr. 1.538–40: 171
  Fr. 1.692–94: 171
  Fr. 7: 47n57
*Kolax*
  117: 156, 167
*Parakatathêkê*: 37
*Perikeiromenê*
  497: 108n61
*Samia*: 17, 47, 100–101, 160n133

Menander (cont.)
   30–31: 47n56
   80–84: 63
   137–45: 47n56
   234–36: 46n45
   373: 63, 178
   381: 63, 178
   381–82: 100–101
   390: 64
   392–94: 64
   394–95: 64
   748–49: 47n56
   Fr. 296–97 (Kassel—Austin): 135
   Fr. 337 (Kassel—Austin): 148
   Fr. 338 (Kôrte / Thierfelder): 25n1

Naevius
   Fr. 2: 147n105

Pausanias
   1.22.3: 30n35
   1.23.2: 30n37
   1.37.5: 11n55, 31n42
   9.27: 63n157

Petronius
  *Satyricôn*
   7.1: 142

Pherekratês
   Fr. 70 (Kassel—Austin): 135
   Fr. 142: 45n40

Philêmôn
   Fr. 3 (Kassel—Austin): 29n31, 30n36, 165

Phôtios
   s.v. ματρυλλεῖον: 140

Pindaros
  *Olympian Odes*
   1.85: 163n42
   10.16–21: 87
   10.99–105: 87

Plato
  *Alkibiadês*
   126e: 50n82
  *Gorgias*
   483b: 107n57
  *Kharmidês*
   154a–c: 87n97
   163b4–5: 42
   163b5–8: 3n12, 81n68
   163b6–8: 39
   163c1–8: 39
   163c3–8: 40
  *Kritôn*
   50d: 21
   52d9–e3: 105n48
  *Lysis*
   204e: 87n97
   208d–e: 50n82
  *Menexenos*
   236b5: 36n70, 62
   236b7–c1: 62n154
  *Nomoi*
   805e–806a: 50n82
   823e: 39n1
   836a7: 58n125
   840d–841e: 28
   846d–847b: 132n8
   849e: 105–106
   889d: 25n1, 42n17
   915d6–e2: 106n53
   918d8–e3: 132
   919d3e2: 132
   920d: 105n48
   920d1–5: 113
  *Politikos*
   289e: 25n3, 42n17
  *Prôtagoras*
   347c: 25n3, 42n17
  *Republic*
   371c: 25, 42n17
   373a: 176
   451d: 134

## Index of Passages Cited

455c: 50n84
458d–461b: 28
462d: 128n66
563b: 23n106
573d: 176n116
574b–c: 176n116
*Symposion*
  176e: 163
  182a7–9: 1, 6, 81
  183b3–c4: 86–87
  184d4–d7: 86–87
  184e5–185a5: 87n96
  196c2–3: 104
*Theaitêtos*
  149a–50b: 135
  149a1–4: 122
  150a1–4: 122

Plautus
  *Asinaria* 98–99, 141–42, 147n105
    127: 149
    163–65: 149
    171: 149
    195: 149
    229–36: 149
    230: 99
    238–40: 99
    751–54: 98–99
  *Bacchides* 98n9, 99–100, 148n109
    46: 99
    590: 99
    896: 99n15
    Fr. 10: 99
    Fr. 19: 99n15
  *Cistellaria* 17
    36–39: 148
    41–50: 148
    89–93: 148
  *Curculio* 98n9
  *Epidicus*
    556: 100
  *Menaechmi* 17

  *Mercator*
    533: 100n20
    536: 100n20
    536a: 100n20
    537: 100n20
  *Miles Gloriosus*
    105–108: 149
  *Mostellaria* 17
  *Persa* 98n9
  *Pseudolus* 17, 98n9, 144
  *Trinummus* 98n9
  *Truculentus* 149
    224: 142
    392–93: 100
    401: 142

Pliny the Elder
  *Naturalis historia*
    35.10.6: 63n156
Plutarch
  *Erôtikos*
    759f9: 119n18
  *Moralia*
    122d: 39n1
    349a: 177n120
    400f–401b: 63n157
    753: 63n157
    830c: 50n84
    849e: 63n156
  *Symposiakôn Problêmatôn*
    693c9: 119n18
  *Camillus*
    19.6: 158
  *Periklês*
    24: 36n70
    24.2–10: 62n153
  *Phôkiôn*
    6: 158
  *Solôn*
    1.3: 87
    1.23: 119n17
    15.2–3: 37n74

Plutarch (cont.)
    18.3: 128n66
    22.1: 42
    23.1: 27n15, 120, 121n26
    23.1–2: 168
    23.2: 116n7, 168–69

Pollux
    1.80: 46n45
    3.77: 45n41
    3.82: 41
    4.7: 48n68
    4.7.22: 48n70
    4.22: 48n68
    7.20.2: 117n8
    8.31: 106n56
    9.29: 117n8
    9.59: 165

Polyainos
    3.11.2: 158
    5.2.13: 117n8

Polybius
    2.2.9: 132n5
    4.86.4: 132n5
    5.16.5: 132n5
    10.17.6: 132n5
    20.9.4: 132n5

Quintilian
    *Institutio Oratoria*
    10.1.69: 156

Sêmonidês
    7.49: 47

Seneca the Younger
    *De beneficiis*
    3.22.1: 41n11

Sôphrôn
    Fr. 69 (Kassel—Austin): 140
Suda
    s.v. ἀρρηφορία: 51n91

Telês
    Fr. 4b (Hense): 172n97

Terence
    *Andria* 17
        74–79: 57
    *Eunuchus* 17, 142
        119–20: 100, 149n116
        131–36: 149n116
    *Heauton Timoroumenos* 17
        prol. 39: 143n83
        96–98: 149
        245–48: 178
        451–52: 178
        739: 178
        751: 178
    *Hekyra*
        87–95: 100

Theophilos
    Fr. 11.2
        (Kassel—Austin): 146

Theophrastos
    *Kharaktêres*
        6.2–10: 27n20
        6.4–5: 143–44
        28: 141n71
        30.15: 172n97
        30.17: 172n97

Theopompos of Chios
    Fr. 114 (Jacoby): 11n53
    Fr. 213: 10n51, 29n29
    Fr. 253: 48
    Fr. 254: 10n52

Thucydides
    2.37.3: 128
    2.40.1–2: 42
    2.65.9: 89
    4.59.2: 132n5
    7.13.2: 43n27
    8.65.3: 26n11

Timoklês
  Neaira
    Fr. 25
      (Kassel—Austin): 63n155
    Fr. 33: 56n113

Turpilius
  Com. Fr. 112
    (Ribbeck Leuc.): 100

Xenarchus
  Fr. 4 (Kassell—Austin): 3n13

Xenophon
  Anabasis
    1.3.16: 163n42
    4.3.19: 10n49
    5.4.33: 10n49
  Apomnêmoneumatôn 160–62
    1.1.1: 61n142
    1.2.22: 176n116
    1.3.11–12: 176n116
    1.6.13: 7, 25, 81n68
    2.2.4: 29n29
    2.7.12: 51n87, 137
    2.7.4: 48n70
    2.8.4: 39n1
    3.7.6: 25
    3.9.11: 50n82
    3.11: 61, 108n61
    3.11.1: 60
    3.11.4: 60, 61, 74
    3.11.4–5: 61, 138–39, 146
    3.11.9–15: 61
  Athênaiôn Politeia
    1.10: 23n105
    1.10–11: 172n97
    1.13: 177n119
    1.17: 172n97
  Hellênika
    5.4.4: 169
    5.4.60–61: 158
    6.2.1: 177n120
    6.2.23: 25
  Kynêgetikos
    2.2: 163n42
  Lakedaimoniôn Politeia
    1.3: 50n82
  Oikonomikos
    1.1: 48n68, 48n70
    1.5: 92n120, 133n16
    1.13: 176n116
    1.16–17: 41n14
    2.6–7: 177n120
    2.7: 56n113
    3.14: 36n70
    3.15.1–2: 137
    3.15.3–5: 137
    5.1: 25n1
    6.4: 133n16
    7.33: 141n71
    7.35–43: 134
    7.41: 48n69, 56n114
    7.6: 43n29, 50n84
    9.14–17: 134
    12.3: 41n14
    12.4: 48n69
  Poroi
    4.4: 118n14
    4.14: 171n92
    4.14–15: 172n97
    4.19: 172n97
    4.23: 172n97
    4.25: 118n14
    4.28: 118n14
  Symposion
    3.10: 40n4, 122, 123, 142
    4.30–32: 177n120
    4.34: 134n19
    4.52–54: 144
    4.56: 40n4
    4.56–61: 122
    4.56–64: 142
    4.59: 49n72
    4.60: 123n33
    4.62: 119n18, 122
    4.64: 122, 123

**Papyri and Inscriptions**

*Berliner Griechische Urkunden*
  I 202.10: 84n78

*Inscriptiones Graecae*
  I³
    474–76: 164
    1032: 43n27
  II²
    400: 159n21
    499: 159n21
    903: 161n34
    1214: 177n118
    1388.61–62: 41n12
    1492.137: 41n12
    1553–78: 53
    1553.7–10: 55n112
    1553.20–23: 55n112
    1554: 55n109
    1556.28: 50n85
    1556 B27–29: 55n112
    1557 B105–107: 55n112
    1558 A37–43: 55n112
    1558 A37: 136n34
    1559 A II 26–31: 55n112
    1561.22–30: 137
    1566 A27–29: 55n112
    1568 B18–23: 55n112
    1569 A III 18–21: 55n112
    1570.24–26: 55n112
    1570.57–62: 55n112
    1570.78–79: 43n31
    1570.82–84: 55n112
    1571.8–11: 55n112
    1672.12: 164n51
    1672.26–28: 164n51
    1672.31–32
    1672.64: 135
    1672.70–71: 43n26
    1672.71: 135
    1672.110–111: 164n51
    1672.159–60
    1672.190: 43n26
    1672–73: 136n33
    1672–73.28–30
    1673.32–34: 164n51
    1673.44–46: 164n51
    1673.60–62: 164n51
    2747–49: 171n92
    2751: 171n92
    2825: 55n109
    4570: 30n35
    4574–85: 30n35
    6873: 135
    10892: 146
    11793: 145
    12026: 146
  III¹
    App. 69: 137
  XII
    7.27: 114n88
    7.67: 114n88
    7.76: 114n88

*Monumentum Ancyranum*
  9.10: 84n78

*Orientis Graeci Inscriptiones Selectae*
  139.20: 84n78

*P Berol.*
  9772: 134

*P Hamb.*
  133: 130n77

*P Mag.*
  1.2366: 163n42

*P Oxy.*
  1012 C Fr. 9 col. ii.14: 71n9
  1012 C Fr. 9 col. ii.15: 102n33
  1176 Fr. 39, col. xi: 134.
  1606: 130n77
  2891: 145n94

PRev. Laws 159n22

P Teb.
    703.176: 159n21

Supplementum epigraphicum Graecum
    (1923–)
    18.36 A335, 339: 55n109
    18.36 B2 50n85
    24.154: 159n21

26.72: 41n12
26.72.49–55: 83n76
27.261: 88

Sylloge Inscriptionum Graecarum³
    1177: 137

Urkunden der Ptolemäerzeit 1
    (1922–27), 2 (1957)
    162.vii.21: 84n78